AN IRISH CENTURY

An Irish Century
Studies 1912–2012

edited by

BRYAN FANNING

UNIVERSITY COLLEGE DUBLIN PRESS

PREAS CHOLÁISTE OLLSCOILE
BHAILE ÁTHA CLIATH

First published 2012
by University College Dublin Press
Newman House
86 St Stephen's Green
Dublin 2
Ireland

www.ucdpress.ie

ISBN 978-1-906359-65-2

Cataloguing in Publication data available from the British Library

Typeset in UK in Plantin and Fournier by Ryan Shiels
Text design by Lyn Davies
Printed on acid-free paper in England by
Antony Rowe, Chippenham, Wilts

For my parents, Matt and Mary

★

Contents

Acknowledgements   *xi*

1 Introduction: *Studies* 1912–2012   *1*
   BRYAN FANNING

2 John Redmond (2009)   *21*
   STEPHEN COLLINS

3 Some Aspects of Irish Literature (1913)   *31*
   PATRICK PEARSE

4 Votes for Youth (1915)   *40*
   ARTHUR E. CLERY

5 Thomas Kettle (1966)   *45*
   DENIS GWYNN

6 I Remember 1916 (1966)   *54*
   SEÁN F. LEMASS

7 The Canon of Irish History: A Challenge (1972)   *57*
   FRANCIS SHAW SJ

8 The Fate of the Irish Flag at Ypres (1919)   *70*
   HENRY V. GILL SJ

9 Lessons of Revolution (1923)   *78*
   GEORGE RUSSELL (AE)

10 The Suppression of the Carrigan Report: A Historical Perspective
   on Child Abuse (2000)   *83*
   FINOLA KENNEDY

11 National Self-Sufficiency (1933)   *93*
   JOHN MAYNARD KEYNES

12 Adolf Hitler (1933)   *105*
    DANIEL A. BINCHY

13 The Jesuits and the 1937 Constitution (1989)   *119*
    DERMOT KEOGH

14 Daniel O'Connell and the Gaelic Past (1938)   *133*
    MICHAEL TIERNEY

15 Reply to Tierney (1938)   *146*
    DANIEL A. BINCHY

16 The Economist and Public Policy (1953)   *150*
    PATRICK LYNCH

17 Uniting Ireland (1957)   *161*
    DONAL BARRINGTON

18 Fifty Years of Irish Writing (1962)   *187*
    SEAN O'FAOLAIN

19 Inherited Dissent: The Dilemma of the Irish Writer (1965)   *200*
    AUGUSTINE MARTIN

20 Pluralism and Northern Ireland (1978)   *210*
    JOHN BRADY SJ

21 Upstairs, Downstairs: The Challenge of Social Inequality (1983)   *223*
    JOHN SWEENEY

22 T. K. Whitaker (1984)   *238*
    RAYMOND CROTTY

23 Moving Statues and Irishwomen (1987)   *244*
    MARGARET MAC CURTAIN

24 Reflections on Current Discontents (1989)   *253*
    TOM GARVIN

25 Growth and Decline of Churchly Religion (1994)   *262*
    TONY FAHEY

26 Catholicism and National Identity in the Works of
John McGahern (2001)   271
EAMON MAHER

27 Forty Years On (2003)   283
MARY KENNY

28 Paisleyism: A Theological Inquiry (2004)   290
NEIL SOUTHERN

29 The Doghouse No Longer Feels Lonely (2008–9)   301
FERGUS O'DONOGHUE SJ

30 Immigration and Social Cohesion (2009)   308
BRYAN FANNING

31 No Cheap Grace: Reforming the Irish Church (2010)   318
SÉAMUS MURPHY SJ

Index   330

Acknowledgements

First and foremost, I owe a debt to thank Fergus O'Donoghue SJ whose invitation onto the editorial board of *Studies* immersed me in this project. This volume would not have been possible without the work of his editorial predecessors, Thomas Finlay SJ, Timothy Corcoran SJ, Patrick Connolly SJ, Roland Burke-Savage SJ, Peter Troddyn SJ, Brian Lennon SJ and Noel Barber SJ. *Studies: An Irish Century* marks their contributions and that of the Society of Jesus to the cultural and intellectual life of Ireland. I owe a debt to a number of academic colleagues at University College Dublin, in particular Professor Tom Garvin and Professor Michael Laffan, and wish above all to thank the contributors, their families and executors.

BRYAN FANNING
University College Dublin
November 2011

CHAPTER I

Introduction

Studies 1912–2012

Bryan Fanning

The Jesuits launched *Studies* in March 1912; this anthology marks its unbroken centenary. It draws from some 400 issues containing more than 3,000 essays. The one per cent solution distilled here was selected to exemplify and reflect a century of debate and analysis of Irish social and political change. The focus is on nine decades of Irish independence and the crucial decade beforehand that witnessed seismic change. In its first decade *Studies* reflected the Catholic constitutional nationalism that became displaced by Sinn Féin. After the War of Independence and the Civil War it hosted the mainstream social, economic, constitutional and political debates that shaped the new state. Both the conservative and liberal wings of the Catholic bourgeois who dominated politics and academia set out their thinking in *Studies*.

A catholic intent was signalled by its initial subtitle: *An Irish Quarterly Review of Letters, Philosophy and Science*. The stated objective of *Studies*, set out in the first issue, was to 'give publicity to work of a scholarly type, extending over many important branches of study, and appealing to a wider circle of cultured readers than strictly specialist journals could be expected to reach.' Specifically, it sought to address general modern literature, comprising both critical and original work; Celtic, Classical and Oriental subjects; historical questions that had some bearing on religious and social issues; philosophy, sociology, education and the experimental and observational sciences. In 1912 Catholic intentions hardly needed to be advertised. In time the subtitle became shortened to *An Irish Quarterly Review* with the accompanying explanation of the remit of *Studies*: 'It examines Irish social, political, cultural and economic issues in the light of Christian values and explores the Irish dimension in literature, history, philosophy and religion.'

In the pages of *Studies* the Manichean distinctions between Catholicism and liberalism claimed by some accounts of Irish modernisation break down. The Irish century it exemplifies reveals symbiosis as well as conflict between both intellectual traditions. Catholicism had found political common ground with nineteenth-century liberalism; in the decades after independence both favoured a minimal state; Catholics were economic liberals and visa versa. In *Studies*, prompted by the northern conflict, clerics came to advocate constitutional pluralism on issues such as divorce. *Studies* had moved well to the left of the political mainstream by the 1980s; its critique of the economic crisis of that decade focused very much on the damage to social cohesion engendered by market forces.

Many leading academics published extensively in *Studies*. For example, Michael Tierney, Professor of Classics and later President of University College Dublin contributed 55 articles between 1922 and 1953. These accounted for most of his academic output and included many public intellectual contributions to Irish debates. George O'Brien, the leading economist of his generation, published 33 articles in *Studies* between 1914 and 1947. Timothy Corcoran SJ, the dominant educationalist of his day, contributed 38 essays between 1912 and 1941.

In recent decades *Studies* can legitimately claim outsider status; the decline of Catholic power and expansion of various media moved the centre of Establishment debates elsewhere. Tierney's successors in twenty-first century university management actively dissuade Irish scholars from contributing to Irish periodicals like *Studies*. Instead they are expected to exclusively target international specialist journals; by definition 'international' excludes Irish periodicals; inadvertently such an international focus sponsors provincialism. In recent decades Catholic ideas have found expression as dissidence where once these represented the Irish status quo. Scepticism about neo-liberalism and commitment to social justice set *Studies* apart from the rightward shift of the Irish political mainstream. In an Ireland stifled by damaging complacencies its new place outside the mainstream has been both honourable and interesting. In selecting the essays that make up this anthology a number of aims collided. These included a desire to include some of the best, best-known and most influential essays, to represent key debates and recurring themes, and to capture a century of social, political, cultural and economic change.

Corcoran, the first editor, was close to Eamon de Valera and a mentor to the future Archbishop John Charles McQuaid.[1] In the post-1912 period he was unofficial leader of the Sinn Féin caucus at the university.[2] In this he was at odds with the main thrust of political opinion within *Studies*, as exemplified by his fellow professors (and former students at Clongowes) Thomas Kettle and Arthur Clery. The political culture into which *Studies* was born is captured by Stephen Collins's 2009 essay on John Redmond, the intellectual one by Denis Gwynn's 1966 article on Kettle. Both are included here.

However, in 1916 *Studies* became temporarily caught up in the wave of emotion that followed the post-Rising executions. It responded with a series entitled 'Poets of the Insurrection'. Thomas McDonagh's patriotism, as evident in his poems, was described as a 'furnace glow of passion'. Joseph Mary Plunket drew admiration for proclaiming that he was dying for God and the honour of Ireland.[3] John F. MacEntee was described as 'a genuine if immature poet', who hated 'all that the word "England" means to an enlightened and patriotic Irishman', yet was passionately fond of English literature, architecture and art.[4] Each was described at the time as an exemplar of Catholic piety and true patriotism. McEntee, who survived 1916, changed his first name to Seán and set aside poetry for a long career in politics. The summer 1916 verdict on Patrick Pearse was that he was a better short story and prose writer than he was a poet. Some of his poems were 'so simple that one may not say much about them'.[5] However, he was portrayed as a brilliant educationalist (subsequent appraisals in *Studies* would say propagandist) in his use of school pageants to foster simultaneously a patriotic and religious spirit amongst his pupils. Later scathing reappraisals – enough to comprise a hefty anthology – saw nothing Christ-like in Pearse's invocation of patriotic blood sacrifice, a theme Pearse was gearing up to in his sole contribution to *Studies*, 'Some Aspects of Irish Literature' in 1913, that is included here in abridged form. The best-known attack in *Studies* on such ideas, 'The Canon of Irish History: A Challenge' by Francis Shaw SJ (1972) is also included here. Also selected is a 1966 eyewitness account of the Rising by Seán Lemass. In 'I Remember 1916' Lemass recalled encountering Eoin MacNeill on Easter Monday in Rathfarnham before he headed into town to join the fighting. MacNeill 'seemed agitated and depressed' and 'very clearly unhappy about the whole situation'. Four other Irish Prime Ministers, W. T. Cosgrave, Garret FitzGerald, John Bruton and Bertie Ahern have also published articles in *Studies*.

Tom Kettle perished on the Western Front within weeks of the Rising. As Professor of Political Economy and essayist he exemplified the distinctive fusion of Catholic and liberal ideas which influenced much that *Studies* published about economics for half a century. Arthur Clery's obituary in *Studies* described him as 'the most brilliant mind of the generation that succeeded Parnell'. Kettle, Clery emphasised, was 'at all relevant times a constitutionalist, a parliamentary nationalist, but with a highly developed dramatic sense', rooted in the orthodoxy of the Irish Party of Davitt and Parnell, but also part of a cosmopolitan movement, that existed as an undeveloped alternative to the 'Irish-Ireland' ideology of which D. P. Moran was the prophet. A casual observer, Clery argued, would describe this incorrectly as 'socialistic'. What this amounted to was 'an effort to apply cosmopolitan ideas of regeneration (often without any clear idea of what they were)' to social conditions – 'in fact, an aspiration towards modern "progress" of the less brutal kind.'

One of Clery's contributions to *Studies*, 'Votes for Youth' (1915) exemplified such progressive liberalism; Clery's concern was with finding a political mechanism to provide an impetus against the exploitation of children in the Irish labour market. The context was the campaign of the suffragettes whose demands both he and Kettle supported. The alternative to Romantic nationalism presented in *Studies* was one that emphasised no practical reform in the living conditions of Irish people. The solutions to Ireland's problems, a 1919 article on the housing conditions of dock workers implied, lay more in better urban planning than political ideology.[6] In the decades that followed with the rise of communism and fascism abroad and threats to parliamentary democracy at home, *Studies* held fast to its focus on reform of a less brutal kind. Clery's eulogy for Kettle appeared in December 1916. He described meeting his friend in Dublin following the executions, just weeks before his own death in France: 'his whole conversation was of MacDonagh and the others who had been put to death in Low Week, of the fortitude they had shown. He felt very bitterly ... He died in a different way for a different cause.'[7]

Other appreciations for Kettle followed. The 1966 one republished here by Denis Gwynn places him within the social and intellectual milieu from which *Studies* also emerged. Gwynn published 30 articles in *Studies* between 1922 (the first on French foreign policy), and in 1966 the essay included here first appeared. He had been a pupil of Kettle's at UCD and also one of Pearse's at St Edna's; he came from similar bourgeois stock; his father had been an Irish Party MP. Gwynn was wounded on the Western Front and invalided home in 1917. John Redmond's son died in France.

In 1920 *Studies* published an article by Henry Gill SJ, a much-decorated former member of the Irish Guards (DSO and MC), which described events during his time as Catholic chaplin to the 2nd Royal Irish Rifles. His account of his quest referred to the death of another Jesuit chaplain to the Irish Guards, a fellow aficionado of the history of Irish regiments. Such commemoration of Irishmen who died in the Great War, Catholic Redmonites as well as Protestants, was driven underground by the versions of nationalism that came to dominate ideologically post-1912 Irish politics. Hostility to the commemoration of Armistice Day and Remembrance Sunday became, to some extent, institutionalised within the new state.[8] In 1993, the seventy-fifth anniversary of the Armistice, an Irish Head of State attended a Remembrance Sunday service for the first time.

The First World War, the Irish War of Independence and the subsequent Civil War received little contemporary attention in *Studies*. An article assessing the journal on its seventy-fifth anniversary in 1986 attributes this to an early decision that *Studies* should be characterised by reasoned and detached criticism. One exception was Daniel Corkery's eulogy 'Terence MacSwiney: Lord Mayor of Cork' (1920), following MacSwiney's death from hunger strike in Brixton prison. Corkery saw him as cut from the same cloth as Pearse when it came to patriotic fervour and self-sacrifice.[9] AE's sober 'Lessons of Revolution' (1923) was more characteristic of the *Studies* viewpoint. The champions of physical force, he argued in an essay reproduced here, had poisoned the soul of Ireland: 'The very children in the streets play at assassination, ambush and robbery.'

After independence *Studies* published many articles on the implications of Catholic social thought as set out in the papal encyclicals *Rerum Novarum* (1891) and *Quadragesimo Anno* (1931). A key contributor here was Alfred O'Rahilly, Professor of Mathematics and later President of University College Cork. Article after article struggled with the practicalities of corporatist and vocationalist alternatives to socialism and capitalism. Whilst many articles disparaged socialist political experiments, many were genuinely informative. Whilst Catholic social thought proposed a conservative political project this should not be mistaken for a crude anti-modernist one. O'Rahilly's first article in *Studies* had been a defence of Darwinism from a Catholic perspective. His second contribution was a very fine survey of works by Nietzsche that had yet to become available in English.

Virginia Crawford's 'The Rise of Fascism and What it Stands For' (1923) noted the apparently successful corporatist restructuring of trade unions and the establishment of vocationalist councils, all along lines mooted by Catholic thinkers. However, this was leavened by a scathing account of Fascist terrorism. Their methods 'were those of the Black and Tans'. She described how lorries filled with armed Fascisti would concentrate at a given signal on a Socialist municipality, setting fire to Labour Halls and Co-operative Stores, destroying and looting property unhindered. Mussolini, she reported, had restored religious teaching in the schools ('not that he is a practising Catholic but he accepts Italy as a traditional Catholic country and believes that religion is beneficial for the masses') but any Irish admirers she argued, would be wise to copy the extreme caution of the Vatican in its dealings with the new Italian state.[10]

By the time a corporatist state (the replacement of democracy with vocational representation) was mooted by General O'Duffy it found little support in *Studies*. Significantly, Michael Tierney, a key intellectual figure in *Cumann na nGaedheal* and a founder of *Fine Gael*, wrote nothing in *Studies* in the course of some 55 articles that advocated corporatism or vocationalism. In 1935 O'Rahilly argued that the corporate state was dead as a political idea, and rightly so. There was no real point to a vocational senate with, say, one doctor, one professor, a few industrialists, some farmers, shopkeepers and workers and so on. *Dáil Éireann* was, as things stood, probably just as diverse. Instead the emphasis had to be on the adoption of a Christian constitution protecting, as he put it, 'our natural and religious rights and embodying our social aspirations.' The main institutional success of Catholic social thought lay with the insertion of natural law principles into the sections of the 1937 Constitution on family (Articles 40–44) and into the preamble of the Constitution. Dermot Keogh, in 'The Jesuits and the 1937 Constitution' (1989), reproduced here, assesses the nature and extent of Catholic influence.

In March 1933 Daniel A. Binchy, who had been the Irish Minister to Germany from 1929 to 1932, published an astute article on Adolf Hitler. It was written before the March 1933 elections which cemented Hitler's political domination over Germany. Binchy had first heard Hitler speak in Munich in 1921. At the time he described Hitler to a friend as 'a harmless lunatic with the gift of oratory'. His friend retorted: 'No lunatic with the gift of oratory is harmless.' Binchy detailed plans, outlined in *Mein Kampf*, for the withdrawal of citizenship from Jews and the confiscation of their property. Subsequent articles in *Studies* also contested Nazi racial theories. 'The Nazi Movement in Germany' (1938) by Revd Denis O'Keeffe, then Professor of Ethics and Politics at UCD, rubbished Nazi racial theories as 'pseudo-scientific nonsense'. He described their claims as characteristic of extreme forms of nationalism (what a social scientist might now call essentialism). There was, he observed, 'a natural tendency for nations to seek an escape from the inadequacies of the present in a mythical past. This is a common experience in all countries. But it requires a portentous absence of humour to accept the theory in the form given to it in Nazi literature – in this form it is altogether pathological.'[11]

Post-independence Irish Catholicism is now often depicted as monolithically repressive. Yet a strong distaste for any the authoritarian political experiments of the twentieth century – extreme nationalism at home, fascism and communism abroad – characterised the early decades of *Studies*. A large number of articles examined the rise of state socialism. Most were inevitably critical; many were genuinely informative about Marxist ideas; some were clearly awed by the Soviet experiment. In 1926, 1929 and 1932 *Studies* published reports by visitors to Soviet Russia. The first example, 'Two Months in Soviet Russia' by Violet Connolly described a delightful 'pulse of life' behind the shabby character of day-to-day existence, noting only in passing that prospective émigrés recounted alarming stories about 'the latest communist enormities'.[12] In 'Reflections After Visiting Russia'

(1929) Peter Somerville came away by no means certain that Communism would be an economic failure.[13] In 1932 the economist John Busteed insisted that the Soviets had accomplished colossal tasks.[14]

A 1938 symposium in *Studies*, whereby a number of writers responded to an article by Michael Tierney, adroitly captures the then intellectual politics of cultural nationalism and isolationism. Tierney's essay along with a response by Daniel Binchy is reproduced here so as to illustrate both sides of the debate. Tierney's piece was an attack on the intellectual legacy of Daniel O'Connell. Binchy to some extent sided with Sean O'Faolain whose book on O'Connell, *King of the Beggars*, was the object of discussion. O'Faolain had in turn challenged the core arguments of Daniel Corkery's *The Hidden Ireland*, the most celebrated intellectual defence of cultural isolationism. Both books were proxies for post-independence ideological conflicts between liberals and cultural isolationists.

Like Corkery, Tierney championed a Catholic cultural 'restoration' that would turn back the clock on nineteenth-century utilitarianism and liberalism and other 'great heresies' of the last three hundred years. Both imagined in their respective thought experiments reversing the influence of the Reformation and on the post-Reformation destruction of Gaelic Catholic culture. Tierney found little fault with O'Faolain's account of the genesis of the modern Irish nation. Gaelic League platforms were built on 'faked tradition' but this did not, he argued, warrant a denunciation of the older Gaelic society that preceded the political Irish nation. The foundations of modern Ireland laid down by O'Connell were ones built on an indigenous cultural vacuum. O'Connell's Benthamite ideas justified the abandonment of Gaelic for the 'superior utility of the English tongue'.

Tierney's solution, like Corkery's, was to promote a cultural Restoration even though he accepted that whatever might be restored would not be authentic. Many successful civilisations were built, Tierney explained, on attempts to 'recover literary, linguistic and artistic traditions that were not always genuinely ancestral to them'. The vanished Gaelic past then, however unreal, was a necessary ideological bulwark against the cultural void of individualism and utilitarianism. But Tierney also acknowledged that such cultural restoration did not fulfil the institutional needs of a nation state. The invocation of a mythic past sometimes worked as symbolic politics but not as a basis of policy making.

After independence Irish economic policy was anti-protectionist. A punctilious observance of British economic orthodoxies, including the doctrine of free trade, prevailed. For example, a 1924 article by C. H. Oldham, Professor of National Economics at UCD, lambasted the assumption that protectionist tariffs would foster industrial development. Oldham pointed to the incapacity of the Irish home-market to absorb the whole of industrial output. Exports were crucial for the survival of Irish manufacture. Protectionism would be inflationary because imported raw materials were needed. Economic development, he argued, could only be sustained by *laissez faire* policies and by resisting a sentimental chauvinism towards Irish goods.[15] In 1927 John Busteed advised that tariffs 'were part of a larger complex problem and in themselves produced endlessly complex reactions'. On their own they could not solve the problems of the Irish economy.[16]

One volume of Robert Skidelsky's biography of John Maynard Keynes is subtitled *The Economist as Saviour*.[17] In the Irish case such accolades are usually reserved for T. K. Whitaker. But Whitaker had, in Patrick Lynch, a John the Baptist who was much more than a herald. His 1953 essay 'The Economist and Public Policy', republished here, reveals Lynch as intellectual midwife to Irish developmentalism. Many writers on the Irish twentieth century presume or imply that the publication of Whitaker's *Economic Development* in 1957 represented day zero of a new economy and society. The actual document itself would disappoint readers expecting some grand manifesto. Most of it refers to agricultural productivity; its novelty and importance consists of an appendix of correspondence between Whitaker, head of the Department of Finance and Seán Lemass. The direction that Whitaker proposed can be traced through a series of articles published in *Studies* by various Irish economists in the preceding two decades.

From the outset *Studies* was very much preoccupied with economics; its behind-the-scenes founder Thomas Finlay SJ went on to become UCD Professor of Political Economy. In 1932 Finlay's protégé and successor at UCD, George O'Brien, invited John Maynard Keynes to give the first memorial Finlay lecture: this was published the following year in *Studies*. The lecture had been attended by de Valera and his Cabinet as well as by W. T. Cosgrave and former members of his government. Keynes, when later recalling his visit to Dublin, described Cosgrave as very much the nineteenth-century liberal.[18] His lecture as published in *Studies* warrants inclusion here as an historically important statement of ideas that came to profoundly influence subsequent Irish economic and policy debates.

In 1953, *Studies* gave a platform to Patrick Lynch to argue for Keynesian planning and offer reassurances about growing state activism. *Studies* published a number of seminal articles advocating an economic develop-mental role for the state. Lynch argued for realistic debate stripped of ideological polemic about the necessity for some state activism. Many critics of state interventionism sheltered behind 'the lingering shadows of economic liberalism to deny positive economic functions to a government'. Their views were, he argued, based on an incorrect reading of classical economics and on a convenient disregard of economic history. Economic arguments were one thing – these depended on time and place – and ideology was another. Lynch quoted Keynes: 'Practical men who believe themselves to be quite exempt from any intellectual influences, are usually the slaves of some defunct economist.' Indeed much of what he had to say owed much to Keynes. Economic liberalism had been bankrupt since the Great Depression. Lynch emphasised the impracticality of *laissez faire* ideology – 'the only untried utopia' – because it had never naturally occurred in the world. In a 1963 article Lynch described his preferred approach as 'non-doctrinal state activity'.[19] It was one distinctly derived from the ideological models of liberal Keynesian economics and Catholic social thought. His influential argument was that when it came to state planning and development there was no conflict of interests between Church and State.

A number of articles in *Studies* had railed against the spectre of a welfare state. The 1951 'Mother and Child Scheme' as proposed by Noel Browne was vilified in a number. But nuanced analyses of the British post-war plans were also published. In 1944 George O'Brien contributed three such articles. None of these are reproduced here but their contents warrant recollection. The first, 'Capitalism in Transition' argued that the great age of capitalism had passed. Reform had won out over revolution; future societies would be more egalitarian than before, with less poverty and no 'pauperism'. This new social security would, he suggested, come at a cost to society:

> People will be less forward-looking. Social security will provide against the risks and hazards of life … The falling birth-rate and the gradual ageing of the population will reduce the importance of the family as a unit in the social structure. Saving, the typical Victorian virtue, will cease to arouse applause. The accumulation of a fortune, the dearest Victorian ambition, will no longer command respect.[20]

In his second article in 1944 O'Brien examined the White Paper produced by the British Government in response to the Beveridge Plan. He noted that Seán Lemass had commended the British document – *Full Employment in a Free Society* – to members of the Dáil as a useful guide to dealing with Irish conditions.[21] His third promoted F. A. Hayek's *The Road to Serfdom* as an antidote to its likely excesses.[22] O'Brien's attempt to Catholicise Hayek suggested profound ambivalence indeed to social democracy even if he was convinced as an economist of the need for a stronger state role. In 'New Views on Unemployment' (1945) O'Brien summarised the thesis of Keynes's *General Theory of Employment*, the theory underpinning the Beveridge Report. O'Brien had long championed Keynes. The *General Theory* argued, amongst other things, that free trade could no longer be trusted to maximise the volume of production. There was then a *prima facie* case for state intervention in the economy. The state, Keynes argued and Beveridge accepted, could alleviate chronic unemployment by stimulating demand through state expenditure. That is, it could break past cycles where high unemployment and high saving coexisted. By spending more than its current revenue, it could add to the total expenditure of the community. It could add directly to consumption, that is, stimulate economic demand by subsidising goods through schemes of public investment or by redistributing income from the rich to the poor.[23] O'Brien endorsed the validity of Keynes's paradigm and, for all his reservations, Beveridge's proposals based upon it. In subsequent articles on the welfare state clerics invoked Hayek just as economists had routinely cited papal encyclicals in their contributions to *Studies*. What Lynch successfully proposed in 1953 was to shift this conservative consensus towards accepting greater levels of state activism.

The IRA 1956 Border Campaign prompted some soul searching about the notion of a united Ireland, a hitherto taken-for-granted aspiration of constitutional nationalists writing in *Studies*. Donal Barrington's 'Uniting Ireland', reprinted here, argued that prevalent nationalist thinking was impoverished. It blamed partition on British rule and claimed that what Britain had done it must undo. She must take home her money, her men and her influence, liberate the six occupied counties and re-unite Ireland. The paradox was that nationalists ultimately demanded that the British army force all Irishmen to live together. Partition, he argued, was not forced on Ireland by Britain but necessitated by the conflicting demands of the two parties of Irishmen. It was Ireland's crime against itself rather than England's crime against Ireland. Barrington's article was republished in 1959 as the first pamphlet by *Tuairim*, a collective of young – all were under 40 years of age – progressive academics and policy makers.

Barrington was fiercely critical of how de Valera, John A. Costello and particularly Seán MacBride had sought to lever international opinion in favour of Southern claims. This, Barrington implied, restated the old demand that the British should impose Irish unity. The scale of Southern misunderstanding of the North was huge. Southern efforts (the 'ill-fated Mansion House Committee') sought to fund the campaigns of anti-partition candidates. This met with a backlash in the 1949 General Election. It gave the Unionist Party its biggest victory to date and 'wiped out' the Northern Ireland Labour Party. For the first time the latter then came out against partition. At the same time no effort had been made to engage with Unionists.

In his *Memoir*, Conor Cruise O'Brien, recalled life as a Foreign Affairs civil servant under MacBride, who, in 1951, was the Minister in charge of such propaganda.[24] O'Brien was tasked to establish an Irish News Agency to put out stories comparing the British 'occupation' of the North with Soviet occupation of Eastern Europe. O'Brien recalled a pamphlet designed for

Irish-American consumption supposedly authored by the American League for an undivided Ireland but ghost-written by McBride. McBride's successor Frank Aiken deemed this policy of 'brandishing the sore thumb all over the world' to be unproductive. In the same issue containing 'Uniting Ireland' O'Brien contributed a seminal article (in terms of his own subsequent political and ideological engagement with Unionists). 'A Sample of Loyalties' (1957) analysed 'the ideas and feelings contained in a batch of essays written towards the end of 1953 by a class of 26 boys, aged 13 to 14 years of age attending a large Protestant secondary school in the Six Counties'. The set topic of the essay was 'Ireland'. The value of the exercise for O'Brien was 'an unguarded candour and clarity' unlikely from 'older or more intellectual members of that community'. Twenty of the essays expressed various degrees of positive feeling towards Ireland as homeland: many were attached to some sense of Irishness. As put by one boy who professed to like the poetry of Yeats: 'I am sort of a way attracted to its music its famousness and its green fields. We should be proud of it.' Another wrote; 'Ireland is a good country in spite of their overcrowded towns and their slums and the Roman Catholic inhabitants.' Nine of the 26 boys stated a preference for unification. Just one of the boys came out unequivocally against it. Only four went into any specifics about what they meant by reunification. One concluded it would be good if Northern Ireland and 'Éire' were brought together under the Queen's rule. The second maintained that reunification should be under the British flag. The third suggested that Ireland should be a separate nation with a king. For the fourth, it required forgetting the seventeenth century.[25]

These responses were far removed from nationalist understandings of what was meant by the unification of Ireland. A degree of religious sectarianism was identifiable but O'Brien cautioned reading too much into some of the misconceptions the boys demonstrated about Catholicism. A similar exercise conducted amongst Southern Catholic schoolboys would produce similar howlers. That said, O'Brien left the teacher to whom he owed his article anonymous lest, 'in the grim words of one of his essayists, he be silently disposed of.'

The next major debate on nationalism occurred in the 1966 issue that marked the 50th anniversary of the 1916 Rising. Shaw's article on the Rising was refused publication in 1966; the then editor Ronald Burke-Savage SJ considered it too controversial for what was meant to be a commemoration. When it was finally published in 1972 the accompanying editorial by Peter Troddyn SJ described it as a 'tract for the present troubled time'.[26] Weighing in with more than 17,000 words – several times the length of usual contributions to *Studies* – Shaw savaged the account of Irish history mobilised by Pearse, and attacked subsequent 'myths' that had grown up around the actual events of 1916. Tone aside (and puns; there was much criticism of Wolfe Tone), Shaw said little that had not been advanced in critiques of Pearse and analyses of Irish history published in *Studies* in 1966. Burke-Savage's 1966 editorial had defended, as did Shaw, the patriotism of Eoin MacNeill who had opposed the Rising at the last moment.[27] David Thornley emphasised Pearse's obsession with the idea of blood sacrifice. He quoted Pearse from December 1915 as writing about the European war:

> The last sixteen months have been the most glorious in the history of Europe. Heroism has come back to Earth ... The old heart of the earth needed to be warmed with the red wine of the battlefields. Such august homage was never before offered to God as this, the homage of millions of lives given gladly for love of country.[28]

Shaw quoted this also. In the same 1966 issue Augustine Martin picked out another example of Pearse's 'terrifying' rhetoric also cited by Shaw:

> We may make mistakes in the beginning and shoot the wrong people; but bloodshed is a cleansing and a sanctifying thing, and the nation which regards it as the final horror has lost its manhood. There are many things more horrible than bloodshed; and slavery is one of them.[29]

Perhaps the most trenchant critique published in *Studies* in its 1966 'commemoration' came from Garret FitzGerald. He admired the courage of the men who died but insisted that they hardly warranted admiration as thinkers:

> This almost mediaeval respect for the letter of what had been written or spoken between 1913 and 1916 by the leaders of the Rising is misconceived. Even if these men had been political or social thinkers of world standing, their thoughts on the Ireland they knew could not have stood up to such prolonged and unthinking veneration, but they did not regard themselves – nor were they in fact great thinkers.[30]

They had, FitzGerald argued, few clear-cut ideas of political or social philosophy. There had been, for instance, deep differences between Pearse and Connolly over the 1913 strike. But neither went into the GPO with a coherent intellectual, political or social programme; political freedom was an end in itself. To treat then the Proclamation of 1916 as a great source of political or social doctrines was to misunderstand what it meant to those who wrote it. Granted, it contained noble ideals, the wish to secure political freedom expressed in an enduring language, but no clear ideas. It was a mistake for Irish people half a century later to ask themselves of what they might do or say on any issue: 'Their views on modern Ireland would be no more valuable than many of their colleagues still alive, and probably less valuable than many of our contemporaries.' FitzGerald's argument was that Ireland could not be administered on a day-to-day basis by the dead.

The Northern conflict came to preoccupy *Studies* to a considerable extent. Debate and analysis in *Studies* emphasised that the need to foster ecumenism and pluralism in the North required reform down South. Here criticism emerged of those very constitutional provisions successfully promoted by the Jesuits in 1937. In 'Constitutional Aspects of Pluralism' (1978) Mary Redmond observed that it was relatively easy to single out various phrases and provisions that might be said to offend against a pluralist society. Her list included the preamble where the people of Éire were proclaimed in effect to be a Catholic nationalist people, Articles 2 and 3, which claimed the North, Article 8 which proclaimed a Gaelic ethos in addition to the nationalist one and, of course Articles 41 to 44 which reflected Catholic teaching.[31] Her remedy included gradual change by Referendum. In the same issue in 'Cultural Pluralism', Liam de Paor argued that time would solve many of the problems rooted in the different origins of the two main communities on the island. English at the end of the day was the common language, the Republic had abandoned the culturally isolationist preoccupations of the post-colonial era, and even in the North there was ample common cultural ground.[32]

In a 1978 piece John Brady SJ argued that citizens of the Republic must emphasise that they did not wish to govern Northern Ireland against the wishes of the majority. In many respects Brady updated Barrington's argument for unification by consent. He maintained that there was a need to modify those aspects of law and public administration that seemed to give the state a markedly Catholic character. These included issues such as divorce and contraception. A carefully framed divorce law would, he argued, be for the common good. The Irish prohibition on the sale of contraceptives in the wake of the 1973 McGee ruling was described as 'bizarre'. Brady argued that to abstain completely from all efforts to influence the decisions of mixed marriages – the abandonment of *Ne Temere* – would be 'an appropriate gesture'. Inter-denominational schooling was needed in the North. Children could be taken to separate classes for religious education, but there was a case for pilot work on the ecumenical teaching of religion using the same textbooks for Protestant and Catholics which would explain divergences in understanding and the existence of a common Christian heritage. In his winter 1985 editorial Brian Lennon SJ also argued that the state should not prohibit divorce.[33]

From the 1960s *Studies* was at the vanguard of progressive social debate. It published articles by members of *Tuairim*, the new rising generation in

Irish public life (*Tuairim*'s charter stipulated that members should be under 40 years of age; Ireland was at the time still run by the 1916-era gerontocracy). In addition to Donal Barrington and Patrick Lynch these included Garret FitzGerald and David Thornley. The new mood found expression within the editorials and articles of Ronald Burke-Savage. In the forward-looking 'Ireland: 1963–1973' he called for a new openness to the disparate intellectual traditions that had shaped Irish society:

> The best of the Protestant Anglo-Irish tradition has much to offer us in its concern for civic responsibilities, for virtues of truthfulness and hard work, and for its concern for the appreciation and cultivation of arts and letters. Our national ideal would be a poor one without these qualities. Thinking in Ireland has been much influenced by English welfare liberals and socialists. Again many of their ideas must find a place in our national ideal, ideas which often find a firmer foundation and a stronger motive-power in the authentic Christian tradition than in the premises from which their formulators derived them.[34]

Even socialist ideas, Burke-Savage implied, could be claimed for Christian social justice; he referred to the socialist traditions of Methodism and Nonconformism (which were subsequently much emphasised in the United Kingdom by New Labour). The early 1970s witnessed an alliance between post-Vatican II clerical advocates of social justice and left anti-poverty activists. This found influential expression in the 1971 Kilkenny Conference of the Council of Social Welfare. The new radical Catholic mood was exemplified by Sr Stanislaus Kennedy's *One Million Poor? – The Challenge of Irish Inequality*.[35] In *Studies*, Frank Sammon SJ published several articles depicting poverty as a structural problem, one resulting from inequality of power and resources, as a problem that could not be solved just by economic growth.[36]

The winter 1982 editorial had proclaimed a 'radical shift' in future editorial policy. 'We aim,' it began, 'to be non-academic in future, reacting more to the problems of the day, while maintaining the traditional interest of *Studies* in general Irish culture.' However, such a shift had been building for a number of years. The editorial view from the late 1970s onwards was that *Studies* had misplaced its *raison d'être*.[37] The new emphasis was to be upon the perceived dislocations resulting from social injustices, secularisation and loss of political legitimacy. These were understood as somehow intertwined with the problem of declining Catholic influence in the Republic, but also with conflicts in the North. The focus on poverty and inequality was then, to some extent, about reacquiring moral capital. But the new radical emphasis on social justice was also heartfelt. Galvanised by third-world liberation theology Gerry O'Hanlon SJ criticised the preoccupation of Northern clergy with doctrinal orthodoxy at the expense of secular welfare.

He argued that social justice was a burning issue for Northern Catholics, whilst the sermons of their clergy tended to focus on matters of personal piety.[38] Down South relevance was equated with radical commitment to addressing social inequalities.

With neo-liberalism ascendant, Hayek's *The Road to Serfdom* had many new admirers in the West, but none in *Studies*. Various articles around this time argued that the market was a good servant, but a poor master. The state, Kieran Kennedy urged in 1985, should not allow the market to dominate when it produced socially unacceptable results. A 1985 editorial by Brian Lennon SJ urged the Church to position itself to the left of the political mainstream. Now market forces rather than the state were the enemies of social cohesion. In another editorial the same year Lennon professed regret that Irish socialism had been stillborn. Yet another 1985 article (by Emmet Larkin) concluded that the current Irish labour movement had 'produced the most opportunistically conservative Labour Party anywhere in the known world'.[39] This victory of Catholic thought in the early years of *Studies* was now to be regretted.

A 1985 editorial described the reality of Dublin working-class parishes where less than 10 per cent attended Sunday mass regularly. A review article in the same year by Tom Inglis defined secularisation as 'the decline of traditional religious practices that produce a shared meaning and consciousness amongst members of society'.[40] In the same issue Michael Paul Gallagher SJ argued that 'under the open conditions of Irish modernity' faith could no longer be imposed. The decline of traditional authority meant that it could not be accepted passively. Faith had become, like many other things, a matter of individual choice.[41]

In this context *Studies* promoted anti-authoritarian solidarity rather than a return to obedience. Themed issues such as spring 1983's *Upstairs, Downstairs* by John Sweeney emphasised the need to challenge social inequality. Autumn 1983's *'Private' Property* emphasised 'the ever widening gap between the managerial class and the Irish worker'. Spring 1984's issue *A Solution to Homelessness* outlined the history of vagrancy laws and their current use against homeless people who had been denied social housing. In a number of articles *Studies* captured the mixture of anger and despair that to some extent characterised the 1980s.

The hallucinogenic despair of the 1980s has more than a little relevance to the Ireland of 2012. Three articles included here address different aspects of social and economic dislocation. In the first, from 1983, Sweeney argued that neo-liberalism had blithely permitted huge levels of social inequality; this he warned would drive disaffected unemployed people into the arms of Sinn Féin. Sweeney argued that the economic success that followed *Economic Development* in 1958 had created an Irish society that was more relatively unequal than before. In the second 1984 review Raymond Crotty lacerated the veneration of Whitaker, 'Ireland's most influential civil servant'. Whitaker in his various roles (first Secretary of the Department of Finance, then Governor of the Central Bank) had, according to Crotty, contributed much to the current economic crisis. The great defining political event of the early 1980s – the 1983 Constitutional Referendum on the Right to Life of the Child – vindicated the influence of Catholic conceptions of human rights, even if religious observance had gone into decline. A 1981 article 'Pessimistic Origins of the Anti-Life Movement' speculated that the prevalence of abortion in wealthy capitalist society was an existential response to materialism born out of secular despair. The third examination of 1980's anxiety included here, a 1987 article by Margaret Mac Curtain, examined the moving statues phenomenon as a kind of atavistic religion response to social change. *Studies* also published articles criticising economic fatalism including one, republished here, by Tom Garvin, which emphasised the concrete economic and social gains of the post-1950s era.

The 1990s saw some important debate on the future of Catholicism and the emergence of a neo-conservative critique of social liberalism following what Tony Fahey called in an article reprinted here, a post-1960s 'flirtation with liberal thought'. Fahey's 1994 sociological analysis of the apparent decline of Catholicism (the main theme of Irish sociology for decades) stood out from the pack by focusing astutely on the options now facing the Irish Church. Simply put, it could dilute itself by spreading itself thinly across the whole of Irish society, for example by continuing to run most of the primary and secondary school system or it could choose to focus on the needs of a smaller devout population: quality, so to speak, over quantity.

Studies remained to the left of the political mainstream when it came to the pursuit of social inclusion for some marginal groups. Various articles by Peter McVerry SJ and others were critical of the inadequacy of state responses to the needs of the homeless and other vulnerable people. But it also developed a conservative critique of the impact of social liberalism on Irish society. This perspective is represented in this anthology by Mary Kenny's autobiographical essay on forty years of Irish feminism. *Studies* remained, as always, preoccupied with Christian ideas and religion in Irish society. In keeping with its long-standing pluralist ethos it published in 2004 an article on the political influence of Protestant theological ideas on Unionist politics. The very first issue of *Studies* in 1912 had contained an article on Islam.

In the last decade some new fields of debate stand out alongside the many other articles that continued to be published on various aforementioned themes. There has been a recurring focus on the crisis of accountability in Irish life. Many articles have addressed topics such as the institutional abuse of children and other vulnerable persons in Irish society. Finola

Kennedy's 2000 article on the suppression of the 1931 Carrigan Report depicts a long history of state institutional failure in protecting children from abuse. As Arthur Clery suggested in 1915 the exploitation (and abuse) of children was most likely where they were rendered powerless and there was no obligation to be accountable for how they were treated.

In June 1994 Father Brendan Smyth was convicted on 17 counts of sexual abuse of children over a period of 30 years. Smyth, according to Harry Ferguson, perpetrated appalling acts of violence against children and deserved to be demonised. Yet Ferguson was preoccupied with the vilification of celibate clerics. His underlying argument was that masculinity and male sexuality needed to be better understood and openly discussed in order to separate out the causes of sexual abuse from the moral panic that surrounded it.[42] An accompanying article in the same 1995 issue argued that some Church leaders, in their arrogance and hubris, had chosen to deny the seriousness of what was taking place and did not take steps to stop the behaviour of paedophile clerics.[43] There was, Noel Barber SJ argued in his editorial, too much concern about the 'good name' of the Church and too little concern for victims.[44] The winter 2005 issue contained several articles criticising responses by the institutional church to the scandal of abuse. The final 2010 essay included in this volume, 'No Cheap Grace' by Séamus Murphy SJ, is taken from a special issue of *Studies* published in response to the Ryan and Murphy reports on child sexual abuse. Murphy bluntly started with 'three simple facts'. A large number of priests sexually assaulted children during the last 40 years. Their superiors made no serious effort to punish or prevent them. If it were not for media *exposé*, it would still be going on.

The twenty-first century saw the emergence of immigration as a social and political issue in the Republic of Ireland. My own involvement with the journal (as a member of the editorial board) came about when a suggestion I made to the editor Fergus O'Donoghue SJ to publish a special issue on the topic was warmly received. Since then *Studies* has published articles on human trafficking, the treatment of asylum seekers, the participation of immigrants in politics, critiques of multiculturalism and analyses of immigration policy. It has similarly addressed a range of other contemporary social issues.

In a 2009 *Irish Times* interview Colm Tóibín, commented that the entire of Irish society 'has become as introspective and dull, almost as *Studies* magazine'.[45] Fergus O'Donoghue, responding on his editorial blog and in the best Jesuit tradition, took this as a back-handed compliment. O'Donoghue, for his part, preferred the word reflection to introspection. Tóibín also said that what Ireland needed was a period of very deep introspection. Tóibín, O'Donoghue noted, lived around the corner from Leeson Street where *Studies* was edited. He could be seen doing mundane things like queuing to be served in the local pharmacy, entering the newsagents, waiting for a traffic light to change, or even simply walking along the street. Reading this at the time, I imagined Colm Tóibín as a minor character in James Joyce's *Ulysses*, a bit like the Jesuit John Conmee, out walking in another part of Georgian Dublin with his fleeting thoughts of a book that he might write.[46] Joyce wove such banal perambulations into an epic, taking in the surface detail but also the inner lives that lay beneath. *Studies* has published many essays on Joyce.

What then of the more cutting charge: dullness. *Studies* cannot compete with the mainstream media in all its glittering twenty-first century forms, although it now has a state-of-the-art website. Yet, for decades it has functioned as a kind of metablog on Irish affairs where instead of throwaway comments the long essay form has prevailed. Many of these have been dull and worthy. Far fewer have been trivial. The best have been very good, and some have been very important. On dusty library stacks or readily accessible in digital form these are revealed as a century-long river of arguments and reflections on the changes, crises, culture, politics, passions and poetry of Irish society.

Notes

1   John Cooney, *John Charles McQuaid: Ruler of Catholic Ireland* (Dublin, 1999), p. 43.

2   Louis McRedmond, *To the Greater Glory: A History of the Irish Jesuits* (Dublin, 1991), pp. 236–7.

3   Peter McBrien, 'Poets of the Insurrection III: Joseph Plunkett', *Studies* vol. 5, no. 20 (1916), pp. 536–49.

4   Padric Gregory, 'Poets of the Insurrection IV: John F. MacEntee', *Studies* vol. 6, no. 21 (1917), pp. 70–9.

5   Ibid.

6   Lambert McKenna SJ, 'The Housing Problem in Dublin', *Studies* vol. 8, no. 30 (1919), pp. 279–95.

7   A. E. Clery, 'Thomas Kettle', *Studies* vol. 5, no. 20 (1916), pp. 503–15.

8   L. Leonard, 'The Twinge of Memory: Armistice Day and Remembrance Sunday in Dublin since 1919', in G. Walker and R. English (eds), *Unionism in Modern Ireland* (Dublin, 1996), pp. 107–9.

9   Daniel Corkery, 'Terence MacSwiney: Lord Mayor of Cork', *Studies* vol. 9, no. 36 (1920), pp. 512–20.

10 Virginia M. Crawford, 'The Rise of Fascism and What it Stands For', *Studies* vol. 12, no. 48 (1923), pp. 539–52.

11 Revd Professor Denis O'Keeffe, 'The Nazi Movement in Germany', *Studies* vol. 27, no. 105 (1938), pp. 1–11.

12 Violet Connolly, 'Two Months in Soviet Russia', *Studies* vol. 17, no. 69 (1923), pp. 64–78.

13 Peter Somerville, 'Reflections After Visiting Russia', *Studies* vol. 18, no. 72 (1929), pp. 556–68.

14 John Busteed, 'Soviet Russia', *Studies* vol. 21, no. 84 (1932), pp. 531–48.

15 C. H. Oldham, 'After the Fiscal Inquiry Report', *Studies* vol. 13, no. 49 (1924), pp. 1–13.

16 John Busteed, 'Foreign Trade and National Policy', *Studies* vol. 16, no. 61 (1927), pp. 69–85.

17 Robert Skidelsky, *John Maynard Keynes: The Economist as Saviour, 1920–1937* (London, 1992), p. 476.

18 Ibid., p. 479.

19 Patrick Lynch, 'Escape From Stagnation', *Studies* vol. 52, no. 206 (1963), pp. 136–63.

20 George O'Brien, 'Capitalism in Transition', *Studies* vol. 33, no. 129 (1944), pp. 37–44.

21 O'Brien, 'Stability of Employment: Its Possibility as a Post-War Aim', *Studies* vol. 33, no. 131 (1944), pp. 304–15.

22 O'Brien, 'A Challenge to the Planners', *Studies* vol. 33, no. 130 (1945), pp. 210–15.

23 O'Brien, 'New Views on Unemployment', *Studies* vol. 34, no. 133 (1945), pp. 33–56.

24 Conor Cruise O' Brien, *Memoir: My Life and Themes* (London, 1998), p. 160.

25 Cruise O'Brien, 'A Sample of Loyalties', *Studies* vol. 46, no. 184 (1957), pp. 403–10.

26 Peter M. Troddyn SJ, 'Editorial', *Studies* vol. 61, no. 242 (1972), pp. 110–12.

27 Ronald Burke-Savage SJ, 'Current Comment', *Studies* vol. 55, no. 217 (1966), pp. 1–6.

28 Patrick Pearse, *Peace and the Gael*, December 1915 cited in David Thornley, 'Patrick Pearse', *Studies* vol. 55, no. 217 (1966), pp. 110–28.

29 Augustine Martin, 'To Make a Right Rose Tree: Reflections on the Poetry of 1916', *Studies* vol. 55, no. 217 (1966), pp. 38–50.

30 Garret FitzGerald, 'The Significance of 1916', *Studies* vol. 55, no. 217 (1966), pp. 29–37.

31 Mary Redmond, 'Constitutional Aspects of Pluralism, *Studies* vol. 67, no. 265–6 (1978), pp. 39–59.

32 Liam de Paor, 'Cultural Pluralism', *Studies* vol. 67, no. 217 (1978), pp. 77–87.

33 Brian Lennon SJ, 'Editorial: Church and State', *Studies* vol. 74, no. 296 (1985), pp. 369–70.

34 Burke-Savage, 'Ireland: 1963–1973', *Studies* vol. 52, no. 206 (1963), pp. 117–18.

35 Sr Stanislaus Kennedy (ed.), *One Million Poor? – The Challenge of Irish Inequality* (Dublin, 1981).

36 Frank Sammon SJ, 'The Problem of Poverty in Ireland', *Studies* vol. 71, no. 281 (1982), pp. 1–13.

37 Brian P. Kennedy, 'Seventy-Five Years of *Studies*', *Studies* vol. 75, no. 300 (1986), pp. 361–77.

38 Gerry O'Hanlon SJ, 'Images of God: Northern Ireland and Theology', *Studies* vol. 73, no. 292 (1984), pp. 291–99.

39 Emmet Larkin, 'Socialism and Catholicism in Ireland 1910–1914', *Studies* vol. 74, no. 293 (1985), pp. 66–92.

40 Tom Inglis, 'Sacred and Secular in Catholic Ireland: A Review Article of *Irish Values and Attitudes: The Irish Report of the European Value Systems* – Study by Michael Fogarty, Liam Ryan and Joseph Lee' (Dublin, 1984), *Studies* vol. 73, no. 293 (1985), pp. 38–43.

41 Michael Paul Gallagher SJ, 'Secularisation and New Forms of Faith', *Studies* vol. 74, no. 293 (1985), pp. 16–17.

42 Harry Ferguson, 'The Paedophile Priest', *Studies* vol. 84, no. 335 (1995), pp. 247–56.

43 Peadar Kirby, 'The Death of Innocence: Whither Now?', *Studies* vol. 84, no. 335 (1995), pp. 257–335.

44 Noel Barber SJ, 'Editorial', *Studies* vol. 84, no. 335 (1995), pp. 237–8.

45 *Irish Times*, 25 Apr. 2009.

46 See chapter 10 (the wandering rock episode) of James Joyce, *Ulysses* (open cit.).

CHAPTER 2

John Redmond (2009)

Stephen Collins

Studies was launched in 1912, the year that the Irish Party politics it exemplified began to decline in influence within political nationalism. Collins's article depicts the enduring political influence of the milieu from which *Studies* emerged. Collins argues that modern Ireland is far closer to Redmond's political dream than it is to the messianic visions of the 1916 leaders, and that the values of democratic politics, epitomised by Redmond, prevailed over those epitomised by the 1916 Rising. At the time of writing Stephen Collins was Political Editor of the *Irish Times*.[1]

INTRODUCTION

John Redmond died in March 1918, a political failure and a broken man. In the years that followed his death the tolerant values of parliamentary politics that he stood for were, temporarily, pushed aside in a bloody tide of revolutionary violence. While an independent Irish state was established on sound democratic principles, after a vicious civil war, Redmond's memory was systematically buried and his contribution to the independence movement ignored. The 1916 leaders, who had effectively rebelled against him, and not simply against the British Government, became the icons of the new state. Their cult of blood sacrifice was adopted as the national myth even though the Free State quickly developed into a functioning parliamentary democracy that owed very little to the revolutionary values of 1916.

Redmond, as his modern biographer, Dermot Meleady, points out in the first volume of his fine, ambitious work, has managed 'the difficult feat of becoming at once a neglected and controversial figure'. From time to time his reputation has been dusted down and his contribution to the creation of our democracy acknowledged, but the rehabilitation phase has never lasted very long. This is mainly because Fianna Fáil, the dominant party of Irish politics since 1932, cannot bring itself to acknowledge his political legacy without casting doubt on the myths of 1916. Political opponents of Fianna Fáil who adopted a more inclusive form of nationalism than the traditional variety were regularly dismissed as 'Redmondites', even when Fianna Fáil itself finally came around to Redmond's basic approach.[2]

Fine Gael is more inclined to give some recognition to Redmond, because his political heirs in the Centre Party were involved in the formation of the new party in 1933. The former Fine Gael leader, John Bruton, had a picture of Redmond on the wall of the Taoiseach's office during his spell in power, but it was quickly relegated to the basement by Bertie Ahern, who restored Padraig Pearse to pride of place when he took over in 1997. Paradoxically, in his approach to the North, Ahern actually adopted a policy that owed far more to Redmond's belief in a democratic accommodation between Ireland and Britain and between the two traditions on the island, than it did to traditional Republican ideology.

There was a rare acknowledgement of Redmond at the ninetieth anniversary commemoration of the first Dáil in the Mansion House on 20 January 2009. All of the party leaders paid tribute to the Irish democratic tradition at a special sitting of the thirtieth Dáil, to mark the occasion, but the Fine Gael leader, Enda Kenny, went a step farther and acknowledged the debt Irish democracy owed to the party of Parnell, Redmond and Dillon:

> It is easy to forget the enormous part they played in the shaping of Irish parliamentary democracy. For 40 years it was the voice of nationalist Ireland and for 40 years its goal was an independent Irish Parliament. For all of this it got little thanks. The great Seán MacEoin, the Blacksmith of Ballinalee, expressed it well in 1938 when he said, 'The old Sinn Féin members should apologise to the members of the old Irish Party ... We blackguarded them up and down the country because we were not aware of the facts.'

It is ironic that MacEoin, one of the most successful IRA leaders in War of Independence, should have come around to almost precisely the same view as that of Augustine Birrell, one of the last British politicians who had the task of governing Ireland. Birrell wrote of the Government of the Free State in the late 1920s:

> They have entered into their inheritance by the efforts of and great personal sacrifice and risks of the Irish Parliamentary Party, they have since flung upon the scrap heap. Politicians seldom deserve gratitude and never get it.

EARLY CAREER

John Redmond was born in South Wexford, at Ballytrent House near Carne, on 1 September 1856, the eldest son of William Archer Redmond, nationalist MP from a well-established Catholic gentry family in the county. He was educated at Clongowes Wood College and Trinity College Dubli, and became a clerk in the House of Commons.

Determined on a political career, Redmond applied to Parnell, was selected as a candidate for New Ross and elected to the Commons in 1881. An able speaker, he quickly established a reputation for himself as a solid Irish Party MP, but was not immediately admitted to the front rank of a very talented party. He made his reputation during a successful trip to Australia, a trip designed to collect funds and build a political organisation among the Irish community there. At a succession of meetings across Australia, Tasmania and New Zealand, Redmond spelled out a compelling argument for constitutional nationalism and raised a considerable sum for the Irish Party to boot. It was also a success on a personal level as it was in Australia that he met his first wife, Johanna Dalton.

While he took part in the Land War and Plan of Campaign and was briefly imprisoned in 1888 for incitement, Redmond always opposed the use of violence to achieve political ends. He was never very comfortable with Parnell's alliance with the Fenian 'hillside men' and remained committed to political change by constitutional means. He had a deep respect for the House of Commons and its traditions and was naturally an enthusiastic supporter of Gladstone's First Home Rule Bill.

'He did not easily adopt the role of the rebel or fanatic; his natural pose was that of the eighteenth-century patriot, a Grattan or a Flood,' according to his obituary in the London *Times*. His ambition, at all stages of his political career, was Irish self-government as part of the British Empire, with acceptance of the Crown as head of state. The heady sensations generated by Gladstone's First Home Rule Bill in 1886 gave Redmond the conviction that his goal was achievable and it sustained him through the barren years that followed.

PARTY LEADER

After the bitter Parnell split and the death of 'the Chief', Redmond emerged as the leader of the minority Parnellite wing of the Irish Party. While he was widely regarded as a fine speaker, his reserved personality meant that he remained aloof from the squabbles that divided the Irish MPs in the 1890s, following the failure of Gladstone's Second Home Rule Bill in 1893. When the Irish Party was reunited in 1900, Redmond, with the support of John Dillon, the leading figure in the anti-Parnellite wing, became the leader ahead of more notable figures like William O'Brien and Tim Healy. The very qualities that made Redmond remote from many of his colleagues were the ones that also made him into a leader all of them could accept. Determined to avoid another serious split in the party which might get in the way of the ultimate goal of Home Rule, he responded cautiously to political developments.

For instance, in 1903 Redmond was personally inclined to accept the Wyndham Land Act, having signed the report of the land conference on which it was based. However, he sided with Dillon and other critics of the legislation against O'Brien, who stood by a commitment to back the legislation, and as a result, was forced out of the party and marginalised. Redmond repeated the performance on the Irish Council Bill of 1907, which was designed to implement administrative home rule. He privately backed the measure, but did a rapid u-turn when it was denounced by rank and file party members at a national convention.

In the House of Commons, Redmond, by this stage, had not only established himself as one of the leading figures, he led a disciplined party that actively participated in every aspect of parliamentary life. The political atmosphere of the period and the day-to-day work of the Irish Party is brilliantly captured in John Pius Boland's *Irishman's Day*, a chronicle of the everyday activity of the Irish Party, written by a man who served as MP for Kerry South from 1900 until 1918.

The victory of the Liberals in the general election of 1906 ended more than a decade of Conservative domination of British politics. The new government was well disposed to Ireland and this was reflected in the policies of the new Chief Secretary, Augustine Birrell, who introduced a range of reforms, including a new land act and the establishment of the National University of Ireland, which were manna from heaven to the Irish Party. For the following decade, Ireland was effectively ruled by an alliance of Birrell, Redmond and Dillon.

HOME RULE

The holy grail of Home Rule, however, remained on the long finger, until the two general elections of 1910 resulted in a political stalemate that put Redmond and his party in a pivotal position in British politics. Not only did the Irish Party have the balance of power for the first time in two decades, but Liberal Prime Minister, Asquith, was committed to abolishing the House of Lords' veto and to following that up with Home Rule for Ireland.

Redmond, however, like Parnell before him, totally underestimated the strength of opposition among Irish Protestants, who were overwhelmingly opposed to Home Rule. In north-east Ulster, where they were in a majority, they were determined to resist it at all costs. That aspiration was fully supported by the Conservative Party, which embarked on a potentially treasonous course to stop Home Rule becoming a reality.

The culmination of Redmond's career came in 1912 with the passage of the Third Home Rule Bill through the Commons. The bill was a relatively modest proposal, providing for an Irish Parliament to run local affairs while leaving taxation and foreign policy as the preserve of the Government in London. Still, in the right circumstances it could, like the Anglo Irish Treaty of 1921, have been the stepping stone to the establishment of a genuine Irish democracy, albeit one within the Empire.

While the Bill was, as expected, defeated in the Lords after its passage through the Commons in 1912, the ending of the veto meant that it only had to pass twice more through the Commons in order to become law. That made 1914 the deadline for the introduction of the measure. However, the strength of opposition in the North, backed by Conservative agitation, brought the Liberal government around to the view that it would be impossible to impose Home Rule on the whole island. Despite Redmond's furious opposition, Asquith and his ministers came to the conclusion that they had no option but to consider partition. This view hardened after the Curragh mutiny in the spring of 1914, when it became clear that elements of the Army would refuse to impose Home Rule in Ulster when the bill became law later in that year.

By that stage nationalist Ireland had responded to the militancy of Ulster, with the formation of the National Volunteers. Founded by Eoin MacNeill, the Volunteers sought to emulate the UVF who had imported guns from Germany. The Volunteers were infiltrated by the IRB, who regarded them as the vehicle for their long desired armed revolt. Alarmed by the development, Redmond and the party took control of the Volunteers, but the IRB militants bided their time until they could seize control.

In May 1914 the Home Rule Bill passed through the Commons for the third time, but there was one important exemption: Redmond reluctantly accepted that six counties in Ulster could be allowed to opt out of Home Rule for six years, on an individual basis. Full-scale civil war in Ireland and a constitutional crisis for the whole United Kingdom loomed, and in July, King George V called a constitutional conference at Buckingham Palace. The leaders of the Liberals and Conservatives, Unionists and Nationalists met for weeks, but failed to reach agreement. However, an event that had already taken place in Sarajevo, in Bosnia, was to sweep the Irish issue and the prospect of partition away from the centre of British politics. The assassination of the Austrian Archduke Franz Ferdinand, by a Serb militant, set off a chain of events that culminated in the German invasion of Belgium and France and the beginning of the First World War in August 1914.

THE GREAT WAR

When the war started, Redmond came to a momentous decision aimed at delivering 32-county Home Rule at the war's end. After the Foreign Secretary, Edward Grey, made his famous speech in the Commons about 'the lamps going out all over Europe' Redmond intervened in the debate:

> Today there are in Ireland two large bodies of Volunteers. One of them sprang into existence in the North. Another has sprung into existence in the South. I say to the Government that they may tomorrow withdraw every one of their troops from Ireland. I say that the coast of Ireland will be defended from foreign invasion by her armed sons and for this purpose armed Nationalist Catholics in the South will be only too glad to join arms with the armed Protestant Ulstermen in the North. Is it too much to hope that out of this situation there will spring a result which will be good, not merely for the Empire, but good for the future welfare and integrity of the Irish nation.

The speech electrified the Commons and Redmond was applauded on all sides.

If Redmond had left it at that, all might have been well, but a month later he went a step further. In September 1914, when the Home Rule Act was formally placed on the statute book he made a speech at Woodenbridge in Co. Wicklow pledging the Volunteers to the war effort.

> The war is undertaken in the defence of the highest principles of religion and morality and right and it would be a disgrace forever to our country, and a reproach to her manhood, and a denial of the lessons of her history, if young Ireland confined their efforts to remaining at home to defend the shores of Ireland from an unlikely invasion.

The belief that involvement in the war would lead to Irish unity was clearly a strong motivating factor in Redmond's call to arms, but it was not the only one. Like many middle-class Irish nationalists, he was deeply upset at the atrocities perpetrated by Germany on the Catholic people of Belgium in the early days of the war. His niece, who was a nun in Belgium, gave him a first-hand account of the suffering inflicted on the population and he was deeply moved. After the war reports of German atrocities were widely dismissed as British propaganda, but modern historical scholarship has shown that the atrocities were very widespread.

Redmond also believed that, by defending the right of a small nation like Belgium to exist against the power of Prussian totalitarianism, Irish soldiers would vindicate the right to freedom for their own country. 'I am speaking the truth when I say of the Irish race as a whole that they would feel covered with humiliation if when this war is over they had to admit that their rights and liberties had been saved by the sacrifices of other men while Irishmen remained safe at home and took no risks,' he said. He also fatally under-estimated the potential of his opponents, dismissing Sinn Féin as 'a handful of pro-German shirkers'.

If the war had ended in a few months, as all the experts predicted at the time, Redmond's tactics might have worked, but it went on and on and the carnage of the Western Front cast Redmond's encouragement to enlist in a very different light. After the Woodenbridge speech, the Volunteers split. Redmond initially held on to the vast majority, with 150,000 nominal members compared to the 5,000 or so who left to form the new Irish Volunteers. Eoin MacNeill headed the breakaway group, but, more sig-nificantly, the Irish Republican Brotherhood (IRB) dominated its executive. As the war dragged on, the National Volunteers declined, through enlistment or demoralisation, while the Irish Volunteers flourished, joining with Sinn Féin in opposing recruitment and ultimately supporting the notion of a German victory.

In 1915 the British political situation changed with the inclusion of the Conservatives in a coalition government to prosecute the war. Asquith was still prime minister but the pro-Irish Liberals were no longer in control. The Ulster Unionist leader, Carson, joined the cabinet and became an influential member. Asquith did offer a cabinet post to Redmond, but he refused to accept it, in the belief that it would undermine his authority as the leader of Irish nationalism. Redmond was undoubtedly right in his assessment, but his position was undermined in any case. Although he had achieved a political victory by having all of Ireland excluded from the imposition of conscription, the public became steadily more disenchanted with the war as it dragged on through 1915 and into 1916.

1916 AND AFTERMATH

Then in 1916 came the Rising that changed the political situation utterly. The Rising was the project of a minority within a minority. The plot was devised by a select band of IRB militants, without the knowledge of the wider IRB and in defiance of MacNeill's authority. It was far from being a popular revolt, but the destruction of central Dublin, the courage of its leaders and, most importantly of all, the executions that followed its defeat, turned the tide of public opinion. It marked the end of Redmond's authority as the political leader of Irish nationalism. As the London *Times* noted, the Sinn Féin movement 'from the first was directed as much against Mr Redmond and the nationalist Party as against Great Britain'.'

Redmond was shattered by the Rising, which came as much of a surprise to him as to the British Government. In the Commons he expressed feelings of 'detestation and horror' at what he regarded as a German plot and 'treason to Home Rule'. He also pleaded with Asquith for restraint and rightly forecast that the executions' policy would make martyrs of the rebels. His point was proved in a series of by-elections in 1917, when supporters of the Rising defeated the Irish Party candidates. Redmond then suffered two devastating and inextricably linked blows, one personal and the other political. His brother Major Willie Redmond, an MP for Clare, was killed on the Western Front. To make matters worse, the resultant by-election was won by Eamon de Valera, the senior surviving commandant from the Rising. John Redmond died prematurely at the age of 62 in March 1918, knowing that his political life had ended in failure.

After 1916 Redmond had few illusions and realised that everything he stood for was about to be swept away. Speaking to Lady Fingall, not long before he died, he advised her: 'Do not give your heart to Ireland, for if you do you will die of a broken heart.' As Lady Fingall remarked: 'He spoke truly of himself, alas.'

ASSESSMENT

On the face of it, Redmond exemplifies the dictum that all political careers end in failure. He has to take some of the blame for that failure, for mistakes at various stages of his political career. His political caution prevented him from taking advantage of the real prospect of conciliation between moderate nationalists and unionists in the early years of the twentieth century. Despite his own personal inclinations towards a rapprochement, he shied away to appease more truculent colleagues like Dillon. A bolder approach might have paved the way for Home Rule on the basis of conciliation and consent favoured by William O'Brien.

When Home Rule did materialise, Redmond completely underestimated the strength of Unionism, and initially persuaded Asquith and his cabinet to accept his flawed analysis. Then his reluctant acceptance of partition as a temporary expedient undermined his authority and fuelled more extreme nationalism. Redmond's enthusiastic encouragement of Irishmen to join up in the first 18 months of the war further weakened his authority, when the war continued for far longer than he, or almost anybody else, had anticipated. Redmond also fatally underestimated the strength of extreme nationalism, represented by the IRB and Sinn Féin. His advice to Birrell not to clamp down on the Volunteers paved the way for the 'success' of the Rising. The result was that his enemies swept the Irish Party into the dust heap of history in 1918.

Yet, for all his shortcomings, it is arguable that modern Ireland is far closer to Redmond's political dream than it is to the messianic visions of the 1916 leaders. The modern Irish State is a smooth running parliamentary democracy, committed to the rule of law and an enterprise economy. Ireland is an outward looking country, rather than the introverted 'ourselves alone' society developed by his Republican opponents during the first half of the independent State's existence.

More importantly, the values of democratic politics, epitomised by Redmond, ultimately prevailed over the cult of violence epitomised by the 1916 Rising. While the shadow of the gunman has never quite vanished from Irish life, and continues to prove a fatal attraction for a tiny minority, the norms of parliamentary democracy have withstood the challenge in successive generations.

Irish sovereignty has been pooled through the European Union and not within the British Empire, as Redmond had hoped but, after many decades of suspicious and sour co-existence, relations with Britain are now excellent, with the two governments working closely together to deal with the residual problems of Northern Ireland.

The endurance of Irish democracy, which has made it one of the oldest continuous parliamentary democracies in the world, is a tribute to the roots put down in Irish soil by Redmond and his predecessors, Parnell and O'Connell. Redmond would surely feel at home in the Dáil chamber, even if his oratory was of a higher quality than that usually on offer in Leinster House.

By contrast, it is hard to believe that leaders of the 1916 Rising, who seized control of Irish nationalism from Redmond, would be quite as happy with the way things turned out. Modern Ireland is hardly the Gaelic-speaking, devoutly Catholic, anti-materialist nation dreamed of by Padraig Pearse when he made his blood sacrifice. Neither is it the dictatorship of the proletariat envisaged by James Connolly.

The distorted version of history that traces Irish independence solely to 1916, and the Fenian tradition from which it sprang, has had an unhealthy impact on Irish democracy and provided ideological cover for the minority in successive generations who have tried to destroy it. In his pioneering reassessment of modern Irish history, written for *Studies* in 1966, but only published in 1972, Fr Francis Shaw SJ pointed out the layers of contradiction inherent in the popular myth of modern Irish history, which is still fostered by those in power. Not only does it condemn the majority of the population, who had no sympathy with the Rising when it happened, it also 'asks us to praise in others what we do not esteem in ourselves' by disowning the democratic values that have underpinned the history of independent Ireland.

Restoring credibility to those democratic values, after the excesses of the Celtic Tiger, is the most important task facing the present generation of Irish politicians. The country is currently facing a deep crisis that will pose a challenge to the authority and legitimacy of all its major institutions. The values of integrity and democratic political moderation epitomised by Redmond are as important today as ever.

Notes

1   Originally published, Stephen Collins, 'John Redmond: Discarded Leader', *Studies* vol. 98, no. 390 (summer, 2009).

2   The following sources were drawn upon: Paul Bew, *John Redmond* (Dundalk, 1996), John Pius Boland, *Irishman's Diary: A Day in the Life of an Irish MP* (London, 1942), S. J. Connolly, *The Oxford Companion to Irish History* (London, 1998), Elizabeth Countess of Fingal, *Seventy Years Young* (London, 1937; reissued 1991), Charles Lysaght (ed.), *Great Irish Lives* (London, 2008), Fr Francis Shaw SJ, 'The Canon of Irish History: A Challenge', in *Studies* vol. 61, no. 242 (spring, 1972), pp. 113–53.

CHAPTER 3

Some Aspects of Irish Literature

(1913, abridged)

Patrick Pearse

Patrick Pearse's sole essay in *Studies* claimed greatness for the Gaelic epic. Pearse's benchmarks were both classical (he argued that the *Táin* exceeded the Greek) and modern (Gráinne was the Hedda Gabler of Irish literature). His article criticised sentimentality within Irish literature but argued that there was a place for symbolism with the caveat: 'there can be no excuse for using symbols in which you do not yourself believe.' Many subsequent articles in *Studies* criticised the symbolism in which Pearse believed.[1]

Now that the libraries have yielded up so much of the buried treasures of Irish literature and that so much more which has not yet seen the light of day has been surveyed and appraised by competent authorities, one is better able than one was even so recently as ten years ago to fix a value and attach a definition to Ireland's contribution to the world's vision of beauty. One is able to form some idea of what distant horizons have been scanned by Irish-speaking men, what heights scaled, what depths sounded. And when our knowledge is just a little wider and deeper than it is at present it will be found that an amazing thing has happened. It will be found that the literary history of the world, what is commonly accepted as literary history, has left out of account one of the great literary peoples. Just as the rediscovery of the buried cities of the East has made it necessary for us to rewrite social and political history, so will the rediscovery of this buried literature of the West make it necessary for us to rewrite literary history. And it will mean not only a re-writing of literary history, but a general readjustment of literary values, a general raising of literary standards. The world has had a richer dream of beauty than we had dreamed it had. Men here saw certain gracious things more clearly and felt certain mystic things more acutely and heard certain deep music more perfectly than did men in ancient Greece. And it is from Greece that we have received our standards.

How curiously might one speculate if one were to imagine that when the delvers of the fifteenth century unearthed the buried literatures of Greece and Rome they had stumbled instead upon that other buried literature which was to remain in the dust of the libraries for four centuries longer! Then instead of the classic revival we should have had the Celtic revival; or rather the Celtic would have become the classic and the Gael would have given laws to Europe. I do not say positively that literature would have gained, but I am not sure that it would have lost. Something it would have lost: the Greek ideal of perfection in form, the wise calm Greek scrutiny. Yet something it would have gained: a more piercing vision, a nobler, because a more humane, inspiration, above all a deeper spirituality. One other result would have followed: the goodly culture and the fine mysticism of the Middle Ages would not have so utterly been lost. And, thinking of the effect of literature upon men's lives and conduct, one may add that the world might not have proved so untrue to so many of its righteous causes.

Now I claim for Irish literature, at its best, these excellences: a clearer than Greek vision, a more generous than Greek humanity, a deeper than Greek spirituality. And I claim that Irish literature has never lost those excellences: that they are of the essence of Irish nature and are characteristic of modern Irish folk poetry even as they are of ancient Irish epic and of mediaeval Irish hymns. This continuity of tradition amid all its changing moods (and the moods of Irish literature are as various as the moods of the Irish climate) is one of the striking things about it; the old man who croons above a Connacht hearth place the songs he made in his youth is as definitely a descendant of the elder bards as a Tennyson is of a Chaucer. I propose to illustrate what I mean, and to show how an attitude characteristic of Irish-speaking men in the days when they shaped the *Táin* is reproduced in the song in which an Irish peasant woman of today reproaches her lover or keens over her dead child.

What I have called here clearness of vision is part of a great sincerity, a great feeling for ultimate reality, which the supreme poets always have. The clear sheer detection and statement of some naked truth, the touching of some deep bedrock foundation, the swift sure stroke at the very heart of a thing: that is what I mean. There is sometimes a harshness in the relentlessness of this truth telling, a pain in the pleasure of this revelation. The heart shakes, because for a moment one sees with the awful clearness with which God sees.

The passage in the tale of *The Sickbed of Cúchulainn and the only Jealousy of Emer* in which Fand and Emer both beg to be rejected by Cúchulainn, whom they love, because neither will have half his love, shows this understanding and this sounding of the depths. 'If thou followest this woman,' said Emer, 'I shall not refuse thee to her. For indeed everything red is beautiful, everything new is bright, everything high is lovely, everything common is bitter, everything we are without is prized, everything known is neglected, till all knowledge is known. O youth,' she said, 'I was at one time happy with thee, and we should be so again if I were pleasing to thee.' 'Thou art pleasing to me,' said Cúchulainn, 'and thou shalt always be pleasing to me.' Then said Fand: 'Let me be rejected.' 'Nay, it were fitter to reject me,' said Emer. 'Not so,' said Fand, 'it is I who shall be rejected, and long have I been in peril of it.' And Fand bade farewell to Cúchulainn, and went back to her own country.

This seems to me to be the authentic note of great imaginative psychology. And I find equally authentic, albeit startling in the audacity of its sincerity, the psychology and the imagination which in the tale of the *Tragic Fate of Cúchulainn*, when the hero is being drawn forth to his doom by the din of phantasmagoric battles, make Emer, in the last forlorn hope of saving him, send to him that very Fand – the woman whose power over him she had such good reason to know. How differently inferior artists would have imagined either of these episodes! How a conventional sentimentality would have baulked at making Emer capable of that great sacrifice!

Sheer clear naked truth, the great reality of love and sacrifice, the miracle of the sacrifice by love of itself, the breaking down of strong barriers in the presence of some awful issue – again and again through the centuries have Irish-speaking men seen and described these things [. . .].

The Irish strength and truth where the artists of a more sentimental people like the English would have carefully provided a lachrymose ending stand out conspicuously in the conclusion of that surpassing tale, *The Pursuit of Diarmuid and Gráinne*. This was pointed out in a fine study contributed by the late Father O'Carroll to the *Irish Ecclesiastical Record* a good many years ago. The unknown novelist (for *Diarmuid and Gráinne* is in all essentials what we now call a novel) did not make Gráinne die of grief for Diarmuid. She had wooed Diarmuid and may have loved him, and his death had come from that wooing. But love was not the greatest thing in Gráinne, if indeed there was love in her at all. Irish literature had given memorable types of woman's love, Deirdre and Emer and Fand and Leadan and Crede, enduring types of the love that is faithful even unto death. But Gráinne was no Deirdre or Emer. She is the Hedda Gabler of Irish literature, the woman who craved to have her destinies interwoven with those of a strong splendid man: when Diarmuid's red cheek was white in death and his clustering hair had mingled with the dust Gráinne turned to Fionn, the strong subtle man who had slain him. It is entirely in keeping with her character as conceived by the novelist that after Diarmuid's death she should purchase power and splendour by wedding Fionn. 'I trow, O Fionn,' quoth Oisín, 'that henceforth thou wilt keep Gráinne safely.' Whereat, concludes the storyteller, Gráinne bowed her head in shame. This grimly ironic note is not struck in European literature again until the last half of the nineteenth century.

No great literature has shown a subtler understanding of women than Irish literature. Alike in the *Táin* and in the fugitive love songs of the manuscripts and of the countrysides we come upon profound intuitions or flashes of imagination which reveal more than many modern novels and much modern poetry. Some of the passages I have quoted will stand as illustrations. And take the couplet of a peasant cradlesong which Mr Yeats has elaborated into a charming little lullaby. A mother says to her child:

> *Cad déanfaidh mé gan mo ghiolla beag,*
> *Nuair bheidh tu mór is críonna?*
> (What shall I do without my little lad when you will be big and grown?)

Or, as Mr Yeats has it:

> I kiss you and kiss you,
> My pigeon, my own;
> Ah! how I shall miss you,
> When you have grown!

There is a real poignancy there which one does not often meet with in poems of motherhood and childhood. Many mothers must have thought just that: only a great poet could have imagined it. One finds the same yearning of motherhood but in a note of high tragedy in the mediaeval *Lament of the Mothers for the Slaughtered Innocents*. Think of what obvious things you and I should have made the mothers say, and then note that the Irish poet makes them say the things that were not obvious, but which when we hear them we yet recognise to be the inevitable things. The second woman cries (I give Mr Graves's translation):

> 'Tis my own son that from me you wring,
> I deceived not the King.
> But slay me, even me,
> And let my boy be.
> A mother most hapless.
> My bosom is sapless,
> My eyes one tearful river,
> My frame one fearful shiver,
> My husband sonless ever,

And I a sonless wife
To live a death in life.

O my son! O God of Truth!
O my unrewarded youth,
O my birthless sicknesses
Until doom without redress.
O my bosom's silent nest,
O the heart broke in my breast.

In an article on *The Personal in the New Poetry* contributed to *An Macaomh* my friend Mr MacDonagh recently pointed out that the dramatic lyric is almost as old in Irish as poetry itself, and that poetry had to revolve through a whole cycle before the form came back to Ireland again in modern Anglo-Irish poetry. He quotes the monologue of Eve published by Dr Kuno Meyer in *Eriu* as a good example of the early Irish dramatic lyric, 'telling in those vivid nervous lines of the *dán díreach* clear and simple thoughts of passion or emotion – poems that translate so literally into all languages that in translation they appear almost too simple.' Mr MacDonagh translates this poem almost word for word:

I am Eve, great Adam's wife,
I that wrought my children's loss,
I that wronged Jesus of life,
By right 'tis I had borne the cross.

I a kingly house forsook,
Ill my choice and my disgrace,
Ill the counsel that I took,
Withering me and all my race.

I that brought the winter in
And the windy glistening sky,
I that brought terror and sin,
Hell and pain and sorrow.

I quote the poem as an example of the Irish power of clear vivid unadorned statement. Mr MacDonagh regards it as typical of the early Irish dramatic lyric – only modernly, he thinks, has the dramatic lyric had the intense human thrill of individual subtle character. Yet surely that greatest of Irish dramatic lyrics (and it is as old as the tenth century) has that thrill: I mean *The Old Woman of Beare*. No doubt that old woman speaks the universal language of old age; no doubt she might say to any old sad woman with memories of a splendid youth what every poet can in a sense say to every reader: 'Unless these words are as much to you as they are to me they are nothing and less than nothing.' And yet she is not a mere type. There is an individuality there, a subtle self-characterisation. We know her; her sorrow is unforgettable, and the phrases in which she expresses her sorrow linger in the mind, as do the phrases of Shelley's *Flight of Love* or the phrases of Ronsard's *Quand vous serez bien vieille*. I would place this dramatic lyric among the greatest dramatic lyrics of all literature. Like Deirdre, *The Old Woman of Beare* will pass into many literatures, and poets in many tongues will vie with one another in giving new breath to her sorrow.

I have spoken of the Irish power of clear vivid unadorned statement. Some of you, remembering the rich and royal redundance of a good deal of later Irish verse, will ask whether clear vivid unadorned statement is really an Irish characteristic. It is. It was an Irish characteristic from the beginning and remained an Irish characteristic as long as *Dán Díreach* verse ruled, and longer; for it remains a characteristic of the best of the peasant poetry. The reserve and severity of the early Irish *I am Eve, great Adam's wife* are as apparent in the seventeenth-century poem of Keating, *A bhean lán de stuaim*:

> O woman full of subtlety,
> Keep from me thy hand.

The strength and brevity of the language here are as striking as the candour and energy of the thought. Yet Keating was one of those who ushered in the new school in poetry.

There is no such thing as sentimentality in Irish literature. One finds in the later literature, especially in the later poetry, bad taste of various kinds, but never that particular kind of bad taste. The characteristic faults of the later poetry spring from various causes. First, the metres, which had been elaborated, became a snare. And secondly, Irish poets, most conservative of races, retained an obsolete machinery and an outworn set of symbols long after the machinery had become unnecessary and the symbols had ceased to be convincing. There is a place for symbols in literature, but there can be no excuse for using symbols in which you do not yourself believe. That way lies insincerity, and without sincerity there can be no literature. Let me illustrate what I mean by a parallel thing which has taken place in recent Anglo-Irish poetry. Either Mr Russell or Mr Yeats discovered a certain symbolism in certain white birds spoken of in connection with Angus in one particular passage of early Irish literature. They straightway let loose those birds upon Anglo-Irish poetry, and for many of us since the music of Anglo-Irish poetry has almost been drowned by the needless flapping of those white wings. You never open a new book of Anglo-Irish verse but the birds of Angus fly out. It almost reminds one of the nursery rhyme: 'When the pie was opened the birds began to sing.' When the book is opened the birds begin to fly. And the curious thing to us who know *Irish* literature is that the birds of Angus never trouble us there at all. They are the most unobtrusive fowl imaginable.

Irish poetry has of course its symbols, and much of the later Irish verse is fully symbolic – *Eamonn an Chnuic*, for instance, and *An Druimfhionn Donn Dílis*, and *An Draighnean Donn*, and, as I believe, *An Bunán Buidhe*. But here I am concerned with the employment of outworn symbols and the retention of obsolete conventions. So many of the elegies of the eighteenth-century poets are insincere and unconvincing on this account. But there were always poets individual enough to stand apart from this tendency: Seán O'Neachtain, for instance, who used the rich and elaborate metres without allowing himself to be caught in their snare, and who went back from artificiality to the joyous artlessness of the first notes of Irish poetry. And my contention here is this: that alike in early Irish literature and in the finest songs of the later peasant poets there is absolutely nothing of this make-believe, but always the clear strong expression of a genuine emotion. The make-believe phase was merely a phase that affected only two or three generations, and not all the poets even of those generations. The style of the eighteenth-century school has no more right to be regarded as nationally characteristic than the costume of the eighteenth century to be regarded as a national costume. Both were phases, and in both Ireland shared to a certain extent with the Continent.

The *aisling* and the *caoineadh* – the vision and the elegy – are the forms in which the dead conventions are most persistent and most wearisome. But what noble vision poetry early Irish literature had produced! And how reserved, how sincere, how true and right, how free from false sentiment are such early elegies as – I will not take the supreme ones, those of Deirdre and Crede – but the Dirge of Congall Claen in the *Book of the Dean of Lismore*, or that of Gormley for Niall Glundubh, or those of Mac Liag and Mac Giolla Caoimh for Brian Bóroimhe, or the later elegy on the Irish princes dead at Rome. In these poems there is no conventional machinery, no repetition of outworn symbols. And one finds the same characteristics, the same rightness and sincerity, in elegies made by peasant men and women for their dead lovers or their dead children [. . .].

When I said in the beginning that had Irish literature been rediscovered four centuries ago instead of Greek and Latin literature, modern letters might have received a nobler, because a more humane, inspiration than they did actually receive, what I meant to suggest was this: that the Irish chivalry and the Irish spirituality which would then have commenced to percolate the literatures of Europe was a finer thing than the spirit of the old classic literatures, more heroic, more gentle, more delicate and mystical. And it is remarkable that the most chivalrous inspiration in modern literature does in fact come from a Celtic source: that King Arthur and the Knights of the Round Table have meant more to modern men than the heroes who warred at Troy or than Charlemagne and his Paladins. But how much richer might European literature have been had the story of Cúchulainn become a European possession! For the story of Cúchulainn I take to be the finest epic stuff in the world: as we have it, it is not the most finely finished epic, but it is, I repeat, the finest epic stuff. I mean not merely that Conor and Fergus and Conall and Cúchulainn are nobler figures, humaner figures, than Agammemnon and Hector and Ulysses and Achilles; not merely that Macha and Meadhbh and Deirdre and Emer are more gracious figures, more appealing figures, than Hecuba and Helen; I mean also that the story itself is greater than any Greek story, the tragedy as pitiful as any Greek tragedy, yet at the same time more joyous, more exultant. The theme is as great as Milton's in *Paradise Lost*: Milton's theme is a fall, but the Irish theme is a redemption. For the story of Cúchulainn symbolises the redemption of man by a sinless God. The curse of primal sin lies upon a people; new and personal sin brings doom to their doors; they are powerless to save themselves; a youth, free from the curse, akin with them through his mother but through his father divine, redeems them by his valour; and his own death comes from it. I do not mean that the *Táin* is a conscious allegory: but there is the story in its essence, and it is like a retelling (or is it a foretelling?) of the story of Calvary. Whether you agree with me or not, you will agree as to the greatness of the theme, stated thus in its essentials; and you will no longer, I hope, think of the *Táin* as the tale of an ancient Cattle Drive.

In that glorious Anthology *The Bards of the Gael and Gall* Dr Sigerson long ago pointed out that the story of Deirdre fell naturally into the five acts of a great tragic drama. Since then four dramatic poets, three in English, and one in Irish, have given us tragedies on the Deirdre story. But the whole Ulster epic falls just as naturally into a great trilogy of tragedies, with a prologue and an epilogue. The Prologue tells of the primal sin and the Curse of Macha; the three great tragedies are, in order, Deirdre, the *Táin*, and the Death of Cúchulainn; the Epilogue is the Death of Conor. Each of the great tragedies is complete in itself, yet through the whole cycle unrolls in inevitable sequence the doom of Ulster.

It may be said of the Homeric gods that they are too nearly akin to men, but of the Irish heroes that they have in them always something of the divine. The unseen powers have always been very close to Irish-speaking men. I have known old people who lived in familiar converse with the unseen; who knew as it were by sight and by the sound of their voices Christ and Mary and many familiar saints. Now that intimacy with spiritual things is very characteristic of Irish literature. One finds it in the mystical hymns of the Middle Ages; one finds it in the folk-tales of the Western countrysides; one finds it in many exquisite folk songs. As Mr Colum has pointed out, Christ and Mary have been incorporated into the Gaelic clan; and Irish peasant women can keen Christ dead with as real a grief as they keen their own dead. I have many times seen women sob as they repeated or listened to *The Keening of Mary*. The strange intimacy that connects certain places in Ireland with the scenes of Christ's birth and life and death, and links certain Irish saints and heroes with the joy of the Nativity and the tragedy of the Passion – this is the true Irish mysticism, the mysticism which recognises no real dividing line between the seen and the unseen, and to which the imagined experience is often more vivid than the real experience. A people so gifted must bring in their turn a very precious gift to literature; for is it not the function of literature by making known the real and imagined experiences of gifted souls to reveal to common men all the hidden splendours of the world and to make vocal its silent music?

Notes

1   Originally published, Patrick Pearse, 'Some Aspects of Irish Literature', *Studies* vol. 2, no. 5 (March, 1913, abridged), pp. 810–22.

CHAPTER 4

Votes for Youth (1915)

Arthur E. Clery

Arthur Clery's article made the case for extending the franchise to persons aged
12 years and older as a serious response to the prevalent exploitation of child
labour. Rather than being encouraged to stay in school many children were
pressed into unskilled work and effectively discarded on maturity. The wider
context here was demands to give the vote to women, backed by Clery and
other 'Irish Party' intellectuals such as Tom Kettle. The emphasis on concrete
examples of exploitation contrasts with the essentially abstract conceptions of
Irish freedom which had come to dominate the political agenda. Clery be-
friended Kettle at Clongowes, a Jesuit boarding school in County Kildare; he
later became a Professor of Law at University College Dublin.[1]

Like ping-pong and roller-skating, the art and pastime of voting is for the
moment somewhat out of vogue. At least it is so in Europe. Nevertheless,
this has not prevented the inauguration of at least one suffrage movement. I
take courage to suggest another. After all at the present time one can be a
propagandist with less danger to life and limb than usual, since no one really
cares what your views are, on any subject save the one. The absence of free
institutions is moreover in some respects rather a help to the spread of novel
opinions, an absolute government having, as has often been remarked, by no
means the same facilities for hunting down and slaying new ideas that a well-
established democracy possesses. The Renaissance and the French Revolution
were each of them the product of unfree institutions. Women's claim to the
suffrage and the further claim I now venture to put forward are but carrying
the second of these movements to its logical conclusion.

It is a trite saying that the three stages of any reform movement are
ridicule, indignation, and acquiescence. Home Rule is (outside Ulster) in
the third stage; women's suffrage was recently in the second; we can all
remember when it was in the first. The proposals here put forward have yet

to reach even the first stage, of attentive ridicule. But let me say that, though it may perhaps have the good fortune to excite wide-spread derision, this article is not intended to be humorous. It is not for instance written as a satire upon the movement for women's suffrage, as might readily be suspected. On the contrary the suggestions it contains are put forward as a serious remedy for a great body of admitted social evil.

Modern social enquiry seems to be steadily reaching the conclusion that the human race is in large part ruined in its 'teens'. Physically, no doubt, civilised humanity is corrupted at a still earlier age by underfeeding, bad housing, and want of medical attendance; and the community realising this has entered on a policy (limited no doubt) of housing the poor, free meals, and medical inspection for school children. (By the way, speaking of free meals, I wish some economist with classical qualifications would make an independent investigation into the subject of *panem et circenses* [bread and circuses] and ascertain whether this state policy of a great empire was really the evil thing, that middle-class authorities have so often represented it to be). The physical ruin of the poor comes early; their moral and intellectual degeneration comes in the second decade of life. I need not enlarge on such topics as child-labour, the sudden stoppage of education, the want of technical training and 'blind-alley occupations', nor yet on these worse snares and evils which a modern city provides in unchecked profusion for the young. The former class of evils has been pointed out by all recent social investigators. It was the subject of a very able lecture by Professor Corcoran some time ago in which he advocated certain palliatives, such as extension classes. The latter kind of evils fall under that axiom of modern state-craft, that 'the Devil has his rights and they are not lightly to be interfered with'. Humanity between the ages of twelve and twenty is surely the site of his most extensive possessions.

The evils themselves are admitted. How are they to be dealt with? The remedy for social evils is commonly not sociological. Of course it is simple enough to combat evil; you have only to do good. But doing good, in a *public way*, is about the hardest thing in the world. It is commonly the most unpopular. For one thing, you trench on the vested rights alluded to in the last paragraph. One must look to politics for the answer to the problems of sociology. The evils of the Irish land system for instance were known for more than a century. Royal Commissions had discovered them. Philanthropists had wept over them. Economists had set them forth in treatises. It required Michael Davitt and the Land League to put an end to them. The social sciences seldom go beyond a treatment of symptoms. You must employ the surgery of the politician to effect a radical cure.

There is one other proposition which has come to be looked upon as an axiom of democracy; that nobody can look after a man's interest as well as the man himself. Of course there are always other people ready to take charge of them. Before 1793, while Catholics still lacked the franchise, there were not a few benevolent Protestants ready to promote and foster their interests in every way, to be more Catholic than the Catholics themselves. Wolfe Tone for one was wholly disinterested. Still the Catholics preferred to do the voting themselves; they felt they could safe-guard Catholic interests better than even their most eager well-wishers. And this has been the view of all disfranchised classes, a view commonly borne out in the result. It is of course one of the strongest grounds upon which women's claim to the suffrage is usually based.

Now, as there were Protestants who looked after Catholic interests before 1793, as there are Members of Parliament at present who look after the interests of women, so there are by no means wanting philanthropists, who take an interest in the welfare of the young, men who devote themselves to such questions as 'blind alley occupations' or 'child-labour', and honestly seek a remedy for them. There are friends of youth, just as there are friends of Ireland, and friends of labour. But my point is that the interest of such persons in these questions and their influence for good in solving them is much less than the interest and influence of the classes affected would be if they were themselves allowed a voice in the matter. Philanthropy is a weak battle-cry as compared with self-interest. And though any one individual may be neglectful of his own interests, a class hardly ever is. Give boys the vote, and they will of a surety use it, like other classes, to promote the interests of their kind, to solve the problems of boyhood, to punish the outrages that are perpetrated on their age.

The wrongs inflicted by adults upon voteless adolescents are very considerable, and yet like most such things readily laughed away. Laughter is the best defence for the indefensible. Some of them, such as the problems of boy-labour, have already been alluded to. The system which to suit the convenience of their elders turns the city street into an occasion of sin, is an evil scarcely less crying, though perhaps less perceived. But even in small matters it is remarkable how the adult constantly sacrifices the interest of the young to his own most trifling convenience. The English monetary system and system of spelling are two of the most glaring examples. Here the interest of the young is in direct conflict with the inertia of the adult, and the adult does not hesitate to inflict years of useless drudgery upon the school-boy or school-girl in order to avoid the three or four weeks of discomfort that would be caused by the change to a more rational system. Here again laughter is the defence. American adults laughed as loudly at Roosevelt's spelling changes as English adults would laugh at a proposal to introduce dollars and cents as a basis of computation.

The young too have certain of the other marks of a servile class. With procurers and garotters they remain the only sections of the community still liable to torture by stripes. Laughter again tends to be the defence. And the jokes about flogging boys bear a close family resemblance to the jokes about flogging adult slaves, with which readers of Terence and Plautus are familiar. It is only in comparatively recent times that the same treatment has come to be looked upon as no longer suitable for women. Some such phrase as 'it is good for them', or perhaps even 'they like it' is in such matters usually thought a sufficient justification. That for which a class beyond all else needs the vote, is to protect itself from degradation.

Of course it will be said that if the young had the vote, they would not know how to use it, that schoolboys are not the persons most fit to decide questions of foreign policy for instance. Are agricultural labourers? Youths under twenty-one have those qualities which are perhaps most lacking in modern statecraft, honesty and enthusiasm. They would form an incorrupt element in every electorate. Honesty – public honesty – is the quality of the 'teens and the early twenties. It is all but gone by the thirties, surviving later perhaps in a few chosen individuals, in men like Davitt for instance, who have had their principles preserved in the antiseptic atmosphere of a British gaol.

Nor have boys shown themselves in any way lacking in those other qualities that make the good citizen. In Ireland at least, taking them one with another, they certainly work harder than adults, and their work is more disinterested. They have a far keener desire for intellectual improvement, and are more interested in serious questions. They read serious books for pleasure. Not one adult in a hundred does. Until contaminated by some of the sources of corruption already alluded to, they are more religious and much less vicious than adults. In our time, in such bodies as the boy scouts, they have shown a remarkable capacity for patriotism and organisation. Irish boy scouts have at least one very striking achievement to their credit, in quite recent times. The 'military' argument commonly urged against the female vote cannot be used in this case. Whilst on the other hand a well-known argument for women's suffrage, that the highest type of woman is immeasurably superior to the lowest type of male voter, applies with even increased force in the case of boys. A well-educated and clever boy has faculties immensely superior to those of the lowest type of adult voter. Yet even were this not the case, the objection would be irrelevant. It is not because of his capabilities as a governor, but because of his rights as one of the governed, that modern democracy gives an individual the vote.

Finally, it may be asked, what is the concrete proposition? Are voters in arms to be carried to the poll by their nurses, for instance? This is the *reductio ad absurdum* of the proposal. The propositions of practical politics always admit of a *reductio ad absurdum*; it in no way impairs their validity. There is a limit. But one can be damned at seven. I propose to give the vote at twelve, or at all events at fourteen, when the individual incurs full criminal respon-

43

sibility, and a large degree of civil responsibility for his acts. In the Roman Empire the privilege of citizenship was acquired about this age. In other words the interests of the school population, so much talked about, so little really attended to, would receive a real representation in the Commonwealth. Educational questions would at least be looked at from the point of view of those who are to be educated, instead of from every other point of view under heaven. Nor would this point of view resolve itself into a mere demand for idleness, as the cynic may suggest. Boys as a class are no more fools than anyone else, in fact rather less so. It might, however, easily resolve itself into a demand that learning should be associated with humanity.

It remains to deal with a few rather obvious objections. 'They have shown no desire for the vote, they don't want it.' As this objection is a standard one against all franchise and emancipation movements whatever, I need only refer the objector to the well-known answers, which are now almost as definitely in stereotype as the objection. 'They would not use it if they got it', 'it would bring ruin and ridicule on the commonwealth.' 'It is too ridiculous to be seriously discussed.' To these the same remark applies. Finally, the subtle humorist, if he be of a logical turn of mind, can urge something really original. 'Why stop short in your democracy? Why not give votes to the other excluded classes, criminals and lunatics?' Well, as for lunatics, any politician must admit, nay he has perpetually stated, that they are fully represented – on the other side. Whilst as for criminals, many of them in fact have the vote; but in any event criminals belong commonly not so much to the classes that vote, as to the class that is voted for. To take the most famous instance, the hero of Victor Hugo's 'Story of a Crime' received the almost unanimous suffrages of the people.

I cannot, of course, hope for an immediate acceptance of these proposals. I shall be satisfied if I awake some first faint stirring in the political conscience of the community, even though that stirring should take its rise in the risible faculty.

Notes

1   Originally published, Arthur E. Clery, 'Votes for Youth', *Studies* vol. 4, no. 14 (June, 1915), pp. 279–85.

Thomas Kettle (1966)

Denis Gwynn

Arthur Clery's 1916 obituary of Tom Kettle in *Studies* described him as 'the most brilliant mind of a generation, the generation that succeeded Parnell and Yeats'. Kettle died at the Somme just weeks after the executions that followed the 1916 Rising. Denis Gywnn's article is one of a number of subsequent appreciations of Kettle which appeared in *Studies*. Like Kettle, Gwynn was born into the Irish Party (his father Stephen Gwynn was MP for Galway); during 1916–17 he served on the Western Front in the Munster Fusiliers. Subsequently he became editor of the *Dublin Review*. He was appointed as a Professor of Modern Irish History at University College Cork in 1948. He wrote several books on modern Irish history; these included biographies of Roger Casement, Daniel O'Connell and John Redmond.[1]

T. M. Kettle, one of the first and most distinguished professors of University College Dublin, was killed in action in France just 50 years ago. In September 1916 he fell while leading his company of the Dublin Fusiliers with conspicuous gallantry to the capture of a strongly held village on the Somme.

He was only 36 when he gave his life for the causes which had inspired him since boyhood: the necessity for closer relations between Ireland and Europe, and the obligation to defend justice and freedom. His extraordinary gifts of intellect, wit, originality and courage were apparent during his brief public career. In Clongowes he had been an outstandingly brilliant student. At the University he became the central and most attractive of a group of young men who were to attain many distinctions and become the architects of the national triumph which Tom Kettle did so much to promote but did not live to see. He would have been a born leader of the generations who were then actively preparing to assume the tasks of self-government.

Few now survive of those who knew him as Professor of National Economics at University College. One of that dwindling group, I sat under him during his first years in the chair which had been specially created for him. I had other contacts with him. My father, then MP for Galway City, had been a member of the statutory commission for the new National University and a close colleague of Kettle's under John Redmond in the Nationalist Party. I was directly aware of Kettle's vigorous co-operation in organising the Irish Volunteers. And when war came I followed him to serve in France with one of the many Irish regiments in what he called the 'Army of Freedom'. To understand and appreciate Kettle fully one needs to have shared his experiences in the trenches. 'I have seen war and faced modern artillery and know what an outrage it is against simple men,' he wrote in a letter, 'I want to live to use all my powers of thinking, writing and working, to drive out of civilisation the foul thing called war, and to put in its place understanding and comradeship.'

Yet Tom Kettle was no pacifist. He had inherited traditions of unflinching courage. Born in 1880, in north County Dublin, he was the third son of Andrew J. Kettle, one of the principal founders and organisers of the Land League. The Kettles had been strong farmers in the Swords–Malahide area for generations. Andrew Kettle, known throughout Ireland as a determined and self-sacrificing champion of the tenant farmers, was the close confidant of Parnell and Michael Davitt. Of high moral courage and strong convictions he was also a man of great physical strength, once in the course of an argument lifting a blacksmith's anvil over his head and throwing it backwards. His son Tom had not these physical endowments but he had inherited his father's courage and devotion to public service.

Though farming good land and relatively prosperous, Andrew Kettle deeply sympathised with the victims of landlord exactions in the West and other poor areas. His practical knowledge as an industrious and successful farmer was invaluable to Parnell, who relied heavily on his advice. Kettle's predominance in the Land League brought him threats of eviction but his friends rallied round him; in north County Dublin he formed an important group in the appeals for a national tribute to Parnell and he was imprisoned in Kilmainham for his Land League activities – an indignity his son Tom always remembered with pride.

Tom Kettle never ceased to share his father's devoted loyalty to Parnell after the disastrous split. He was 11 when Parnell died. Less than 20 years later he expressed his idea of what Parnell gave Ireland in lines published when the Parnell monument in O'Connell Street was unveiled. I quote in part:

> Signed with a sign, unbroken, unrevealed,
> His Calvary he trod;
> So let him keep, where all world wounds are healed
> The silences of God.

Yet is he Ireland's too: a flaming coal
Lit at the stars, and sent
To burn the sin of patience from her soul,
The scandal of content.
A name to be a trumpet of attack;
And in the evil stress,
For England's iron No to fling her back
A grim granitic Yes.
He taught us more, this best as it was last:
When comrades go apart
They shall go greatly, cancelling the past,
Slaying the kindlier heart.
So freedom comes, and comes no other wise:
He gave – 'the Chief' – gave well.
Limned in his blood across your clearing skies
Look up and read Parnell!

In 1894, after a few years with the Christian Brothers at Richmond Street, Tom Kettle went to Clongowes. He arrived at the University, a University College kept alive since 1883 by the Jesuits, in 1897. There he was one of a remarkable group. His close friends included James Joyce, Hugh Kennedy, the first Chief Justice under national government, Arthur Clery and James Murnaghan who became professors of Law in the new University, John Marcus O'Sullivan who was its first Professor of History. There was Constantine Curran, later Registrar of the Supreme Court and the greatest expert on Georgian architecture in Ireland, and Felix Hackett, another professor who became President of the RDS and has held other eminent positions.

Some of this group decided on a symbolic protest against the delay in replacing the moribund Royal University – merely an examining body – with a new national University. They were also agitating for improved conditions and planned to interrupt the annual conferring of degrees. The plan was to seize the organ and prevent the playing of 'God save the King', then an integral part of the proceedings. A students' manifesto declared that 'we wish to protest against the unjust, wasteful and inefficient government of which that air is a symbol'. Kettle's connection with the incident was so obvious that he was held partly responsible.

From the beginning of his undergraduate days his leadership and personal popularity among the students was evident and it was no surprise when he was elected auditor of the 'L&H'. In 1902 he entered the King's Inns as a law student and was called to the Bar in 1905. While at the University he was editor of a students' magazine called *St Stephen's*. Contributions which showed promise of future accomplishment included an essay by Joyce on James Clarence Mangan.

In 1904 Kettle was elected president of the newly formed Young Ireland branch of the United Irish League. His friends, including Cruise O'Brien and Frank Skeffington, determined to assert through this new branch the right to criticise and protest against the general somnolence of official nationalist policies. Kettle delivered his presidential address when he was only 24. It revealed the striking maturity of his mind and outlook and his capacity for self-expression.

The leader of his brilliant contemporaries, in 1905 he founded and edited the weekly *Nationist* to publish the restless opinions of his friends. The eccentric title was chosen in an effort to avoid repeating the traditional slogan. It could scarcely have survived long, and Kettle's career was deflected when in 1906 – the year of the great Liberal triumph in British politics – he was invited to contest an almost hopeless constituency in East Tyrone. He won by 16 votes and represented that constituency for the next three years. This experience, in such a marginal constituency, gave him an insight invaluable in the following years. It strengthened his conviction that reconciliation between the Ulster Unionists and the rest of Ireland must be accomplished as a first priority in national politics. (One of his last letters, written from the trenches, shows him still devoted to the duty of working this out.)

As a young MP, elected for an apparently hopeless constituency, he could well have hoped for rapid success in practice at the Irish Bar. He was already highly popular in the Law Library where his social instincts and talents found immediate welcome. But legal practice never appealed to him; indeed he felt repugnance towards the legal system as he saw it on circuit and in the Dublin courts. Apart from the congenial life of the Law Library and the circuit journeys the life of a barrister did not appeal to Tom Kettle. He realised that his special gift was for politics. The wide scope of political activity, the exercise of his natural flair for debate, his power to attract audiences at public meetings, all combined to satisfy him. He was soon sent to the United States with Richard Hazelton, to represent the younger men in the Nationalist Party. This tour was a great personal success for Kettle. He enjoyed it and learned much from contact with American politics. At Westminster he soon made his mark, as a magnetic speaker and witty debater. A born orator, he has left in the introduction to his *Selection from the Irish Orators*, a brilliant description of the talents that make an orator. Unfortunately, in the early years of this century, politics as a profession was almost impossible for young nationalists, however gifted. There was no remuneration for Members of Parliament, the party fund going to subsidise elections and to help those in extreme need. Young representatives of Irish constituencies were obliged to find other means of livelihood. For Kettle that meant journalism and writing books – literary work that yielded very meagre returns.

At the British general election of 1906 the Liberal landslide had raised hopes that Home Rule might soon become a practical prospect, with many openings for young Irishmen. For Kettle, however, a different prospect offered when the Liberals established the National University with its three constituent colleges. By unanimous decision he was chosen as one of its first professors, the new chair of National Economics being created for him. It was a full time professorship which yielded him a secure though modest income, and enabled him to work among some of his ablest friends and contemporaries to create a real university life in Dublin and to establish a higher academic prestige.

Soon afterwards he married and thus became one of a group of nationalist politicians closely related by marriage. His wife was Mary Sheehy, daughter of David Sheehy, MP, a Land League veteran. A sister of Mary Sheehy married Frank Skeffington who, with his strong convictions about women's rights, changed his name thenceforth to Sheehy Skeffington. A third sister married Cruise O'Brien. The young men, with their brother-in-law, Eugene Sheehy, had all been prominent in the agitation for a new university and in the college debating societies. Before long Kettle found that his duties as professor absorbed most of his time, so he resigned his seat in Tyrone.

In many ways he had wider scope than formerly. He was happily married. He had an assured regular income. But it was inevitable that he soon began to miss the House of Commons, where exciting battles over Home Rule were about to begin. However, he soon entered the fray from the wings, replying to Kipling and other British publicists who were campaigning against Home Rule. When Kipling claimed that Ulster should be treated as a different country and race Kettle retorted in scathing verses with the telling line, 'Ulster is ours, not yours.'

Some public men regarded Kettle with suspicion because of his dislike for isolationism. But, deprived of opportunity to become a national spokesman, it was inevitable that Kettle should experience a growing sense of frustration. Even his professorship was something of an anticlimax, since National Economics did not figure among the subjects prescribed for ordinary degrees. The total number of students in the new university was then little over a thousand and subjects like Kettle's attracted very small classes. In his first year he had only four students, but they were all men of high calibre, one being the future Professor of Economics, George O'Brien. A few years later I was one of Kettle's class of five. Such small classes gave our professor little scope for his energy and activity. His first big chance came during the protracted labour troubles in Dublin in the summer of 1913. Using his status as an expert on Irish economics and making full use of his wide range of

49

friendships, Kettle convened a Citizens' Peace Committee and was elected its chairman. The Committee pressed for some kind of negotiated settlement, but its efforts produced no result. Kettle later wrote an illuminating appreciation of the whole dispute in the quarterly *Dublin Review*. After a general description of Dublin's economic and social structure he continues:

> The great body of the workers are engaged in low wage occupations. Not less than one fourth of the population is constantly below the human minimum. Housing is particularly bad. . . . The labour propaganda had hardly reached the mass of the unskilled; organisation was almost unknown to them. On this terrain appeared suddenly the disturbing figure of Mr Larkin, picturesque, eloquent, prophetic. At once dictatorial, and intimate, he was, as he might say himself, the very man for the job. The Dublin worker is not a natural revolutionary, but he is a natural soldier. Mr Larkin, appealing at once to all his instincts, organised not so much a union as an army. . .

Kettle described briefly the Dublin employers and the progress and subsidence of the conflict, concluding with the comment:

> Nobody supposes that things in Dublin have swung back to anything like stable equilibrium. If there is peace in Dublin it is the peace of industrial anaemia, not that of a healthy civilisation.

The Peace Committee's failure to obtain a settlement in the labour dispute, combined with the growing threat to Home Rule while Carson invoked resort to rebellion, left Kettle disillusioned and frustrated. His health deteriorated and he was sometimes absent from work but always kept in touch with College activities. But events were moving fast and Kettle was not to be kept indefinitely in the background. With his shrewd experience of national politics and his close connection with the Nationalist Party he had a vital part to play. He had formed an intimate friendship with Joseph Devlin, recognised leader of the Ulster nationalists and Catholics and, in view of the Ulster situation and the vanishing hopes for Home Rule, was in constant consultation with him. The Ulster Volunteers were being enrolled in tens of thousands and were parading openly, with full encouragement from the highest official authorities. They were still without arms, but in Tyrone, Kettle's former constituency, new threats of armed violence increased, as it did in all constituencies where Nationalists and Unionists were of almost equal strength. Conditions in the northern province grew more tense from week to week. The Nationalists soon insisted that they were entitled to defy the Government as freely as the Orangemen. Behind the scenes the organisers of the revived IRB were seeking opportunities to create a definitely illegal revolutionary force. Opportunity came suddenly when Professor Eoin MacNeill, an Antrim Nationalist, published in the Gaelic League's weekly organ, *An Claidheamh Soluis*, an article entitled 'The North Began': this article openly welcomed the example set by the Ulster Volunteers in asserting their rights, as Irishmen, to arm.

Almost immediately the small IRB junta decided to organise a national Volunteer force with MacNeill as a figurehead. A provisional committee was formed to arrange for the first public appeal for volunteers. Larry Kettle, Tom's brother, was organising secretary to this committee. It is deplorable how little credit subsequent historians have given the Kettle brothers for their part in organising the Volunteers; all suggest that the organisation of the Irish Volunteers was entirely due to the IRB. I attended that first historic meeting in the Rotunda in November 1913, the meeting to launch the Volunteers. When Larry Kettle, Dublin City Engineer, was called upon to read the resolution, pandemonium broke out. This arose from the fact that Andrew Kettle, Larry's farmer father, had been in collision with Larkin's Transport Workers' Union. When Larkin called out all Kettle's farm workers neighbours helped him to get in his harvest. In the bitter atmosphere of the time all the Kettle family were denounced as 'scabs' and 'blacklegs'.

I remember the courage and determination with which Larry Kettle faced the tumult in the Rotunda. Finally Pearse rose as a supporting speaker; his austere presence and resonant voice saved the meeting from utter collapse, though very few of the immense audience had any idea of who he was.

The Volunteer movement spread rapidly, especially in Ulster. Tom Kettle, whose ill health had precluded him from active work when he was invited to join the original committee, was nevertheless in close touch with the Volunteers through his brother Larry and through Joe Devlin. By mid-May, 1914, the Irish Volunteers numbered 100,000, one third of these being in Ulster and one third in Leinster. When on 25 May 1914, the Home Rule Bill passed finally through the House of Commons, the troops in Belfast were confined to barracks for fear of violence.

During these exciting months Kettle recovered his strength and I saw him regularly at the University. Many of us students were already drilling and marching with the Volunteers. I asked Kettle one day whether the Irish Party could continue to remain aloof from the movement. He replied, 'They have already come into the movement so heavily that there is danger of their swamping the ship.'

At Volunteer meetings he used to insist with vehement eloquence that Carson should not be allowed to browbeat and overwhelm the forces of Irish Nationalism. When the Carsonite Volunteers got a large cargo of rifles landed, without official resistance, at Larne, this cleared the way for a similar exploit on the part of the Irish Volunteers, though it meant gun-running in open defiance of the law and naval forces. In pursuance of a plan made under the aegis of the reorganised committee, Tom Kettle was sent to Belgium at the end of July 1914 to obtain arms for the Volunteers.

In his book, *The Ways of War*, published after his death, he tells of how the war broke out while he was in Belgium on this mission:

> On the 6th of August 1914 I wrote from Brussels in the *Daily News* that it was a war of 'civilisation against barbarians'. I assisted for many overwhelming weeks at the agony of the valiant Belgian nation. I have written no word and spoken none that was not the word of an Irish Nationalist who had been to the trouble of thinking for himself.

As an accredited war correspondent for the *Daily News* Kettle wrote descriptions of what he actually saw in Belgium during these agonising weeks. He believed it impossible that England 'would go to fight for liberty in Europe and Junkerdom in Ireland'. The Tsar's announcement that Russia would liberate Poland when the war ended stirred him deeply, for he had always been conscious of the parallel between Poland and Ireland. In Belgium that August he wrote the verses entitled *A Nation's Freedom*. By September, when he returned to Ireland, the German invasion had advanced almost within striking distance of Paris. He applied for a commission in the Dublin Fusiliers to serve with the new Irish Division then being formed. He took part in recruiting campaigns, appealing vehemently throughout the country for Irishmen to fight German aggression in Europe. He was passionately convinced (as some chapters in *Why Ireland Fought*, written at this time, show) that Irish traditions would be disgraced if Ireland did not take an active part in the war. He was also convinced that England could never go back on the Home Rule settlement and would certainly enlarge its scope.

Training in Ireland during 1915 he had much cause for disappointment at the actions of the British Government. But no one expected then that a rising would erupt suddenly in 1916. Kettle had no intimate friends among the promoters of the Rising, although he knew MacDonagh and Plunkett and Pearse slightly. He admired MacNeill as a scholar and leader of the Volunteers, and could understand, though he did not sympathise with, MacNeill's policy in regard to the Volunteers. But he had no sympathy whatever for the Rising when it came and used to say bitterly that they had spoiled his 'dream of a free united Ireland in a free Europe'. Nevertheless, he was appalled by the brutality of the British military repression. Most of all he felt a keen personal loss in the execution without trial of his brother-in-law, Sheehy Skeffington, a lifelong pacifist, and wrote a fine obituary tribute to him.

Kettle had asked to be sent out to France at once, although not fit for service in the trenches. It has been widely stated, especially by Padraic

Colum, that he had lost faith in the ideals that sent him to his death on the Somme. Colum ought to have known better, but was misled. Kettle's last letters disprove these statements.

He was thrilled by the fine spirit and high courage of his Dublin Fusiliers. In the trenches, before leading his men to the attack on Ginchy he wrote the famous sonnet to his daughter, the concluding lines of which are inscribed on his memorial in St Stephen's Green. At midnight they advanced through a devastated waste of bombarded ground, Kettle directing and holding his soldiers together under deadly fire. He was hit twice and died instantly. His body was never recovered.

Before his death he drafted a last Political Testament. Within six years after Tom Kettle's death every item in this document had been fulfilled.

Notes

1   Originally published, Denis Gwynn, 'Thomas M. Kettle 1880–1916', *Studies* vol. 55, no. 220 (winter, 1966), pp. 384–91.

CHAPTER 6

I Remember 1916 (1966)

Seán F. Lemass

At the time of writing Seán Lemass was Taoiseach; he was little more than a schoolboy when the events he described took place. The winter 1966 editorial in *Studies* described his account as 'an unpretentious story of the events he witnessed and took part in' that 'quite unconsciously revealed something of his distaste for the dramatic gesture.'[1]

On Easter Monday, 1916, my elder brother, Noel, and I, having had no orders or information about what was going to happen, since Professor MacNeill's cancellation of the Parade of Volunteers on Easter Sunday, went for a walk in the Dublin mountains with our friends Jim and Ken O'Dea. We walked to Glencree and returned in the afternoon. I was then 17 years of age and my brother 19.

Around 5 p.m. and some distance outside Rathfarnham, we met Professor MacNeill and two of his sons riding on bicycles outwards from the city. We had a slight acquaintance with the MacNeill boys and they dismounted and spoke to us. It was from them that we first learned of the Rising.

Professor MacNeill seemed agitated and depressed. He informed us that the Volunteers had occupied various positions in the city, but that he had no information as to further events. He was very clearly unhappy about the whole situation.

There were no trams running from Rathfarnham so we had to walk into the city. We went to Jacobs factory, which was the first position occupied by the Volunteers which we came to, but the windows were barricaded and we could make no contact with the defenders.

Noel and I got up early the next morning and, with no word to our parents, left home determined to take part in the Rising. We went first to the Four Courts which was the position nearest to our home in Capel Street,

54

where we were informed that our own unit, the Third Battalion, was in the Ringsend direction. We decided to make our way there, but when passing the GPO we met a friend, Volunteer Hugh Holohan, on sentry duty and he brought us inside where we were absorbed into the garrison and given arms.

Noel was despatched across the street to the Imperial Hotel where he was wounded in the subsequent fighting. I was sent to a position on the roof of the GPO, at the corner nearest the Pillar, where there was a group of eight or ten Volunteers, including a couple of Citizen Army men, under the command of a Volunteer Officer named Cremin who had come from London to take part in the Rising.

At this position on the roof there was a number of rather crude bombs made out of billycans and equipped with slow-burning fuses. The idea was that, in the case of a mass assault on the GPO, we were to light the fuses and throw them on the attackers in the street below.

We remained in position on the roof until Thursday, when we were ordered down into the building. The stage of serious fighting was beginning at the GPO and there was tremendous activity inside preparing for the attack which was assumed to be pending. Later on that day, the shelling started, and activity was directed to fire fighting, although the initial damage done by the exploding shells was surprisingly slight.

The shelling continued on Friday, and later on that day as the building became well alight the word went around that its evacuation was to begin. O'Rahilly and his men had made their gallant but ill-fated charge up Moore Street, and it had been decided to work up this street by tunnelling through the houses so that another charge on the British barricade at the Parnell Street end of it could be attempted. We were given to understand that the general objective was to occupy a new position in Williams and Woods factory in Parnell Street.

Many people have claimed to have helped in carrying the wounded Connolly from the GPO. In fact, the process was so slow and so frequently interrupted, that almost everyone in the GPO helped in it at some stage. Personally, I assisted to carry Connolly's stretcher for a short distance to a small door opening on Henry Street, where however I was ordered, with all those around, to proceed at the run up the small back street, Moore Lane, opposite to the GPO.

Another back street running parallel to Moore Street intersected this lane and down this a continuous flow of machine-gun and rifle fire poured. Those who were first across the intersection, of whom I was one, escaped unharmed, but some of the main body following us were killed or wounded here.

A house at the corner of Moore Street was entered and all that night relays of men tunnelled through the walls up the street. Moore Street was littered with dead people, including some of the Volunteers who died in the O'Rahilly charge and, much more numerous, men, women and children who had tried to leave their homes.

The next day the tunnelling process ended in a warehouse yard not very far from the British barricade. Those Volunteers who possessed bayonets for their rifles, of whom I was one, were directed to this yard, and I arrived there when various obstacles which had been blocking the doorway were being quietly removed, so that the way would be cleared for us to pour out in the intended charge.

During the week I had eaten very little and slept hardly at all. Surprisingly enough, however, while waiting in the yard I experienced both hunger and fatigue. I ate a tin of preserved fruit from a shop through which we had passed, and while seated on the stairway into the yard, watching the obstacles being removed, I fell asleep for a few moments.

When I awoke, Seán McDermott had come into the yard and had begun to address us, to tell us of the decision to surrender. He spoke briefly but very movingly and many of those present were weeping. Some time after he had departed, we were paraded in single column and marched out of the yard into Moore Street, headed by Captain M. W. O'Reilly and a Volunteer bearing a white flag.

We marched back up Moore Street into Henry Street, which was littered with debris from the burning and destroyed buildings, and into O'Connell Street.

In O'Connell Street, under the guns of the British military lining the street, we laid down our arms. We spent that night in the open, crowded into the gardens outside the Rotunda, and were marched the next morning, in long columns under guard, to Richmond Barracks in Inchicore.

Notes

1 Originally published as, Seán Lemass, 'I Remember 1916', *Studies* vol. 55, no. 217 (spring, 1966), pp. 7–9.

CHAPTER 7

The Canon of Irish History

A Challenge (1972, abridged)

Francis Shaw SJ

This article was written for the commemorative issue of *Studies* aimed at marking the fiftieth anniversary of the 1916 Rising. However, it was spiked as 'untimely and even inappropriate' for what was intended as a commemorative volume. It was subsequently published in 1972 and described in an accompanying editorial as a 'tract for the present troubled time'. Pearse had claimed that nationalism and holiness were one and the same. Shaw insisted that this 'false equation of the patriot with Christ' was in conflict with the whole Christian tradition. Shaw marshalled his own 'religious' imagery in attacking the canon of nationalist history sanctified by Pearse by likening him to a prophet of its New Testament. The Old Testament, now to be written out of existence, included everything in the real Irish past that could not be yoked to revolutionary nationalism. Fr Shaw was Professor of Early and Medieval Irish at UCD.

In the right corner virgin Éire, virtuous and oppressed, in the left the bloody Saxon, the unique source of every Irish ill and malaise; round eight, the duration of each round a hundred years: this might be said to be the accepted *mise en scène* of the Rising of Easter Week, and it may be added that the seconds in the English corner are usually degenerate Irishmen. It is a straight story of black and white, of good 'guys' and bad. The truth of course is different: there are many qualifications and complexities, and this essay is concerned with some of them.

Clarke, Pearse, McDermott, MacDonagh, Colbert, Connolly, these names are known to all. Less well known is the fact that these same names are those also of men who in Easter Week of 1916 were decorated, wounded or killed, fighting on the side of the British Crown forces in Ireland.

Kilmainham Jail, we were told, was the Irish Bastille: in 1916 it was empty, and had been unused for many years. In 1916 it was not necessary to storm the Irish Bastille or any other prison, because there were no prisoners to release. On Monday afternoon of Easter Week, 1916, notwithstanding the very recent attempt to bring in a consignment of arms from Germany, the highest-ranking British officer on duty in Dublin was an adjutant. The city of Dublin was virtually unguarded: the routine guard on the General Post Office had rifles but no ammunition. These three curiosities of the Rising may serve as an introduction to the contention that the story of Easter Week is not as straightforward a tale as we are asked to believe.

One of the commonest occupations in the Ireland of today is the plying of sleeping dogs with tranquillisers. In this study of the Easter Rising in relation to Irish history an accepted view is challenged, a canon of history which has come into being, has been carefully fostered and was newly consecrated in the massive State-inspired and State-assisted Commemoration in 1966. The final seal on the Easter Rising is to be seen today on the walls of our schools in which the proclamation of Easter Monday is presented as the charter of our freedom and of our State.

The canon of history of which I speak stamps the generation of 1916 as nationally degenerate, a generation in need of redemption by the shedding of blood. It honours one group of Irishmen by denying honour to others whose merit is not less. In effect it teaches that only the Fenians and the separatists had the good of their country at heart, that all others were either deluded or in one degree or another sold to the enemy. This canon moulds the broad course of Irish history to a narrow preconceived pattern; it tells a story which is false and without foundation. It asks us to praise in others what we do not esteem or accept in ourselves. It condemns as being anti-Irish all who did not profess extremist nationalist doctrine, though it never explains how it is possible to be judged to be against your own people when the views you hold are those which they overwhelmingly support. This canon is more concerned with the labels and trappings of national politics than with the substance, which wisely used political action can bring. It sets more store on what people profess themselves to be than on what they are.

It is urged here that Irishmen of today owe it to their fathers and grandfathers to think again before accepting a facile judgement which charges a whole people with national apostasy. Pearse may have been entitled to judge as he did because he took his stand on the infallible teaching of Wolfe Tone, but those who do not admit Pearse's premises should not endorse his conclusion. Further, Irishmen of today owe it to many generations of their countrymen to reject the myth in accordance with which the Rising of 1916 was, as it were, the beginning and the end of Ireland's struggle for freedom.

And those who will allow no credit for any achievement to the constitu-
tionalists, but who insist that every good that was achieved was won by force
of arms, are inclined to overlook the inconvenient truth that militarily the
Rising was a complete failure, that all the arms and ammunition of the
Volunteers throughout the whole country, which had been obtained with
such difficulty, were handed over to the British authorities, and that when
the fighting started again it had militarily to start from scratch.

In the commonly accepted view of Irish history the Irishman of today is
asked to disown his own past. He is expected to censure as unpatriotic the
common Irishmen who were not attracted by the new revolutionary ideas,
but who adhered to an ancient tradition. Irishmen of today are invited at least
implicitly to apologise for their fellow-countrymen who accepted loyally the
serious guidance of the Church to which they belonged. Irishmen of today
must despise as unmanly those of their own countrymen who preferred to
solve problems, if possible, by peaceful rather than by violent means.

It is my contention that some attempt should be made to challenge this
chain of error in Ireland's history. The views expressed here may surprise
many readers; I hope they will offend none. It is no tribute of honour to the
brave men of 1916 to accept their words and their works in an unthinking
and uncritical spirit. They were men who differed very widely from the vast
majority of their own people, and they did not fear either controversy or
contradiction. Sentiment is a poor substitute for intellectual honesty and
sincerity. To examine and to re-examine the foundations of our political and
national institutions is a duty never to be shirked. The 'troubles' of the
decade which followed 1916 may be in part at least responsible for the fact
that today, over 50 years after the Rising, there is no mature, comprehensive,
objective study of the political philosophy and the ideals of the men of 1916.

THE COMMON IRISHMAN

It is high time that the common Irishman should come again into his own; it
was he in any case who always bore the brunt of the struggle. The business
of revolution was usually an Anglo-Irish affair: it flourished principally in the
Pale. Tone's *Autobiography* shows the common Irishman as less than a pawn
in a game of high politics. If Tone had landed at Bantry in 1796 he might
have found himself in the extremely embarrassing position of not being able
to communicate with the people he had come to save. It may be recalled that
in 1798 the English-speaking insurgents in Wexford found themselves facing
in battle the Gaelic-speaking militia of North Cork. In 1916, MacNeill, the
Antrim countryman, warned Pearse, the Dublin city-man, that Dublin and

Ireland were not the same, and he told Connolly that he could see no further than the city roof-tops.

In 1916, half-a-dozen men decided what the nation should want. The deception of MacNeill by such extreme measures as lying and forgery was not for reasons of security or secrecy; it was because MacNeill and his fellows, together with the overwhelming majority of the Irish people, were known to be opposed to extremist action. In fact the Rising could only begin by bringing men out to fight who had no way of knowing to what they were summoned; and this had to be done in violation of the constitution of both the Irish Republican Brotherhood and of the Irish Volunteers.

One of the most important historical features of Easter Week is the role played in it by the Citizen Army led by James Connolly. In this essay it is left out of account, not because it is judged to be of little consequence, on the contrary. It is omitted because it would require an essay as long again as this to do it justice. But it can be omitted because basically it is more a part of world history than of Irish history. In *Labour in Ireland* Connolly strove to show that all Irish revolutionary efforts had been socialist, and he was satisfied that the Gaelic mode of life was democratic; he apparently believed that the capitalist system had been introduced to Ireland by the British, and that before that disaster there had been no private ownership of the land in Ireland. His book shows that some curious blooms can be grown most successfully in a vacuum.

The action of Easter Week as seen in retrospect over a half-century stands in stark isolation. It had no strong link with the past: it was universally condemned by contemporaries: and the ideals which inspired it have not worn well; they have been quietly but firmly side-stepped by the Irish people: they are ideals which are proclaimed on the understanding that they remain as such. The 'gallant allies in Europe', the Germans, have won no special relationship with the Irish people, and our friends in America in 1916 could not prevent the Government of the United States from transmitting to Britain the secret documents of the Irish revolutionaries which were taken from the German Embassy in Washington. Within a few years of 1916 the Irish cause in America went up in the flames of a series of bitter personal feuds. And in the Second World War in spite of the protests of the Irish Government the Americans joined with the British in occupying the Six Counties of Northern Ireland while the American Ambassador in Dublin worked steadily to persuade his Government to violate the neutrality of the 26 Counties, and the British Ambassador worked steadily to avert such a catastrophe.

THE POLITICAL PHILOSOPHY OF PEARSE

The Main Themes

Leaving Connolly aside, there was only one of the signatories of the proclamation who set down in writing at any length his political and national doctrine and that was Patrick Pearse. To some degree he was spokesman for the others. Although his writings are strongly coloured by his own peculiar and unusual cast of thought, yet his exposition of the separatist and Republican creed may be taken as broadly reflecting the mind of the Irish Republican Brotherhood, the secret and oath-bound body which planned and brought about the Rising of 1916.

Pearse was a man of complex character. Nobody would seem to have known him intimately, not even his boys at St Enda's. To some he appeared to be cold and withdrawn, although much of what he wrote suggests that he was warm-hearted and sentimental. He is often described as a mystic or a dreamer, and in his management of St Enda's he gave the impression of being impractical. He wrote well and on the whole his thinking is clear and incisive. In controversy he could be sharp and even bitter. His ideas on education were stimulating and, for Ireland at least, novel. He was neither profound in his thinking nor was he for the most part original. This is peculiarly true of his political philosophy. In his earlier years the Gaelic League stimulated an interest in the Irish language and in the culture and tradition enshrined in it. Pearse was especially attracted by the folk songs which the work of Hyde at the time was making known. To judge by his writings Pearse's knowledge of the Gaelic past of the country was slight rather than profound. The three addresses to the Irish Literary Society which he delivered in 1897 and 1898, and which were later printed, are not of much import; they are rhetorical and immature. In the fashion of his time he made many exaggerated and uncritical claims for Irish literature, and he created for himself a highly romantic image of early Ireland which had only a slight relation to reality.

In the course of his life Pearse's political views changed considerably; in the last three or four years of his life the rate of change accelerated rapidly. The progress was from moderate nationalist to extremist republican and separatist. One feels that by temperament Pearse was a conservative. In his religious beliefs he was strongly traditionalist. He was a revolutionary *malgré lui*. He wrote fiery words about shooting people; but he did not himself use any weapon; and we would be surprised if he had. It is not difficult to discover the sources of Pearse's later political thinking. He makes it clear himself that he had nothing new to offer. He declares without qualification that on the subject of Irish nationalism everything that needed to be said had already been said. To use his own words, what he called 'the gospel of Irish nationalism' had its canon and its canonical writers. These were 'the four evangelists' of Irish nationalism: Wolfe Tone, Thomas Davis, Fintan Lalor and John Mitchel. Of these, by a long way, the most important was Tone. In the writings of Davis, Pearse found support for his ideal of a Gaelic Ireland. There was nothing of this in Tone. Finally, Pearse was especially attracted by Lalor's idea that the land and soil of a country were the property of the State. This had been to some degree expressed earlier by Tone. When the successful revolution came all land-owners were dispossessed while a new distribution of the land to the deserving members was effected by the newly-formed State. Pearse found support for this idea in the belief, which incidentally was without foundation, that in early Ireland there had been no private ownership of the land.

In 1912 Pearse had spoken in favour of Home Rule at a public meeting in O'Connell Street, Dublin. Soon after that he became a wholehearted separatist; and in the last years of his life he became impatient with all who did not share his extremist views. In spite of the need for some circumspection, Pearse's later political writings plainly have only one message: the separatism of Tone must be effected quickly, and this must be done by the use of physical force. Tone had hoped that the ideal of complete separation could serve to unite the whole people of Ireland. In 1916 it must have been apparent that separation from England could only divide the nation more deeply. Even the most modest measure of Home Rule for the whole country was wholly unacceptable to the Carson-led Ulstermen. In 1914 an armed soldiery stood between Ireland and its destiny; but that body was not the British army; it was the Ulster Volunteers. Logically the Rising of 1916 should have been in Belfast, and it should have been directed against those who illegally and by the use of force opposed the acceptance by the Irish people of the considerable degree of self-determination for 32 counties which was being offered to them. But the Rising was not in Belfast; on the contrary, the north-east was not to be disturbed. In effect, this was perhaps the first time that partition was recognised by Dublin and the south. It is difficult to find anything which throws light on Pearse's mind at this time about the effect of the Rising on the unity of Ireland. Both the Irish Republican Brotherhood and the Volunteers were pledged to avoid any action which would cause disunity. On the fall of the dice which was cast in 1916 there were different possibilities, but amongst them the unity of Ireland did not figure.

'To break the connection with England, the never-failing source of all our political evils.' More than once Pearse declared that these words of Tone said all that needed to be said about the national objective. Though he said that nothing needed to be added to them, in fact Pearse did add two important themes. The first was the sanctity of nationalism, especially of

Irish nationalism; with this may be joined the notion of the sacredness of warfare and blood-shedding. The second theme is that the new Ireland should be separated from England, not only politically and economically, but also culturally and linguistically: the new Ireland should be Gaelic as well as free.

NATIONALISM AND HOLINESS

The idea that dedication to one's country is a good thing, a Christian duty, is a commonplace, but Pearse introduced a new idea, a startling one: the idea that patriotism and holiness are the same, that they are convertible concepts. This idea is most unambiguously expressed by Pearse in the oration at the grave of Tone in Bodenstown in 1913:

> We have come to the holiest place in Ireland; holier to us even than the place where Patrick sleeps in Down. Patrick brought us life, but this man died for us . . . He was the greatest of Irish Nationalists; I believe he was the greatest of Irishmen. And if I am right in this I am right in saying that we stand in the holiest place in Ireland, for it must be that the holiest sod of a nation's soil is the sod where the greatest of her dead lies buried (*How Does She Stand*, pp. 53–4).

There is no ambiguity here: nationalism and holiness are identical.

Pearse's solemn and alarming words at Bodenstown were not due to oratorical exaggeration. We find the same sentiment again and again in his writings. I do not know whether Davis is considered to be a holy man in the conventional sense, but Pearse says: 'The highest form of genius is the genius for sanctity, the genius for noble life and thought. That genius was Davis's.' (*The Spiritual Nation*, p. 328)

But it is even more disturbing to find that consistently and deliberately and without reservation Pearse equates the patriot and the patriot-people with Christ. I accept without question the sincerity and the subjective reverence of Pearse in this matter, but one has to say that objectively this equation of the patriot with Christ is in conflict with the whole Christian tradition and, indeed, with the explicit teaching of Christ. The prayer of Pearse:

> O King that was born
> To set bondsmen free,
> In the coming battle,
> Help the Gael
> (Christmas 1915, *Plays*, etc., p. 340).

is aggressively unorthodox. In the sense in which Pearse uses the words they are false. Christ was not born to set bondsmen free from any chains other than those of sin. In the Judea of his day, Christ was set down in a situation comparable to that of the Ireland of 1916. Christ made it unmistakably plain that he was not a national saviour, and his words to his disciples on the day of the Ascension expressed his sorrow that those who knew him and who loved him could continue so long in error.

Pearse had no misgivings. In *The Singer* the patriot-martyr explicitly professes the doctrine of the blood sacrifice in terms of the Gospel:

> You should have kept all back but one. One man can free a people as one Man redeemed the world. I will take no pike, I will go into battle with bare bands. I will stand up before the Gall as Christ hung naked before men on the tree! (*The Singer*, pp. 43–4).

For Pearse, Tone is the prophet of the Lord: 'God spoke to Ireland through Tone' (*The Separatist Idea*, p. 293); and of Emmet's death Pearse says: 'It is the memory of a sacrifice Christ-like in its perfection. This man was faithful even unto the ignominy of the gallows, dying that his people might live, even as Christ died' (*How Does She Stand*, p. 69 and p. 71). When he speaks of war and blood-shedding (against a tradition as old as Christianity), Pearse applies the words of Our Lord thus: 'The Christ that said: "My peace I leave you, My peace I give you," is the same Christ that said: "I bring not peace but a sword"' (ibid., p. 77); in another place he says: 'Ireland will not find Christ's peace until she has taken Christ's sword' (*Peace and the Gael*, p. 218). He never cited the words of Christ to Peter: 'Put up thy sword; he who takes the sword will perish by the sword.' The doctrine of separatism is 'the New Testament of Irish nationality'. Incidentally there are many things in the writings of Tone and his fellow evangelists other than their doctrine of separatism, but it is to that doctrine, almost exclusively and par excellence, that Pearse gives the name of gospel. 'John Mitchel's *Jail Journal* (is) is the last gospel of the New Testament of Irish Nationality, as Wolfe Tone's *Autobiography* is the first' (*From a Hermitage*, p. 168). 'This gospel of the Sovereign People that Fintan Lalor delivered is the shortest of the gospels' (*The Sovereign People*, p. 346). The notion of expressing politico-national ideas in terms of the Christian faith became an obsession with Pearse, as when he writes: 'Like a divine religion, national freedom bears the marks of unity, of sanctity, of catholic city, of apostolic succession' (*Ghosts*, p. 226).

Possibly the most extreme example of this obsession is the extraordinary idea which Pearse expresses in his lecture entitled 'Aspects of Irish literature', given in 1912. Pearse is speaking of the old Irish epic the *Táin Bo Cúailnge* and of its hero Cúchulainn, whom he always looked on as the great prototype of the Irish patriot-martyr:

> The story of Cúchulainn I take to be the finest epic stuff in the world . . . the story itself is greater than any Greek story . . . the theme is as great as Milton's in *Paradise Lost*: Milton's theme is a fall, but the Irish theme is a redemption. For the story of Cúchulainn symbolises the redemption of man by a sinless God . . . it is like a retelling (or is it a foretelling?) of the story of Calvary (*op. cit.*, p. 16).

But it is when Pearse comes to speak of the nation rather than of the individual patriot that he seems to abandon all reserve and all restraint:

> The people itself will perhaps be its own Messiah, the people labouring, scourged, crowned with thorns, agonising and dying, to rise again immortal and impassible. For peoples are divine and are the only things that can properly be spoken of under figures drawn from the divine epos (*The Coming Revolution*, November 1913, pp. 91–2).

> The people who wept in Gethsemane, who trod the sorrowful way, who died naked on a cross, who went down into hell, will rise again glorious and immortal, will sit on the right hand of God, and will come in the end to give judgement, a judge just and terrible (*The Sovereign People*, p. 345).

It is hard to imagine anyone reading those words today without a shudder.

With the Messianic view of nationalism is connected the unqualified glorification of blood-shedding and war. In reading Pearse's words about this, however, we should keep in mind the enormous change which has taken place in the world in the last half-century in regard to war. Nonetheless, one must admit that, for a man of obviously gentle and sensitive disposition, the writer Pearse is very bloody-minded. He does 'not know how nationhood is achieved except by armed men' (*How Does She Stand*, p. 75); and 'When war comes to Ireland, she must welcome it as she would welcome the Angel of God' (*Peace and the Gael*, p. 217). The famous essay *Ghosts* ends with the grim application of scripture taken from Mitchel: 'That thy foot may be dipped in the blood of thine enemies, and that the tongue of thy dogs may be red through the same' (p. 255). At times Pearse seems to hold human life cheaply as when he says: 'We may make mistakes in the beginning and shoot the wrong people; but bloodshed is a cleansing and a sanctifying thing . . .' (*The Coming Revolution*, p. 98). In Easter Week, 1916, 56 Volunteers were killed in action. The number of civilian non-combatants killed was over 200.

The most frightening passage is in *Peace and the Gael* (p. 216); it was written in December 1915, it says:

The last 16 months have been the most glorious in the history of Europe. Heroism has come back to the earth . . . It is good for the world that such things should be done. The old heart of the earth needed to be warmed with the red wine of the battlefields. Such august homage was never offered to God as this, the homage of millions of lives given gladly for love of country . . .

and to this is added the relevant gloss: 'Ireland has not known the exhilaration of war for over a hundred years' (*Peace and the Gael*, p. 216 and p. 217).

I refrain from any comment on these passages. They speak for themselves. About this time, it is of interest to note, Casement was recording his horror at the suffering caused by the war.

It would be dishonest on my part if I were to pass from this subject without stating that the most potent ingredient in the separatism which Pearse adopted was hatred of England. In three of the four 'gospels' it is as assuredly the motive force as love is that of the Gospel of Christ. Tone's hatred of England was implacable. He says himself, 'I was led by a hatred of England so deeply rooted in my nature that it was rather an instinct than a principle.' Tone preached an undying hatred: 'The truth is, I hate the very name of England; I hated her before my exile; I hate her since; and I will hate her always' (*Autobiography*, by R. Barry O'Brien (ed.), II, p. 146). England, 'the never falling source of all our political evils', must be hated always even after Ireland has achieved her complete freedom. Tone looked to 'the pleasure of revenge in humbling a haughty and implacable rival'. These words are cited by Pearse, and it is in this place that Pearse says that 'God spoke to Ireland through Tone' (*The Separatist Idea*, p. 293).

'Irish hate of the English', Pearse tells us in 'Songs of the Irish-Rebels', is a 'holy passion'. In *O'Donovan Rossa: A Character Study*, Pearse writes: 'O'Donovan Rossa was not the greatest man of the Fenian generation, but he was its most typical man.' In his eulogy of Rossa, Pearse then says:

To him the Gael and the Gaelic were splendid and holy, worthy of all homage and all service; for the English he had a hatred that was tinctured with contempt. He looked upon them as an inferior race, morally and intellectually; he despised their civilisation; he mocked at their institutions and made them look ridiculous (*op. cit.*, pp. 127–8).

Speaking in praise of Davis, Pearse wrote: 'To him the English language was "a mongrel of a thousand breeds"', and Pearse blesses Davis for the petty observation that 'modern English literature was "surpassed" by French literature' (*The Spiritual Nation*, p. 317). Pearse must have been a little unhappy in this commendation of Davis, for not many writers of his time showed forth so splendidly in writing the power of the English tongue, and these sentiments about the English language and English literature are different from the views which Pearse expresses in *The Story of a Success*.

It is true that nowhere does Pearse teach as explicitly as Tone the duty of hate, and it is true that Pearse follows Mitchel in the classical (but usually ineffective) distinction between hating the person and hating the evil done – nonetheless it is regrettably evident that 'the gospel of the New Testament of Irish nationality' was essentially a gospel of hate [. . .].

THE GAELIC LEAGUE: A SPENT FORCE

From 1913, the intensity of Pearse's single-minded purpose becomes progressively more evident. It was in that year that he was admitted as a member of the Irish Republican Brotherhood. (Clarke had opposed his admission. He had been shocked by Pearse's speech in 1912 in favour of the promised Bill of Home Rule.) From 1913 onwards Pearse had only one end in view, an armed revolt. To this end everything was subordinated, one may even say, sacrificed. In this Pearse was quite ruthless. And it would seem that he was satisfied that the end in this case justified means which otherwise would have been most unacceptable to him. The most evident in stance of this is Pearse's deliberate and sustained deception of his friend, Eoin MacNeill. Of this Pearse said simply: 'It was regrettable but necessary.' The full consequence of the destruction of the unity and power of the Volunteers as a national force has never been assessed, perhaps never can be. But the wrecking of the Gaelic League as a result largely of Pearse's obsession with physical force may have had consequences even more tragic for our people, consequences which Pearse himself would surely have regretted.

In 1912 the Gaelic League was still a growing and powerful force. In a wonderful way the ideals of this comprehensive movement had appealed to Irishmen of every creed and of every class. These worthy national and cultural ideals inspired especially the young, and we know that it was from the ranks of the Gaelic League that the national movements of the time drew many of their adherents. But the League had to be sacrificed on the altar of extremism and in the interest of the physical force movement. Pearse himself leaves us in no doubt about this. His words are clear:

> Our Gaelic League education ought to have been a preparation for our complete living as Irish Nationalists . . .
>
> I have come to the conclusion that the Gaelic League, as the Gaelic League, is a spent force; and I am glad of it . . .; I had and I hope that you all had an ulterior motive in joining the Gaelic League. We never meant to be Gaelic Leaguers and nothing more than Gaelic Leaguers. We meant to do something for Ireland . . .

> Our Gaelic League time was to be our tutelage . . .; we do not propose to remain
> schoolboys for ever (*The Coming Revolution*, pp. 91–3).

The idea of physical force and bloodshed takes precedence over everything
now – 'to do something for Ireland'; and in Pearse's new scale of values the
high and noble ideals of the Gaelic League are judged to be the things of a
child. They are a ladder to be kicked away when it had served its use. 'I want
a missionary,' Pearse wrote in 1913:

> I want a missionary, a herald, an Irish-speaking John the Baptist, one who would
> go through the Irish West and speak trumpet-toned of nationality to the people in
> the villages. I would not have him speak of Gaelic Leagues . . . I would have him
> speak of Tone and Mitchel (*From a Hermitage*, p. 169).

In an article in *Barr Buadh*, May 1912, Pearse makes it plain that he held no
high opinion of those who found in the ideals and work of the Gaelic League
a fulfilment of their patriotic inclinations:

> Do ghabh dream eilee dhíobh ag saothrughadh na Gaedhilge agus do mheasadar
> go rabhadar ag coímhlionadh dualgaís deagh-fheadmannach dá bhfoghluímeo-
> chaidís an teanga nó dá scríobhfaidís cúpla mion-leabhar nó dá gcuirfildís roinnt
> Craobh de Chonnradh na Gaedhilge ar bun (*Schríbhinní*, p. 234).

> (trans) Another group took up the study of Irish. They believed they were fulfilling
> their obligations as patriots if they learned the language, or if they wrote a few
> booklets or if they founded some branches of the Gaelic league.

The words of Pearse are plain. It is not even a question of relative values; the
making through the Gaelic League of an Ireland culturally worthy of her
past was for MacNeill an end towards which self-determination and political
independence were a means; for Pearse the relation of end and means is
reversed: the Gaelic League was a means to produce men ready to fight for
political freedom.

In pursuit of his objective Pearse was ready to sacrifice even his close
friends. He could tolerate no other view but his own. The Irishman who did
not accept his doctrine was a coward, and in an unbelievably bitter judgement he declared: 'But the (Gaelic) League was too busy with resolutions to
think of revolution, and the only resolution that a member of the League
could not come to was the resolution to be a man' (*The Coming Revolution*,
p. 98, written in November 1913). A few months earlier in that year, Pearse
had bewailed the fact that 'the exhilaration of fighting has gone out of

Ireland' and the passage which follows seems to suggest that fighting in itself is an end to be pursued:

> When people say that Ireland will be happy when her mills throb and her harbours are warm with shipping, they are talking as foolishly as if one were to say of a lost saint or an unhappy lover: 'That man will be happy again when he has a comfortable income.' I know that Ireland will not be happy again until she recollects . . . that laughing gesture of a young man that is going into battle or climbing to a gibbet . . . an eternal gesture in Irish history.

Three years earlier Pearse had said, and the words are of peculiar interest in relation to Yeats's famous poem: 'It is murder and death that make possible the terrible beautiful thing we call physical life' (*The Story of a Success*, p. 76 and p. 61).

The Gaelic League had to be sacrificed so that 'a terrible beauty' should be born. The realistic vision of Hyde and MacNeill had to yield place. It was in any case no part of Tone's teaching, and his doctrine contained all that was needed. In its place, by way of doing something for Ireland, the people were offered the husk of separatism and the synthetic mythology of 'the Celtic Twilight' [. . .].

Notes

1   Originally published as F. Shaw, 'The Canon of Irish History: A Challenge', *Studies* vol. 61, no. 242 (summer, 1972), pp. 113–53.

2   The page references to Pearse's writings throughout are to the *Collected Works of Padraic H. Pearse* vols: 1–5: *St Enda's and its Founder* (including 'The Story of a Success'); *Political Writings and Speeches* (including 'The Murder Machine'); *Songs of the Irish Rebels etc* (including 'Some Aspects of Irish Literature' and 'Three Lectures on Gaelic Topics'); *Plays, Stories and Poems* (including 'The Singer') and *Schríbhinní Phádraig Mhic Phiaras* (Dublin, Cork, Belfast, numerous editions from 1917 onwards).

CHAPTER 8

The Fate of the Irish Flag at Ypres (1919)

Henry V. Gill SJ

In 1920 *Studies* published an article by Henry Gill SJ, a much decorated former member of the Irish Guards (DSO and MC), which described his unsuccessful efforts to retrieve the flag of the Irish Brigade from the Convent of Les Dames Irlandaises in Ypres, at the time a deserted ruin 'being heavily bombarded by gas shells almost every night'. The flag in question was a 'relic' of the Irish Brigade which had fought in the Battle of Ramillies in 1706 under Lord Clare. Irish regiments fought on both sides of the 1706 battle. Clare's Brigade fought against the British. His account of his quest referred to the death of another Jesuit chaplain to the Irish Guards, a fellow aficionado of the history of Irish regiments. In all Gill published five articles in *Studies*; the others focused on scientific theory (including one on Einstein's theory of relativity) and on the teaching of science in schools.[1]

The object of this paper is to put on record the effort made by the writer to find and if possible save from destruction the flag which the Irish Brigade had deposited at the Convent of *Les Dames Irlandaises* of Ypres. It is hoped that this account will clear up certain misunderstandings which still exist as to its fate. There seems to be no doubt that the precious relic has shared in the destruction of the town and the convent. It will be best to put this statement in the form of a personal narrative.

I arrived in France in November 1914, and joined the 2nd Royal Irish Rifles, to which I had been attached as Catholic chaplain at the beginning of December. During the heavy bombardment which had taken place about this time enormous damage had been done to the town of Ypres. Many of the inhabitants had gone away, and many dwelling places and public buildings had been destroyed. But the town was far from being altogether deserted. During the lull which succeeded the onslaught in October and November many of those who had fled returned to their homes, some of the shops were re-opened, and a certain amount of trade was done with the French troops in the neighbourhood.

In January 1915, an opportunity presented itself which enabled me to make my first visit to Ypres. It was a beautiful day; overhead hardly a cloud was to be seen in the sky, save the white puffs of smoke from shrapnel shells exploding around aircraft. The condition of the roads was absolutely unthinkable. Seated in the front seat of a motor ambulance, one could not but be amused at the good-natured way in which soldiers and civilians alike fled to escape the splash of the wheels as the car floundered through the deep ruts – an experience with which I had been taught to sympathise.

My first care on arriving at Ypres was to make my way to the Irish Convent, in order that I might at least get sight of this building around which so many historic memories are grouped. The Community had already left the Abbey, which had suffered from shell fire. A great shell had badly damaged the Chapel. I need not dwell on the condition of the once spotlessly clean convent where some French soldiers were billeted. There is little difference between the general methods of the soldiers of one nation and of another; none of them are very tender in their treatment of the houses in which they are quartered. An old man still inhabited the kitchen and acted as caretaker. He shook his hands in despair when he looked round him. The idea at the back of every soldier's head when in billets in the war zone is that, as the place will almost certainly be burnt and destroyed before long, he may as well make himself as much at home as possible while he is in the land of the living. In this instance the calculations of the soldiers were only too well justified, as the sequel will show. At this time the Convent was by no means a complete wreck. The upper rooms appeared to be intact. They were locked up and were filled with the nuns' belongings. Notices in French were attached to the doors, signed by military authorities, forbidding anyone to enter. I need hardly say that my object in this visit was not to seek the flag. As I learned afterwards, I had in my wanderings through the house passed within a few feet of its hiding place.

I dined at mid-day in the cellar of a college, and there met a priest who was, I understood, the Spiritual Director of the Convent. I asked him if the flag of the Irish Brigade had been saved. He replied that it had always been guarded with the greatest care, and had recently been made doubly secure. This assurance had to suffice for the time. I did not then learn whether the flag had been removed from Ypres.

After this I had neither occasion nor opportunity of visiting Ypres for many months, though later I was to become acquainted with every corner of the ruined town. The second and more severe bombardment took place in April and May 1915, and continued with more or less intensity during the summer and autumn. It was the period of the first gas attacks, and of the repeated efforts of the German Army to get through to Calais. Without warning the massed guns of the enemy opened fire on the town and rained in shells of all sizes. Soldiers and civilians were literally blown to pieces; hundreds of men, women and children were killed. For days the town was in flames; at night the blaze could be seen for miles around. During the daytime the dense black clouds caused by the explosion of the great shells were visible from all sides on the flat plains. Incendiary shells completed the destruction. Every civilian was forced by the military authorities to evacuate the town. Ypres became a city of the dead. Under certain conditions civilians were allowed to return to take away any of their property which had escaped destruction. They could only enter the town when accompanied by Belgian gendarmes and when furnished with a special pass.

About this time I had heard that the Irish flag had *not* been removed from Ypres, and I began to feel anxious. I had learned that M. Delaere, the Curé of the Church of St Pierre, Ypres, had been told by the Director of the Irish Convent that the flag had been walled up in a hiding place in one of the cellars. I had the good fortune to meet this devoted priest at Poperinge, on 26 May 1915. He had for some time been working with the greatest activity to save as much as possible of the valuable property which abounded at Ypres. He told me that the Director had informed him that the nuns had placed the most valuable of their treasures in three walled-up hiding places, and that the Irish flag was in one of them; he did not know in which. I accompanied the Curé to Ypres on that day, and on many future occasions had opportunities of visiting the ruins of the Convent.

The change which had taken place since my first visit was a sad one. The Convent had been completely gutted by fire. All the inner rooms and flooring had been burnt away. The walls still remained, but nothing else. With a sad exception, the cellars had escaped. In order to penetrate into these cellars it was necessary to descend through a shell hole in the brick floor of one of the lower rooms. By cautiously creeping down an iron girder one reached the basement. In one of these cellars a walled up space had been found a day or two before; it was still smoking when I first saw it. This hiding-place reached from the ceiling to within two feet of the floor. It was about 4 1/2 feet long, 3 feet high, and 2 feet deep. As soon as a small hole had been made in the brickwork a volume of flame issued out which had to be extinguished by water. We proceeded to enlarge the aperture, and began to remove such of the contents as could be recognised. Gold and silver chalices, ciboriums and montsrances, blackened and destroyed by fire, half melted glass vessels, blackened pieces of an ivory crucifix, and such like remnants were found. Other objects, such as half-burnt books and manuscripts, were also found. These were carefully collected and forwarded in a tin box to Paris, and have since been restored to their owners.

We succeeded in locating the other two hiding-places. They had altogether escaped the flames. Their contents, or at least the more valuable
objects, were collected hastily and removed. It must be remembered that
during all this period shells were falling in the town, and at least on one
occasion when I was in the cellar shells actually struck the building. It was,
therefore, impossible to do more than save objects of special value. One
modest little paper parcel which I passed out was labelled 'Lace of Mary
Stuart'. But no trace of the flag could be discovered.

It now remained to find out definitely in which of these places the Irish
flag had been placed. I wrote to the Mother Abbess, who was in England. I
described some of the objects we had found in the burnt-out hiding place
already referred to, and asked if the Irish flag had been placed there. In reply
the Mother Abbess wrote me very fully:

> The hole in which you found the ciborium, etc., and the books you mention is the
> one where the flag was hidden. We put it in a large tin canister this shape. . . . The
> pedigree and genealogy of Lady Arthur which you speak of was in the same tin,
> with the nuns' vows (written on parchment), the Patent Letter with seal of James
> the Second, and other very valuable manuscripts, and in the middle of these papers
> the flag was placed. It was a piece of blue stuff with a golden harp painted on it and
> a lion rampant.

All the objects referred to in this letter had been found in the cavity,
including a mass of very white flaky ashes, which was evidently the remains
of the formulae of vows. There was also the remains of a metal box. But no
trace of the flag.

It seemed, therefore, only too probable that the flag had perished, but
perhaps some portions might have escaped. I spent many hours alone in the
cellar and turned over the ashes as systematically as possible. I carefully put
aside any remnants of cloth which might possibly have been the remains of
the flag. I sent portions of these pieces of cloth to the Mother Abbess, asking
her if she could recognise them as being the remains of the flag. In reply I
received a postcard, followed by a letter. In the former, dated 19 June, the
Mother Abbess wrote:

> The only thing really important is to let you know that what you sent is certainly
> not what we are looking for. You will perhaps have received by now my last letter,
> in which I enclosed a (picture) postcard. This will give you the exact colour, it may
> be a little deeper blue. The stuff was light, between calico and silk – rather soft, the
> harp was painted on it in yellow and gold (on both sides) . . .

I admit that this card was a disappointment to me, as I had found a piece of stuff, almost completely destroyed by the fire, which did appear to have been once blue, and on which there were evident signs of gold paint. This piece was, however, proved to be of much more modern material.

On further inquiry I was told that a tin box had been sent to Paris which contained some burnt papers, etc. This was a box in which we had placed small objects saved from the fire. I felt sure that no portion of the flag was in it. I wrote, however, to the Conservateur Belgae, Baron H. Kervyn de Lettenhove, at the Petit Palais, where Belgian property was stored, telling him the state of affairs and asking him for particulars. In reply I received a most kind letter from him, in the course of which he said:

> Alas, your fears are only too well justified! Nothing remains of the precious flags. The box – an iron one – was sent to Paris. We found in this box pieces of burnt wood, small pieces of ivory blackened by fire which had the appearance of coal, belonging to a crucifix, and different pieces of the silver abbatial cross, ornamented with precious stones, blackened by fire, but intact. Then ashes, ashes in which I have not found the slightest vestige of a flag or of any cloth whatever . . .

These investigations extended over almost a year, and could of course only be carried out during intervals snatched from other more important work. I removed some of the ashes from the last resting place of the famous flag. This would seem to be all that remains of the precious relic of the old Irish Brigade.

It will be useful to add a few words as to the history and nature of the Ypres flag, especially as certain obscurities seem to exist. The regiment of the Irish Brigade under Lord Clare took part, along with the French cavalry, in covering the retreat of the French at the Battle of Ramillies in 1706. In one of the rearguard actions the Irish captured two and probably three flags from the enemy. These flags were deposited by the Brigade in the Irish Convent at Ypres.[2]

Even before the outbreak of war the flags had met with vicissitudes. It appears that towards the early part of the last century the number of nuns of Irish birth in the Ypres Convent was very small, and that for a time there were none. During the regime of an English Mother Abbess, Dame Elizabeth Jerret, the flag or flags were removed from the choir, where they had been in a place of honour, and put elsewhere. The story goes that some German lay sisters were preparing to celebrate the feast of their Patroness, St Martha, and began to cut up the flags in order to make decorations. One of the nuns came up in time to save portion of the flag. This portion was, as has been shown, in existence at the beginning of the war.

The question arises as to the nature of this flag. Dom P. Nolan gives a coloured illustration in his work, which is from a photograph. This represents a golden harp on a blue ground. An animal in gold was a separate piece. In addition, the following passage occurs in the work referred to:

> The flag, or rather the portion of it which is left, is of a dark blue colour, with a large harp of Erin in reddish gold thereon. A small detached figure of an animal, apparently that of a lion, of a reddish gold colour, is still preserved as part of the original flag. A venerable nun, who remembers the flag in its original entire state, assures me that the colours were blue, yellow, and red. The blue being in the place of honour next the staff. She remembers seeing the figures 17 – and the name 'Ramillies' inscribed on the flag.

Fr J. Gwynn SJ, who was killed while chaplain to the Irish Guards, took much interest in the Irish Brigade, and some years before the war visited the Convent at Ypres. I have found amongst the lantern slides of his lecture on the Brigade a coloured representation of what was evidently the flag in question, and also a large drawing from which the slide was made. This figure consists of a long rectangle, the extremity of the narrow end away from the mast being in the shape of a B. The half of the rectangle near the mast represents a blue flag with the harp in gold or yellow. The outside half of the rectangle is divided longwise into two smaller rectangles. The upper portion is red, with three animals similar to that referred to by Dom Nolan; the lower rectangle is yellow. Thus the colours correspond to the description quoted above.

The question arises as to the origin of this flag. No mention is made of any flag being deposited at Ypres except those captured at the Battle of Ramillies. But the flag is evidently Irish. Was it therefore captured from one of the Irish regiments fighting on the English side? The two Irish units present at the Battle of Ramillies were the 5th RI Dragoons, now the 5th Lancers, and the 18th Royal Irish. The former regiment was clearly in the fight. They seem to have carried a flag with a harp, for their regimental badge has a harp similar to that on the Ypres flag. We are told that in these mounted regiments 'Silken Guidons were carried until 1834, when they were ordered to be discontinued, and the badges and honours to be displayed on the appointments instead'. The flag, as represented in the slide referred to, has the peculiar B-shaped form which is certainly to be found on other 'guidons'.

The 18th Royal Irish have a blue silk flag with the number of the battalion in the upper corner near the flag-staff, axed in each of the others an escutcheon of the arms of Nassau – a golden lion on an azure field. A harp occupies the centre. It is probable that this flag is at least similar to that of the regiment in 1706. It is to be noted that the lion is not the same as that associated with the flag. The following from Gretton's *History of the Royal Irish Regiment*, explains their part in the Battle of Ramillies:

> There is a curious conflict of evidence as to the part played by the Royal Irish in this battle. According to Kane and Parker, the xviiith was among the British regiments which, in the extreme right of the allied line, stood all day on a hill without firing a shot. Stearne, on the other hand, records in his journal that the regiment was 'greatly mauled' at the attack of the village of Ramellies; and Millner, at the end of his casualty return (in which the losses of the different nationalities is not given), mentions that 'upwards of three hundred of our Horse and Dragoon horses were killed or disabled at the head of the Royal Regiment of Foot of Ireland'. If Stearne and Millner are correct, it would appear that the xviiith was not only employed in the attack on Ramellies but was also in close support of the mounted troops during some part of the pursuit.

There is no doubt that Clare's Dragoons were very hotly engaged with the British. At one time it needed the personal influence of Marlborough himself to encourage his troops. Whether they were ever at close quarters with their countrymen on the other side is not certain. It does not appear probable that one of the flags of the two Irish regiments referred to was captured, for we learn from 'A letter to the Rt Hon. Sir Robert Sutton for disbanding the Irish Regiments in the service of France and Spain' by Forman, 8 August 1727, states that the only colours lost in the Battle of Ramillies were those of the Scotch Regiment in the Dutch service, and of the English Regiment of Churchill – the present 'Buffs'.

The only reasonable explanation is that the flag destroyed at Ypres was in reality that of the Irish Brigade which was carried by them at Ramillies, and that it, along with the captured colours, was left at the Convent of the Irish Nuns.

I have on several occasions visited Ypres since these days; the last time was in May 1918, nearly three years after the date of the events I have recorded. The Germans then seemed to be closing in on the famous ruins, and were only about a mile distant. It was practically deserted, even by troops, being heavily bombarded by gas-shells almost every night. The smell of gas hung around the place. I went to see the Irish Convent; some of the walls were still standing, but the cellars were full of water. It was a time of real anxiety, and the silence and gloom of desolation hung over the dust of the once beautiful town. Happily these forebodings were not fulfilled, and now the *urbs invicta* can be visited in safety.

Notes

1   Originally published as Henry Gill SJ, 'The Irish Flag at Ypres', *Studies* vol. 8, no. 29 (March, 1919), pp. 119–28.

2   For a full account of this foundation see *The Irish Dames of Ypres* by Dom P. Nolan OSB (Dublin, 1908).

CHAPTER 9

Lessons of Revolution (1923)

George Russell (AE)

AE offered a pessimistic assessment of the failure of the revolution to overthrow the British legacy. Free State Ireland had 'hardly deflected a hair's breadth from the old cultural lines'. Preoccupation with material reconstruction would, he argued, thrust all spiritual and cultural ideas out of sight. The champions of physical force, he continued, had unintentionally poisoned Ireland. They had squandered a spirit created by poets, scholars and patriots: 'spending the treasure lavishly as militarists in all lands do', to give 'a transitory gilding to their propaganda'. AE was a major figure within the Irish Literary Renaissance, as mentor, poet and mystic, and, when this article first appeared, had been the editor of the *Irish Homestead* for almost two decades.[1]

I have found few people in Ireland deeply concerned about the ethics of civil war or revolution. The majority accept the principle that it is lawful to use physical force in support of high ideals. Their questioning is about the justice of the cause; and, if that be admitted, they seem to think the right to use physical force to secure its triumph follows in logical and unquestionable sequence. I will not discuss the morality of civil war or revolution. I remember a man, tired of ideal ethics, who cried out at a meeting many years ago: 'Let us hear no more of the good man or the bad man. Let us speak of the wise man and the foolish man.' I am like that man. I desire to question the wisdom of a policy rather than discuss the original rightness of a cause.

A policy is wise if, in operation, it secures the triumph of the ideal. It is unwise if, in destroying opposition, it does not at the same time establish in the hearts of men the lovable and desirable life for which the struggle was begun. I think few disinterested thinkers dispute the moral justice of the ideals of the Russian revolutionaries who desired to bring about such a control and use of the natural resources of their country that none would be poor or hungry or neglected. Was the policy adopted wise as the ideal was right? Did it succeed? Could it have succeeded even if there was no blockade or foreign intervention? Lenin and Bukharin have learned wisdom. They confess to great errors. Where lay the unwisdom?

Bukharin says it lay in this, that they provoked a revolution without the technical competence to realise their ideal. On the plane of physical force they won. On the intellectual plane they were defeated. Bukharin admits that, to save the economic situation, they had to restore the control of industry to the enemies of the revolution. Intellect, science, administrative ability could not be improvised, being evolutionary products. The revolutionaries now fall back on evolution and declare their hope lies in education. They begin again in the neglected sphere of culture.

The Irish revolution, which began in Easter Week, has also triumphed solely in externals. Our spiritual, cultural, and intellectual life has not changed for the better. If anything, it has retrograded. Nothing beautiful in the mind has found freer development. In so far as anything is done efficiently, it is done by administrators, educationists, officials and guiders of industry, who maintain, so far as permitted by circumstances, the habits engendered before the war for independence. The Anglicisation of the Irish mind remains unaffected. The Gaelic movement was the one movement in Ireland with a truly national character. It began its work in the soul, not on the body. It inspired a few heroes to fight; but the transfer of energy to the plane of physical conflict weakened it; and now, when there is theoretical possibility of a Gaelic state, there are not Gaels in numbers and intellect competent to take control. The mass of people in the country continue to think as they did before the revolution.

If the Republicans succeeded in establishing a republic, the country would be as Anglicised as ever, because the Republic, no more than the Free State, could improvise culture, experience, intellect or administrative ability. It is practically certain that after a period of muddle, for their leaders have even less administrative experience than the Free State politicals, they would be forced like the Russians to fall back on the technical components of the old order to prevent chaos. The Gaelic state cannot be established unless there are Gaels in multitude to administer it. The momentum of the old order carries us along in Ireland hardly deflected a hair's breadth from the old cultural lines. It would carry us along despite the legal establishment of a Republic, – a purely external thing, just as that human momentum ignored the legal establishment of a Free State.

Inevitably also, after a victory brought about by the wreckage of the economic life of the people, the preoccupation of all with the work of material reconstruction would thrust all spiritual and cultural ideals out of sight. It would give people a sense of nausea to have them discussed. The moods by which high spiritual, political or cultural ideals are appreciated are engendered in times of peace. The Free State came into being with popular feeling stagnant. Why was this? Seven years of sensation had dulled the heart and made it insensitive. If a Republic were proclaimed in Ireland next year or the year after, would there be any more exultation? I think not. Another year or two of civil conflict and the heart would have been unhappy so long that it would have become fixed in sadness. The citizens would gaze with the same apathetic dullness on Republican deputies going to Dáil meetings that they now display when deputies attend the Free State assembly.

A deep mistrust exists in Ireland about the wisdom, character and intelligence of its politicals. As regards some of them this mistrust is, I believe, unjustified. In other times these men might have won the rightly-placed confidence of the people; but they cannot, and it is not their fault, win affection or excite enthusiasm in seared and cynical hearts. Our over-long employment of physical force has prohibited the spiritual genius from manifestation among the people. It has almost become atrophied from disuse. The triumph of spiritual or cultural ideals cannot be brought about by physical force, but only by labours of the imagination and intellect. We have not laboured long enough in that field, and this is the cause of our failure in Ireland, of the moral depression, and why we seem immeasurably more distant from a spiritual nationalism than we were in 1914. We would not use the intelligence with which nature had so abundantly endowed us. We hated reading and thinking like the old Turks. How many bookshops are there outside Dublin, Cork, and a few other towns? We have set up the machinery of self-government. The body is fashioned, but the Gaelic soul is incapable of functioning.

The champions of physical force have, I am sure, without intent, poisoned the soul of Ireland. All that was exquisite and lovable is dying. They have squandered a spirit created by poets, scholars and patriots of a different order, spending the treasure lavishly as militarists in all lands do, thinking little of what they squander save that it gives a transitory gilding to their propaganda. With what terrible images have they not populated the Irish soul as substitutes for that lovable life! The very children in the streets play at assassination, ambush and robbery. Manhood maintains in new forms the spirit of the games of youth. What future lies before the present generation? Modern psychology, after long years of research and experiment, has come to attach the utmost importance to the images in the mind. Once an image is implanted, an energy latent in the being operates through the image, as the earth gives energy to whatever seed may be flung in the clay. If these are images of health, the energy works through the image and the body becomes as the mind. If these are images of despair, the body itself grows listless. But if the images are of assassination and destruction, what follows? Thoughts and moods breed true to type, as do birds and beasts and fishes.

Where is it to end? If it be lawful for a section of the people, simply because they hold their ideal to be the highest, to use force to impose that ideal on the rest, every other group may consider itself justified in following the precedent. Why should not the proletarians in Ireland, suffering far more than middle-class nationalism has ever suffered under British rule, also use physical force to upset a social order which has never brought them physical plenty or intellectual life? Why should not Catholics or Protestants, holding sincerely to the truth of their religion, make war on those who differ from them to prevent injury to immortal souls surely worse than injury to bodies, I could name a dozen causes all of which could be made to appear as shining in the sight of Heaven and humanity as the political idealism which is now wrecking Ireland. If politicians refuse the democratic solution of our troubles, if they insist on force, we will have proletarian wars and religious wars. Does not recent history show how easy it would be to excite such passions, how ready they are to flare up with an accompaniment of burning houses? The end of it all would be that the most ruthless militarism would conquer; and how long might it be before the tiniest flower of the soul could push up through that ice to begin a new spring in the heart?

We can establish Irish nationality only by building in the heart and the imagination. When we fight we level life to that of the primitive savage, before the imagination had built up the high poetry, arts, architecture and sciences which make civilisation and distinguish race from race. We extinguish national characteristics, for there is no difference between killers in any country. They are all beasts for the time – being Russians, Germans, French, English, Irish – all the same. It is easy for a nation to break with its past in a few tragic years. The Great Famine made such a break in Irish life. The heart was too dead to grow its flowers, and beautiful traditions and customs withered with human life out of memory. The civil conflict which is devastating Ireland, if it does not end speedily, will part us from what was saved of lovable national life and character. In the Apocalypse a spirit blows a trumpet, and a third part of life perishes. Another trumpet is blown, and the waters of life turn bitter and men die because of the bitterness. These images might stand for the tragedy which is past and for the tragedy which is to come.

I cannot understand the faith of those who act on the belief that a nation is immortal and can survive any strain. Nations are no more immortal than individuals. The dust of the desert is over great cities whose inhabitants loved their country with no less a passion than Irish nationalists have loved theirs. Earth is dense with traditions of perished nationalities. If a nation is like a dissolute youth who impairs his vitality by excesses, it will perish as surely and by as inexorable a law of life as the debauchee. There comes a point where recovery is impossible. Something – a skeleton or larva – may survive, but not the nation with confident genius. There will always be herdsmen to look after the bullocks; but the genius of the Gael, if this conflict continues for much longer, will have vanished from its place of birth. The curious in psychology may seek to trace a flash of character here and there in some state of the new world to a possible Gaelic ancestry –

> 'a phrase,
> As in wild earth a Grecian vase.'

Notes

1   Original published as AE, 'Lessons of Revolution', *Studies* vol. 12, no. 45 (March, 1923), pp. 1–6.

CHAPTER 10

The Suppression of the Carrigan Report

A Historical Perspective on Child
Abuse (2000)

Finola Kennedy

Writing about behind-the-scenes debates in 1930 and 1931 Finola Kennedy suggests that then-prevalent attitudes towards children and vulnerable women exemplified a social and moral climate that allowed child abuse to be ignored by the State. Her article examines the suppression of a report in 1930 on the Criminal Law Amendment Acts 1880–5 and Juvenile Prostitution. It first appeared in a 2000 issue of *Studies* focused upon child sexual abuse. Finola Kennedy, an economist, has contributed several articles to *Studies* on social history, and has written extensively on Irish social policy.[1]

The full story of the establishment of the Carrigan Committee and the suppression of its Report is one which has never been told.[2] It is, I believe, of some importance at the present time when the spotlight has been turned on cases of sexual abuse of young people, and when a high premium is being placed on openness in every aspect of public life. This article provides an outline of the Carrigan story.[3]

On 17 June 1930 a Committee was appointed by the Cosgrave-led government to consider if the Criminal Law Amendment Acts of 1880 and 1885 required modification, and to consider if new legislation was required to deal with juvenile prostitution. Pressure for change in the law had come about as a result of statutes passed for England and Scotland in 1922 and 1928 and for Northern Ireland in 1923, which resulted in the law with regard to sexual offences against young persons being more lenient in the 26 Counties (Irish Free State) than in Great Britain and Northern Ireland. The Chairman of the Committee was William Carrigan, KC. The other members were

Revd John Hannon SJ, Very Revd H. B. Kennedy, Dean of Christ Church, Surgeon Francis Morrin, Mrs Jane Power, a Commissioner of the Dublin Union, and Miss V. O'Carroll, Matron of the Coombe Hospital. The Committee thus included one clergyman from the Roman Catholic Church and one from the Church of Ireland; of the four lay members, two were women. It was, by any standards, balanced in its composition.

The Committee viewed itself as operating in a distinct context, emphasising the 'secular aspect of social morality':

> Under the terms of our Reference we had to consider the secular aspect of social morality which it is the concern of the State to conserve and safeguard for the protection and well being of its citizens (Carrigan, 1931: 4).

Those who gave evidence to the Committee included George Cussen, Senior Justice of the Metropolitan District Court, who would act as chairman of the Committee of Inquiry into Reformatories and Industrial Schools 1934–6, Dr Dorothy Stopford Price, representing the Irish Women Doctors' Committee, Miss Edith Tancred of the Women's Police of Great Britain, representatives of several women's organisations, Mr Frank Duff of the Legion of Mary and a number of clergymen.

William Carrigan had acted as prosecuting counsel in a celebrated case a few years earlier when a medical doctor, Dr Purcell, and a former Garda superintendent, Leo Dillon, were charged with the murder of Lily O'Neill, a prostitute known as 'Honour Bright'. Both men were acquitted. In the course of prosecution Carrigan described the murder as 'a sordid tale of debauchery by a pair of moral degenerates'. This contrasted with the defence led by Joe O'Connor, KC, who asked:

> Is it because they go on a spree, and fall victim to the two things that men have fallen victims to from the beginning of time – wine and women – that you are not to judge them by ordinary standards, but to treat them as human vampires? (*Irish Independent*, 4 February 1926).

Among the findings of the Carrigan Committee, which reported on 20 August 1931, was the following, based on evidence of the Commissioner of the Civic Guard, regarding sexual crimes against children:

> That there was an alarming amount of sexual crime increasing yearly, a feature of which was the large number of cases of criminal interference with girls and children from 16 years downwards, including many cases of children under 10 years;

That the police estimated that not 15 per cent of such cases were prosecuted, because of:

(1)   the anxiety of parents to keep them secret in the interests of their children, the victims of such outrages, which overcame the desire to punish the offenders;
(2)   the reluctance of parents to subject their children to the ordeal of appearing before a public court to be examined and cross examined;
(3)   the actual technical embarrassments in the way of a successful prosecution of such offenders owing to (a) the difficulty of proof, from the private nature of the offence, usually depending on the evidence of a single witness, the child; (b) the existing law, or the rule of practice in such cases, requiring corroboration, or requiring the Judge to warn the Jury of the danger of convicting the accused upon the uncorroborated evidence of the witness (Carrigan, 1931: 14).

The Carrigan Report pointed to the ways in which the prevailing judicial processes operated to the detriment of children, leading to their sometimes being treated as accomplices in a crime, rather than victims of an outrage (ibid., 28). The Report pointed to the fact that procedures were protracted and put:

. . . a strain upon the child, under which not infrequently she or he breaks down, and the prosecution fails or must be abandoned. . . . Indeed it may be believed that the frequency of assaults on young children is to some degree attributable to the impunity on which culprits may reckon under this protection (ibid., 26).

Among the 21 recommendations made by the Carrigan Committee were: that the age of consent be raised from 16 to 18 years; that the time for commencing a prosecution under the Criminal Law Act be extended; that the offence of solicitation be redefined in an enactment which would be applicable to men as well as women; that girls when discharged from Industrial Schools be placed under the supervision of a Probation Officer until the age of 18 years; that the sale of contraceptives should be prohibited except under exceptional conditions; that a staff of not less than 12 Women Police be established for the Metropolitan Police District.

When the *Report of the Committee on the Criminal Law Amendment Acts and Juvenile Prostitution* (Carrigan Report) was circulated to each member of the Executive Council (Cabinet) on 2 December 1931 it was accompanied by a memo from the Department of Justice which said that it might not be wise to give currency to the damaging allegations made in Carrigan regarding the standard of morality in the country. The Department of Justice strongly advised against the publication of the Carrigan Report. At the Cabinet meeting that day the Executive Council requested the 'considered views of the Minister on the matter'.

A general election was called in February 1932 and a new government led by Eamon de Valera took over from the government led by W. T. Cosgrave. Mr James Geoghegan was appointed Minister for Justice. On 27 October 1932 a 14-page foolscap memorandum from the Minister for Justice was delivered to the Executive Council. It was severely critical of the Carrigan Report and firm in the judgement that the Report should not be published. It started its attack with the suggestion that only one side of the case had been heard, claiming that the views of many witnesses were known already; that there had been no *advocatus diaboli*, and that no evidence had been heard from a Circuit or High Court Judge (Department of the President S5998, Memorandum: 10, 27 October).

About the proposal of Carrigan to raise the age of consent to 18 years, the memorandum from the Minister for Justice said that, while it would have some beneficial effects, it:

> . . . would produce an enormous increase in the number of crimes committed in the country of which only a small proportion will come to light. In most of the cases which will come to notice, the reason will be that the girl has become pregnant and it is not unlikely that the final result will not be a police prosecution, but a forced marriage (ibid.).

The memorandum suggested that raising the age of consent to 18 years would increase opportunities for blackmailing men and expressed doubts in regard to the Carrigan recommendation to abolish grounds for acquittal based on 'reasonable cause to believe' that a girl was above the age of consent, even if she were not so in fact. At the time a man who was charged with carnal knowledge of a girl under 16 could be acquitted if he satisfied the jury that he had reasonable cause to believe that the girl was over 16. That defence had been abolished in Northern Ireland and restricted in Great Britain, where it was permitted for young men up to the age of 23 years. While Carrigan argued that the proviso in Great Britain conferred protection on 'young reprobates', the memorandum from the Minister for Justice said:

> The wording of this remark casts doubts on the judicial temper of the authors. The defenders of the proviso might say 'it confers a measure of protection on unsophisticated young men against the wiles of designing hussies'. Either remark is mere vituperation and unhelpful. The parties may be 'reprobates' or 'hussies' or both, but it is certain that the blame is not invariably on one side (ibid., 4).

On the proposed appointment of women police officers, the memorandum observed:

> The Committee recommend the appointment of additional women Probation Officers and women police. Doubts have frequently been expressed as to whether women police are of any real value (ibid., 13).

In a telling remark concerning the evidence of children, the memorandum said:

> It is understood that many competent authorities have grave doubts as to the value of children's evidence. A child with a vivid imagination may actually live in his mind the situation as he invented it and will be quite unshaken by severe cross-examination (Department of the President, S5998, Department of Justice memo, 27 October 1932: 10).

A clear difference in approach and tone had emerged between Carrigan and the Minister for Justice. Carrigan painted a bleak picture of the standard of 'social conduct' in the country, which the Minister and the Department thought was exaggerated. Carrigan favoured a considerable tightening of the law to protect women and children, while the view of the Department was that it was unbalanced to be too severe on men, while overlooking the shortcomings of women in these matters, and the, at times, highly coloured imaginations of children. Following the receipt of the memorandum on the Carrigan Report from the Department of Justice at the end of October 1932, the Executive Council decided to set up an all-Party Committee of Deputies to consider on a 'strictly confidential' basis what action should be taken in light of Carrigan. The Committee was chaired by James Geoghegan, Minister for Justice.

The Seventh Dáil was dissolved on 22 December 1932, and following a general election early in 1933, Mr Patrick Ruttledge was appointed Minister for Justice. Mr Geoghegan, still a Dáil deputy, chaired the new Committee of Deputies dealing with the Carrigan Report, as he had done with the Committee of the previous Dáil. The Geoghegan Committee commended a less stringent approach than Carrigan, opting for 17 rather than 18 years as the age of consent. When it became known that the Geoghegan Committee recommendations fell short of Carrigan, the National Council of Women of Ireland, whose President was Professor Mary Hayden, convened a meeting. They passed a motion in favour of raising the age of consent to 18; removing 'reasonable cause to believe' that a person was older than the age of consent as a complete defence; recommending that solicitation laws should be equal between men and women and that there should be women police. All of these items had been recommended by Carrigan. An identical resolution was passed by the United Council of Christian Churches and Religious Communions in Ireland. Both were sent to the Minister for Justice (Department of Justice 8/20/1, 10 November 1933).

Under the Criminal Law Amendment Act 1935, the age of consent was raised to 17, not 18 years. Unlawful carnal knowledge of a girl between 15 and 17 years would be a misdemeanour, not a felony, as would attempted unlawful carnal knowledge with a girl under 15 years. In contrast to Carrigan, the language of the Act sounded dismissive in its reference to 'only attempted carnal knowledge', while the content implied that attempted carnal knowledge of a girl under 15 might constitute a 'minor offence':

> A justice of the District Court shall have jurisdiction to try summarily any charge of an offence which is declared by any of the foregoing sections of the Act to be a misdemeanour where the offence charged is only an attempted carnal knowledge, and the Justice is of the opinion that the facts proved against the person so charged constitute a minor offence fit to be tried summarily, and such person (inquiry having been made of him by the Justice) does not object to being so tried (Criminal Law Amendment Act, 1935, 5(1)).

The Act also differed from Carrigan in regard to responsibility for the offence of prostitution. Carrigan recommended that the offence of solicitation be redefined in a general enactment applicable to men as well as women, while the Act imposed fines and terms of imprisonment on 'Every common prostitute', depending on whether it was a first, or a second or subsequent offence.

If the recommendations of the Geoghegan Committee, combined with the attitude of the Department of Justice, led to a less stringent approach to sexual offences against young people than Carrigan recommended, there was one matter on which *both* Carrigan, Geoghegan and the Memorandum from Justice were all *less* drastic than the subsequent provisions of the Criminal Law Amendment Act 1935. That matter concerned contraceptives. The Carrigan Committee suggested that contraceptives should be dealt with under an enactment similar to the Dangerous Drugs Act 1920. The precise wording of their recommendation was, 'That the sale of contraceptives should be prohibited except under exceptional circumstances.' In an addendum Revd John Hannon SJ argued that the Committee did not intend contraceptive 'appliances' to be covered by 'exceptional circumstances'. The memorandum from the Department of Justice found 'difficulty in ascertaining the relevance of this subject to the terms of reference' (Department of the President S5998, 27 October 1932: 13). The Geoghegan Committee held that a complete ban on contraceptives might be unduly severe.

A letter dated 13 November 1933 from S. A. (Stephen Roche, Assistant Secretary of the Department of Justice), to the Secretary of the Executive

Council was accompanied by a short memorandum, dated 10 November 1933, which referred to 'a difficulty which has arisen' regarding the Criminal Law Amendment Bill which was then in draft form. According to the memo, the Geoghegan Committee recognised that drugs used for contraceptive purposes were also used with other objectives and decided that there should be no prohibition of drugs or substances capable of use for contraception, and limited their recommendations to contraceptive appliances:

> They felt, however, that it would be unduly severe on persons who did not regard the use of such appliances as improper, and who were advised by their Doctors to employ them, to prohibit completely the importation and sale of such appliances. Head 16 (of the proposed Bill) accordingly contemplates that qualified medical practitioners may prescribe and supply such appliances to their patients (Roinn an Taoisigh S6489A, 10 November 1933).

Under the proposed Head 16 it was provided that there should be a general prohibition against the sale or distribution, and importation for sale or distribution, of contraceptive appliances (in the resultant 1935 Act contraceptives would be dealt with under Head 17). Qualified medical practitioners should have power to prescribe and to supply such appliances to their patients. The quantities required by such practitioners would be imported under licence granted by the Minister for Local Government and Public Health. Registers of supplies received and prescribed would be required to be kept by doctors and should contain full particulars of the persons to whom such appliances were supplied.

According to the communication from Roche to Geoghegan, when the draft Heads of the Bill were circulated to the Department of Finance and to the Department of Local Government and Public Health, they were agreed by the Minister for Finance, Seán MacEntee, but an objection to Head 16 was raised by the Minister for Local Government and Public Health, Seán T. Ó Ceallaigh. The Roche memo says:

> The Minister for Local Government and Public Health has, however, informed the Minister for Justice that he is unable to concur in head 16 insofar as it empowers qualified medical practitioners to prescribe and supply the appliances in question to their patients (Roinn an Taoisigh S6489A, 10 November 1933).

On 14 February 1934 John Duff, the Secretary to the Geoghegan Committee, and subsequently Secretary of the Department of Justice, wrote to James Geoghegan communicating the decision of the Executive Council on the matter of contraceptives:

The question of contraceptives seems to have given a very considerable amount of trouble and it is only in the last few days that a decision was finally reached. It has not been communicated to us in writing but it amounts to this: all appliances and substances for contraception are to be definitely prohibited and no exceptions whatsoever are to be made (Department of Justice 8/20, 14 February 1934).

It may be of significance that Duff says that the decision of the Executive Council had not been communicated in writing, as it seems that time was allowed for the Geoghegan Committee to react. On 19 February 1934 the Minister for Local Government and Public Health sent a hand-written note to the Minister for Justice, enquiring if in fact the Geoghegan Committee had met to reconsider their position on contraceptives:

Has the Dáil Committee on Criminal Law Act been summoned yet to reconsider the matter of contraceptives? If so, has it come to any decision? I am being pressed to speed up the matter (Department of Justice 8/20, 19 February 1934).

Ruttledge replied on 21 February, saying that the Committee members had been notified, but that he was not sure what they would do. He said that he intended to go ahead with the main Bill and that Ó Ceallaigh could sponsor a separate bill on contraceptives. Four months later, on 15 June 1934, the Criminal Law Amendment Bill was approved by the Executive Council. On Saturday 16 June at 11 a.m. Stephen Roche received a phone call from Seán Moynihan, Secretary to the Department of the President, in which Moynihan said that the Executive Council decided at its meeting on the previous evening that, before the text of the Bill was circulated to deputies, members of the Geoghegan Committee should be given the chance of 'meeting and formally approving' the Bill (Department of Justice 8/20, 16 June 1934). The Geoghegan Committee met a few days later on 19 June in Room 106 in Leinster House. Present were: the Chairman, James Geoghegan, the Attorney-General, Conor Maguire, Desmond Fitzgerald, William Davin, James Dillon and James Fitzgerald-Kenney, that is, all members were present except Dan Morrissey. Professor Thrift of Trinity College said that the Section dealing with contraceptives did not follow the recommendations of the Committee. He disapproved of the Section. It was finally decided by the Committee not to make any recommendation on the subject to the Executive Council. The way was now clear for the Bill to be introduced in to the Dáil and this was done on 21 June 1934.

In the course of the Dáil debate Deputy Rowlette, a medical doctor, argued that contraception is a 'matter, which she (a woman) herself must decide by her own conscience' (PDDE, 53, 2019). He pointed out that there were a number of people in the country who did not view the use of contraceptives as contrary to morality, and that 'It is questionable whether it is either feasible or just to try to enforce moral principles by statute' (ibid., 2019–20). On 9 August the Bill was passed by the Dáil and sent to the Senate. On 12 December the Bill was referred to a special committee. The nine-member committee, chaired by Senator Brown KC, was appointed on 20 December. Again the issue of contraceptives was to the fore. On a motion proposed by Mrs Clarke, the committee voted 5: 3 in favour of the deletion of the Section on contraceptives. In the Senate debates she was strongly supported by Senator Gogarty, but her view did not prevail. A graphic illustration of the secrecy which enveloped the entire findings of the Carrigan Committee is found in the fact that on 3 January 1935, the Assistant Clerk of the Senate, Mr D. Coffey, wrote to the Department of Justice to seek a copy of the Carrigan Report to help the work of the Senate special committee. On 8 January Stephen Roche replied to Coffey saying that permission was granted to let the committee see the Carrigan Report. Roche said that very few copies of the Report had been printed and that Roche would lend his own copy to Coffey, but that he wanted it back (Roinn an Taoisigh S6489A, 3, 8 January 1935).

On 20 February 1935 the Criminal Law Amendment Act passed both Houses of the Oireachtas and the King's Assent was sought from Domhnall ua Buachalla who had been appointed *Seanascal* in place of the Governor General, James MacNeill.[4] On 28 February the Act was marked 'Signighte ag an seanascal' and initialled by the Private Secretary to Domhnall ua Buachalla. The Clerk of the Dáil agreed to accept it provided the Secretary to the Department (of the President of the Executive Council) agreed, which he did.

Tantalising questions present themselves about the way in which the Carrigan Report was dealt with by de Valera, his Ministers and by key civil servants both regarding the decision not to publish, and the decision not to follow its recommendations. To pose just one specific question. If Carrigan had been debated in public would public awareness of the prevalence of child sexual abuse have ensured that the relevant authorities took appropriate action? If, as Bentham said, 'publicity is the soul of justice', perhaps the answer to the question is in the affirmative.

Notes

1 Originally published as Finola Kennedy, 'The Suppression of the Carrigan Report: A Historical Perspective on Child Abuse', *Studies* vol. 89, no. 356 (winter, 2000), pp. 354–63.

2 Carrigan (1931), *Report of the Committee on the Criminal Law Amendment Acts* (1880–5), and *Juvenile Prostitution* (Chairman William Carrigan KC). A small number of copies of the report were printed by the Stationary Office, but the Report was never released to the public.

3　The author recorded thanks to Liam Cosgrave who first obtained a copy of the Carrigan Report for her, and to Patrick Lynch who encouraged her research.

4　*Seanascal* translates as high steward or major domo. It was the term used by de Valera in lieu of Governor General, just as *Taoiseach* was used in lieu of Prime Minister.

CHAPTER II

National Self-Sufficiency (1933)

John Maynard Keynes

In 1933, *Studies* published the text of the first Finlay lecture at UCD, delivered by John Maynard Keynes. Keynes spoke at the invitation of George O'Brien who had championed his work at UCD. Keynes's theme in 'National Self-Sufficiency' was his own personal shift away from being a doctrinaire liberal free-trader of the nineteenth century mould. It endorsed the protectionism of the new Fianna Fáil Government. The world, Keynes observed, was embarking on a variety of politico-economic experiments and different ones appealed to different national temperaments and national environments. No one could yet foresee which of the new economic systems would prove to be the best. National self-sufficiency, he argued, was not an end in itself but one that enabled other ideals to be pursued.[1]

I

I was brought up, like most Englishmen, to respect Free Trade not only as an economic doctrine which a rational and instructed person could not doubt, but almost as a part of the moral law. I regarded ordinary departures from it as being at the same time an imbecility and an outrage. I thought England's unshakeable Free Trade convictions, maintained for nearly a hundred years, to be both the explanation before man and the justification before Heaven of her economic supremacy. As lately as 1923 I was writing that Free Trade was based on fundamental truths 'which, stated with their due qualifications, no-one can dispute who is capable of understanding the meaning of the words'.

Looking again today at the statements of these fundamental truths which I then gave, I do not find myself disputing them. Yet the orientation of my mind is changed; and I share this change of mind with many others. Partly, indeed my background of economic theory is modified; – I should not charge Mr Baldwin, as I did then, with being 'a victim of the Protectionist fallacy in its crudest form' because he believed that, in the existing conditions, a tariff might do something to diminish British unemployment. But mainly I attribute my change of outlook to something else – to my hopes and fears and preoccupations, along with those of many or most, I believe, of this generation throughout the world, being different from what they were. It is a long business to shuffle out of the mental habits of the pre-war nineteenth-century world. It is astonishing what a bundle of obsolete habiliments one's mind drags round even after the centre of consciousness has been shifted. But today at last, one third of the way through the twentieth century, we are most of us escaping from the nineteenth; and by the time we reach its mid-point, it may be that our habits of mind and what we care about will be as different from nineteenth-century methods and values as each other century's has been from its predecessor's.

So here today, delivering the first of a series of lectures, which will have many successors but no predecessor, delivering it in Ireland, which has lifted a lively foot out of its bogs to become a centre of economic experiment and stands almost as remote from English nineteenth-century Liberalism as Communist Russia or Fascist Italy or the blond beasts in Germany, – I feel it appropriate to attempt some sort of a stocktaking, of an analysis, of a diagnosis to discover in what this change of mind essentially consists, and finally to enquire whether, in the confusion of thought which still envelops this new-found enthusiasm of change, we may not be running an unnecessary risk of pouring out with the slops and the swill some pearls of characteristic nineteenth-century wisdom [. . .].

What did the nineteenth-century Free Traders, who were amongst the most idealistic and disinterested of men, believe that they were accomplishing?

They believed – and perhaps it is fair to put this first – that they were being perfectly sensible, that they alone of men were clear-sighted, and that the policies which sought to interfere with the ideal international division of labour were always the offspring of ignorance out of self-interest.

In the second place, they believed that they were solving the problem of poverty, and solving it for the world as a whole, by putting to their best uses, like a good housekeeper, the world's resources and abilities.

They believed, further, that they were serving, not merely the survival of the economically fittest, but the great cause of liberty, of freedom for personal initiative and individual gift, the cause of inventive art and the glorious fertility of the untrammelled mind against the forces of privilege and monopoly and obsolescence.

They believed, finally, that they were the friends and assurers of peace and international concord and economic justice between nations and the diffusers of the benefits of progress.

And if to the poet of that age there sometimes came strange feelings to wander far away where never comes the trader and catch the wild goat by the hair, there came also with full assurance the comfortable reaction:

I, to herd with narrow foreheads, vacant of our glorious gains,
Like a beast with lower pleasures, like a beast with lower pains!

II

What fault have we to find with this? Taking it at its surface value, – none. Yet we are not, many of us, content with it as a working political theory. What is wrong? We shall discover the source of our doubts, I think, not through a frontal attack, but by perambulation – by wandering round a different way to find the place of our political heart's desire. Nevertheless I will try to relate the new orientation as closely as I can to the old.

To begin with the question of peace. We are pacifist today with so much strength of conviction that, if the economic internationalist could win this point, he would soon recapture our support. But it does not today seem obvious that a great concentration of national effort on the capture of foreign trade, that the penetration of a country's economic structure by the resources and the influence of foreign capitalists, that a close dependence of our own economic life on the fluctuating economic policies of foreign countries are safeguards and assurances of international peace. It is easier, in the light of experience and foresight, to argue quite the contrary. The protection of a country's existing foreign interests, the capture of new markets, the progress of economic imperialism – these are a scarcely avoidable part of a scheme of things which aims at the maximum of international specialisation and at the maximum geographical diffusion of capital wherever its seat of ownership. Advisable domestic policies might often be easier to compass, if the phenomenon known as 'the flight of capital' could be ruled out. The divorce between ownership and the real responsibility of management is serious within a country, when, as a result of joint stock enterprise, ownership is broken up between innumerable individuals who buy their interest today and sell it tomorrow and lack altogether both knowledge and responsibility towards what they momentarily own. But when the same principle is applied internationally, it is, in times of stress, intolerable – I am irresponsible towards what I own and those who operate what I own are irresponsible towards me. There may be some financial calculation which shows it to be advantageous that my savings should be invested in whatever quarter of the habitable globe shows the greatest marginal efficiency of capital or the highest rate of interest. But experience is accumulating that remoteness between ownership and operation – what is historically symbolised for you in Ireland by absentee landlordism – is an evil in the relations between men, likely or certain in the long run to set up strains and enmities which will bring to nought the financial calculation.

Take as an example the relations between England and Ireland. The fact that the economic interests of the two countries have been for generations closely intertwined has been no occasion or guarantee of peace. It may be true, I believe it is, that a large part of these economic relations are of such great economic advantage to both countries that it would be most foolish recklessly to disrupt them. But if you owed us no money, if we had never owned your land, if the exchange of goods were on a scale which made the question one of minor importance to the producers of both countries, it would be much easier to be friends. I sympathise, therefore, with those who would minimise, rather than with those who would maximise, economic entanglement between nations. Ideas, knowledge, science, hospitality, travel – these are the things which should of their nature be international. But let goods be homespun whenever it is reasonably and conveniently possible, and, above all, let finance be primarily national. Yet, at the same time, those who seek to disembarrass a country of its entanglements should be very slow and wary. It should not be a matter of tearing up roots but of slowly training a plant to grow in a different direction.

For these strong reasons, therefore, I am inclined to the belief that, after the transition is accomplished, a greater measure of national self-sufficiency and economic isolation between countries, than existed in 1914, may tend to serve the cause of peace rather than otherwise. At any rate the age of economic internationalism was not particularly successful in avoiding war; and if its friends retort that the imperfection of its success never gave it a fair chance, it is reasonable to point out that a greater success is scarcely probable in the coming years.

Let us turn from these questions of doubtful judgement, where each of us will remain entitled to his own opinion, to a matter more purely economic. In the nineteenth century the economic internationalist could probably claim with justice that his policy was tending to the world's great enrichment, that it was promoting economic progress, and that its reversal would have seriously impoverished both ourselves and our neighbours. This raises a question of balance between economic and non-economic advantage such as is never easily decided. Poverty is a great evil; and economic advantage is a real good, not to be sacrificed to alternative real goods unless it is clearly of an inferior weight. I am ready to believe that in the nineteenth century two sets of conditions existed which caused the advantages of economic inter-nationalism to outweigh disadvantages of a different kind. At a time when wholesale migrations were populating new continents, it was natural that the men should carry with them into the New Worlds the material fruits of the technique of the Old, embodying the savings of those who were sending them. The investment of British savings in rails and rolling stock to be installed by British engineers to carry British emigrants to new fields and pastures, the fruits of which they would return in due proportion to those whose frugality had made these things possible, was not economic internationalism remotely resembling in its essence the part ownership of the A. E. G. of Germany by a speculator in Chicago, or of the municipal improvements of Rio de Janeiro by an English spinster. Yet it was the type of organisation necessary to facilitate the former which has eventually ended up in the latter. In the second place, at a time when there were enormous differences in degree in the industrialisation and opportunities for technical training in different countries, the advantages of a high degree of national specialisation were very considerable.

But I am not persuaded that the economic advantages of the international division of labour today are at all comparable with what they were. I must not be understood to carry my argument beyond a certain point. A considerable degree of international specialisation is necessary in a rational world in all cases where it is dictated by wide differences of climate, natural resources, native aptitudes, level of culture and density of population. But over an increasingly wide range of industrial products, and perhaps of agricultural products also, I become doubtful whether the economic loss of national self-sufficiency is great enough to outweigh the other advantages of gradually bringing the producer and the consumer within the ambit of the same national, economic and financial organisation. Experience accumulates to prove that most modern mass-production processes can be performed in most countries and climates with almost equal efficiency. Moreover, with greater wealth, both primary and manufactured products play a smaller relative part in the national economy compared with houses, personal services and local amenities which are not equally available for international exchange; with the result that a moderate increase in the real cost of the former consequent on greater national self-sufficiency may cease to be of serious consequence when weighed in the balance against advantages of a different kind. National self-sufficiency, in short, though it costs something, may be becoming a luxury which we can afford, if we happen to want it.

III

Are there sufficient good reasons why we may happen to want it? There are many friends of mine, nurtured in the old school and reasonably offended by the waste and economic loss attendant on contemporary economic nationalism in being, to whom the tendency of these remarks will be pain and grief. Yet let me try to indicate to them in terms with which they may sympathise the reasons which I think I see.

The decadent international but individualistic capitalism, in the hands of which we found ourselves after the war, is not a success. It is not intelligent, it is not beautiful, it is not just, it is not virtuous; – and it doesn't deliver the goods. In short, we dislike it and we are beginning to despise it. But when we wonder what to put in its place, we are extremely perplexed.

Each year it becomes more obvious that the world is embarking on a variety of politico-economic experiments, and that different types of experiment appeal to different national temperaments and historical environments. The nineteenth-century Free Trader's economic internationalism assumed that the whole world was, or would be, organised on a basis of private competitive capitalism and of the freedom of private contract inviolably protected by the sanctions of law – in various phases, of course, of complexity and development, but conforming to a uniform type which it would be the general object to perfect and certainly not to destroy. Nineteenth-century protectionism was a blot upon the efficiency and good sense of this scheme of things, but it did not modify the general presumption as to the fundamental characteristics of economic society.

But today one country after another abandons these presumptions. Russia is still alone in her particular experiment, but no longer alone in her abandonment of the old presumptions. Italy, Ireland, Germany, have cast their eyes or are casting them towards new modes of political economy. Many more countries after them, I predict, will seek, one by one, after new economic gods. Even countries such as Great Britain and the United States, which still conform *par excellence* to the old model, are striving, under the surface, after a new economic plan. We do not know what will be the outcome. We are – all of us, I expect – about to make many mistakes. No-one can tell which of the new systems will prove itself best.

But the point for my present discussion is this. We each have our own fancy. Not believing that we are saved already, we each would like to have a try at working out our own salvation. We do not wish, therefore, to be at the mercy of world forces working out, or trying to work out, some uniform equilibrium according to the ideal principles, if they can be called such, of *laissez-faire* capitalism. There are still those who cling to the old ideas, but in no country of the world today can they be reckoned as a serious force. We wish – for the time at least and so long as the present transitional, experimental phase endures – to be our own masters, and to be as free as we can make ourselves from the interferences of the outside world.

Thus, regarded from this point of view, the policy of an increased national self-sufficiency is to be considered, not as an ideal in itself, but as directed to the creation of an environment in which other ideals can be safely and conveniently pursued.

Let me give as dry an illustration of this as I can devise, chosen because it is connected with ideas with which recently my own mind has been largely preoccupied. In matters of economic detail, as distinct from the central controls, I am in favour of retaining as much private judgement and initiative and enterprise as possible. But I have become convinced that the retention of the structure of private enterprise is incompatible with that degree of material well being to which our technical advancement entitles us, unless the rate of interest falls to a much lower figure than is likely to come about by natural forces operating on the old lines. Indeed the transformation of society, which I preferably envisage, may require a reduction in the rate of interest towards vanishing point within the next 30 years. But under a system by which the rate of interest finds a uniform level, after allowing for risk and the like, throughout the world under the operation of normal financial forces, this is most unlikely to occur. Thus for a complexity of reasons, which I cannot elaborate in this place, economic internationalism embracing the free movement of capital and of loanable funds as well as of traded goods may condemn my own country for a generation to come to a much lower degree of material prosperity than could be attained under a different system.

But this is merely an illustration. It is my central contention that there is no prospect for the next generation of a uniformity of economic system throughout the world, such as existed, broadly speaking, during the nineteenth century; that we all need to be as free as possible of interference from economic changes elsewhere, in order to make our own favourite experiments towards the ideal social Republic of the future; and that a deliberate movement towards greater national self-sufficiency and economic isolation will make our task easier, in so far as it can be accomplished without excessive economic cost.

IV

There is one more explanation, I think, of the reorientation of our minds. The nineteenth century carried to extravagant lengths the criterion of what one can call for short 'the financial results,' as a test of the advisability of any course of action sponsored by private or by collective action. The whole conduct of life was made into a sort of parody of an accountant's nightmare. Instead of using their vastly increased material and technical resources to build a wonder-city, they built slums; – and they thought it right and advisable to build slums because slums, on the test of private enterprise, 'paid', whereas the wonder-city would, they thought, have been an act of foolish extravagance, which would, in the imbecile idiom of the financial fashion, have 'mortgaged the future'; though how the construction today of great and glorious works can impoverish the future, no man can see until his mind is beset by false analogies from an irrelevant accountancy. Even today I spend my time – half-vainly, but also, I must admit, half-successfully – in trying to persuade my countrymen that the nation as a whole will assuredly be richer if unemployed men and machines are used to build much needed houses than if they are supported in idleness. For the minds of this generation are still so beclouded by bogus calculations that they distrust conclusions which should be obvious, out of a reliance on a system of financial accounting which casts doubt on whether such an operation will 'pay'. We have to remain poor because it does not 'pay' to be rich. We have to live in hovels, not because we cannot build palaces, but because we cannot 'afford' them.

The same rule of self-destructive financial calculation governs every walk of life. We destroy the beauty of the countryside because the unappropriated splendours of nature have no economic value. We are capable of shutting off the sun and the stars because they do not pay a dividend. London is one of the richest cities in the history of civilisation, but it cannot 'afford' the highest standards of achievement of which its own living citizens are capable, because they do not 'pay'.

If I had responsibility for the government of Ireland today, I should most deliberately set out to make Dublin, within its appropriate limits of scale, a splendid city fully endowed with all the appurtenances of art and civilisation on the highest standards of which its citizens were individually capable, convinced that what I could create, I could afford – and believing that money thus spent would not only be better than any dole, but would make unnecessary any dole. For with what we have spent on the dole in England since the war we could have made our cities the greatest works of man in the world.

Or again we have until recently conceived it a moral duty to ruin the tillers of the soil and destroy the age-long human traditions attendant on husbandry, if we could get a loaf of bread thereby a tenth of a penny cheaper. There was nothing which it was not our duty to sacrifice to this Moloch and Mammon in one; for we faithfully believed that the worship of these monsters would overcome the evil of poverty and lead the next generation safely and comfortably, on the back of compound interest, into economic peace.

Today we suffer disillusion, not because we are poorer than we were – on the contrary even today we enjoy, in Great Britain at least, a higher standard of life than at any previous period, but because other values seem to have been sacrificed and because they seem to have been sacrificed unnecessarily, inasmuch as our economic system is not, in fact, enabling us to exploit to the utmost the possibilities for economic wealth afforded by the progress of our technique, but falls far short of this, leading us to feel that we might as well have used up the margin in more satisfying ways.

But once we allow ourselves to be disobedient to the test of an accountant's profit, we have begun to change our civilisation. And we need to do so very warily, cautiously and self-consciously. For there is a wide field of human activity where we shall be wise to retain the usual pecuniary tests. It is the state, rather than the individual, which needs to change its criterion. It is the conception of the Minister of Finance as the Chairman of a sort of joint-stock company which has to be discarded. Now if the functions and purposes of the state are to be thus enlarged, the decision as to what, broadly speaking, shall be produced within the nation and what shall be exchanged with abroad, must stand high amongst the objects of policy.

v

From these reflections on the proper purposes of the state, I return to the world of contemporary politics. Having sought to understand and to do full justice to the ideas which underlie the urge felt by so many countries today towards greater national self-sufficiency, we have to consider with care whether in practice we are not too easily discarding much of value which the nineteenth century achieved. In those countries where the advocates of national self-sufficiency have attained power, it appears to my judgement that, without exceptions, many foolish things are being done. Mussolini may be acquiring wisdom teeth. But Russia today exhibits the worst example which the world, perhaps, has ever seen of administrative incompetence and of the sacrifice of almost everything that makes life worth living to wooden heads. Germany is at the mercy of unchained irresponsibilities – though it is too soon to judge her.

Ireland? – well I know so little about Ireland that it ought to be no effort for me to be discreet? Let me, nevertheless, risk a few rash sentences, asking beforehand the pardon of my readers for an incursion for which I have but too little warrant.

I feel myself greatly divided in my sympathies. It will be obvious from what I have just said that, if I were an Irishman, I should find much to attract me in the economic outlook of your present government towards greater self-sufficiency. But as a practical man and as one who considers poverty and insecurity to be great evils, I should wish to be first satisfied on two matters.

My first question is fundamental. I should ask if Ireland – above all if the Free State – is a large enough unit geographically, with sufficiently diversified natural resources, for more than a very modest measure of national self-sufficiency to be feasible without a disastrous reduction in a standard of life which is already none too high. I believe, I should answer that it would be an act of high wisdom on the part of the Irish to enter into an economic arrangement with England which would, within appropriate limits, retain for Ireland her traditional British markets against mutual advantages for British producers within the wide field which for long to come will not interfere with Ireland's own developments. I should see nothing in this the slightest degree derogatory to her political and cultural autonomy. I should look on it merely as an act of common sense for the preservation of the standard of life of the Irish, at a level which would alone make possible the country's new political and cultural life. Today it is not too late to accomplish this and it would be in the interests of both countries. But with each delay it will be more difficult, inasmuch as the exclusion of Irish agricultural produce suits extremely the present trend of British agricultural policy.

But if for a complexity of reasons, good or bad, idealistic or political, I were to reject this, and were deliberately to decide to work out the economic destiny of the country on other lines, having made, so to speak, my moral decision, I should sit down to the problem with the best brains I could command to work out a slow series of experiments. No one has a right to gamble with the resources of a people by going blindly into technical changes imperfectly understood. Russia stands before us as an awful example of what ruin and desolation ill-judging and obstinate experimentation can work in an agricultural people, so that men are actually starving today in what was a little time ago one of the greatest food-producing areas of the world. Agricultural processes have deep roots, work themselves out slowly, are resistant to change and disobedient to administrative order, and yet are frail and delicate, so that when they have suffered injury they are not easily restored. What a wound would have been inflicted on the fair face of Ireland if within two or three years her rich pastures were to be ploughed up and the result were to be a fiasco! Could a man forgive himself for such a thing if he had acted, before ascertained knowledge and careful experiment had first shown beyond reasonable doubt that the project was a practicable success – I do not say at no cost – but at no undue cost.

Meanwhile those countries which maintain or are adopting straight-forward protectionism of the old fashioned type, refurbished with the addition of a few of the new-plan quotas, are doing many things incapable of rational defence. Thus, if the World Economic Conference achieves a mutual reduction of tariffs and prepares the way for regional agreements, it will be matter for sincere applause. For I must not be supposed to be endorsing all those things which are being done in the political world today in the name of economic nationalism. Far from it. But I bring my criticisms to bear, as one whose heart is friendly and sympathetic to the desperate experiments of the contemporary world, who wishes them well and would like them to succeed, who has his own experiments in view, and who, in the last resort, prefers anything on earth to what the City reports are wont to call 'the best opinion in Wall Street'. And I seek to point out that the world towards which we are uneasily moving is quite different from the ideal economic internationalism of our fathers, and that contemporary policies must not be judged on the maxims of that former faith.

I see three outstanding dangers in economic nationalism and in the movements towards national self-sufficiency. The first is Silliness, – the silliness of the doctrinaire. It is nothing strange to discover this in movements which have passed somewhat suddenly from the phase of midnight high-flown talk into the field of action. We do not distinguish, at first, between the colour of the rhetoric with which we have won a people's assent and the dull substance of the truth of our message. There is nothing insincere in the transition. Words ought to be a little wild for they are the assault of thoughts upon the unthinking. But when the seats of power and authority have been attained, there should be no more poetic licence.

We have, therefore, to count the cost down to the penny which our rhetoric had despised. An experimental society has need to be far more efficient than an old established one, if it is to survive safely. It will need all its economic margin for its own proper purposes and can afford to give nothing away to softheadedness or doctrinaire impracticability. When a doctrinaire proceeds to action, he must, so to speak, forget his doctrine. For those who in action remember the letter will probably lose what they are seeking.

The second danger – and a worse danger than silliness – is Haste. Paul Valery's aphorism is worth quoting: 'Political conflicts distort and disturb the people's sense of distinction between matters of importance and matters of urgency.' The economic transition of a society is a thing to be accomplished slowly. What I have been discussing is not a sudden revolution, but the direction of secular trend. We have a fearful example in Russia today of the evils of insane and unnecessary haste. The sacrifices and losses of transition will be vastly greater if the pace is forced. I do not believe in the inevitability of gradualness, but I do believe in gradualness. This is above all true of a transition towards greater national self-sufficiency and a planned domestic economy. For it is of the nature of economic processes to be rooted in time. A rapid transition will involve so much pure destruction of wealth that the new state of affairs will be, at first, far worse than the old; and the grand experiment will be discredited. For men judge remorselessly by early results.

The third risk, and the worst risk of all three, is Intolerance and the stifling of instructed criticism. The new movements have usually come into power through a phase of violence or quasi-violence. They have not convinced their opponents; they have downed them. It is the modern method – but very disastrous I am still old-fashioned enough to believe – to depend on propaganda and to seize the organs of opinion; it is thought to be clever and useful to fossilise thought and to use all the forces of authority to paralyse the play of mind on mind. For those who have found it necessary to employ all methods whatever to attain power, it is a serious temptation to continue to use for the task of construction the same dangerous tools which wrought the preliminary house-breaking.

Russia, once again, furnishes us with an example of the crushing blunders which a regime makes when it has exempted itself from criticism. The explanation of the incompetence with which wars are always conducted on both sides, may be found in the comparative exemption from criticism which the military hierarchy affords to the high command. I have no excessive admiration for politicians, but, brought up as they are in the very breath of criticism, how much superior they are to the soldiers. Revolutions only succeed because they are conducted by politicians against soldiers. Paradox though it be – who ever heard of a successful revolution conducted by soldiers against politicians? But we all hate criticism. Nothing but rooted principle will cause us willingly to expose ourselves to it.

Yet the new economic modes towards which we are blundering are, in the essence of their nature, experiments. We have no clear idea laid up in our minds beforehand of exactly what we want. We shall discover it as we move along and we shall have to mould our material in accordance with our experience. Now for this process bold, free and remorseless criticism is a *sine qua non* of ultimate success. We need the collaboration of all the bright spirits of the age. Stalin has eliminated every independent, critical mind, even when they are sympathetic in general outlook. He has produced an environment in which the processes of mind are atrophied. The soft convolutions of the brain are turned to wood. The multiplied bray of the loud speaker replaces the inflections of the human voice. The bleat of propaganda bores even the birds and the beasts of the field into stupefaction. Let Stalin be a terrifying example to all who seek to make experiments. If not, I, at any rate, will soon be back again in my old nineteenth-century ideals, where the play of mind on mind created for us the inheritance which we today, enriched by what our fathers procured for us, are seeking to divert to our own appropriate purposes.

Notes

1   Originally published as, John Maynard Keynes, 'National Self-Sufficiency', *Studies* vol. 22, no. 86 (June, 1933), pp. 177–93.

CHAPTER 12

Adolf Hitler (1933)

Daniel A. Binchy

Professor Daniel Binchy, Irish envoy to Germany from 1929 to 1932, published an astute article on Adolf Hitler. It appeared just as Hitler had cemented his political domination of Germany in March 1933. Binchy had first heard Hitler speak in Munich in 1921. With 'all the arrogance of twenty-one', he described Hitler to a friend as 'a harmless lunatic with the gift of oratory'. His friend retorted that no lunatic with a gift for oratory was harmless. Binchy's scrupulous refutation of anti-Semitism and his analysis of Nazi ideas influenced a number of subsequent articles published in *Studies* during the 1930s.[1]

I first saw Hitler on a murky November evening in 1921. A Bavarian fellow-student in the University of Munich had induced me to accompany him to a meeting of what he described as 'a new freak party' in the Burgerbraukeller. The hall was not quite full, the audience seemed to be drawn from the poorest of the poor – the 'down and outs' of the city: indeed, except for a sprinkling of obvious ex-soldiers, I might well have believed myself assisting at a continuation of a Communist meeting which I had attended in a neighbouring hall a few nights previously. Hitler was the principal speaker, and as he sat on a platform waiting for the very prosy chairman to conclude, I remember wondering idly if it would be possible to find a more commonplace-looking man. His countenance was opaque, his complexion pasty, his hair plastered down with some glistening unguent, and – as if to accentuate the impression of insignificance – he wore a carefully docked 'toothbrush' moustache. I felt willing to bet that in private life he was a plumber: a whispered query to my friend brought the information that he was a housepainter.

He rose to speak, and after a few minutes I had forgotten all about his insignificant exterior. Here was a born natural orator. He began slowly, almost hesitatingly, stumbling over the construction of his sentences, correcting his dialect pronunciation. Then all at once he seemed to take fire. His voice rose victorious over falterings, his eyes blazed with conviction, his whole body became an instrument of rude eloquence. As his exaltation increased, his voice rose almost to a scream, his gesticulation became a wild pantomime, and I noticed traces of foam at the corners his mouth. He spoke so quickly and in such a pronounced dialect that I had great difficulty in following him, but the same phrases kept recurring all through his address like motifs in a symphony: the Marxist traitors, the criminals who caused the Revolution, the German army which was stabbed in the back, and most insistent of all – the Jews. There were some interruptions, and I gathered from Hitler's attempts to deal with them that he was utterly devoid of humour. But there could be no doubt of his ascendancy over the vast majority of the audience. His purple passages were greeted with roars of applause, and when finally he sank back exhausted into his chair, there was a scene of hysterical enthusiasm which baffles description. As we left the meeting my friend asked me what I thought of this new party leader. With all the arrogance of twenty-one I replied: 'A harmless lunatic with the gift of oratory.' I can still hear his retort: 'No lunatic with the gift of oratory is harmless.'

I saw Hitler again nine years later at a meeting in the Sportpalast in Berlin to celebrate the success of his party in the general election of September 1930. I found little change in his appearance beyond a marked increase in his waist-line: 'the twentieth century Siegfried,' as one of his followers called him, had developed a very unheroic *embonpoint*. In his speech I found no change at all. Allowing for the altered place and circumstances, it was substantially the same address which I had heard in the Burgerbraukeller. There were the same denunciations, the same digressions and the same enthusiasm. At the conclusion of his speech the vast throng cheered itself hoarse. The obscure housepainter was now the leader of the second largest party in Germany. In the interval which has since elapsed, he has gone from strength to strength, and today he is Chancellor of the Reich. One may well ask: what manner of man is this?

There are several books in several languages which purport to answer this question. The prophet himself has contributed one of them, written during his enforced retirement in the fortress of Landsberg after the Munich Putsch of November, 1923.[2] It would be interesting to know how many of his followers have really waded through the two volumes of *Mein Kampf*: I strongly suspect that among the true believers the so-called bible of 'National Socialism is' – as was said of Klopstock's *Messias* – 'more admired than read.' It certainly has given more ammunition to Hitler's enemies than to his friends, and any unprejudiced outsider who has the patience to finish the work is bound to conclude that its author is a self-educated man of very limited intelligence. Written in a maddeningly wooden style, in which hackneyed *clichés* alternate with windy rhetoric, full of rambling digressions and hysterical denunciations, it affords no insight whatever into Hitler's own life and development. Anything he tells us about himself is merely introduced, as a peg on which to hang some political or ethnological dissertation. Commonplaces of history, politics and sociology are paraded as new and epoch-making discoveries; long-discarded theories are rescued from the lumber rooms of science and enunciated with all the pompous omniscience of a village schoolmaster. At times one is almost disarmed by the author's *naiveté*; occasionally, too, one meets a gem of entirely unconscious humour. But for the most part the book makes sad reading, and anyone who has even attempted the task readily can understand why Hitler exalts the spoken over the written word.

This so-called 'autobiography' contributes very little to our knowledge of Hitler's life and previous history. Accordingly it will be necessary to supplement the information which it gives from other sources.

Adolf Hitler was born on April 20, 1889, in Braunau on the Inn, a village in Upper Austria, close to the Bavarian frontier. His father was a typical Austrian *petit fonctionnaire*, a customs official who had worked his way from grinding poverty up to what he considered a post of eminent respectability. His one ambition was that young Adolf should also serve the King-Emperor, if possible in a more exalted capacity; but the boy had other ideas, and a serious conflict between father and son was only averted by the sudden death of the older Hitler when Adolf was just 14 years old. Two years later he lost his mother also. Of her he tells us practically nothing (whereas he has much to say about his father), and this strange silence lends colour to the statement of his political opponents that she was a Bohemian of Czech nationality, who up to her dying day could only speak broken German. Certainly this man, who claims to represent, 'all that is best and purest in the German race', is neither in appearance nor in character a typical German.[3] Yet, so strange is the psychology of the masses, this whispered story of his half-foreign parentage seems to have increased rather than hampered his prestige.

The modest family savings barely sufficed to pay the expenses of his mother's last illness and funeral and a few days later young Hitler took the train for Vienna, carrying his entire fortune of 50 gulden in a leather wallet. What was to be his career? The few years he had spent at a *Realschule* near Linz had been utterly wasted, either because (as Hitler says) he was too high spirited to learn anything except what interested him, or because (his enemies' version) he was too stupid to learn anything at all. His great ambition was to become an artist or an architect, and he believed that he had a marked talent for sketching. This belief was not shared, however, by the examiners of the Vienna Academy of Art (were they, perhaps, Jews?), who rejected his candidature for admission. The 50 gulden, a respectable sum in Braunau on the Inn, were quickly spent in Vienna, and Hitler had to abandon his artistic ambitions and seek work as an unskilled labourer. For four years he belonged to the poorest stratum of the Viennese proletariat, living in grinding poverty, frequently unemployed, always unhappy. Yet they were not wasted years, for during them he obtained that insight into the social problem and the psychology of the proletariat which has since stood him and his movement in good stead. He was not popular with his fellows. They thought him haughty and distant, and his refusal to join a Socialist Trade Union cost him more than one job. Thus, isolated from the society of his kind, he passed a lonely, cheerless adolescence, growing more introspective every day. Problems of all kinds – social, political, religious – began to obsess him, and in quest of their solutions he read feverishly and without much discernment everything that came into his hands. During his periods of unemployment he haunted the public libraries; while he was working, he often sat up most of the night reading by candlelight (his economical landlady having turned off the gas) some cheap edition, the purchase of which had cost him his supper. There is something pathetic in the picture of the friendless lad of 18, weak with hunger and blind with sleep, building up his *Weltanschauung* on haphazard, half-digested reading. For, he tells us proudly, his complete philosophy of life was formed during this period, and since then he has found 'nothing to subtract from and little to add to it'. How different from Mussolini, to whom his admirers would fain compare him! Mussolini was for years a convinced socialist and internationalist, far from striving to conceal his changes of views, he glories in proclaiming them. To Hitler, on the other hand, consistency is a fetish: he is quite willing to admit that he has learned nothing since the age of 18 in return for the privilege of being styled 'constant as the Northern Star'.

Nowadays we are too prone to think of pre-war Vienna in terms of a Strauss operette. But cheek by jowl with all the elegance and gaiety there flourished a social misery unparalleled in any other European capital. In the slums all the races of the heterogeneous Habsburg Empire were represented, and their incessant quarrellings with one another were but a mirror of the larger political squabble, which menaced the continuance of the Dual monarchy. Hitler had always regarded himself, however questionable his right to do so, as a thorough German: for the rabble of 'lesser breeds' which surrounded him he had nothing but contempt. More than this, he believed that the policy of the Court was to 'de-Germanise' Austria by relegating to the background the German element which had hitherto run the Empire, or at least its Austrian half. Hence his first political conviction was hatred of the Habsburg house. To him Germany was the true fatherland, and he looked forward to the day when Bismarck's Reich would abandon the alliance with the 'treacherous Habsburg' and absorb the 'separated' Germans of Austria in a greater German Empire. Incidentally, he forgets to thank the group of Jews, freemasons and financiers who (he tells us) engineered the world war against Germany, for bringing this ideal appreciably nearer to realisation.

Holding such views, it was natural that Hitler should first be attracted to the Pan-German Party of Austria, then led by Georg von Schoenerer. But he soon discovered that this movement, while revolutionary from the national standpoint, was conservative to the point of reaction in social policy. Strange though it may seem, he was much more impressed by a leader in the opposite camp, Dr Karl Lueger, Mayor of Vienna and head of the Christian Social Party of Austria.[4] Despite his detestation of the strictly Austrian policy of the Christian Socialists, Hitler had the greatest admiration for their chief. The two great merits which he ascribes to Lueger are his strong social sense and his anti-Semitism. Here was a man who (unlike the Pan-Germans) could reach the masses and had a programme to uplift them, a man who could fight Marxian Socialism on its own ground with its own weapons and beat it. Further, he had correctly diagnosed the evil from which society was suffering – the forces of Jewry. But Hitler's attitude to the Jewish problem, which I shall have to discuss presently, is utterly different from that of Lueger, and the parallel which he draws between the latter and himself is fantastic. Lueger was not a professional anti-Semite: his opposition to the Jews was neither racial nor religious, but was exclusively due to the obstacles which Jewish financial concerns, aided by the Jewish press, sought to place in the way of his social reforms.

In April of 1912 Hitler, now aged 23, shook the dust of Vienna from his feet and came to live in Munich, where he set up as a housepainter and decorator. Here, for the first time in his life, he tells us, he felt 'at home', and to this day he has continued to reside in the Bavarian capital, 'the best city in Germany' – probably the only preference which he shares with the present writer. But it was just as difficult to make a living 'at home' as it had been in 'the putrefying Habsburg Babel'. It was even more difficult to secure an audience for the schemes for the regeneration of the fatherland with which his head was humming, and accordingly the outbreak of the world war found Hitler poor and unknown – not even a *Prophet im kleinen Kreise*. The war he hailed with joy and thankfulness as a sign that 'the days of heroism were not yet over', as he had been inclined to fear. Scorning to wear the Habsburg uniform, he enlisted by permission of King Ludwig III in the 16th Bavarian Regiment. Hitler fought bravely throughout the war, but not more bravely than thousands of other Germans (and Jews for that matter) whom he now denounces as traitors because they support 'the parties of the Revolution'. It is characteristic of his book that it should tell us practically nothing of his own personal experiences during those terrible years when, 'a human cypher', he faced death constantly: the author is too busy explaining the shortcomings of the Kaiser's government and contrasting their inefficiency with the clever propaganda of the Allies. Of himself he has merely time to mention that he was promoted lance-corporal early in 1915, received the Iron Cross, was wounded in October, 1916, and invalided home to Germany, where he was horrified at the 'defeatism' of Berlin and Munich. In March, 1917, he returned to the Western Front, and about a month before the armistice he was practically blinded by an English gas attack. In the little hospital of Pasewalk, in Pomerania, Lance-Corporal Hitler, still compelled to wear a bandage over his eyes, received tidings of the Revolution. Perhaps the only moving passage in his long book is the description of this scene: the old Protestant rector telling the news in faltering accents and the half-blind soldier, unable to hear it out, rushing from the room to weep for the first time since his parents died.[5]

On that day, he tells us, he decided to enter politics. But which party was he to join? Back in Munich, with his sight restored, he weighed all parties in the balance and found them wanting. By pure chance he attended one evening a meeting of the newly formed German Labour Party (*Deutsche Arbeiterpartei*), the total membership of which was six, and while totally disapproving of its 'bourgeois' methods, Hitler consented to be enrolled as the seventh member. As might have been expected, Number Seven soon radically transformed the programme and procedure of the party – not without grave internal dissensions, in the course of which the majority of the six founders resigned. He also changed its name to the 'National Socialist Labour Party of Germany' and gave it the challenging flag which has since become so familiar. The use of the adjective 'Socialist' and the adoption of red as the basic colour of the flag were designed to emphasis the break with the tradition of bourgeois nationalism and to bid for the support of the proletariat. But the latter showed no inclination to hearken to the new gospel, and the average attendance at Hitler's meetings for most of the year 1919 did not exceed 20. But his genius for propaganda in time bore fruit. The flaming red posters, designed by Hitler himself, with the swastika symbol at each corner and the intriguing notice, 'Jews not admitted' (*Juden ist der Zutritt verboten*), were well calculated to arouse interest or curiosity. Gradually the meetings grew larger and the party received swarms of new recruits, mostly ex-soldiers who found themselves out of sympathy with all the older parties. Their presence was useful in the times that followed. The Munich Communists, realising that the new movement was sufficiently like their own to become a possible competitor, decided to attend *en masse* and break up a meeting advertised for 17 January 1920. Hitler had expected, indeed hoped for this development, and had organised a strong bodyguard to meet it. For the first time since the Revolution the Communists were publicly routed and compelled to fly for their lives. The result was more publicity and more recruits. At a mass meeting in the Hofbrauhaus on 24 February, the party programme was submitted to an audience of 2,000 and adopted with enthusiasm. Hitler had found his platform.

The subsequent fortunes of the National Socialist Party cannot be recounted in this article. Even the party programme does not concern us here except in so far as it bears the impress of Hitler's *Weltanschauung* as formulated in his writings and speeches. To unravel his political theories from the masses of rhetoric, which envelop them and to present them in some coherent form is indeed a formidable task, but one which cannot be shirked.

Hitler's study of history – one may be pardoned for wondering about its extent – has convinced him that the chief lesson to be learned from it is the vital importance of preserving racial purity. The destruction of great empires and civilisations may be always traced to some contamination of the ruling race with inferior foreign blood. Among the races of mankind history shows one to have been predominant over all others in war, politics, morality and culture: the Aryan race. But here we meet a difficulty. Hitler does not seem to know the meaning of the word Aryan: indeed he is not even sure of the meaning which he himself intends to attach to it. Some times he uses it to denote the western branches of the Indo-European race (a sense in which it is never used) as opposed to the Semites and the Hindus! But on the very next page he speaks of Slavs, Latins, and other members of the western. Indo-European stock as 'inferior races', denying them the august title of Aryan. The latter is usually reserved for the peoples of Germanic race, or, to use the phrase made fashionable by pseudo-ethnologists of the last century, the 'Nordic' peoples. The Nordic race is the flower of humanity, the *Herrenvolk*, born to rule the world. But being few in numbers compared with the swarms of 'lesser breeds' which surround it, it can only hope to retain its leadership of civilisation by jealously preserving its racial purity from foreign inter mixture. In this task the German people have a special responsibility; for Germany is the largest Nordic country in Europe and apparently possesses the Nordic virtues in special degree. The theory is by no means new: it counted adherents in Germany long before Hitler was heard of and, ironically enough, its chief apostles were two foreigners: the Frenchman Gobineau and the Englishman Houston Stewart Chamberlain.[6] The latter's influence is manifest in Hitler's ethnological dissertations; and I should not be surprised if his reading on the subject has been confined to Chamberlain's *Die Grundlagen des neunzehnten Jahrhunderts*. That this extreme theory has been refuted a thousandfold by history it is hardly necessary to state. Hitler may possibly believe it; his more intelligent followers certainly do not. They merely use it as a cloak to cover their crude anti-Semitism.

For anti-Semitism is the chief practical consequence which Hitler deduces from his theory. The greatest danger to racial purity comes from the

Jews. They are the parasites of humanity, the leeches which batten upon the noble Nordic blood. They are united in 'one increasing purpose': the destruction of the superiority of the Nordic peoples and particularly of Germany. To secure this aim they are willing to adopt any and every device. Some of the devices with which Hitler credits them are more than passing strange: indeed they seem to be self contradictory. Thus they are at once the leaders of international capital and of the Bolsheviks who seek to destroy it. They are equally responsible for the curse of parliamentary government and for the dictatorship of the proletariat which has abolished it. In Germany they dominate both the Social Democrats, and their sworn enemies the Communists. The pages which Hitler devotes to the exposure of 'the Jewish conspiracy' against Germany teem with similar absurdities. But his followers are mainly interested in his practical measures for defeating the conspiracy. They are at once simple and attractive: confiscation of all Jewish capital and landed property, suppression of the Jewish press, withdrawal of citizenship and all public positions from Jews. The policy is clever in that it appeals to the lowest instincts of the mob, its jealousy and cupidity, while cloaking them over with the 'racial' argument. No impartial observer will deny that the Jewish problem is more complicated in Germany than elsewhere, but to make this a pretext for advocating wholesale robbery is hardly consonant with those high Nordic virtues of which Hitler purports to be a shining example. Yet Gottfried Feder, the party 'economist', is probably right in declaring that 'anti-Semitism is the foundation of our movement'.

But the expropriation of the Jews does not exhaust the state's duties towards the sacred principle of racial purity. Indeed, the very *raison d'être* of the state is the preservation and development of the race. The worth of the state is to be tested, not by its form of government, but by the 'ruthless energy' with which it repels the enemies of the race and fulfils the other conditions under which Nordic stock may flourish. It matters little whether the state calls itself republic or monarchy: Hitler has no sympathy with the Monarchist Conservatives, and some of his choicest abuse has been hurled at the very leaders of Junker nationalism who now constitute the majority of his colleagues in the Cabinet. But there are certain baneful institutions, invented by the Jews, which, being essentially alien to the Nordic temperament, cannot be tolerated. Chief among them is parliamentary democracy. Apparently our textbooks err in attributing this institution to the genius of the Anglo-Saxon race, for Hitler declares it to be utterly un-Nordic: for the old Germanic constitution of personal leadership and individual responsibility it substitutes government by counting heads. The most successful of modern demagogues has a profound contempt for the majority upon which he exercises his unrivalled powers of agitation: it is stupid, volatile, treacherous. Hitler believes rather in the aristocratic principle, not indeed as expressed by the 'Judaised' nobility of pre-war Germany, but by an aristocracy of character. From this the 'natural leaders' of the people are to be drawn, who, scorning the subterfuges of representative government, will answer personally for their actions. To whom they must answer we are not told.

The 'natural leaders' of the Nordic state have not merely to maintain but also to improve the race. To secure this, drastic measures must be adopted. Hitler does not go as far as some of his friends, for example Alfred Rosenberg, editor of the Party's official organ the *Volkischer Beobachter*, who seeks to atone for his Jewish name by exceeding all others in anti-Semitism. Rosenberg advocates the sterilisation of all Jews and defective Nordics, the recognition of a 'limited' polygamy, and even, if necessary, the establishment of what one can only describe as human stud farms. Hitler's own programme is more modest. He would forbid all marriages of pure Germans with Jews. For the rest, he would have those who are racially pure and physically sound unite with their peers at about the age of 18, so that they may produce a numerous and healthy stock. But what of those Nordics who, while racially above suspicion, are either corporally or mentally unfitted to have vigorous offspring. Hitler would give the state power to effect the sterilisation of such persons, assuming that they cannot be induced to serve the paramount interests of the race by voluntarily renouncing marriage. In this all-important matter his youthful followers, looking for guidance to the leader himself, must be somewhat bewildered: Hitler did not marry at 18, and even today, at the age of 43, he is still a bachelor.

To secure that every healthy German youth will be in a position to marry and found a family, it is necessary to revolutionise the existing social order. The capitalist system, a Jewish invention, must be replaced by a state regulated economy which will accord equal opportunities to every pure German. Hitler is convinced – and herein lies the real strength of his movement – that there can be no racial and national regeneration of Germany until the claims of the proletariat have been fully satisfied. His quarrel with Marxian Socialism is not that it is Socialist, but that it is internationalist and pacifist. It has degraded and denationalised the German worker: witness its 'stab in the back' in 1918 just when Germany was about to win the war (our military histories are also in need of revision). In its place must be established a Germanic socialism, a national socialism, under which the exploitation of the Nordic workman will cease. How far this new brand of socialism differs from the orthodox type I do not propose to discuss here, for Hitler does not even profess any knowledge of economics and is content to leave the formulation of the party's economic policy to others. Or perhaps the silence of the prophet is calculated. The masses can only be won by a socialist programme, but the party funds are largely dependent on 'big business'.[7] In order that the latter may not be scared, it is useful to be able to represent the extreme doctrines of Feder or Rosenberg as 'unofficial'. This is one of the most difficult parts of Hitler's tasks, and its difficulties will be increased a thousandfold when he is forced to put his economic programme into action.[8]

Perhaps even more difficult is the religious question. Hitler's parents were pious Catholics (he even informs us that his earliest ambition was to be a priest), but his book shows clearly that personally he is no longer a *croyant*. Yet he has resolutely set his face against any attempt to use his movement in the interests of a new *Kulturkampf*, and has unsparingly denounced the introduction of 'confessional differences' into the party. The various 'racist' movements of which National Socialism is the successor had all a strong anti-Catholic, sometimes even an anti-Christian bias. Hitler has tried hard to exorcise this spirit, but only with limited success. He has proclaimed that the party favours a 'positive Christianity', without declaring in favour of either Catholicism or Lutheranism. He has dissociated himself from the crazy religious speculations of his editor-in-chief, Rosenberg. He has broken with the racists *strictioris observantiae* led by General Ludendorf, who seek to replace Christianity by the old Germanic cult and who now (amusingly enough) denounce Hitler as a 'serf of Rome'. The condemnation of his movement by the German episcopate he seeks to explain as due exclusively to the machinations of the Centre Party. There is no doubt that, while he must know that the Church will never accept the unchristian implications of his racist theories, he is desperately anxious to avoid an open breach. Not so his more extreme followers, led by the notorious Goebbels (himself an ex-Catholic), who daily bespatter the Church and the episcopate with the vilest abuse. As a result, Hitler finds himself losing ground in all the Catholic parts of Germany: the vast army of new recruits is composed of either Protestants or dissidents.[9] He makes no secret of his concern at this development: even if his study of history be as slight as I suspect, he must realise that the Church has faced and beaten greater movements than his.

A considerable portion of Hitler's book is devoted to questions of foreign policy. His criticisms of the Imperial government's sins in the pre-war period may be dismissed as wisdom after the event; and in any case the clumsy Machiavellism which he propounds as an alternative policy would have neither averted the war nor won it for Germany. Of more practical interest are his proposals for the future. A firm believer in the inevitability, nay even the desirability of war, he is concerned to find suitable allies for Germany, and as a *Realpolitiker* he would seek them among those nations which, for their own reasons, are opposed to the present hegemony of France. England, another Nordic country, would be the most desirable ally, and as the price of its friendship Germany should definitely consent to abandon her colonies and the policy of naval and colonial expansion. But England is traditionally cautious; and besides, the Jews are high in its counsels: no doubt they were responsible for the frosty reception accorded to Herr Rosenberg during his unofficial 'mission' last year. Italy, though racially inferior, offers brighter prospects. The admiration felt for Mussolini by Hitler and his followers and the sympathy extended to the Nazis in the Fascist press encourage hopes of close cooperation. The price which Hitler is prepared to pay for this is heavy: the final abandonment of Southern Tyrol, the home of Walther von der Vogelweid, perhaps the fairest of all German-speaking lands. But most remarkable of all is Hitler's attitude towards the Soviet. Far from entertaining any idea of alliance with Russia, he looks forward to its complete disintegration as the signal to resume the old Germanic policy of pushing eastward. By forcible colonisation at Russia's expense, Germany may hope to gain more territory than she has lost by the Treaty of Versailles and to solve the problem of her surplus population, acute enough under present circumstances, but destined to become infinitely more so under Hitler's schemes for early marriages. With marked emphasis he declares that the new movement is not committed to the restoration of Germany's pre-war frontiers in so far as they included territories, such as Alsace-Lorraine, where the race was not predominantly German. But then why provide for another war with France? Is it to be fought merely for the purpose of demonstrating Nordic superiority?

The reader who has had the patience to follow this summary of Hitler's doctrines may well ask – does young Germany really take him seriously? It is sometimes stated that he is a mere puppet managed by clever men, that he is only the loud-speaker of the party apparatus. Personally I have seen no evidence of this. On the contrary, I believe that Hitler's influence is paramount. He has smashed all attempted rebellions against his authority, and a few of them looked very serious for a time. From the 'Brown House' in Munich his writ runs all over the Reich and his word is obeyed unquestioningly. The rank and file of the 'Storm Troops' have proved their loyalty to 'the Chief' in the face of revolts by their immediate commanders. No doubt many of the newer leaders of the party have infinitely more ability than their leader and are privately inclined to laugh at him. But there can be no question of ousting him from power, for his personality alone is capable of holding together all the – discordant elements in the Nazi camp. Without Hitler the party would certainly fall asunder, the larger section going over to the Communists, and a minority to the old Nationalist party. He has shown considerable skill in driving his ill-assorted team, though the necessity of conciliating all sides has introduced extraordinary discrepancies into his public pronouncements. Thus the Nazi programme provides for the liquidation of all big corporations and trusts. Hitler now adds: 'except such as have definitely benefited the nation' – a loophole for Thyssen, Krupp and other subscribers to the party funds. He has affirmed on oath that his movement will pursue its aims solely by constitutional means; yet a few months later he could telegraph to the seven Nazis accused of the Beuthen murders (perhaps the most brutal in the annals of political crime in Germany): 'You are not murderers, but my comrades.' His approach to office has made it still more difficult to tie him down to any definite policy, and his first broadcast message to the German people as Chancellor is a study in the art of saying nothing at great length.

How explain his ascendancy over the masses? To millions of normal Germans he is a prophet and a hero. On what is this reputation based? Obviously not on his intelligence. Nor can it be on his political record, which makes poor reading. He has been invariably outwitted by more experienced statesmen and sometimes made to look intensely foolish. He has made bad mistakes in tactics: witness his decision to oppose Hindenburg for the presidency in March of last year. By this action he secured for the old Field Marshal a solid block of 20 million votes and therewith the claim to speak for the absolute majority of the German people. The story of the frantic endeavours to make him a German citizen in time for the fray raised much laughter at his expense.'[10] And even now, before being entrusted with the Chancellorship, he has had his wings firmly clipped by the President. He has had to accept as colleagues most of the 'Government of Barons' which he was hysterically denouncing a few months ago. In addition he has the chief of the Conservative Nationalists, whose meetings were consistently broken up by the Nazis during the last election campaign, as well as the chief of the *Stahlhelm*, with which his Brown Army has had many a skirmish. He can hardly expect these men to swallow his programme. Accordingly his choice will be unenviable: either to scrap his more crazy objectives and govern Germany along bourgeois conservative lines, thereby risking the secession of his proletarian supporters, or to stage a fight with his 'reactionary' colleagues and return to the wilderness once more.

Some have attempted to explain Hitler's ascendancy by his eloquence, others by his genius for propaganda, others again by the fact that he stands on the same intellectual plain as the bulk of his followers. While these are contributory factors, the personality of the man himself cannot be left out of account. His personal honesty and disinterestedness are not disputed by any sincere opponent. But the real secret of his power lies in his fanatical, almost mystic belief in himself and his mission. 'I am only forty-three years old,' he told his followers on the day after his defeat in the presidential election, 'and I am in perfect health. I am convinced that nothing can happen me, for I know that I have been appointed to my task by a higher power.' There are only two barriers to megalomania in public life: intelligence and a sense of humour. Either of these qualities would suffice to prevent it, but I believe Hitler to be lacking in both, and thus faith in himself and his mission has become for him a kind of religion. Such fanatical belief can easily be communicated to the masses, especially when it is accompanied, as in his case, by the gift of eloquence. It is not merely the right sort of faith which is capable of moving mountains.

I write while Germany is in the throes of the most bitter election in her history. Until the result is known, it would be idle to speculate as to the new Chancellor's future. But, whatever be the result of the gambler's throw, he himself will deserve the continued attention of the student of comparative politics. For the phenomenon of Hitler is not peculiar to Germany.

Notes

1 Originally published as Daniel Binchy, 'Adolf Hitler', *Studies* vol. 22, no. 85 (March, 1933), pp. 29–47.

2 *Mein Kampf* by Adolf Hitler (Munich, 1925).

3 Professor von Gruber, the Munich anthropologist, who is a strong Nationalist (though not of the Hitlerite persuasion), described him in 1926 as follows: 'Face and skull reveal racial inferiority. Obviously he is the product of cross-breeding.' See E. Lengyel, *Hitler* (London, 1932) where other equally unflattering opinions are cited.

4 For an account of Lueger (1844–1910) and his political and social achievements see *Studies*, Sept 1914 and June 1915.

5 Quite characteristically Hitler does his best to spoil the effect of this simple narrative by appending five pages of hysterical rhetoric.

6 Count Joseph Arthur Gobineau (1816–82): *Essai sur l'inégalité des races humaines* (1853), Houston Stewart Chamberlain (1855–1926): *Die Grundlagen des neunzehnten Jahrhunderts* (1890).

7 Lengyel (*op. cit.*, chp. XIV) has collected some interesting statistics about the financing of the Nazis by German captains of industry, and believes that the latter has been privately reassured by Hitler that the party's 'socialism' need not be taken too literally.

8 Under the Papen and Schleicher governments, Hitler's tendency was to emphasise the proletarian character of his movement against the 'feudalist reactionaries'. He even gave his blessing to a strike of Berlin Municipal workers organised by Nazis and Communists jointly last November. It will be interesting to watch his attitude now that he is to govern along with the 'feudalist reactionaries'.

9 Thus his adopted city, Munich, the cradle of his movement, now gives him less votes than any of the other large cities. Already there are demands from some quarters for 'a bold anti-Roman front'.

10 As Hitler declined to apply for naturalisation in the ordinary way, his friends sought to smuggle him into citizenship by getting him appointed to some nominal position in the public service of one of the federal states which had Nazi ministries. First, Dr Frick, then Minister of Education in Thurgina and now Minister for the Interior in Hitler's Cabinet, proposed to make him Professor of Education in the University of Jena, but the faculty protested. Frick then

proceeded to nominate him head constable of the police in the little village of Hildburghausen, but amid general laughter the nomination was held to be unconstitutional on the ground of secrecy. Finally, Dr Klagge, the first Nazi minister in Brunswick, found the solution. Hitler was appointed attaché to the Brunswick 'Legation' in Berlin, a post which involved neither work nor salary, but only an oath of allegiance to the Weimar Constitution, which the new official apparently found no difficulty in taking.

CHAPTER 13

The Jesuits and the 1937 Constitution (1989)

Dermot Keogh

This article analyses the role of the Jesuits in the drafting of the 1937 chapters following correspondence between Edward Cahill SJ and Eamon de Valera; Cahill whom de Valera regarded as a friend offered to 'get the opinion' of other Jesuits on the draft constitution. Keogh's article offers a detailed analysis of the nature and extent of Jesuit influence on the wording of the final Constitution, particularly the preamble and articles 40 to 44 which reflect Catholic social thought. Read alongside Finola Kennedy's analysis of the Carrigan Report (1930) Keogh's analysis reveals more than a few similarities with the working practices of civil servants who influence legislative debates behind the scenes today. The author is a Professor of History at University College Cork.[1]

INTRODUCTION

The opening of the Eamon de Valera papers on the drafting of the Constitution, in summer 1987, has helped put into focus many of the theories surrounding those important events. The role of John Charles McQuaid, later to become Archbishop of Dublin in 1940, has already been written about quite extensively.[2] However, the modest role played by the Irish Jesuit community is less well known. At the invitation of de Valera, they went so far as to draft their own constitution and have it forwarded to government buildings. I would like to provide a detailed account here of the involvement of that order in the process which led up to the enacting of the 1937 Constitution. It is an important episode in modern Irish history. Edward Cahill, a member of the Jesuit Order, had been known to de Valera through his activities in the late 1920s as a founder of *An Rioghaght*, an Irish organisation designed along the same lines as the Catholic Action movement in France and Italy. He was a man of many enthusiasms.[3] Cahill could never be described as a confidential adviser to Eamon de Valera. It was rather that the Jesuit's friendship and loyalty through the years deserved recognition. In the wake of the Irish Civil War, loyalty was a virtue which de Valera held in high esteem.

BACKGROUND TO JESUIT SUBMISSION

On 4 September 1936, Cahill wrote to de Valera from the Imperial Hotel, Lisdoonvarna, where he had been sent unexpectedly by his superior. He explained how the drafting 'of the suggestion which I had in mind' took much longer than he had anticipated and apologised about sending them along in such rough condition. On his return to Dublin, he volunteered if de Valera was interested to 'get the opinion of some few others of the fathers who are interested in these matters and revise the present draft'.[4]

In his submission, Cahill encouraged de Valera to 'make a definite break with the Liberal and non-Christian types of state'. The latter had been 'forced upon us by a foreign, non-Catholic power'. That imposition was:

> exotic, unnatural and quite foreign to the native tradition. It tends in innumerable ways to cramp and paralyse the free development of the people's Catholic life and culture. It causes lamentable and sometimes very dangerous confusion of thought upon public questions of the highest importance; and it leaves the door open to still graver dangers.

Cahill was concerned that the Irish, who were 'probably among the best Catholics in Europe', could be subject to the influence of 'the most anti-Christian or degrading or even blasphemous doctrines or practices or writings' from groups who enjoyed the protection of the Executive under the Constitution. He referred to a recent judgement of a member of the Supreme Court 'which denied the existence of a natural Law superior to all human enactments' and further 'rejected the idea of indefeasible personal rights which no positive statutes can invalidate'. That judge, according to Cahill, 'is given in the Irish Freemason Calendar as a Freemason of one of the very highest degrees, who consequently must have taken the impious and more or less blasphemous oaths which I refer to in my book.'

Cahill was of the opinion that 'a constitution for Ireland should be, if not confessedly Catholic (which may at present not be feasible) at least definitely and *confessedly Christian*'. The precept 'Seek ye first the Kingdom of God and His Justice and all other things shall be added unto you' applied to states as well as to persons. Cahill felt that it was especially important to pursue such a line 'when the anti-Christian and disruptive forces of the world are apparently being mobilised for a determined effort to destroy the Church and what is still left of Christian civilisation; and change radically the whole system of life and thought which has developed under Christian influence and teaching'. Cahill continued in a very emotional tone to argue that de Valera had a unique opportunity to introduce a Christian constitution which otherwise would be to betray 'in a very grave manner the sacred trust committed to them by providence and will deservedly suffer an irreparable loss of prestige in the minds of the best of their own people and of the Catholic people of Europe'. Cahill explained the philosophical basis of his objections to the 1922 Constitution as follows:

> It is commonplace to assert that the English Protestant culture and the English economic and fiscal system which have been forced on Ireland will, unless eliminated, prove fatal obstacles to the real emancipation of the country from a foreign yoke. The same thing is true of the unchristian Liberalism which has been introduced from the same source into the public life of the Irish people. But political Liberalism contains within itself much greater danger than either English culture or individualistic capitalism. It is in fact the underlying philosophy and the unifying element of all the movements mutually antagonistic in many details, which are now making for the destruction of Christianity. Again, our people have never freely accepted the unchristian Constitution under which they have been forced to live since the English conquest.

Cahill felt that the basic lack of respect prevalent in the country for legitimate civil authority would be removed if a Christian constitution were introduced. He pointed out that all the Irish people, including those in the Northeast counties, 'are with the exception of a negligible minority (such as the Hebrew element) professing Christians; and the overwhelming majority are not only professing but practical Catholics, whose religion is dearer to them than anything else on earth.' Cahill wanted to see a strong President and executive emerge under a new constitution. He wanted an executive independent of the legislature, as in Salazar's Portugal. With proper safeguards against the abuse of the executive, he felt 'the unnatural party system would then disappear'.

De Valera was appreciative of Cahill's help. He wrote on 19 September 1936 enclosing the manuscript:

> (I) have read it over carefully. It is very useful as indicating the principles which should inspire all governmental activity so as to make it conform with Catholic teaching. The difficulty is to decide how much can be or should be embodied formally in the new constitution.

However, de Valera did not find the document in its present form particularly practical. He suggested:

> If you could find time to put into the form of draft articles, with perhaps a draft preamble, what you think should be formally written into the Constitution, it will be very helpful. I could then arrange, when I have seen your draft, to have a chat with you about it.[5]

Cahill took up the offer: 'I will willingly do what you suggest', he wrote to de Valera on 21 September 1936. But he was afraid that it might take some time – some weeks: 'as I would like to secure the advice and help of some others.'[6]

MEETINGS OF JESUIT 'BEST HEADS'

True to his word, Cahill brought the matter to the immediate attention of his superiors. Obviously, he stressed the urgency of the matter and may have requested special leave to work exclusively on the draft requested by de Valera. However, the matter was taken very seriously by the superiors of the Order who realised that the standing of the Society would be judged by the quality of the document. It was decided, therefore, to set up a committee to draft a formal submission which would be sent to de Valera as an official presentation from the Irish Province of the Jesuits. Cahill was appointed to the committee. Some of the 'best heads' the order had 'in matters of this kind' were selected to serve on the committee along with Cahill P. Bartley was to act as president; J. McErlean was appointed secretary, J. Canavan and E. Coyne were also appointed.

The committee met for the first time on 24 September 1936. Fr Bartley presided. The secretary, Fr McErlean, was absent on retreat. A decision was taken to draft a preamble on the model of the preamble in the Polish Constitution. Articles were to be prepared on the following subjects:

The rights of the family, particularly with regard to the education of children.
Religion to be taught in all schools, which were to be denominational whenever there was no insuperable obstacle.
The State could not dissolve a valid marriage.
The relations between the Catholic Church and the State were to be defined by a Concordat.
Freedom of religious worship.
Ecclesiastical property.

Private property.

Freedom of speech and of the press, and the limitations of that freedom.

Any other matters that might be suggested by a study of concordats and existing constitutions.

The next meeting of the committee, on 1 October, discussed three drafts of the preamble submitted by Cahill, Canavan and Coyne. They were discussed clause by clause, and certain changes were approved. It was to be considered in its new form at the next meeting.

At this meeting, it approved 'with slight modifications' an article on Church and State drawn up by Bartley. But drafting the article that declared that the State could not dissolve a valid marriage was difficult. Various attempts were made to find a satisfactory wording that would embrace all possible cases, and further consideration was held over until the next meeting, when drafts on private property, and freedom of conscience, of the press and of association were to be discussed.

At the meeting of the committee on 8 October 1936, many drafts were considered and approved with slight modification. The article on Church–State relations was passed with an addition proposed by Canavan. On Catholic marriage and the State, everyone except Canavan accepted Bartley's draft. It was decided to include Canavan's draft as an alternative. Bartley also drew up the articles on freedom of worship and freedom of the press. Canavan suggested an article on freedom of cinema, radio, theatre and suchlike, and it was decided to include it. The same control was to be exercised by law for these media as for the newspapers. A draft by Coyne on the family was approved. Coyne and Bartley drafted an article on parents and education of children in schools. The article on religion in school was to be taken, with slight changes, from the Polish Constitution. There was also progress on articles on private property, religious property, family and living wage. Coyne was entrusted with the task of working in that area. Canavan gave some help. The committee drew heavily on the Polish Constitution. Bartley wrote to the Provincial on 11 October, reporting that he hoped the work of the committee would be concluded within a week. He proposed to hand over 'our suggestions to Fr Cahill, who will deliver them in the proper quarter. It is of the utmost importance that no time should be lost if our recommendations are to be in before the official draft is completed'. Bartley told his superior that the 'work has been very harmonious so far. Fr Cahill is in full agreement with it, and has shown no desire to veto anything'. If any such difficulties were to arise, he thought they would have to be 'met by diplomacy: and I think it can be so met'. But there was one problem which only the Provincial could address:

Fr Cahill will almost certainly want to add recommendations of his own to those approved by the committee. Now these recommendations, partly by their sheer bulk and partly by their singular character, are likely to bring discredit on the very solid findings of the committee, especially if they are delivered at the same time as the committee's findings.

Bartley suggested that Cahill be told that he was to add nothing when he delivered the committee's findings. He should be free later to send in additional recommendations, provided that these were approved by any two of those who had served on the committee with him. By that time, the committee would have ceased to exist. Bartley referred to what he was recommending as 'censorship', which he considered justified:

> The source of Fr Cahill's recommendations will be quite well known to a small number of very important people. The reputation of the Society will be involved; and the Provincial has the right to watch over that reputation.

Bartley was a master of understatement. What he had said about Fr Cahill was not pure conjecture: 'I know for certain that he is preparing voluminous recommendations and that some of them at least are rather singular.'

Bartley had been entrusted with the job of controlling Cahill and preventing him from being too 'singular' in his ideas. Contrary to what might have been expected, Cahill appears to have played a rather passive role on the committee. He produced a draft preamble but did not make a substantial contribution to the drafting of any of the articles. It may have been that Cahill was aware of the 'policeman' role of the committee and determined to save his ideas for an individual submission. He obviously did not keep secret from Bartley the fact that he was preparing 'voluminous recommendations' for de Valera.

Meeting again on 15 October, the committee proceeded steadily with the work. Bartley read the articles as amended 'by previous decisions of the committee, together with a few additions and modifications handed in by Fr Cahill'. These changes were mostly verbal. In the article on private property, 'the right to productive and non-productive property' was outlined. The state was to aim at a wide distribution of private productive property, especially in land. The committee approved an article on private schools. Typed copies of the entire document were to be distributed to all members within a few days. They were at liberty to add any further comments they considered advisable as well as references to existing foreign Constitutions tending to confirm important clauses.

THE FINAL SESSION

After the meeting Bartley wrote to the Provincial again, reporting that 'our committee finished its collective labours today'. The committee had 'maintained our harmony to the end though I was prepared for some dissension in the last session'. Bartley was preparing the final report and Cahill was going to type it. They intended to meet again on Sunday, 18 October to 'give this report a final look over'. Bartley explained how he had told Cahill that the committee was 'authorised by Your Reverence to deliver this report through him in the proper quarter'. Bartley told Cahill that the Provincial had some instructions to give him regarding the report. 'I did not profess to know,' Bartley wrote, 'the nature of these instructions.' However, Bartley advised that the instructions should be sent at once: 'I am now more convinced than I was before that they are necessary. They should reach him on Saturday at latest.'

Two days before the committee met for the last time on 18 October, the Provincial wrote to Cahill, giving him exactly the same instructions as Bartley had recommended:

> Now as that document will be the product of the best heads we have in matters of this kind I think it would be well if it were presented as it stands by your Reverence to Mr de Valera.

The Provincial picked up Bartley's suggestions exactly. Cahill was not to submit any of his own material with the main Jesuit draft. Neither was he to send anything to de Valera at a later stage without first submitting it for 'censorship to any two you may select of the committee members'.

All members of the committee were present at its final meeting on 18 October 1936. The preamble was changed slightly so as to read:

> In the Name of the Most Holy Trinity and of our Lord Jesus Christ, the Universal King, we the people of Ireland so full of gratitude to God who has so mercifully preserved us from innumerable dangers in the past; hereby, as a united independent Christian Nation, establish this Sovereign society of the Irish people . . . and so in accordance with the principles laid down we freely and deliberately to the glory of God and honour of Ireland, sanction this constitution and decree and enact as follows.

The committee agreed that reference to the Constitution and concordats of Catholic states should be added to the various 'assertions' made in the document so 'that those who have the task of drawing up the Constitution may come to know what the Catholics of other European States have already secured'. Cahill was to type the document and submit it without any additions of his own.[7]

On 21 October 1936, Cahill wrote to de Valera enclosing the committee's preamble and articles. The letter accompanying the submission was an indication of just how much Cahill had bridled at the idea of turning his original initiative into a society one. Towards the end of the letter, he wrote:

> I have, in drawing up the drafts which I am sending you, availed myself of the advice and assistance of three or four others, some of whom have made a special study of these matters; although not specialists, they are pretty well informed on them, and are men in whose judgement I have confidence.

In fact, there is no mention that the material he was giving to de Valera came from the society as a whole. Quite the contrary. He wrote:

> I have, in drawing them up, confined myself to the minimum that I would consider necessary to realise a Christian Constitution, as I feared to outstep the limits of what you asked me to do.[8]

The document which emerged from the committee is of considerable historical importance in itself. The question as to whether it influenced de Valera and the Irish Constitution will be dealt with later. The Jesuit document offers an important insight into the world view of the Irish Jesuits in 1937. The document in question drew heavily on the Portuguese, Polish, and Austrian Constitutions. The Austrian Concordat was also consulted.[9]

A MINIMALIST DOCUMENT

The document was minimalist in construction. It was divided into six articles: Religion, Marriage, the Family, Education, Private Property, and Liberty of Speech. In essence, the document guaranteed freedom of religious worship to all, in public and in private, within the limits of public order and morality. The Catholic Faith, which was 'the faith of the vast majority of the nation, and which is inseparably bound up with the nation's history, traditions and culture', occupied in the country 'a unique and preponderant position'. (This was based on Article 114 of the Polish Constitution.) Relations between Church and State were to be determined by 'an agreement to be entered into with the Holy See'. The relationship between the State and other religious bodies 'may be determined by an agreement between the State and official representatives of the bodies in question'. There was a clause defending the right of religious institutions to 'freely manage' their own affairs, 'own and acquire movable and immovable property, administer and dispose of the same, possess and enjoy its revenues and endowments, and maintain institutions for religious, educational and charitable purposes.'[10]

On marriage, the draft article upheld that the civil power could not 'dissolve a marriage validly contracted'.[11] Part (b) sought to bring civil and ecclesiastical law into unison:

> The conditions required for the civil validity of the betrothals and marriages of Catholics shall be identical with those laid down in the Code of Canon Law of the Catholic Church. The competent authority of the Catholic Church shall, where a member of that Church is concerned, decide finally all questions as to the existence or non-existence of the marriage bond. All such decisions, when they have been duly communicated to the State, shall be registered by it and given civil effect.[12]

An alternative wording was also provided if the former was not suitable:

> Seeing that the Catholic Church has its own marriage laws, the State shall, after agreement with the Holy See, bring its marriage laws into conformity with the Canon Law, where one or both parties to a marriage are members of the Catholic Church.

The article on the family recognised it as 'a natural society, and being the fundamental unit of Civil Society, possesses natural, inalienable, and imprescriptible rights, prior and superior to all positive law'. The family, being as the article termed it 'indispensable to the continuance, strength, and well-being of the Nation', would have 'its right respected and in a very special way protected by the State and its laws'.[13]

The article on education protected the parents' right to choose freely a school for their children and defended the right of all citizens and all associations of citizens to found, own, and administer schools 'provided that they fulfil the conditions required by law relative to the welfare, physical and moral, of the children, and provided that they are well disposed to the State'. Religious teaching within school hours was to be obligatory. The teaching was to be under the direction of the religious body to which the pupils belonged. The State had the duty and the right to assist in the work of education and to supplement private effort as far as the public good required.[14] Schools maintained by the State were to be 'in principle denominational; and, except in special circumstances, to be defined by law, boys and girls of adolescent age shall be educated separately'.[15] Primary education was to be compulsory.[16]

The right of individuals to own private property was acknowledged and guaranteed by the Constitution. There were limitations to that right:

The right of property has, however, a double aspect, individual and social. Hence the State has the right and duty to see that neither the acquisition nor accumulation of private ownership, especially in land, takes place in such a way as to injure the common good. It is also the right and duty of the State to see that the use which owners make of their property, especially goods of a productive nature, is in accord with the common good and with social justice.[17]

The Jesuit constitution further stipulated that suitable laws should be introduced to prevent the natural resources of the country, such as land, mines, fisheries, waterways, etc., from being unduly held up by private individuals or syndicates. The State was to 'so adjust property rights as to secure that these are duly developed and utilised in the interests of the common good.'[18] The State was also to guarantee 'the protection of private property, and may not limit or abolish individual or collective private property, except when the law so provides for reasons of public utility and with fair compensation.'[19] It was further envisaged under the Constitution that the State should assume the role 'to promote a wide distribution of private property, especially in land'.[20]

Liberty of speech and the press was 'conceded to all within due limits', but it was not to be extended to 'the utterance, publication, or circulation of anything that is subversive of the Christian religion, of Christian morality, or of public order in the State'.[21]

Was this document successful in influencing de Valera and the others engaged in drafting the Constitution. I would argue that it was quite influential in a number of different ways. There is an interesting correlation between the Jesuit submission and the structure of Articles 41 to 45: the Family, Education, Private Property, Religion, and Directive Principles of Social Policy. Perhaps the Jesuit submission had the advantage of being the all important first draft on which both Hearne and de Valera worked. There is certainly a similarity between some of the wording in particular with reference to the article on religion. Compare the wording submitted by the Jesuits and the final wording:

> Freedom of Religious worship (in public and private) is guaranteed to all within limits of *public order and morality.*
>
> The Catholic Faith, which is the faith of the vast majority of the nation, and which is inseparably bound up with the nation's history, traditions and culture, holds among religions in our country a unique and preponderant position.

When de Valera was casting around later for the wording of Article 44, he may have remembered the content of what he would have regarded as Cahill's submission.

De Valera rejected a number of the specific ideas in the Jesuit draft. In particular, he did not warm to the suggestion of regulating Church-State relations through a concordat. However, the Catholic social principles underlying the submission did become part of his final document. The titles of the Articles and the structure of the Jesuit submission may also have influenced de Valera. There were places where de Valera might have been better advised to listen to the Jesuits, particularly in the area of private property.

It was not until 13 November that Cahill was in a position to submit his follow-up suggestions. He must have been delayed by the two Jesuit censors as most of his work had been completed by 21 October 1936. Cahill told de Valera that he was anxious that his idea about the establishment of rural committees should be taken up. Heavily influenced by Salazar's Portugal, he wanted to establish committees in the countryside based on the family – elected by the heads – and the principal ministers of 'any considerable religious body within the parish would be *ex-officio* members'. In that way, rural and agricultural organisation would be established and the natural basis of the family and the parish saved 'from the corruption and robbery, which apparently prevailed in the previous rural councils which were based on an artificial and individualistic basis'.

He also wanted his articles on denominational public hospitals adopted which would 'serve to undo a very grave injury to our poor, practically all of whom are Catholic, and who naturally desire to have a proper religious environment when they are ill or dying'. He believed his scheme would serve also 'to anticipate the danger which has proved so real in Continental countries of an undue ingerence (*sic*) of non-Christian aliens into the medical profession'. As a supplement to the article on religion, Cahill argued that 'hospitals, mental homes, houses of refuge, etc., maintained or subsidised from public funds, shall be in principle denominational'.[22] He also wanted to strengthen the earlier provisions by making the State explicitly responsible for the 'moral protection and religious ministration to citizens with whom it is directly concerned in public institutions such as educational institutions, barracks, hospitals, houses of detention, mental homes, etc'.

Cahill's proposed additions reflected his concern for the poor. Under 'the Family', he wrote that 'the condition of the employment of women and minors in industry shall be fixed by law, in accordance with the interests of the family and the common good'.[23] Under Private Property, he sought the 'voluntary subdivision of larger farms within the limits of economic proportions' and the subsidisation of suitable homesteads in newly formed farms. He also wanted specific facilities for agricultural labourers to acquire independent homes with a specific minimum of land 'of sufficient extent to supply milk and vegetables for the labourer's family'. He had further suggestions to tighten control over the press and freedom of speech. Cahill also wanted to include a section on fundamental duties of the State where the State's duty 'to protect in a special way the interests of the poor and the less favoured social classes' was stressed. There was also an addition from Cahill defining the territory of the State and declaring that 'objects of artistic, historical or national value, officially recognised as such, are under the protection of the State, and may not be injured or alienated in favour of foreigners'.[24] Cahill's new material, except in one respect, was not influential. The section which dealt with the nature and scope of Irish territory was certainly worked over by de Valera. But whether it orientated his mind in the same direction as Cahill is difficult to say with certainty. The voice of Cahill was not a particularly strong or influential one. However, many of his ideas particularly in relation to the urban and rural poor reflected early Fianna Fáil thinking which had been abandoned by the mid-1930s.

EVALUATING THE JESUIT CONTRIBUTION

The historical importance of the Cahill papers and the Jesuit draft constitution is significant at a number of levels. The influence of both Cahill and the draft on the final document has already been assessed. But the papers afford a very interesting glimpse into the mindset of a religious community in Ireland in the 1930s on a range of important issues. The papers also shed light on the relationship between an individual religious – in this case Cahill – and his superiors. The papers show the efforts that were made to curtail Cahill's influence on the writing of the Jesuit submission. Further more, the papers reveal the differences of both political opinion and personality within the Order on the pressing political matters of the day.

What the papers do not expose is any serious attempt by the Jesuit Order to pressure de Valera or his government into taking a particular line. They simply responded reluctantly to the invitation from de Valera and produced the required documentation. The end product was not notably brilliant. But neither was it fanatical or extreme. It was, however, orthodoxly Catholic in every line. It may come as a surprise to some contemporary readers that there was such concern in the document for the lot of the poor.

In a word, the Jesuits were more indirectly influential than I had at first thought. They produced the first draft in the areas where the 1922 Constitution was not particularly expansive. Having set the context and the topics for discussion, the Jesuits were thus quietly influential in the drafting process.

Notes

1 Originally published as D. Keogh, 'The Jesuits and the 1937 Constitution', *Studies* vol. 78, no. 309 (spring, 1989), pp. 82–95.

2 Earl of Longford and T. P. O'Neill, *Eamon de Valera* (London, 1970) and Tomas O'Neilla and Padraig O'Fiannachta, *De Valera* (An Charraigh Dhubh, 1968) provided the first authoritative account of the process. I attempted to develop the argument further in *The Vatican, the Bishops and Irish Politics, 1919–1939* (Cambridge, 1986). Further information is contained in 'The Irish Constitutional Revolution: Analysis of the making of the Constitution', *Administration* (special issue, 1988), pp. 4–88. However, for the latter article, I had not been through the complete Cahill file in the de Valera papers. I would like to thank Fr McGrath SJ, Leeson Street, for first drawing my attention to the personal papers of Edward Cahill. I would also like to thank the Irish Franciscans and Mr and Mrs Brendan MacGiolla Choille for their help while working in the de Valera archive.

3 Cahill Papers, Jesuit House, Leeson Street, Dublin. Following the death of de Valera's son in a riding accident, Cahill found time to write to the President. De Valera sent a hand-written reply on 17 February 1936:

> It was more than kind of you to write when you were so ill, but no letter was needed to tell us we had your sympathy and prayers. I called at 97 to see an old friend, Dr Crehan CSSp, a few days ago and had hoped to see you also, but learned that you were still too ill to see visitors. I am looking forward to seeing you in a few days.

De Valera may have known Cahill from cultural nationalist circles. There is an air of familiarity in the correspondence between the two men in the years 1932 to 1936 which showed that de Valera visited Cahill, who suffered from indifferent health, on a number of occasions. When Cahill published a book or an article, he usually sent a copy to de Valera. When his magnum opus *The Framework of a Christian State* appeared in 1932 Cahill sent a copy to Government Buildings and de Valera responded with a kind letter in Irish on 2 August 1932:

> Taim an-bhuidheach diot i dtaobh coip den leabhar *The Framework of a Christian State* a bhronnach orm. Is fiu é leigheamh agus aaith-leigheamh, agus is minic, dar liom, a raghfar chuige chun comhairle agus treoru 'fhaghail as ins no bliantaa ta le teacht' (Cahill Papers).

4 4 September 1936, de Valera Papers.

5 De Valera Papers, 1095/1 and Cahill Papers.

6 Ibid., 1095/1.

7 All the foregoing can be found in a minute book and letters filed now with the Cahill collection in Leeson St.

8 Cahill to de Valera, 21 October 1936, de Valera Papers, 1095/23.

9 Other documents consulted were the following: *Codex Juris Canonici, Papal Encyclicals,* Shiva Rao (ed.), *Selected Constitutions of the World* (2nd ed., Madras, 1934), Publications of the Catholic Social Guild, Oxford, Catholic Truth Society Publications, especially English

translations of Papal Encyclicals, *The Code of Social Principles* (Malines International Union, CSG), Documentation Catholique (Paris), vol. 32 in particular.

10   This was based on the Polish Article 133, *Selected Constitutions of the World* (*op. cit.*), p. 101, and the Austrian Constitution (1934), Article 2: 9 *Documentation Catholique* (*op. cit.*), col. 81.

11   Papal Encyclicals of Leo XIII, *Quod Apostolici Muneris* (1878), and *Arcanum* (1880).

12   This was based on Article 34 of the Italian Concordat, *Casti Connubii* (1930), Austrian Concordat (17934), Article 7, and Protocol of Article 7.

13   Based on *Rerum Novarum, Casti Connubii* and the Code of Social Principles.

14   Divini Illius, Polish Constitution, Article 120, Austrian Constitution, Article 31 and Article 6, and *Codex Juris Canonici*.

15   Divini Illius.

16   Polish Constitution, Article 99, *Rerum Novarum*, and *Quadragesimo Anno*.

17   *Rerum Novarum, Quadragesimo Anno*, Catholic Truth Society on the Social Order, and Code of Social Principles.

18   Based upon *Quadragesimo Anno* and Code of Social Principles.

19   Polish Constitution, Article 99.

20   *Rerum Novarum* and *Quadragesimo Anno*.

21   Austrian Constitution, Article 26, Norwegian Constitution, Article 100, Pius VII's Post Tam Diuturnas (1814), Leo XIII's *Officiorum Munerum* (1897), and Pius XI's *Casti Connubii* (1930).

22   Cahill to de Valera, 13 November 1936, de Valera Papers, 1095/2C.

23   De Valera Papers, 1095/2C.

24   Ibid.

CHAPTER 14

Daniel O'Connell and the Gaelic Past

(1938)

Michael Tierney

The context here was a symposium on Sean O'Faolain's biography of Daniel O'Connell, *King of the Beggars*. A modern Irish culture, Tierney argued, could be built on the old Gaelic culture but a viable political system could not. O'Connell's contribution to the modern Irish nation was, Michael Tierney argued, a philosophically utilitarian one that readily discarded this legacy. That O'Connell's democratic nation-building occurred alongside Gaelic cultural decline was to be regretted. Tierney was appointed Professor of Greek at University College Dublin in 1922. He became President of UCD in 1947 and oversaw the building of the new campus at Belfield. He contributed some 47 articles to *Studies*, more than any other contributor.[1]

Those engaged on the task of providing an Irish rendering for the abundant products of our legislative activity are familiar with the disconcerting scarcity of native words to correspond with the most ordinary concepts of modern politics. There is a lesson to be derived from the reflection that, for all our long fever of nationality, we have no Irish word for 'nation'. Somehow or other historians, attempting to fit our peculiarities into accepted categories, have managed to blur for us the instructive contrast that must be drawn between medieval Ireland and the Ireland of the nineteenth and twentieth centuries. In spite of all that has been written about the Gaelic state, the strict truth is that no such thing, in any valid sense of the term, has ever existed. And in spite of our modern preoccupation with Gaelic culture, only those who care little for the meaning of what they say can apply the phrase to anything very living or effective in Ireland at present. In Irish history, state and culture have been like the extremes of contradiction. The middle ages possessed the culture, but they neither had nor wanted particularly to have the state. We have the state and are justifiably proud of it, so proud that we sometimes expect it to do duty for everything; but Gaelic culture is with us a romantic dream or a crudely-formed aspiration towards something that we either cannot effectually grasp or would not care much for if we could.

The historical effects of this strange contrast are easily seen in relation to the medieval period, but our self complacency, it is to be feared, rather disguises them in relation to ourselves. In the middle ages the Normans penetrated physically into almost every part of Ireland and held large areas for a long time by force; but culturally they were absorbed into the Irish mass with startling rapidity and completeness, so that some of the greatest names in Irish literature are those of Gaelicised foreigners. We read of this absorption with satisfaction and accept it so readily as to miss its significance. In modern times the pendulum has swung astonishingly the other way; and again, I think, we hardly appreciate the mystery of events. The English have been physically and forcibly extruded from four-fifths of the country; but this extrusion has coincided with a continuously-intensified process of Irish subjection to English culture, in the course of which the Gael has almost disappeared from the world. There is surely little doubt but that the two contradictory extremes are in some way inter-connected. It was not an accident that the emergence of the political nation in the nineteenth century. Coincided with the decay and gradual disappearance of the native ways of thought, life, and expression, any more than it was an accident that in the middle ages the Gaelic power of cultural absorption coincided with a calamitous failure to create or even conceive the idea of a Gaelic state.

The medieval failure is a matter for diagnosis by historians; the full understanding of the causes for the modern failure is the urgent task of all who are concerned about the future of civilised life in Ireland. In both cases the terms of the problem involved must be clearly grasped before there is any chance of a successful solution. One of the greatest disabilities of present-day thought in general is an obsession with politics and economics, studied in isolation from broader and deeper issues. This obsession has its roots in the mentality of nineteenth-century England, and has helped enormously to distort Irishmen's views on their own peculiar history. The complaint is frequently heard that earlier Irish history in particular is an unintelligible jumble of meaningless battles and insignificant dynastic changes, now and again lit up by a glare of inappropriate heroics. One reason for this complaint is that Irish history is essentially non-political and non-economic in character and will not fit easily into these irrelevant modern categories. The same fact has recently been observed about the history of Greece in the sixth and fifth centuries BC. Nineteenth-century historians, with all their learning and skill, often deprived their readers of ability to understand these distant ages by their insistence on searching in them for the play of purely nineteenth-century forces. Thus it was against their reason, so to speak, that able scholars admitted any significance in so great a poet as Pindar, because he wrote about chariot-races and boxing-matches in an idiom and style that eluded modern criteria. Until very recently almost all of them felt about Pindar what Voltaire had openly said:

> Toi, qui modulas savamment
> Des vers que personne n'entend
> Et qu'il faut toujours qu'on admire.

It would be easy to find examples of the same lack of appreciation as applied to the very similar Irish court-poetry of the middle ages.

In order to get a real understanding of Irish history down at least to the Elizabethan period, it should be studied, not from the familiar modern dynamic aspect with its emphasis on evolution, progress, political and economic change, but rather as a comparatively static culture or cultural series. That changes occurred, no one will of course deny; but they were of a different kind and followed a different rhythm from those we look for in modern states. It was the static element that gave its characteristic note to Gaelic civilisation, and we are struck again and again even in the present-day Gaeltacht with the extraordinary persistence of very ancient ways of thought. The true analogy with Ireland – on an entirely different scale of magnitude and value, it need not be said – is to be seen in the great cultures of the Far East like India and China, where again the European historian finds it bewilderingly difficult to apply his politico-economic standards. We are accustomed to a certain contempt for these, static cultures, but it is an obvious error to apply the derogatory term 'backward' indiscriminately to them all. In recent times everything is 'backward' that is not, up to the latest American standards of industrial complexity and financial chaos. The epithet has been widely used by Marxist writers in describing pre-revolutionary Spain, a fact which taken by itself should put us on our guard against such facile condemnation.

Indeed the very facility with which we accept these strictures on a country like Spain is itself the measure of our distance from Gaelic culture. We normally find it almost impossible not to attach to commerce, industry and finance the importance acquired by them in modern England since the overthrow of the Stuarts, or to realise that it was partly against these very powers and the mentality from which they emanated that the Stuart battle was fought and lost. A great many of the criticisms levelled by historians like Richey against the social conditions of medieval Ireland, or even by a magnificent imaginative writer like Standish O'Grady against those of the Elizabethan period, are valid only as coming from and addressed to the same mentality. We do not normally analyse the origin of our ideas, least of all those which are so pervasive as to have become prejudices. In a healthy and vital condition of society such analysis is undesirable and almost impossible. But in present-day Ireland, with its rather terrifying cultural necessities and tasks, and in a period when external influences of all kinds have mingled in our education as never before since the world began, it is very important for us to sort out our ideas and prejudices, find where they have come to us from, and how far they are mutually consistent.

The distressing result of such an inquiry would quite certainly be the discovery that, outside a limited field devoted to religion, our present-day Irish culture is not by any means of Gaelic origin, but almost entirely Puritan and English. Even in the religious field the unnoticed influence of Puritanism on our Catholic practice has been astonishingly powerful. Very many of our commonest prejudices, for example, about the relations between employer and employed or about the validity of moral restraints in business methods, have come to us from the long-developed commercial morality of England. We are accustomed to the accusation of Jansenism from our younger writers, but we never hear of our much more thorough subjection to Puritan ideas. These ideas, of course, have by now had a long history and have gone through many phases. Not merely have they formed the nucleus of English morality, but through the medium of Voltaire and Rousseau they have also supplied most of the doctrinal background for revolutionary France. From France the same ideas often have returned to England, and in one of these reappearances they produced, through the English philosophic radicals, a very powerful movement which combined individualism, utilitarianism and belief in progress into a single stream of thought and action. This last manifestation of Puritanism was the dominant English philosophy of the past century, and its effects have been widespread and little short of catastrophic.

The 'moral chemistry' of the Utilitarians, worked out into a system by self-educated members of the English middle class, was in its essence a denial of traditional culture. On one side it was an English version of French eighteenth-century rationalism; on the other it fitted into the 'dogmatic and austere religion' endemic in England since the Reformation. Although in itself highly anti-religious, it reinforced tendencies already powerful among the numerous sects into which English Protestantism was divided. There were many reactions against Utilitarianism as the nineteenth century wore on, especially when the influence of German philosophy made itself felt, and nowadays it has few intellectual champions. But it corresponded so intimately with the English character and with the circumstances of the age that it gradually came to pervade all English civilisation – and through its expansion that of the whole Western world. Even yet educated men are hardly sufficiently conscious of its connection as a powerful determining cause with the universal modern downfall of taste, not only in architecture, sculpture, painting, music and literature, but in furniture, dress, and all the minor arts of life. Everyone admits that the taste of the late Victorian epoch, when Utilitarianism had reached the peak of its power, was horrible; but it is not so evident that the horror had a very definite doctrinal origin, nor that it has persisted in the artistic and cultural anarchy which we find so bewildering today.

Protests against Utilitarianism have taken many forms, from Carlyle's apocalyptic worship of the Hero to Matthew Arnold's denunciation of the Philistines and the aestheticism of the pre-Raphaelite school. In recent times the reaction has hardened into a cult of self-expression and anarchy and a belief in revolt for its own sake. Nowadays many writers and artists have elevated revolt into a law of general validity without being very particular about what they are in revolt against, or the direction their revolt is taking. Unfortunately all these tendencies, however one may sympathise with their motives, represent only the working-out in new conditions of the same forces as produced Utilitarianism over a century ago. They, like it, spring from the innate tendency of English Puritanism to rebel against the ancient European tradition. All that has happened is that an end has come to the period when they could unite with triumphant commercial and industrial expansion. If they are often found associated with a more or less conscious bias towards communism, that is only because the latter is itself the logical term, the *telos* towards which modern commerce and industry seem inevitably to lead. Karl Marx reviled Jeremy Bentham as 'the insipid, pedantic, leather-tongued oracle of the commonplace bourgeois intelligence of the nineteenth century', and as being among philosophers, what Martin Tupper is among poets. Yet it is significant that Bentham's disciple, John Stuart Mill, became in his later years a distant prophet of communism, just as Marx himself owed a great debt to Bentham's earlier disciple, Ricardo.

Here in Ireland our revolt for the past half-century or so has been against what we usually call Anglicisation. By this term, if we mean anything, we surely mean the whole complex of Puritan and Utilitarian anti-culture, the principal vehicle of which among us is of course the English language. It is, however, a great mistake, into which we too readily fall, to suppose that we have to deal only with a linguistic problem. Our whole life is long since organised on such a purely Utilitarian basis that a mere change of language might now have hardly any real effect at all on our cultural position. The difficulty in which we find ourselves is only made more apparent by the belief that the Gaelic cause is advanced when H. G. Wells, Bram Stoker and the latest American song-numbers are translated into the Irish language. Our customary weapons against Anglicisation are either the purely linguistic zeal which considers it immaterial what we read or say so long as we read or say it in Irish, or else a combination of this zeal with extreme democratic nationalism. Nobody can doubt the power of this combination, which after all has been responsible for Easter Week and the Treaty of 1921, but we may perhaps be justified in remarking that its more recent explosions into civil war and bitter party division have been much less beneficial. As time has gone on, interest in the Irish language has tended to become more and more purely linguistic, while the nationalist side of the combination has grown more superficial, more a matter of slogans and propaganda and less a matter of historically-based conviction than ever before.

The truth is that political nationalism in itself, while it may be an excellent weapon against English government, cannot by its very nature be of any use as a weapon against Anglicisation. There are two reasons for this: first, the obvious one that you cannot quarry rocks with razors; and second, the less widely-realised fact that nationalism, even in Ireland, is itself for the most part a thing of English origin. Its real home is the Dublin of the Ascendancy, and almost all its heroes belonged to the type of Ascendancy younger sons, men who for one reason or another could not fit into the system and who in thoroughly Puritanical style revolted against it, and brought a reinforcement of English and French radical ideas to justify and strengthen their revolt. No one has yet written the history of the Ascendancy impartially, setting it clearly and fairly against its strange background of native Ireland. Lecky in his great work simply ignored the problem by assuming that the Ascendancy, with its limited parliament and its aristocratic transplantation of English culture, was something inevitable, needing explanation neither as to its origin, nor as to its extraordinary development. In the end of the eighteenth century the grievances of the Ascendancy and those of the natives were fused together to make as baffling and variegated a pattern as ever history had to show. From this curious, incomplete, and shifting fusion was born the Irish nation, to describe which there was naturally no word in the ancient native language of Ireland. It was an unfortunate but inevitable consequence of its origin that nationalism could make wholly its own neither the vigorous Protestant culture of the Ascendancy nor the far older native Gaelic culture which Ascendancy had pushed out of its way and to which the new political impetus of the people helped to give the last blow.

Into the vacuum thus created there came the new Utilitarian ideas of the radical English middle class, which entered on its final triumphant struggle for political power shortly after the Union. There was a natural kinship between these ideas and those of the Anglo-Irish in revolt against their own Ascendancy. Both alike owed a great deal to the *philosophes* who during the eighteenth century had given a French colouring to English Puritanical thought. The transition from Godwin and Tom Paine to Jeremy Bentham and James Mill was only a little more obvious than the kinship between Henry Grattan and Wolfe Tone. On the native Irish side also the way had been long prepared for the double *rapprochement* with the left wing of the Ascendancy and with English radicalism. The Stuart collapse had left the Gael politically and socially rudderless; his own traditions were despised and his language, after over a thousand years of classical cultivation, had acquired the stigma of illiteracy. As the pressure of the Penal Laws was gradually lightened, the earliest beneficiaries were those among the native Irish who had money to lend to the extravagant palace-builders of the Ascendancy. It is noteworthy that the first attempt to relieve Catholics was Monck Mason's abortive bill of 1761, permitting them to invest money in mortgages upon land, and that the most effective Catholic leader before O'Connell was the Dublin businessman, John Keogh. The native aristocracy, long the central representatives of Gaelic culture, were scattered over the Continent, while their kinsmen at home had for the most part sunken to destitution. O'Connell was the man who, by his unique genius, effectively combined the Catholicism of the common people with the new nationalism which had developed in Ascendancy circles; and O'Connell, while by birth and early education a member of the old Gaelic aristocracy, was by training and mental outlook a middle-class professional man.

The real foundations of nationalism in its modern form were laid by O'Connell. Since his time it has been immensely strengthened by the incipient Gaelic revival movement, but apart from this its essential characteristics have continued to lie in the operation upon the Catholic multitude of ideas derived from the Protestant nationalism of the eighteenth century. Before O'Connell's time there was no political focus for the common people, once the Stuart cause was lost, except the fires of this Protestant nationalism – fed as to its more extreme elements from revolutionary France. O'Connell first gave the well-to-do Catholics political power and afterwards won the whole people, almost against their wills, for the Repeal of the Union. Before his death Repeal was already beginning, in the name of Federalism, to take the form it afterwards assumed as Home Rule. It was only gradually that Irish democracy, as we know it today, emerged with the widespread extension of the suffrage. This took place, not through any Irish effort, but in virtue of the link, forged by O'Connell and still strong today, between Irish nationalism and English radicalism. Middle-class liberalism, manhood suffrage, and the Land Acts, have between them created an Ireland as different as anything could well be from the Ireland which slowly but inexorably collapsed between the battle of Kinsale and the Treaty of Limerick.

In a very readable and eloquent book, described as 'A Life of Daniel O'Connell, the Irish Liberator, in a Study of the Rise of modern Irish Democracy', Mr Sean O'Faolain has given us a most important new interpretation of O'Connell's part in this strange development. He has done a very valuable service in going to the roots of our present society and compelling us to study and ponder on our destiny as a people. In many ways the future of our political, social, and educational systems must depend on whether or not we agree with what he has said about the significance of O'Connell. At present we seem to be at a resting point where one perilous stage of our journey is completed, and we are rather uncertain which way to turn next. The great importance of Mr O'Faolain's book is that he offers us, in the guise of a study of O'Connell, very definite advice at the crucial moment of choice. His judgement is by no means hasty, superficial, or based upon a one-sided conception of his subject. It is clearly the fruit of mature thought and patient investigation, and is put forward with intense conviction as to its soundness. Yet it seems, in view of our present uncertain position, to be in several respects perverse and apt to mislead. To say this is not by any means to condemn or dispraise his book or to, minimise the profit to be derived from a careful reading of it. Mr O'Faolain is in many ways a pioneer in this work of historical interpretation, and is entitled to the full rights conferred by his own thoroughness and integrity. Even if we are forced to disagree with him, he has much to teach us, not least the need and the capacity to exercise our own judgement upon the case as he presents it and its lessons for ourselves.

His book is rather an effort at imaginative evocation than a biography in the ordinary sense. It must not therefore be pedantically criticised for inaccuracies like '*Eóin* Rua Ó Suileabhain', or the attribution to Plunket of a famous outburst of 'Humanity Dick' Martin's on Ponsonby, or the suggestion that Alvanley and not Disraeli was the 'heir to the impenitent thief on the cross' of O'Connell's diatribe. The method of the novelist naturally lends itself to exaggerations in colouring, and there is no doubt but that Mr O'Faolain exaggerates both the wretchedness of eighteenth-century Ireland and the imbecility of O'Connell's last year of life. The closing pages of the book suggest a painter of the Spanish school, with their ever-deepening gloom illuminated by flashes of more and more riotous folly. All this, however, only means that Mr O'Faolain has found a subject to his taste and has made the most of his opportunities. He has allowed himself rather unnecessarily to go deeply into the question of O'Connell's Deism, only to prove that it is a question not really amenable to his manner of treatment. That he has succeeded admirably in giving a brilliantly vivid sketch of Ireland in O'Connell's lifetime as well as a realistic portrait of the Liberator himself, omitting none of the faults which were as salient as his virtues, and coming as near as writing can do to making the 'wonderful, mighty, jovial, and mean old man' live again for us, all his readers will enthusiastically agree. It is because of the very qualities of the book that what may perhaps be called Mr O'Faolain's principal thesis needs to be carefully criticised. There is a certain danger of our being carried away by the brilliance of his literary power into consenting to a view of Irish history which, if it were to be widely accepted, might be disastrous, especially at the present time.

The central problem of O'Connell's life is no longer his passionate devotion to moral force, which so shocked Mitchel and the Fenians and provoked Meagher's well-known flight of eloquence. That devotion may or may not have been an aberration; as we look back upon it across the interval filled by the Black and Tans, the 1916 Rebellion, and the Land Wars, we need hardly think that its effects were very deep or lasting. What is still of vital importance is his attitude towards, or rather entire lack of understanding or sympathy for, the Gaelic past of Ireland of which he was himself so strangely the physical though not the intellectual product. His lifetime was perhaps the decisive period in which the old native language and tradition were consigned to oblivion over the greater part of the country. If he in his youth, a Catholic gentleman, sprung from an ancient and purely Gaelic stock, had been inspired by the ideas that afterwards were to move the Protestant Davis, descendant of Welsh planters, and educated in Trinity College, there is little doubt but that Ireland might still be Gaelic-speaking and in possession of its native traditional culture – changed perhaps, but still vital and of inestimable value for the future.

There are many considerations which explain O'Connell's failure to see the importance of the Irish language, in spite of the fact that, unlike most of the Young Irelanders, he could speak it fluently. He was, as Lecky has said, a student of men, not of books, a man of action, not a man of letters, and in his time historical knowledge was at a low ebb after the long triumph of rationalism and during the heyday of mechanical and industrial progress. It is not accurate either to praise or to blame him as the sole agent of the Gaelic collapse, whatever be one's point of view. Long before his active career began, Gaelic had been left behind by the rapid changes of the world, and he could only work with instruments that seemed to his mind effective. His preoccupations were first law, then politics, and last economics. Towards Gaelic he was not merely quiescent but almost actively hostile. When Anthony O'Connell, just about the time of Emancipation, brought him the manuscript dictionary compiled by his uncle Peter O'Connell of Clare, O'Curry tells us how 'he suddenly dismissed him, telling him that his uncle was an old fool to have spent so much of his life on so useless a work'. This was in fact probably the attitude of nearly all educated Irishmen, lay and clerical, at the time. The busy and successful political leader was merely the mouthpiece of public opinion, which very likely had far more effect in killing spoken Irish than had Dr Whately and the National Schools, to whom later mythology has assigned so deleterious a part.

Mr O'Faolain, in depicting O'Connell as the 'King of the Beggars', who led his helots out of bondage and created a new Irish democracy on the wreckage of Gaeldom, is entirely uncompromising in his view that the Liberator's attitude towards Irish and all that went with it was sound. His opening chapter is a lively and, to my mind, a wholly wrong-headed account of the Gaelic collapse after Limerick as a background to O'Connell's career. The Gaelic order, he holds, was doomed not merely because it was ineffec-tual, but because it was the creation and the mainstay of a selfish aristocracy, never supported by and always hostile to the people. Its poets were the hangers-on at the tables of the great, ready to cadge on any gentleman who would give them a meal, and despising the common folk who were deserted and left to their fate by the Wild Geese. During the eighteenth century the degenerate remnant of the old poetic class continued to keep up a feeble and ridiculous tradition, still hating the people, fawning on the great, their foolish eyes always turned towards an unreal and impossible past. O'Connell deliberately and with full consciousness put an end to all this – 'he, at least, had no doubts that Ireland was beginning all over again.' The modern Irish people, which he created, is something essentially different from that effete aristocracy 'which had equally despised them, had abandoned them on its fall, and had never contributed to their rise'. The appeal in our days to the sanction of the Gaelic past is 'merely Republicanism . . . faking a tradition for itself independent of, and even contemptuous of, O'Connell's accept-ance of the mingled strain of Anglo-Ireland.'

Now all this denunciation of Gaeldom as effete and undemocratic is very little more than a rather clever notion of Mr Frank O'Connor's, who two years ago published a couple of articles on 'The Gaelic Tradition in Literature'. The charge of being effete merely amounts to a condemnation of something which failed against overwhelming odds. In making it Mr O'Faolain needs to beware of the danger of finding himself, whether he realises it or not, on the side of those: 'whom loud-voiced triumphs acclaim, Victors against the few.' To condemn Gaeldom as effete because it was unable of its own nature to make headway against the triumphant Puritanism and commercialism of England is to misunderstand it as completely as one would misunderstand Chinese art, literature and society if one were to condemn them for their failure against the commercialism of England and America, and the imported Western militarism of Japan. When Mr O'Faolain finds that Gaelic society was 'undemocratic', he is falling into the common error of measuring by English standards, created in the nineteenth century, a form of life to which these standards have no relevance. It would be quite as reasonable to say that Gaelic society could not balance its budget. O'Connell, with his up-bringing and in the circumstances of his time, could not understand the nature of the changes that had taken place before his birth and were entering their final phase during his life. That is no reason why modern intellectuals, with their vastly greater possibilities of knowledge, should applaud his and their misfortune as a consummation devoutly to be wished.

It was not merely circumstances, however, that led O'Connell to take the road he took; his own powerful mind was an originating agent as well. To anyone who reads attentively his letters and speeches, it is clear that he early fell under the intellectual dominance of the Utilitarian philosophy then starting on its victorious march in England. He was the friend of Jeremy Bentham and, even before he became a member of Parliament, was allied with the English Radicals whom Bentham's teaching had inspired. As early as 1825 we find him expressing a theoretical belief in manhood suffrage; he was a convinced Free Trader and an opponent of slavery on principle, and was fond of using Benthamite phrases like 'the greatest happiness of the greatest number'. His interest in legal reform and in the abolition of capital punishment, his opposition to the Corn Laws, his failure to support efforts to end the abuse of child labour, even his very pacifism, all undoubtedly derive from the same sources. If any one of these interests were isolated, we might put it down to his feelings as an Irishman and a Catholic, but here we are really in the presence of a coherent body of doctrine, for much of which Irishmen and Catholics had no necessary sympathy. It may even be a question whether his attitude on duelling, for which Bentham praised and defended him, was not as much the fruit of his Benthamite principles as of his very real Catholicism. Such a coincidence between Catholic morality and the teachings of liberal ideology is not by any means an unknown phenomenon in other cases than his. During the past century it was in many ways a stumbling-block to Catholic thinkers, as coincidences between their thought and that of Fascism are apt to be today. When we find him actually proffering Utilitarianism as his reason for abandoning Irish, our diagnosis is surely complete. On p. 38 of Mr O'Faolain's book will be found a quotation from one of his speeches, prefixed by another in which he claims to be 'a confirmed Benthamite'. These are his words:

> I am sufficiently utilitarian not to regret its abandonment (i.e. that of Gaelic). It would be a vast advantage to mankind if all its inhabitants spoke the same language. . . . The superior utility of the English tongue, as the medium of all modern communication, is so great that I can witness without a sigh the gradual disuse of Irish.

The Abbé Dimnet has recently remarked that, if politicians knew more of history, they would make fewer mistakes. O'Connell was clearly not aware that in his commanding position his attitude towards the Gaelic past was condemning his people to that most dreadful of all fates, the awful emptiness of a nation without a history. Mr O'Faolain is likewise unaware of what was and still is at stake. His view is that of the nineteenth-century radical, intent on politics and economics, contemptuous of tradition, oblivious to the fact that tradition is the nurse of art, literature, and all that makes life civilised. Like Michelet, speaking of the middle ages, he says to his readers 'oublions et marchons'. A century ago the march was towards the world-wide expansion of industry, commerce, and high-finance. Today these things have been found hollow, and we are bidden to face the future with nothing in our hands but the statistical, uncultured, illiberal democracy in which the Utilitarian dream has culminated. Our own past is barred to us, even for our contemplation, as effete and aristocratic. The significance of Mr O'Faolain's book is that it once more raises clearly and frankly the dilemma that inexorably faces modern Ireland. Are we bound to rely for all our culture upon an incongruous mixture of etiolated Catholicism, Puritanical individualism, and commercial utility, or is there no hope of our being able to obtain some light from our vanished Gaelic past to brighten our gloom?

It would be a great pity if any large number of Mr O'Faolain's Irish readers should be led, by a natural irritation with some of the crude and hasty methods now in vogue for reviving the Gaelic language, into concluding as he has done that there is no way out except the choice he presents between a 'fake' and the entire rejection of their own history. Democracy is no substitute for culture, and much of what is most precious and of highest quality in past civilisations was in fact the result of their enthusiastic devotion to, and attempt to recover, literary, linguistic, and artistic traditions that were not always genuinely ancestral to them. After all a surprising amount of what adds most to the savour of life even at present has come to us from the obsession of the seventeenth and eighteenth centuries with the languages and cultures of Greece and Rome. How much poorer would be European literature and art if all the consequences of the Renaissance were suddenly to disappear? Yet the Renaissance was far more a 'fake' even in Italy, which could lay some claim to continuity with Rome, than the Gaelic revival is in the original home of Gaelic culture, whose political destiny even in our own time has been changed by the half-recovered memory of its ancient 'otherness'. The real study of Irish history has only begun, that of Irish literature is still in its infancy; we can as yet have only a dim conception of the artistic ideas or even of the social background of the Gaelic order. It is too soon for us to grow impatient, to decide, because of certain errors of tact or procedure, that the whole movement, to which Ireland owes at least as much as she does to O'Connell, was just a foolish mistake, and abandon ourselves to the shadows of democracy and utility. That writers of high intelligence and skill, like Mr O'Faolain and Mr O'Connor, should give us such advice is, however, a symptom which it would be dangerous to neglect.

Notes

1   Originally published as M. Tierney, 'Daniel O'Connell and the Gaelic Past', *Studies* vol. 27, no. 107 (September, 1938), pp. 353–80. The article was published with responses by Daniel A. Binchy, Gerald Murphy, John Ryan and Sean O'Faolain.

CHAPTER 15

Reply to Tierney (1938)

Daniel A. Binchy

Daniel Binchy, former diplomat now Professor of Roman Law and Jurisprudence at University College Dublin defended Sean O'Faolain's account of Daniel O'Connell as a modernising influence. He criticised the unrealism of Gaelic revivalists and called for a 'sane and honest policy in regard to Irish'. This piece and Michael Tierney's capture the intersection between a range of themes: the valorisation of pre-Reformation Ireland, the role of language in nation-building, the redundancy of linguistic revival once nationality had been achieved, and the influence of nineteenth-century liberalism on the modernisation of Ireland.[1]

Whether or not it was part of the author's intention, not the least of the services performed by Mr O'Faolain's book has been the controversy to which it has given rise. And here it may be well to re-emphasise a fact which emerges clearly from Professor Tierney's criticism: that the one thing which is emphatically not in dispute is the extraordinary merit of *King of the Beggars*. Quite apart from its literary distinction, it represents one of the most solid contributions to the history of modern Ireland that has appeared in our time. It will never, of course, figure among 'official' textbooks: it tells too many unpalatable truths to merit that privilege, and its ruthless honesty would disturb the curiously adjusted balance of *Dichtung und Wahrheit* (artifice and truth) which has now become the 'authorised version' of Irish history. Let us hope at least that it will find its way into the hands of those of the rising generation who will eventually mould the cultural destinies of the Ireland of tomorrow.

Mr O'Faolain describes magnificently the debt of Ireland to O'Connell. While O'Connell did not originate the idea of political nationhood – as Professor Tierney rightly reminds us, that concept was transplanted from England by the colonists – still he is the father of the modern Irish nation, for he harnessed the masses of the native race to the new constellation. He introduced the Catholic 'helots' to the new gospel of personal and political liberty; he gave them a new aim, Ireland as a self-governing entity; a new technique, political agitation – and a new language. Minor shifts of emphasis, changes in the rhythm of physical and moral force should not blind us to the fact that, for better or for worse, Ireland has remained in substance what O'Connell made her, and continues to move along the lines which he laid down for her. He bade her speak the English tongue, and the victorious progress of that tongue is even today overwhelming the last feeble strongholds of the older language. He bade her think in terms of political and economic nationalism, and she has obeyed him but too well. No better instance could be found than the career of the movement for the revival of Irish, which, in its origins a reaction against O'Connell's neglect of cultural nationalism, has eventually become political in the worst sense of the word, operating entirely with the weapons and the methods of political agitation. The very measure of the success which Professor Tierney ascribes to the Gaelic League in revolutionary politics is the measure of its abject failure to achieve the purpose for which it was called into being. It was far less trouble to create a revolution than to restore Irish, and so a stream which should have been kept aloof from and uncontaminated by political strife was mingled almost from its source with the turbid waters of Irish political nationalism. We know the result.

It should be noted that Professor Tierney has no quarrel whatever with Mr O'Faolain's account of the genesis of the modern Irish nation. The theory that the latter has some kind of continuity with the so-called 'Gaelic state' may be a useful fiction for political and Gaelic League platforms; historically it is nonsense, and Mr O'Faolain is perfectly justified in calling it a 'faked tradition'. But one can completely accept his view on this point without joining in his denunciation of the older Gaelic order of society. His first chapter, unforgettable in its literary craftsmanship, which is designed to paint in the background to the coming of the Liberator, exaggerates (with conscious or unconscious artistry) the sombre hues of the past. Oppression, squalor and starvation were the frequent lot of the Catholic peasantry in the eighteenth century, but the picture of 'the unhappy hut dwellers drooping by their peat fires' is moving rather than accurate. The 'hut-dwellers', as they live for us in the tenacious memories of their descendants in the Gaeltacht today, were not unhappy, and were far more given to singing and dancing rather than drooping by their peat fires. There is more justification for Mr O'Faolain's criticisms of political and social conditions under the Gaelic order, but the latter sinned chiefly by refusing to move with the times; in a changing world it remained fossilised, parochial, and ineffective. Further, many of the prerogatives of the noble classes which weighed most heavily on their poorer lieges were not 'Gaelic' in origin at all, having been introduced by the Norman conquerors who, while subsequently discarding their foreign speech and ways, jealously retained those feudal customs which had already given their families power and privilege in England at the expense of the 'villeins'. Their neighbours of the native race were not slow to follow and even improve on their example, and thus the so-called 'Gaelic state' was in reality a curious amalgam of old native law and Norman feudal customs which has never been properly studied, least of all by those who clamour for its 'restoration'. For the rest, while in no sense democratic, it was certainly popular. The touching fidelity of even the humblest classes to the old aristocratic order is warranted not merely by the poets (whose testimony is too lightly discounted by Mr O'Faolain, but by the English state papers. The lowliest liegeman of the MacCarthys would have echoed with a passionate pride and loyalty, the cry of Egan O'Rahilly on his death-bed: 'My fathers served their fathers before Christ was crucified.' (Incidentally we owe to Mr Frank O'Connor this fine translation of a still finer original: *na flatha fá fraibh mo shean roim éag do Chríosd.*) Why did the plain people glory in their immemorial submission to the 'old stock'? Not from servility or cowardice, but because the Gaelic mind (as expressed in its literature) and its laws was essentially hierarchical. It would, in fact, be difficult to find a greater contrast with the mind of modern Ireland as moulded by O'Connell.

The traditional social order was doomed even before O'Connell's day, and Mr O'Faolain has no doubts of his wisdom in cutting the new Ireland away from the moribund past. But would it not have been possible for him at least to save the Irish language from the wreckage and to insert it in his new creation? After all, most countries have managed to assimilate the theory and practice of English utilitarian democracy without jettisoning their native speech. Doubtless Irish would have been radically changed in the process – it would have shed, for example, most of the unreal conventions which repel Mr O'Faolain in the work of the poets; but as it was still the language spoken by the bulk of the people, it would have been strong enough to develop in a natural manner the terminology and idiom of a different order which are now being feverishly pumped into its lifeless veins by the official word-manufacturers referred to in Professor Tierney's opening sentence. O'Connell, native speaker and scion of the purest Gaelic aristocracy, with his unique power over the hearts of his people, might well have united the old language and the new Ireland, although it is only fair to say that this would have meant rowing against the tide, for the popular drift away from Irish had already begun. But to O'Connell as to all educated Irish Catholics, lay and clerical, of his day Irish represented merely the annoying relic of a dead order from which his countrymen must free themselves in order to live; accordingly, far from encouraging it, he hailed the signs of its dissolution with satisfaction. Mr O'Faolain applauds his decision. I deplore it (perhaps because I have less use for political nationalism than he has). But we both recognise its irrevocable effects. They may be summarised in one sentence. English becomes henceforward the 'national language' of the political Irish nation, the language in which its gospel is preached and its concepts formulated, and a thousand latter-day Constitutions (or even 'original' *Bunreachta*) cannot alter that stark reality.

Does this mean that we should 'forget and march on', ignoring all that was Ireland before O'Connell? That is certainly not my view, and I doubt very much, despite Professor Tierney's criticisms, if it is Mr Faolain's either. After all Ireland is far older than the political Irish nation. For centuries before the latter was even thought of Ireland was united, not by Constitutions or Presidents, but by the link of a common culture which transcended the boundaries and the bickerings of all the petty sovereignties. That culture, while neither great nor significant as a contribution to the common stock of humanity, has moulded the Irish *Eigenart*, the 'otherness' of which Professor Tierney speaks. If we lose contact with it we shall have surrendered our identity as a people. Nowhere in Mr O'Faolain's book can I find any rejection of the cultural and spiritual (as opposed to political values) enshrined in Irish literature. True, he deals hardly (in my opinion much too hardly) with Ó Bruadair, O'Rahilly and their like. But his book gives evidence of a more than passing interest in their work – no doubt his acquaintance with it is far wider and deeper than that of the average neo-Gael; and surely neither he nor Mr O'Connor can be blind to the original and haunting beauty which flowers so unexpectedly underneath all the rubble of pedantry, formalism, and artificiality. Even still it would be possible to keep future generations in touch with that beauty, with the real as opposed to the sham Gaelic spirit, if only our educational authorities would have the courage to abandon the 'faked tradition' for the English-speaking seven-eighths of the country, and if our political authorities would concentrate their attention on the rapidly dwindling areas where Irish is – in fact and not in 'fake' – the native language of the people. But a sane and honest policy in regard to Irish is in our day an even more fantastic dream than was the hankering of the poets in the eighteenth century after the vanished Ireland of their fathers.

Notes

1   Originally published as a reply to M. Tierney, 'Daniel O'Connell and the Gaelic Past', *Studies* vol. 27, no. 107 (September, 1938), pp. 353–80. The other respondents to Tierney in this symposium were Gerald Murphy, John Ryan and Sean O'Faolain.

CHAPTER 16

The Economist and Public Policy

(1953, abridged)

Patrick Lynch

In 1953 *Studies* published a symposium on economics and public policy with a lead article by Patrick Lynch. Lynch had been close to T. K. Whitaker in the Department of Finance. As an economist at UCD he became a key public intellectual advocate of state-fostered economic planning. Lynch argued for realistic debate stripped of ideological polemic about the necessity for some state activism. Many critics of state interventionism sheltered behind 'the lingering shadows of economic liberalism to deny positive economic functions to a government'. Their views were, he argued, based on an incorrect reading of classical economics and on a convenient disregard of economic history. Lynch quoted Keynes: 'Practical men who believe themselves to be quite exempt from any intellectual influences, are usually the slaves of some defunct economist.' Indeed what he had to say owed much to Keynes.[1]

[. . .]

Many critics of state intervention shelter, unconsciously perhaps, in the lingering shadows of economic liberalism to deny positive economic functions to a government. Their views are often based on an incorrect reading of classical economics and on a convenient disregard of economic history. To circumscribe the economic role of the state by invoking Jeremy Bentham and John Stuart Mill is to do less than historical justice to either of these men. Mill's doctrine prepared the way for the modern British Welfare State, and Bentham's pointed, if somewhat equivocally, towards George Orwell's *1984*; as economists, both are significant not so much because of their advocacy of unlimited individual rights against the encroachment of the state as of their powerful promulgation of concepts which have had the opposite effect.

The notion that *laissez faire* was ever a dominant political philosophy in England is one of the strangest notions ever conceived about the nineteenth century. During the conflict between the old landed interests and the new manufacturing classes it served as a useful slogan, but it is for the psychologist rather than the historian to explain how the idea of *laissez faire* survived as a kind of Sorelian myth in an age when even British Toryism was favourable to what would nowadays be described as centralised planning. There must have been a quite vigorous concept of economic and social responsibility when successive British governments during the last century introduced Factory Acts, Poor Law Acts, Railway Regulation Acts, Public Health Acts, the Bank Charter Act, the Limited Liability Company Acts, measures for disestablishing the Church, and for achieving the agrarian revolution which expressed itself in legislation between 1870 and 1903 in Ireland. There is little justification, it would seem, for the view that the British State in the nineteenth century conceived the government's role as that of a benevolent night-watchman; there is certainly no sanction for it in the writings of the classical economists; indeed, if anything, their writings, if read in their context, bear out the contention that '*laissez faire* is quite literally the only untried Utopia' [. . .].

Economic freedom was prized by the great classical economists. It animated their writings and inspired their campaigns against the restraints and oppressions of obsolete regulations and the abuse of authority. But their teachings make no sense unless they are read in the context of the theory of law and the function of government then generally accepted. Assumptions which they often took for granted can no longer be accepted. Not even Sir Ernest Benn could suggest today that every free contract is a fair one and that consequently market wages, no matter how low, and market prices, no matter how high, are always in accord with justice.

The modern economist, therefore, has a dual function: he must attempt to contribute to an ever-widening body of theoretical analysis, and he must assist the selection of certain goals of economic policy. The more successfully he performs the first task, the scientific one, the better equipped he will be to undertake the second. A great deal of what comes under the general description of economic thought is quite unscientific in character and must always be so, however much it remains the concern of the economist. These extraneous but necessary interests must never obscure the truth that economic science is not an attempt to generalise human desires or human behaviour, but to generalise the phenomena of price – 'the phenomena of scarcity in relation to demand'. Economic science conceives its materials, says Professor Michael Oakeshott, not in human terms of behaviour, action, desire or satisfaction, 'but in such quantitative terms as those of cost and price, utility and disutility.'[2] Economics is not a science of man or of human behaviour, for these are not scientific concepts. Economic theory, thus narrowly defined, has much to contribute to modern thought and action, but much less than the world often demands. 'Plans for eating our cake and having it too are always plentiful,' says Michael Polanyi, 'and economic theory will always remain the Dismal Science engaged in unmasking such fallacies.'[3] Only by recognising, then, the limitations of the science can the economist help to achieve any effective results. He must depart from its neutrality when he suggests aims of economic and social activity, but if he does not suggest these aims, he may find them stated by persons even less equipped than he is to assess the potentialities of the means available for achieving any aims at all. In its ultimate analysis a theory of economic policy must take its goals from outside economics. The classical writers found criteria for their policies in the principle of utility, which was primarily a philosophical rather than an economic principle; they tested public policy by its effect on human happiness, and in Utilitarianism were found the highly questionable but convenient presuppositions of much classical economic theory. Most of the nineteenth-century economists claimed the absolute validity of Utilitarianism for both economic and ethical conclusions.

Economic liberalism is nowadays little more than a historical phenomenon; the foundations of many of its economic tenets have crumbled and the political and social ends of the public policy that embodied it are widely rejected. The great depression of the 1930s revealed the final bankruptcy of a system which based its faith on unlimited competition. The system was ended in the United States when Mr Roosevelt inaugurated the New Deal: it ended in Britain when total war solved a mass unemployment problem which had hitherto defied solution. In neither country is there the slightest likelihood of a complete return to the old ways of liberal economic organisation, when the private enterprise system was often an excuse for the restrictionism of monopoly and unregulated self-government in industry, when a British milk marketing board disposed of its surplus production by offering to school children at a halfpenny a glass the same milk which cost anyone else a penny and cost the manufacturers of plastic umbrellas half-a-farthing.

The trend towards state-intervention is part of a process which has been operating for a long time; but the pace has accelerated. Contrary to many popular opinions, governments have not begun to undertake extensive economic responsibilities overnight. The pace has increased because changing economic and social needs and new conceptions of government demanded it, not because scheming politicians or power-hungry public servants have been seeking to tempt us down the road to serfdom. It is unhistorical to suggest that this is a new move toward collectivism, and it is folly to believe that a modern social democracy can be effectively administered if one recognises only the negative functions of government.

The society in which certain positive economic and social powers are centrally exercised is sometimes described as a 'welfare state'. The term, however, is somewhat unscientific, because there is no generally accepted definition; it is also emotive and question-begging like other economic and sociological concepts, such as 'utility' or 'subsidiarity'. The 'welfare state' may mean a system in which a government discharges necessary economic and social responsibilities which otherwise may be neglected. But it is often used as a term of censure either by those who are opposed to all but minimal state intervention or to describe the usurpation by a government of functions which if they are necessary at all, can be adequately discharged by individual members of the community for themselves, or by effectively operating sub-sidiary organisations in society. The New Deal was the first democratic attempt to establish a welfare state concerned with necessary economic and social responsibilities which no other existing institution in society could adequately undertake.

The principles of the Roosevelt experiment were deeply rooted in American history. Since the days of Jackson there had been wide, if far from general, acceptance of the view that if government belonged to the people it could be used to advance the public welfare. This view was apparent in the political philosophy of both Theodore Roosevelt and Woodrow Wilson, and it became a fundamental concept of the New Deal. Another feature of that programme was the assumption that the national economy required purpo-sive direction if it was to serve the interests of the people as a whole. Public policy had become too important to be left to the businessmen. If subor-dinate or subsidiary organs were not available or were too weak to operate properly, the state intervened to create or strengthen centrally directed economic and social agencies. The planning of the New Deal became a target for unrelenting criticism, which, indeed, has not yet subsided, although the general structure of Mr Roosevelt's creation has been preserved.

To argue the necessity for equipping a modern government with positive economic and social powers does not pre-suppose a political choice between a completely planned economy and an unplanned one. It is quite unreal to pretend that such a choice is inevitable. Unrestricted *laissez faire* never existed; what some people described as such was really planned *laissez faire*. The concepts of liberty and welfare are not mutually exclusive. Their reconcil-iation may present a problem, but the art of politics, unless the resources of its practitioners are wholly exhausted, must find an acceptable solution. The solution which rejects as discredited the unrestricted operation of the profit motive, must avoid, likewise, the other extreme, a state paternalism which by destroying liberty makes a mockery of welfare. No economic argument can justify undue interference with the rights of individuals or private organ-isations. The difficulty, of course, is to find an acceptable definition of 'undue interference'. Only an unsound Marxist or a doctrinaire liberal can maintain that there is only one correct form of economic order for all stages of history or only one correct form of administration for all industry. Even the question of private ownership of certain instruments of production cannot be decided *a priori*. The distinguished American economist and sociologist, Revd John A. Ryan, DD, of the Catholic University of Washington, wrote that:

> Where the line should be drawn between state ownership of industries which is morally lawful and state ownership which encroaches upon the right of private property cannot be exactly described beforehand. The question was entirely one of expediency and human welfare. . .[4]

Some industries, then, may have to be controlled by the state, some regulated, and some left completely free. The Catholic position was stated quite clearly by Revd Dr Ryan:

> According to the Catholic doctrine, therefore, the right of the individual or of a group of individuals to acquire and hold in private ownership some of the means of production, is in harmony with, and required by, the moral law of nature. . . . Therefore, the state would injure human welfare and violate the moral law if it were to abolish all private property in the instruments of production.
>
> However, care must be taken not to exaggerate the implications of this doctrine. All that it asserts is that the institution of private property in some of the means of production is morally lawful and morally necessary; all that it condemns is the contradictory system which would put the state in the position of owner and manager of all, or practically all, natural and artificial capital.
>
> Therefore, the Catholic teaching does not condemn public ownership of what are called public utilities . . . It does not even condemn public ownership of one or more of the great instruments which are not included in the field of public utilities. . .[5]

The best known modern statement of the economic functions of the state occurs in Lord Keynes's pamphlet *The End of Laissez Faire*:

> The state's functions relate not to those activities which private individuals are already fulfilling, but to those functions which fall outside the sphere of the individual, to those decisions which are made by no one if the state does not make them. The important thing for government is not to do the things which individuals are already doing, and to do them a little better or a little worse, but to do those things which at present are not done at all.[6]

The first economic responsibility of a modern government, it may be suggested, must be to ensure that total expenditure within the economy is sufficient to set up a demand for all the workers seeking employment. Private enterprise by itself cannot ensure at all times a demand for all that industry can produce at a price covering costs. Private enterprise alone cannot ensure that money and finance become the servant of the national economy rather than its master. The ultimate responsibility for arranging that private and public outlay together is sufficient to maintain a high level of employment must be taken by the state. The instrument by which the state can influence investment through outlay and maintain effective demand for the productive capacity of the economy is the annual budget. Modern economic analysis of demand demonstrates the conditions in which an unbalanced budget is economically justified: it also demonstrates, and this is scarcely less important, the uses of a budget surplus to combat inflation or to finance investment if sufficient voluntary savings cannot be secured. Budgetary policy must also concern itself with the balance of payments, for no modern state should permit movements in the foreign balance to cause unnecessary unemployment, deflation or inflation; the old automatically self-adjusting, self-equilibrating economic universe was precipitated through the successive crises of the 1930s to its own extinction. When a high level of employment and persistent deficits in the balance of payments reveal intense inflationary pressure, a budget surplus may be both desirable and necessary. But when large-scale unemployment and emigration persist a temporary budget deficit provides the principal means by which a government can consciously undertake external disinvestment. A budget deficit makes it possible to maintain capital expenditure in excess of current domestic saving, and a deficit in the balance of payments can thus be induced. There is, however, the problem of matching that deficit with a corresponding increase in domestic asset creation. Unless that can be done the foreign assets repatriated may be used merely to boost current consumption at home.

But a government's purposive direction of the economy may require more than supplementing private investment by public investment. When funds are made available by the Exchequer it cannot be assumed that fruitful investment will automatically occur. A high level of demand may not be enough to solve the problem of structural unemployment. There are obvious limits to the risks which private business men are willing to undertake even in a highly-protected economy. Private effort may have to be accompanied by direct state intervention if the process of economic growth is to continue. In a period of unprecedented progress in Ireland between 1946 and 1951 the total number of workers in all occupations increased by only 4,000, or an average of about 4,000 a year; the rate of emigration at the same time was about 24,400 a year. There may well be methods other than extended state activity of solving the economic and social problems associated with high rates of emigration. Many people may be satisfied with a stationary population and prefer to let emigration continue. If so, well and good, but if not, it is evident that the existing organisation of the Irish agricultural and manufacturing industries cannot provide work for 25,000 additional persons every year. It is not, therefore, a question of whether the state plans or not, but of what kind of planning the state undertakes. At present, for instance, there is reason to believe that intelligent central-ised planning could achieve a better balance in the existing state capital programme between socially desirable investment, such as hospitals, and investment that earns revenue directly or indirectly. Until there is real coordination of all forms of investment, public and private, it will be difficult to ensure that the nation's resources are distributed to the best advantage between various investment projects. However essential social improvements may be, the balance of national investment must always be tilted towards what is economically productive.

Public policy can justify the social control or regulation of industries which for political or economic reasons have become or threaten to become monopolies. This is the simplest means of ensuring that the policies of monopolies, whether public utility, or not, such as electricity, gas, railways or milling are in accord with the interests of the people generally, rather than directed primarily towards advancing the interests of private or sectional profit. There must, however, be machinery ensuring that industries, socially owned or controlled, are effectively responsible to parliament. It is quite proper that both the legislature and the government should be precluded from interfering in the day-to-day activities of such industries, but the present system in Ireland and Britain is quite inadequate as a method of enabling either government or legislature to be really conversant with the policies of state or semi-state corporations.

Few economists would deny that there is a *prima-facie* case today for bringing credit under effective public control. This does not necessarily mean that all private commercial banking should be nationalised, or that the Central Bank should become altogether the creature of a Minister for Finance. It does mean that the economic independence of a state is impaired if its credit-creating institutions are so organised that credit, a basic national necessity, is created and controlled by private institutions. These institutions may have established their competency to safeguard the deposits of their customers, but their credit-creating powers have grave public implications. No commercial banking system can be regarded as satisfying modern requirements if it can be subjected to government regulation only remotely and indirectly in its exercise of powers that can influence the welfare of the national economy. And there is a wide agreement among many modern economists that unless the interest rate is controlled by a national public authority, the general level of economic activity is liable to be regulated by the blind arbitrament of chance or by the inopportune vagaries of external forces. If the Irish commercial banks decided voluntarily to mobilise for investment in Ireland even some part of their existing liquid reserves, they would effectively disarm a great deal of the criticism to which they are subjected at present, and secure wider public understanding on the undoubted problems that face them.

There is all but unanimous agreement among economists in regard to monopoly and restrictive practices. These policies have been the result of successful pressure by interested producing or distributing minorities and of the lack of imagination and administrative vitality on the part of the state in the past.

The economist need have little qualm about urging the state to extend productive social services when it can afford them. Indeed, it may be that the state cannot afford not to extend them. A modern community will no longer tolerate the arbitrary selection by impersonal economic forces of helpless individuals for immediate punishment without attempting to aid them. The economist is better equipped than most to appreciate how far a community can afford a further redistribution of income because he realises the economic importance of a high standard of housing, of maintaining and increasing the skill and health of the population, and the necessity for directing investment into human capital in the absence of any commercial motive for doing so. He recognises too, the necessary limits to social services, even productive ones, at any particular time since every economic act involves a choice. The choice, it is hoped, will not again be between guns and butter, but Britain has recently had to choose between free dentures and the restoration of Tudor towers: even Ireland may yet have to choose between milk and butter.

A social policy may be described as a collective term for the public organisation of thrift and for public provision for combating the economic insecurity and the debilitating effects of the modern organisation of society. Aspects of such a social policy may justifiably be subjected to criticism; but other criticism often arises because the real nature of the conditions that demand a state-sponsored social policy are inadequately stated or imperfectly understood. The principles of that policy derive from an obligation inherent in a society based on an extreme division of labour, a concentration of property in fewer hands, and upon the unmeasured productivities of machines. 'When man entered the machine age,' says Mr H. L. Beales, 'he created a new division of labour – the vertical division of labour between man and the machine . . . The social policy of late capitalist states has that derivation it represents a quest for freedom for men, women and children whose lives were becoming nasty, brutish, and short because they were being reduced to the functions, as Samuel Butler put it, of domestic animals attendant upon machines.'[7] This view of social policy is rejected by two groups. The first and more important group does not deny the need for a positive social policy. They look with apprehension, however, on the advancing power of the state which they fear may demoralise the individual for whom it attempts to provide social security, removing his incentives and impairing his sense of personal responsibility. They advocate a fundamental reconstruction of society so that conditions might be created in which a comprehensive system of state-administered social security would be unnecessary. There is some force in this view when it castigates the state for undertaking functions which can be adequately discharged by existing subsidiary institutions in society, or when it criticises the state for not creating conditions favourable to the growth of such institutions. But these subsidiary organs are some-times utopian mirages. The detailed subdivision and specialisation of modern industrial society has created an organised web of complementary relations which make each man more dependent on his neighbours than in a society in which no such subdivisions exist. 'All progress,' writes Karl Mannheim, 'is bound up with additional social organisation. The division of labour subjects the individual to the social coercion which cooperation entails.' The fundamental reconstruction of society contemplated by some critics of state intervention presupposes the ability of society as a whole to achieve a degree of perfectibility which, as an aspiration of an individual member for himself they would regard as a romantic illusion.

Many criticisms of state social policies might be avoided if public men were more modest in their claims for their social reforms. In most demo-cratic countries social legislation is, in reality, less extensive than its political advocates suggest or its critics assume. Despite the boasts of British politicians to have provided social security 'from the cradle to the grave', all the services of the British 'welfare state' made payments in 1952 amounting to no more than 5 1/2 per cent of personal incomes generally, against 4 1/2 per cent in 1938 when social services were uncoordinated and less extensive in coverage, and when women were not entitled to pensions at the age of 60.

Responsible Catholic authorities on sociology state as a first principle that state-sponsored welfare schemes must not unduly interfere with the rights of individuals or families or unduly impair personal responsibility and initiative. It is interesting to observe the extent to which the views of Lord Beveridge were in harmony with that principle when he said:

> The term 'welfare state' was unfortunate in that it suggested to many people that responsibility for the welfare of individuals and families rested with the govern-ment. The right view was that men must depend for welfare on themselves; the aim of the Beveridge report was to secure for everyone an income both when working

and out of work, sufficient to provide the bare necessities of life for the worker and his dependents, leaving the spending of this income as the responsibility of the individual. It also left him to secure by his own efforts income above the minimum.

The aim today should be not a welfare state but a welfare society, with private enterprise and social reform. Incalculable good was done by dynamic social reformers in the nineteenth century, and it was hard to picture any one of them as a Civil Servant under the orders of a political Minister. Such people would be needed as much in future, for the twentieth century could not afford to lag behind the last one in voluntary action for welfare.[8]

Some other critics of contemporary state-administered social policy might not unfairly be described as unrepentant economic liberals. The most distinguished of these is probably Professor F. A. Hayek, who declares that 'the rule of freedom began to retreat from about 1870 onwards, and a different set of ideas, not really new but very old, began to advance from the East.'[9] It should, perhaps, be added that he was referring to ideas of German origin. His remedy is a return to the system of freedom, a dispensing with the need of conscious social control by the state. He admits, it is true, the necessity of unemployment insurance and a minimum of food, shelter and clothing for everybody, but economic liberalism, in his view, offers 'freedom from arbitrary or coercive authority' of the state.

Despite these critics, it is now fairly certain that the large measure of social and economic welfare embodied in contemporary public policy in democratic countries will extend rather than recede. Growing responsibilities and obligations will devolve on the governments that make policy and on the civil servants who administer it. The distinction, however, between the creation of policy and its execution is not a clear one. Constitutionally and legally civil servants remain the advisers of their political chiefs, but in reality it is often difficult to separate the making of policy from its enforcement. state-sponsored economic and social policy took a long time to develop, but it is no accident that economic and social reform in England in the nineteenth century followed closely on the reform of the Civil Service; and that the first great attempts at social reform remain even more closely associated with a few great civil servants such as Taylor, Hume, Chadwick, than with the governments that decided to undertake them. Indeed, the brunt of the odium for nineteenth-century social policy was borne by civil servants. Edwin Chadwick, the architect of the Poor Law of 1834, was so hated that his public life was prematurely ended. Now, over a hundred years later, he is the recipient of eulogistic praise. It has been said of him: 'His motive was neither religious nor benevolent – it was a horror of waste.' One can easily think of some present day Irish public servants who would be satisfied with the same epitaph from posterity [. . .].

Notes

1 Originally published as Patrick Lynch, 'The Economist and Public Policy', *Studies* vol. 42, no. 167 (autumn, 1953), pp. 241–74.

2 Michael Oakeshott, *Experience and its Modes* (Cambridge, 1933), p. 230.

3 Michael Polanyi, *Full Employment and Free Trade* (Cambridge, 1948), p. 141.

4 Revd John A. Ryan, DD: *The Doctrine of Property in Readings in Ethics*, (ed.) J. F. Leibell (Chicago, 1926), p. 589.

5 Ibid.

6 Lord J. M. Keynes, *The End of Laissez Faire* (Cambridge, 1926).

7 H. L. Beales, *The Making of Social Policy*, L.T. Hobbhouse Memorial Lectures, 1945.

8 Lord Beveridge, Report in *The Times*, 23 May, 1953.

9 F. A. Hayek, *The Road to Serfdom* (London, 1944), p. 16.

CHAPTER 17

Uniting Ireland (1957)

Donal Barrington

Donal Barrington, writing as a Nationalist, argued that prevalent Nationalist thinking was impoverished. It blamed partition on British rule and claimed that what Britain had done it must undo. She must take home her money, her men and her influence, liberate the six occupied counties and re-unite Ireland. The paradox was that Nationalists ultimately relied on the British Army to coerce all Irishmen to live together. Partition, he argued, was not forced on Ireland by Britain but necessitated by the conflicting demands of the two parties of Irishmen. He blamed the 'armed raids' of 1956 on the ill-considered propaganda efforts of Southern leaders. His article was riposte to a book by Frank Gallagher, who had been de Valera's Press Secretary during the Second World War. Barrington was the first President of Tuarim and a founder member of the Irish Council for Civil Liberties. He became a Supreme Court Justice and served as the first President of the Irish Human Rights Commission.[1]

Mr Frank Gallagher published recently a book entitled, *The Indivisible Island*. It contains the best written and most fully documented statement of the orthodox case against Partition that has yet appeared, but the very title reveals a weakness that has bedevilled all Nationalist thinking on the Partition problem for the past 40 years: a complete refusal to face unpleasant facts.[2] There is little use telling us that Ireland is an indivisible island when, in fact, it has been divided since before many of us were born and is further from unity today than at any point in modern history. Surely it is time we faced the fact that our country is divided and is in danger of remaining divided forever?

There is another unpleasant fact we must face. It is that all the policies which the South has adopted in the past thirty-five years with a view to ending Partition have, in fact, tended to strengthen and perpetuate it. The purpose of this paper is to inquire why this has happened and to make suggestions towards the formulation of a new policy which may be more successful than the old ones.

In the course of it I shall say some hard things about our Southern leaders so that it is well to make clear that I am adopting two standards of criticism throughout the paper. I criticise the Unionists only when they fall short of the elementary standards of justice, but I judge our Southern leaders by a much higher standard. Irish Nationalists have always claimed to speak for all Irishmen regardless of class or creed. This imposes on our national leaders a duty to show restraint, wisdom and understanding in their dealings with all the people of Ireland. It is not enough for them to be just; they must also be wise, for they claim to be, not merely the leaders of a party or a faction or a sect, but the leaders of a nation. Their aim is not to divide, or to perpetuate division, but to unite; they must display wisdom and greatness of soul proportionate to the task they have undertaken; and those of us who claim to be Irish Nationalists must show the same qualities proportionate to the role we play in society.

One weakness in the Southern approach to Partition in the years immediately after the Treaty was that we never fully faced the danger that Partition might be permanent. As a result, we were rather slip-shod in formulating a policy to deal with it. We started from a few simple assumptions concerning the origin and nature of Partition, assumptions never fully examined to make sure that they were true. Partition, we said, was the greatest injustice which England perpetrated against Ireland. The British Government imposed Partition upon us against the will of the overwhelming majority of the Irish people. Neither the Nationalists nor the Unionists ever wanted it. The British set up a puppet regime in six of our counties and continued to support it with British money and a British army of occupation.

We, therefore, claimed that what England had done, England must undo. She must take home her money, her men, and her influence, liberate the six occupied counties and re-unite Ireland. To force her to do this, we decided to mobilise world opinion. We exposed the injustice of Partition and the iniquities of the puppet regime throughout the world, but, despite all our efforts, Partition remains, and seems stronger today than ever before. When a policy has been such a failure as our anti-Partition policy, the time has come to re-examine the assumptions on which it rested.

RESPONSIBILITY FOR PARTITION

Take first the assumption that Partition was imposed on Ireland against the wishes of all Irishmen, both Nationalist and Unionist. There is no doubt that Partition sprang ultimately from England's policy of divide and conquer and that, in its implementation, the British Government was guilty of treachery and deceit towards Nationalist leaders. Yet, from the time when Gladstone introduced his first Home Rule Bill down until 1914, Partition was not the policy of any party in England any more than it was the policy of any party in Ireland.

The policy of the Liberals was to grant Home Rule to all Ireland and thereby to pacify her, and to encourage her to play a quiet and contented part within the United Kingdom. The policy of the Tories was to defeat any measure of self-government for Ireland and to preserve the Act of Union intact, which was a policy identical with that of the Unionist Party in Ireland.

By 1914 the Orangemen had raised an extremely large, well drilled and well equipped army to oppose Home Rule, and had some of the most experienced generals of the age to lead it. They had something more valuable still which was a complete conviction in the righteousness of their own cause, and a determination to defeat Home Rule no matter what the cost.

The weakness of the Nationalists was that they never fully understood the nature or violence of the Unionist opposition to Home Rule, and never believed that the Unionist leaders would go as far as they subsequently did. Redmond saw Home Rule as something to be won from England rather than something to be created in Ireland. He was prepared to give the Unionists guarantees to protect them against victimisation in a United Ireland, but he did not see what more he could do. Home Rule was something to be implemented by means of an Act of the British Parliament, and, if the Orangemen resisted it, the British army was to coerce them into obedience.

This paradox, that the Irish Nationalists ultimately relied on the British Army to coerce all Irishmen to live together, illustrates the poverty and weakness of the Nationalist position. It was a strange form of nationalism the ultimate sanction behind which was the British army. The United Irishmen and the Young Irelanders had seen that any true Irish nationalism must be based on the unity of Catholic and Protestant and not on the coercion of one of them by the other, or of either of them by the British Government. Indeed, Thomas Davis at one time dreamt of a mighty convention of Orange and Green to meet at the Boyne to negotiate a charter for the whole of Ireland.

Eventually, the British Government ordered the army to move from the Curragh to intimidate the North, only to find that Sir Henry Wilson and his colleagues had undermined the discipline of the army from within. Almost all the officers at the Curragh resigned their commissions rather than move against the North, and the British Government found itself faced with a civil war and a mutinous army. The inevitable had happened. The British army could not be relied on to enforce the claims of Irish nationalism upon unwilling British subjects, and the Protestants of England would not support their Government in an attempt to force the Protestants of the North under a Catholic parliament.

It is not surprising that, under these circumstances, the British Government panicked. Brigadier-General Gough, the leader of the recalcitrant officers at the Curragh, went to London and came back with a guarantee from the British Government that the army officers would not be asked to march against the North. This closed one chapter in the history of Home Rule. The Ulster Unionists had said they would fight against Home Rule and the British Government had said it would not fight for it. That left only two alternatives – to abandon the Home Rule Bill or to exempt Ulster from its, provisions, in other words, to partition Ireland – and it was at this time, accordingly, that Partition first became a serious political issue. The British Government had not, however, to make its choice immediately, for the outbreak of the World War caused the whole question of Home Rule to be shelved. Before peace returned the 1916 Rising had shattered the Act of Union. The first alternative had been destroyed. Some form of Home Rule had now to be granted to Ireland – but to a partitioned Ireland.

It is quite misleading to say that Partition was forced on Ireland by the British Government against the wishes of North and South. It would be more correct to say that Partition was forced on the British Government by the conflicting demands of the two parties of Irishmen. It is true that both North and South were dissatisfied with Partition but that was because the North wanted all Ireland for the Act of Union and the South wanted all Ireland for Home Rule. Both demands could not be met, neither party was prepared to give way and the inevitable result was Partition. In one sense Partition may be England's crime against Ireland, but in a more important sense it is Ireland's crime against herself. Until we recognise this fact, we have little chance of formulating a realistic policy to deal with it.

RELIGION AND PARTITION

Just as we Nationalists have tended to lay all the blame for Partition on England, so we have tended to minimise the importance of the part which religious bitterness played in creating Partition. Irish nationalism in the hands of its ablest exponents has always claimed to transcend race and creed, and to stand for a society in which all Irishmen will be treated equally. Unfortunately for Ireland, however, in the course of the nineteenth century, nationalism and Catholicism became confused, with the result that the cry of the Orange leaders that Home Rule was Rome Rule raised very real fears in the heart of an Ulster Protestant.

The Orange Order is described by its official historian, Mr Sibbett, as 'organised Protestantism'. It had its origin in agrarian troubles between

Catholic and Protestant in County Armagh in the year 1795, but it grew into a powerful body designed to maintain the political ascendancy of those who profess the Protestant religion, and to resist the conspiracies of the Church of Rome. It loudly professed its loyalty to the British King, but made no secret of the fact that this loyalty was conditional upon his supporting the Protestant ascendancy; and it reminded him, occasionally, that if he failed to do this, it would kick his crown into the Boyne.

The importance of religion in Irish politics is illustrated by the fact that the Orange Order was originally very dubious about the merits of the Act of Union. It had, in Grattan's Parliament, a Protestant parliament and it wished to keep it. The Act of Union was regarded at the time as part of a scheme, the other part of which was to grant emancipation to Catholics. For this reason, the Catholic hierarchy, which despaired of ever getting emancipation from a parliament of Irish Protestants, supported the Act of Union. The British Government, however, with all its influence, could only secure the neutrality of the Grand Orange Lodge. The individual Orange Lodges, which passed dozens of resolutions condemning the Union and not one in its favour, were violently opposed to the measure and accused their leaders of having betrayed them.

But the hopes of the bishops and the fears of the Orangemen were alike unfounded, for the British Government failed to fulfil its pledge to the Catholics, and it took another 30 years and a fierce struggle before Catholic Emancipation was won. It was unfortunate that the first great political struggle in Ireland in the nineteenth century should have been a religious one and should have seen the Catholics ranged on one side and the Orange Order on the other.

It was unfortunate, moreover, that Daniel O'Connell, the leader of the movement for the repeal of the Act of Union, should also have been the leader of the Catholics, and that his Repeal Association should have been virtually indistinguishable from the Catholic Association of earlier times. Some of O'Connell's lieutenants, including his son John, often spoke as if they thought nationalism and Catholicism were the same thing, and this identification of nationalism with Catholicism was facilitated by the virtual loss of the Irish language in the second half of the nineteenth century. The Orangemen were quick to perceive, after the Emancipation Act, that an Irish parliament would now be a predominantly Catholic parliament, so they threw themselves into the struggle against Repeal and, subsequently, against Home Rule. Indeed, to the ordinary Ulster Protestant it began to appear that the Home Rule movement was aimed simply at setting up a Catholic government in Ireland, and that the whole thing was a gigantic conspiracy, organised by the Church of Rome.

The Presbyterians

The Orange Order had originally been an Episcopalian Association, and the large body of the Presbyterians had held aloof from it. They were democrats and republicans who took their political principles from the American and French Revolutions, and it was they, through their association, the United Irishmen, who laid the foundations of modern Irish nationalism, and who organised the Revolution of 1798. Yet, when that revolution came, it was strongest in Wexford, where it assumed a character which greatly shocked the Presbyterians, for the Wexford Rebellion was priest-led and had many of the characteristics of a Holy War. The massacre of Protestants at Scullabogue had a profound effect on Protestant opinion in the North and, as the French Revolution progressed from democracy to imperialism, the Irish Presbyterians lost faith in many of the ideas they had previously held. The Emancipation Act removed the Presbyterians' chief grievance, and also the chief barrier between them and the Episcopalians. Their remaining grievances were to disappear with the abolition of tithes and the disestablishment of the Church of Ireland. In 1803 the Government had increased the State endowment of the Presbyterian ministry and accompanied it with conditions which, in fact, gave the Government control over the appointment of ministers. So that the way was gradually prepared for that conservative revolution within the Presbyterian body led by the Reverend Henry Cooke, which was to bring the Presbyterians into alliance with the Episcopalians and ultimately into the Orange Order.

The Orange Card

I have dwelt so long on this aspect of the case because I wish to stress the vital importance of the religious factor underlying Partition, and also the enormous importance of the role which the Orange Order played in Irish politics in the nineteenth century. Nationalist propagandists sometimes talk as if Orange opposition to Home Rule dated from Lord Randolph Churchill's decision to play the Orange card. It is true that Tory leaders came over to Ireland to wake up the Orangemen to the dangers of Home Rule, but the Orangemen did not need much waking up, and little is to be gained by counting all the Tory leaders who came to Ireland to speak to the Orangemen and ignoring all the Orange leaders who went to England to speak to the Tories. It is true that Churchill's speeches in Belfast in 1886 touched off riots which cost many lives, but it is also true that religious riots were a feature of Belfast life long before Churchill ever thought of visiting that city. Churchill decided to play the Orange card, and this was a shameful decision, but we should remember that Churchill could not have played the Orange card if there had not been an Orange card to play.

Orangemen and Catholics

It is difficult for a Southern Catholic to realise that the Orange Order sees, or at any rate saw, the Catholic Church as a world-wide conspiracy aimed at destroying human freedom. Yet this is the picture which Mr Sibbett paints in his official history of the Orange Order, published as late as 1938. A Southern Catholic gasps with astonishment when he reads that the Pope was one of the conspirators who organised the 1916 Rising, and that 'the evil work to which they set their hands . . . might have been expected when the Pope was in the game'. After this, one is hardly surprised to read that the driving force behind Mr de Valera and his party has always been 'unblushing and vengeful Popery', or that Republican ideals are made the instruments of sedition and crime by 'Jesuitical influences' with a view to promoting a 'well known type of ecclesiastical exaltation, predominance and power'. But when Mr Sibbett warns England that the British Foreign Office and the League of Nations have been infiltrated by the agents of the Church of Rome, who are using these institutions to destroy the British Empire, we get a clearer idea of where he stands.

This aspect of the subject is of vital importance because religious bigotry based on fear was the force which partitioned Ireland and which helps to maintain Partition. Part of the answer to Partition, therefore, must be to show that this fear is groundless, and to avoid incidents and speeches which tend to inflame religious bigotry. Unfortunately, we Irish, clergy and laity, have a talent for the sweeping phrase which sometimes causes us to make wild statements in public. A collection of such public statements made over the last ten years makes depressing reading and gives one a very false impression of the Catholic Church in Ireland. It is worth noting that such statements are collected and remembered in the North and help to strengthen Partition.

THE NATURE OF THE PARTITION PROBLEM

The paradoxical result of the Government of Ireland Act 1920 and of the Treaty of 1921 was that Ulster, which had struggled so long against Home Rule, ended by getting Home Rule, but Home Rule for Six Counties, while the rest of Ireland became a Dominion and ultimately a republic. The Treaty settlement left Ireland free but divided. Each part of Ireland was free in the sense that each became master of its own destinies, each acquired the form of government which the majority of its inhabitants demanded, and each was free to develop along the lines which it thought best. After 1922, certainly after 1937, all Ireland was free and *the problem was no longer to free the Irish people but to unite them.*

It is inaccurate to peak of the Northern Government as an English puppet regime. The first Ulster Provisional Government was established as a revolutionary government in defiance of the British Parliament in much the same way as the first Provisional Government of the Republic was established, though, of course, the objects of those who established the two governments were utterly dissimilar. It is hardly more correct to speak of the British having set up the Northern Government than it is to speak of them having set up the Southern Government. Each government was established in Ireland by Irishmen and, in each case, the British merely recognised the logic of a situation which Irishmen had created.

It is true that British troops remained in the Six Counties after 1920, but they remained in conformity to the will of the majority of the inhabitants of that area. It is a sad thing to have to say but the Unionists retained them partly to protect themselves against us – a protection which recent events have tragically demonstrated to be necessary. Under these circumstances it is as absurd to speak of the British troops in the North as an army of occupation, or to refer to the North as unfree or British occupied territory, or to talk about liberating the North from the British yoke, as it would be to speak of the American troops in France as an army of occupation, or to refer to France as unfree or American occupied territory, or to talk of liberating France from the American yoke.

It is also misleading to suggest that the British Government deliberately subsidises the Northern Government for the purpose of maintaining Partition. There is no doubt that the Six Counties do not pay their way. But neither does any other distressed area within the United Kingdom, and the North of Ireland is one of the most distressed areas of all. Were it possible to isolate the accounts relating to parts of Scotland and Wales they would reveal much the same story as is revealed by the accounts relating to Northern Ireland. As long as Northern Ireland remains within the United Kingdom it is entitled to all the privileges which membership of the United Kingdom implies. Indeed, the Isles Report makes clear that it is not at present getting all these privileges and the North, so far from feeling bribed, feels that it is not getting fair play from the British Government.

We, in the South, have persistently refused to face the implications of the above facts. After 1922 we were confronted with an entirely new problem but we never faced up to it. As pointed out above, the problem was no longer to free the Irish people but to unite them. The two traditional weapons of Irish nationalism had been physical force and constitutional agitation but both were equally inappropriate in the new situation: you cannot unite a people with either bombs or abuse. What was needed in 1922 was a revision of all our policies in the light of the new situation but that revision never took place, and has not taken place yet. The result has been that ever since the Treaty we have been travelling along a road which leads only to frustration and civil war.

There were many reasons which helped to obscure the true situation from us. First, the traditional enemy was England, and when something was wrong, it came naturally to Irishmen to assume that England was to blame. This idea was assisted by the treachery the British Government had displayed in the Treaty negotiations, in the setting up of the Boundary Commission and in the implementation of Partition generally. Secondly, the plight of the Nationalist minority in the North, dealt with below, served to keep bitterness alive and to prevent us from seeing the situation in its true perspective. Thirdly, the attitude of the Unionist leaders was so negative that our leaders felt that no agreement could ever be reached with them, so they instinctively decided to ignore the Unionists and to try to persuade the British Government, which they hoped would be more amenable, to do something about Partition.

OUR ANTI-PARTITION POLICIES

Mr de Valera has said, from time to time, that the only way to achieve the unity of Ireland is to create a unity of wills, which in fact means converting 300,000 Unionists to a belief in a United Ireland. Yet, Mr de Valera has never committed himself to this policy, but on the contrary has supported the policy of solving Partition by bringing pressure to bear on the British Government. But, whatever his policy, in the later years of his first Administration, he kept silent about the Partition question, and this silence, if it did little good, did no harm. The benefits of Mr de Valera's silence could be seen in the liberalisation of Northern politics in the years after the war, in the growth in the number of Labour and Independent representatives in the Stormont Parliament, and in the rise to power within the Unionist party of moderate men like Mr Brian Maginess.

For some reason, after he fell from power in 1948, Mr de Valera abandoned his former policy of silence, and made Partition the central issue on the Irish political stage. Mr Costello decided not to be outdone, and Mr MacBride wished to do something dynamic about Partition, so that the politicians were soon launched on a vigorous anti-Partition campaign. Mr de Valera went to the United States and Australia, Mr Costello went to Canada, Mr MacBride toured the world, and they were soon joined in their travels by Sir Basil Brooke. What they hoped they could achieve it is difficult to imagine. They certainly succeeded in putting Partition on the world stage, but to achieve that was to achieve nothing, for Partition is essentially a problem for Irishmen, a purely domestic matter, and will be settled here in Ireland by Irishmen or will never be settled at all.

Out of Mr de Valera's renewed enthusiasm for solving Partition and the Government's reaction to it arose the ill-fated Mansion House Committee, the purpose of which was to raise funds to finance the election campaigns of anti-Partitionist candidates, to publish propaganda exposing the evils of Partition, and generally to coordinate the anti-Partition campaign. I should not like to reflect in any way on the well intentioned men who worked hard for this Committee in the honest belief that they were serving Ireland. But the results of the Committee's activities are plain to be seen. At the general election in the North in 1949 the Unionist Party secured one of the greatest victories in its history; the Northern Ireland Labour Party was wiped out at the polls and after its defeat decided to come out for the first time in favour of Partition; and reactionaries regained the ascendancy within the Unionist Party.

The Ireland Act

But the defeat for our leaders was not yet complete. The campaign ended by the North securing from the British Government a guarantee underwriting Partition, and Mr Costello, in his disillusionment, made his famous speech about hurting England in her pride, her prestige, and her pocket. The wording of the British guarantee to the North is interesting:

> It is hereby declared that Northern Ireland remains part of His Majesty's Dominions and of the United Kingdom, and it is hereby affirmed that in no event will Northern Ireland or any part thereof cease to be part of His Majesty's dominions and of the United Kingdom without the consent of the Parliament of Northern Ireland.

This guarantee means two things which I propose to consider separately. It means, first, that the British Government will not force the people of the Six Counties to join the South without the consent of their Parliament. If the giving of this guarantee infuriated our Southern leaders, it must have been because they aimed to persuade or force England to hand over the Six Counties to the South against the will of the majority of the people of the Six County area, in other words, to coerce the people of the Six Counties to come into the Republic against their will. It never became clear how such a policy was to be implemented, whether by military force or economic sanctions or in what other way. But it is virtually impossible to see how any statesman could have expected such a policy to succeed. Our leaders were attempting to re-fight the battle which John Redmond had fought and lost at the time of the Curragh Mutiny. But no English government will ever again place itself in the position in which the Liberals found themselves in 1914. Protestant England will never expel Protestant Ulster from the United Kingdom. The British army will never be used to coerce Irishmen to live together.

The amazing thing about our demand that England should force the people of the North to come into a United Ireland against their will is not that it should have failed, but that it should ever have been made. Such a demand was utterly reprehensible and ought never to have been made in the name of Irish nationalism, because it represented an appeal by our leaders to England to coerce a group of our fellow-countrymen. The fact that Redmond was prepared to use the British army to coerce the Unionists was mentioned above as illustrating the poverty of parliamentary nationalism. But there was some justification for Redmond because he was operating within the framework of the United Kingdom, and he was attempting to fulfil the declared wish of the vast majority of the Irish people in favour of Home Rule, while the Unionists were attempting to frustrate that wish and to keep all the people of Ireland in bondage. But our present leaders had no such excuse. By 1949 we in the South had established our independent State and were free to pursue any policies we might wish. Under these circumstances the fact that our leaders could think of no other way of uniting Ireland than appealing to the British Government to coerce Irishmen to live together shows that there must be something fundamentally wrong about their whole approach to the Partition problem.

There is a second point covered by the British guarantee to the North: the British Government will not give over any part of the Six Counties to the South without the consent of the Northern Parliament. If the object of the anti-Partition campaign was merely to secure the incorporation into the South of Tyrone and Fermanagh and other Nationalist areas, then that campaign becomes much more justifiable, for every argument used to justify the Unionists opting out of a United Ireland can be used to justify the Nationalist areas adjoining the Border coming in with the South, and the greatest injustice of Partition was putting these large Nationalist areas under the Northern Government against their will. Britain must accept her share of responsibility for this injustice, and it might seem reasonable that Southern politicians should organise a campaign to force England to rectify the wrong she has done. But if the object of the anti-Partition campaign was confined to liberating the Nationalist areas in the North that fact was never stated by any Southern statesman.

Even if the object had been merely to secure the redrawing of the Border with a view to incorporating these Nationalist areas in the South, the campaign would still have been unwise for the following reasons: first, the Unionists would have resisted any attempt to take any part of the Six Counties from them as fiercely as they would have resisted an attempt to take away the whole, and nothing short of overwhelming physical force would have dislodged them from this position. There is no use, therefore, pursuing the liberation of the Nationalist areas of the Six Counties as a separate object of Southern policy, as this object is likely to be as difficult to accomplish as the winning back of the whole of the North, and, if accomplished, would still leave us with a partitioned Ireland. Secondly, if successful, it might cause the remaining Unionist areas to abandon their experiment in Home Rule and go back under the direct rule of the London Government, thereby making Partition permanent. Thirdly, any Southern policy which demands the return of certain areas to the South, because they contain local Nationalist majorities, encourages discrimination or worse, on the part of the Orangemen, with a view to liquidating those majorities. Finally, if we agree that the only way to end Partition is to win over a majority of the people of the Six Counties to a belief in the unity of Ireland, then the fact that one third of those people already believe in a United Ireland can assist us in implementing a properly thought-out policy for national reunion. So whether you conclude that the main object of the anti-Partition campaign was to coerce the Unionists (which I think is the correct view) or to liberate the Nationalists; in either event the campaign was equally futile and misconceived.

The Armed Raids and Southern Propaganda

But we have not yet paid the full price of the folly of that attempt to enlist the support of outside powers to coerce the Unionists to come into the South. When the attempt failed, as it was bound to fail, some of our young men took the matter into their own hands. Anyone who thought at all about the history of Ireland could have expected no other result. This result was made all the more probable by the kind of propaganda which we in the South have always employed in relation to the Partition problem, and to which our young people have been exposed from their earliest days. This propaganda has always employed emotionally charged phrases such as 'occupied Ireland', and 'the British army of occupation' with a view to isolating Britain as the party solely responsible for creating and maintaining Partition. Mr Gallagher in his recent book on Partition refers throughout to the Twenty-six Counties as 'free Ireland' thereby implying that the North is unfree or enslaved.

The logical follow through from such propaganda is a resistance movement. If the North is 'occupied territory' held in subjection by a 'British army of occupation', one need not be surprised if the young men of the North rise in arms against the invader or if the young men of the South go to the assistance of their Northern fellow countrymen. The propaganda is rendered all the more insidious by reason of the fact that the deceit employed by the British Government (referred to above) gives it a certain element of truth. But that propaganda injures the cause of Irish unity by disguising from our people the real issue which is that the Northern Government exists because 800,000 Irish Protestants insist that under no circumstances will they allow themselves to be governed by a predominantly Catholic parliament in Dublin.

A Tragic Situation

Once one accepts that proposition, one sees the present raids not as an attack upon an invader but as an attack upon our fellow countrymen. That is the real tragedy of the situation. The young men who are engaged in these raids are as brave and idealistic as any young men who ever fought for Ireland. But instead of helping Ireland they are doing her great harm. They think they are driving the invader from our soil but, in fact, they are merely increasing the bitterness which already divides Irishmen, and the only effect of their efforts will be to turn the present border into a military frontier and to postpone the unification of Ireland for many years. Indeed, we will be fortunate if they do not provoke some outburst of fanaticism which will never be forgotten. There is a tragic contrast between the deaths of Kevin Barry and Fergal O'Hanlon. Both were young men in their teens. Both were fired by the same burning desire to serve Ireland. But while Barry's sacrifice helped to free Ireland and was therefore heroic, O'Hanlon's merely added to the hatreds which divide Irishmen, and can only be described as pathetic.

It is not enough to deplore the present situation and to continue with the policies which have produced it. For 35 years our leaders have been waging a cold war against the North, and if the cold war has now become a shooting war, those who started and carried on the cold war must accept their share of the responsibility. The policy of our leaders has been to coerce the North through the intervention of England, America, the United Nations or some outside power; the policy of the illegal organisations is to do the job themselves. You may call the former policy a constitutional policy, and the latter a physical force policy, but both are basically policies of coercion. Both policies spring from the same presuppositions concerning the origin of Partition, both refuse to face the facts of the situation, and both are doomed to failure.

Persuasion

If we rule out these anti-Partition policies we have to attempt to put something in their place, and the only thing left is a policy of persuasion. This is also the only policy which has never been given a proper trial. We have had cooperation between North and South relating to the Erne Scheme, the Lough Foyle fishery and the Great Northern Railway, but these have been isolated cases, and the general policy of the South has been to ignore the Northern Government except for the purpose of abuse.

If you accept the premises that our problem is not to free our people but to unite them, all the rest falls into place. If North and South are ever to come together, it must be on the basis of mutual trust and understanding and the task for modern Irish statesmen is to create the conditions in which that trust and understanding can grow. The walls of prejudice and bigotry which separate North and South are so great that it may take 50 years to remove them. There is no point in looking for a short-term solution to the Partition problem because, in the short run, there is no solution. The wounds inflicted and suffered by both sides have been too great. The search for a short-term solution will end only in frustration. Fifty years is not a long time in the life of a nation, and a nation which believes in itself and in its destiny will not hesitate to plan for that time.

DISCRIMINATION IN THE NORTH

It is only when one turns to look at the situation inside the Six Counties themselves that one realises the enormity of the task which confronts those who desire an Irish unity based on mutual goodwill. We in the South find it difficult to appreciate the fears and suspicions which divide Catholic and Protestant in Northern Ireland. There may be in the North a few Catholics who support the Unionist cause, and there may be a few Protestants who are Nationalists, but by and large the terms 'Protestant' and 'Unionist' are interchangeable, as are the terms Catholic' and 'Nationalist'. Moreover, the Unionists are permanently in power while the Nationalists are political outcasts. The cleavage between the groups is not merely political and religious, it is also social and affects business life. By and large it is true to say that each group has its own doctors, its own lawyers, its own shopkeepers and lives within a closed system of its own. I realised this for the first time some years ago while talking to a young Northern Catholic, aged about 25. He came from a small town with a population of about 1,000 souls of whom half were Catholics and half Protestants. He told me that never in his whole life had he exchanged one word with a Protestant boy or girl of his own age. It is this system of *apartheid* which constitutes the real partition of Ireland.

We sometimes refer to the persecution of the Catholic minority in the North but there is no persecution if by that word we mean an organised attempt to prevent people from practising their religion. The North has all the forms of a democratic society and the Nationalists possess full freedom of speech. Yet there is a religious discrimination which reduces those democratic forms to a nullity by perverting them in such a way that they defeat the purpose for which they were set up. This system of discrimination operates in several ways. The first is by interfering with the electoral system. One of the first acts of the Northern Parliament was to introduce the system of gerrymandering, and this system was later to be reinforced at local level by a property qualification which effectively disenfranchised a large number of Nationalist voters, and on both national and local levels by the abolition of Proportional Representation. The ultimate effect of this extraordinarily ingenious system of gerrymandering is to give one Unionist vote the effective voting power of two Nationalist votes, so that Unionists control the local administration even in predominantly Nationalist areas such as Fermanagh and Tyrone.

Once in control of the local councils the Unionists proceed to elect committees to deal with housing, education, etc., and all these committees are overwhelmingly Unionist, though, occasionally, they contain one or two Nationalists as a face-saving device. But even then decisions are not made in committee or at council meetings. All decisions are discussed and made at the local Orange Lodge, and the committee or council meets only to hear the final decision of the Unionist majority and the ineffective protests of the Nationalists.

The second way the system of discrimination operates is in the allocation of county council houses. These allocations usually betray the most flagrant injustices. For instance, on 11 March 1950, the Omagh Rural Council allocated 40 houses at Coneywarren, Co. Tyrone, the first council houses built in the area for several years. The Nationalist members of the council submitted the names of 22 desperately badly housed families. Every Nationalist applicant was rejected and the houses were allocated to 40 Unionists, a majority of whom were unmarried, or married but without children or had but one child. Some of those who were allocated houses were already so well housed elsewhere that they refused to move in. There must be, among the Unionist councillors, some who feel troubled in their consciences when a council house built with public money is allocated to a Unionist ahead of a more deserving Catholic. Such councillors may protest inside the Orange Lodges but their voices are not heard in public so that it is not possible to know how numerous they are.

Thirdly, this system of discrimination operates in the allocation of appointments in the public service. The four counties of Armagh, Derry, Fermanagh and Tyrone have together a population of 232,600 Nationalists to 222,500 Unionists. These councils employ 541 officials on their executive, administrative and clerical staffs. Of these only 55 are Nationalists. That is to say, the Unionist minority get 90 per cent of the appointments at these grades.

The same pattern reveals itself in private business. The Unionists who control the greater part of the wealth of the area will not employ a Catholic if they can possibly avoid it, and an Orangeman who sells his house or farm to a Catholic will almost certainly be ostracised by his fellows. No matter what price a Catholic offers, the Orangeman must sell to a Protestant, and a special Unionist fund was started some years ago, with the encouragement of the Government, for the purpose of buying any property in danger of falling into Catholic hands.

The purpose of this discrimination is explained by two simple quotations taken from Unionist sources. The first is from an editorial from the *Strabane Weekly News* for 11 June 1949, and warns that any Unionist

> who sells a farm or lets a house to an anti-Partitionist is assisting the anti-Partitionists to win the Local Government representation in that area at the next election and their action can only be regarded as treachery to their party.

The second quotation comes from a speech made by Mr E. C. Ferguson at Enniskillen, the capital of the predominantly Nationalist county of Fermanagh, on 9 April 1948. Mr Ferguson is a solicitor and was at that time a Unionist MP. He is reported as follows:

> The Nationalist majority in the County, notwithstanding a reduction of 336 in the year, stands at 3,684. We must ultimately reduce and liquidate that majority. This county I think it can safely be said is a Unionist county. The atmosphere is Unionist. The boards and properties are nearly all controlled by Unionists. But there is this millstone around our necks.

Everything was Unionist except the people. Eighteen months after he had made this speech Mr Ferguson was appointed Crown Solicitor for Co. Fermanagh by the Northern Government.

There is no doubt that the entire Northern system of government is based on a system of discrimination the purpose of which is to prevent Catholics from getting any political or economic power, and to prevent any growth in their numbers by denying them housing and employment, thereby compelling them to emigrate. This has been proved, and anyone still in doubt can consult Mr Gallagher's book where the matter is fully documented and from which most of the examples given above are taken. Worse than the system of discrimination itself is the psychological effect it produces on the Catholics who feel themselves to be outcasts in their own country, and who feel when the Unionists speak of liberalism or fair play that they are merely adding hypocrisy to their other sins. If a revolutionary situation exists in the Six Counties today there can be no doubt that the Unionists themselves are largely to blame.

The Major Cause

Yet this is not the whole story. The discrimination which the Unionists undoubtedly exercise against the Northern Nationalists cannot fairly be considered apart from the policies which we in the South have pursued since 1922. To the Unionists it has always appeared that they were fighting to prevent themselves from being forcibly placed under the power of a Catholic

Dublin parliament, and that in this struggle the Northern Nationalists were fifth columnists who were attempting to sap the foundations of the Northern State, destroy the ascendancy of the Protestants, and deliver them into the hands of the Church of Rome. That is why the Unionist usually classifies the people of the Six Counties as the 'loyal' and the 'disloyal', and why he concludes that the 'disloyal' must be excluded from public office and, as far as possible, deprived of political and economic power. In practice, the test of whether a man is 'loyal' or ' disloyal 'is the very simple one of what Church he attends on Sundays'.

The fears of the Unionists strike us as irrational but we should remember that to the Unionist himself they are very real. Unionist bigotry like all bigotry is based on fear. It is true that we have offered the Northern Protestants adequate constitutional safeguards to protect their rights and to guarantee them equality in a United Ireland, and we have been able to point to the tolerant state we have established in the South. But the Unionists doubt our sincerity, and the fact that we have continually pursued a policy designed to coerce them to join the South against their will has lent substance to their suspicions.

If the argument of this paper is correct, there was never any prospect of Southern coercionist policies succeeding against the North, and the Unionists need not have been unduly perturbed. Yet, it was elementary prudence on the part of the Northern leaders to warn their people of the Southern threat. Moreover, that threat was a godsend to Orange politicians, for as long as the Northern Protestants could be convinced that they were in danger of being coerced to join the South, they would continue to rally around the Unionist Party. So long as this threat continued, reactionary and bigoted Orangemen would continue to control the Unionist Party, and the ordinary Protestant would tolerate acts of discrimination against his Catholic fellow-countryman which he would never tolerate were he not afraid that his own social position and way of life were threatened by the Catholics. In this way, the constant threat from the South has kept alive sectarian bitterness in the North, has prevented the emergence of a Liberal or Labour Party, has defeated the ambitions of liberals within the Unionist Party itself, and so has played right into the hands of those Orange leaders who owe their position to sectarian bigotry.

Mr Gallagher has extracted from the election Manifestos or Eve-of-the-Poll messages issued by the Northern Prime Ministers in each of the seven elections since 1921 the following quotations which show the use the Unionist Party has made of the Southern threat:

The fate of the Six Counties hangs in the balance (1921).
Defeat your enemies, save the Border (1925).

Scatter your enemies. The fate of the country lies in your hands (1929).

Defeat the designs of our enemies . . . Ravenous eyes are concentrating on our province (1933).

Ulster's fate is in your hands . . . Forces . . . are at work to deprive us of our birthright (1938).

Ulster's constitutional position . . . is the supreme issue. It dominates every other question (1945).

Our country is in danger – Ulster's heritage is at stake . . . Loyalists stand to your defences (1949).

Overshadowing all else is the constitutional issue (1953).

Mr Gallagher is outraged at the way Unionist politicians have used the threat from the South to spread panic among the Northern electorate and to deflect its attention from the ordinary political and economic problems which preoccupy the minds of voters in other democratic countries. Yet he has nothing to say of those Southern leaders who for 35 years have adhered to policies which seem to be ineffective for all purposes except that of keeping alive sectarian bitterness in the North and maintaining the Unionist Party in power.

A NEW POLICY

The time has come, accordingly, for us to abandon the coercionist policies we have been following hitherto, and to replace them with policies designed to reduce tension and to create an atmosphere in which a unity of wills can grow. As we are the people who believe in the creation of a United Ireland we must make the first move. We must make it clear that we unilaterally renounce all thought of using coercion against our fellow countrymen in the North, or of asking or allowing anyone else to use it against them. The best way for us to prove that we would respect the wishes of the Northern Protestants inside a United Ireland is by respecting their wishes as long as they want to remain outside it.

As pointed out above, nothing is to be gained by pursuing the liberation of the Nationalist areas of the Six Counties as a separate aim of Southern policy, but if we are formally to guarantee the territorial integrity of Northern Ireland we will want in return effective guarantees to protect the Northern Nationalists against the kind of discrimination they have been suffering from hitherto. If it is true that that discrimination sprang largely from the coercionist policies pursued by the South, then the abandonment of those policies by the South should remove any justification there ever was for that discrimination. To ensure that any guarantees given to Northern Catholics would be effective, we would require tokens of good faith, such as that Proportional Representation should be reintroduced in parliamentary and municipal elections in the North, that the property qualifications for municipal voters should be abolished, and that Parliamentary and local constituencies should be redrawn so as to make them truly representative of the wishes of the people, such a redrawing of constituency boundaries to recur every ten or 15 years, and to be presided over by an impartial judge appointed by agreement between the two governments or by the United Nations.

In return Dáil Éireann would solemnly renounce any intention of using coercion against the Northern Protestants and would guarantee the territorial integrity of Northern Ireland in much the same way as the British Parliament guaranteed it in the Ireland Act; that is to say, that the South would recognise that Northern Ireland would never enter a United Ireland without the prior consent of the Parliament of Northern Ireland. The South would also recognise the Government of Northern Ireland as an Irish government entitled to respect not only from the people of the Six Counties but from all Irishmen.

Such an agreement would be the foundation on which the new policy designed to create a unity of wills would rest. But it would merely be a beginning. It would also be necessary to call off the propaganda campaign which we have been carrying on against the Northern Government throughout the world, and it would also be wise to dissolve the anti-Partition Association, which, for all its good intentions, has done a great deal of harm.

The Northern Nationalists

Inside the Six Counties themselves the Nationalists could take many steps designed to reduce tension. In particular, they could ask themselves if the rigid division in Northern politics between Catholic and Protestant produces anything but evil. There will be little hope of creating a better atmosphere in the North as long as you can tell a man's politics by the Church he goes to on Sunday. It is at least worth asking if the Northern Nationalists should not dissolve their existing political organisations, so as to allow room for the growth of a Liberal or Labour party which could bridge the gulf between Catholic and Protestant. Certainly, it would be wise for specifically Catholic organisations such as the Ancient Order of Hibernians to refrain from interfering in politics, and the clergy should not play an active part in any political organisation. These recommendations may demand great sacrifices from men who have devoted a life of labour to the service of Ireland. But such men have already sacrificed so much for their country that they will not deny her this further sacrifice if they are once convinced that it is wise and necessary.

It would also be wise for the Nationalists of the North to refrain from displaying their sentiments in an unnecessarily provocative manner. One can have great sympathy with the position of the Northern Nationalists and yet see that the aim of Nationalist propaganda should be to create a unity of wills and not to provoke the Orangemen to acts of violence. The same thing applies to the carrying of the tricolour in processions in the North. The tricolour is meant to symbolise the unity of the Irish nation, and there is no point in displaying it in the North until the unity which it is meant to symbolise in fact exists there. Otherwise, the tricolour will merely come to be regarded as a Catholic party symbol, and will become an object of hatred to most Protestants.

Confine Partition to Political Field

Again, while we recognise that Partition exists in the political field, and is likely to continue for a very long time, we must try to prevent it from spreading into the fields of economics, culture and sport. We must localise the area of disagreement. Voluntary organisations with branches on both sides of the Border should ignore the Partition problem as far as possible and should confine themselves to achieving the purposes for which the organisations were founded. It has been the habit of Nationalist members of such organisations to introduce the question of Partition into them by demanding that the organisations should declare themselves in favour of a United Ireland, or should display the tricolour on public occasions even when this was likely to cause offence to Unionist members. As often as not the efforts of such well-intentioned but misguided men have split the organisations in question and thereby extended Partition a little further. Nationalist members of such organisations should avoid introducing politics into them and, if some political question inevitably arises, they should show great understanding of the Unionist position, remembering that the most effective argument against Partition is to demonstrate that Irishmen can live in peace together, and can solve their problems in a spirit of friendship.

Sport

As already pointed out, the real Partition of Ireland consists in the *apartheid* between Catholic and Protestant in the North. Anything which tends to end this apartheid is to be welcomed and the converse deplored. The fields of athletics and sport offer opportunities for Catholics and Protestants to meet in a spirit of friendship. The GAA's ban on foreign games in so far as it tends to prevent such contacts is wholly deplorable. This ban may have been justified in the circumstances which prevailed in Ireland in the past but, as it operates in the North at present, it helps to prevent social contacts between Irishmen and, therefore, to maintain Partition.

Economic Policies

We must also try to avoid any unnecessary rifts between the economies of the two parts of Ireland. The volume of legal trade between North and

South has steadily decreased since 1922. Part of this decrease may have been inevitable, due to the policy of industrialisation pursued in the South and the protective tariffs which went hand in hand with it. The loss in legal trade may have been offset in part by a thriving smuggling industry but even this has been destroyed by the heavy frontier patrols called into existence by the recent armed raids on the North! The fact is that the Southern Government has made very little effort to promote trade between North and South, and we have not even got a trade consul in Belfast. It is surely time we took this matter in hand. The tourist industry in particular deserves attention as an increase in the volume of tourist traffic may help to promote understanding between the people of the two parts of Ireland.

Education

In the educational field there are already some points of contact. Both Unionist and Nationalist students attend Queen's University Belfast, which seems to help in fostering an increasingly enlightened approach to Northern politics. Moreover, several hundred Unionist students come to Dublin each year to study at Trinity College, which can and does play an important part in bringing Irishmen together. A corresponding number of Northern Nationalists come to study at University College Dublin. This makes it all the greater pity that there is so little contact between two universities which are not a quarter of a mile apart. Each University has its own tradition and there may the important reasons why each should retain its independence. But there seems to be a strong case on political, economic and academic grounds for closer cooperation between the two universities, particularly in the faculties of Arts, Law, Medicine and Science.

CULTURE AND NATIONALISM

But the most important contacts between North and South will be cultural contacts. If we can produce a distinctive Irish culture this will be a magnetic force which will tend to draw all Irishmen together. Such a culture should grow out of the conditions of modern Ireland, and should appeal particularly to the people who live in Ireland today.

The problems of Irish culture and of Irish nationalism are allied but, unfortunately, in recent years, both Irish nationalism and what is popularly regarded as Irish culture have tended to become exclusive and narrow. This exclusiveness is seen, on the one hand, in the repudiation of the work of men like Yeats or Synge or O'Casey and, on the other hand, in a tendency to deny to the Unionists of Northern Ireland the title of Irishmen. Both forms of exclusiveness tend to cut Ireland in two, the former by repudiating a cultural heritage common to all Irishmen, and the latter by minimising the importance of the affection which every man feels for the country in which he was born.

We cannot expect the Northern Protestant to interest himself in Irish culture as long as we continue to revile him as an alien and a planter. Here is where the narrow and exclusive nationalism which has been current in recent years shows itself at its worst. It may seem strange to deny the title of Irishman to a man whose people have been living in Ireland since before the 'Mayflower' sailed to America, but that one should do it in the name of Irish Nationalism is quite incredible. There are many Ulster Protestants, not necessarily Nationalists, who claim they are as well entitled to describe themselves as Irishmen as anyone else in Ireland, and such claims should be recognised and respected by us. The Ulster poet, Mr John Hewitt, deals with this very problem in one of his poems:

> Once alien here my fathers built their house
> Claimed, drained, and gave the land the shapes of use.
>
> So, I, because of all the buried men in
> Ulster clay, because of rock and glen
> and mist, and cloud, and quality of air
> as native in my thought as any here, . . .

The Unionist *Belfast Telegraph* also returns to this theme from time to time, and has advised its readers to resist the pressure of those who say that Ulster is not a true part of Ireland, and that Ulstermen have not an Irish birthright. The people of the North, it says, should take advantage of every world to which they have access. An editorial on St Patrick's Day, 1953 opens as follows:

> St Patrick's Day comes as a reminder that although deep-seated differences between peoples and religions have caused it to be divided Ireland still inspires a common sentiment. The sadness is that the festival should be turned to political account when it best can demonstrate that the border has nothing to say against love of country.

The editorial adds that St Patrick himself offers the best hope of ultimate amity and reunion between Irishmen.

The New Nationalism

We need a new culture and a new form of nationalism broad enough to meet the needs of a society of men of different origins and different religions. But it is the Anglo-Irish element in such a culture which, initially at any rate, will be most important for the purpose of bridging the Border. We are fortunate in having such a rich heritage to draw upon from the Irish and the Anglo-Irish traditions, and from the general civilisation which grew up around Christianity in Europe and in the English-speaking world. All this is our common heritage, and it would be a pity to turn our backs on any of it. We, too, must take advantage of every world to which we have access. Our national culture should arise from a happy combination of the various cultural traditions we have inherited, and not from concentrating on one and ignoring all the others. The new Irish nationalism will have to be tolerant and non-exclusive, and to recognise that Irishmen display an infinite variety of gifts and serve Ireland in a bewildering variety of ways. Thomas Davis came nearer to such a concept of Irish nationalism than any other Irishman and that is why his writings form the best point of departure for a new nationalism designed to draw all Irishmen together.

FOREIGN POLICY AND PARTITION

The approach to Partition which we have pursued hitherto has led us to make the ending of Partition the dominant aim of our foreign policy. The argument of this paper has been that Partition has nothing to do with foreign policy, but is a domestic matter for Irishmen. If the people of Ireland wish to unite under one government neither England nor any foreign power will keep them apart. For this reason, it is better that we should not even mention Partition in international assemblies, for our doing so would savour of the old coercionist policy of enlisting outside support against our fellow-countrymen, and, like that policy, would merely irritate without effecting any useful purpose.

There are many objects for Irish foreign policy to pursue. We are interested in international peace and justice, in supporting the United Nations, in the defence of European civilisation, in promoting international trade, in exploring the avenues to European unity, in assisting the countries which are struggling for independence, and in promoting understanding between them and the colonial powers. Like other peoples, we need as many friends abroad as we can get. But none of these things has any direct or immediate bearing on Partition. When the time for establishing a United Ireland eventually comes, we shall need many friends in England in order that the English may be helpful with the economic and financial problems which the ending of Partition will raise, but the best way to get these friends is not by carrying on a campaign against England in international assemblies.

The Commonwealth

In this connection, the question of re-entering the Commonwealth arises. I think most Irishmen feel that re-entering the Commonwealth would be a small price to pay for Irish unity, and that the repeal of the External Relations Act was a mistake, in as much as it broke one of the links between North and South. But it is unrealistic to speak of going back into the Commonwealth again, except as part of a scheme for reuniting Ireland. Those who think we can solve Partition simply by going back into the Commonwealth should reflect upon the fact that we were in the Commonwealth for 27 years during which Partition grew in strength. More significantly still, they should reflect upon the Home Rule Bill of 1912, under which Ireland would have received limited powers of self-government but would have remained within the United Kingdom. Yet the Unionists brought Ireland and England to the verge of civil war rather than accept the Home Rule Bill. It is clear, then, that what the Unionists object to is government by a predominantly Catholic Parliament in Dublin and that they are not prepared to accept this within the United Kingdom much less than within the Commonwealth. So re-entering the Commonwealth offers no hope of solving Partition in the immediate future, though it may form part of the solution when we have brought about a change of heart in the North.

THE ROAD AHEAD

I am aware that I have discussed no concrete proposal for establishing a United Ireland. I have refrained from doing so deliberately. Schemes such as the D'Alton Plan are admirable in themselves but they are premature as there is no hope of their being accepted in the North in the immediately foreseeable future. Our immediate task is to create an atmosphere in which the people of the North will be prepared to consider such plans. It is to create a unity of wills, and once we have created that unity of wills, no great difficulty will be found in giving it practical expression. But the creation of that unity of wills is going to take very many years and during the interval many of the political institutions which we know today may have been transformed completely and a United Ireland may come into existence only as part of a United Europe, or of some other political association, the nature of which we cannot now even guess. All we can say is that if we lay the foundations of peace and goodwill between Irishmen we can look to the future with confidence.

I am aware also that I have not referred to the superior social services which exist in the North, and which are often used nowadays as an argument in favour of Partition. Yet, while these are important, they are not the essence of the Partition problem. If the North ever joins the South, it will want to retain the social services and other economic advantages which it at present enjoys, but that does not mean that we should immediately introduce social services identical with those which prevail in the North. What is of vital importance is that we should streamline and develop our economy in such a way that when the time comes to invite the North to enter a United Ireland, we shall, be sufficiently wealthy to ensure that the North can join us without sacrificing any of the advantages which she at present enjoys.

This paper has underlined the religious problem behind Partition, but it has said little of the economic problem. The Orange Order aims at supporting not only Protestantism but Protestant Ascendancy, and there is little doubt that it has been used by a wealthy and privileged caste to keep the poor at war with each other on the religious issue, so as to prevent them from forming a popular or labour party. But the working of the Welfare State, introduced into the North for tactical reasons to prevent the Unionists falling foul of Mr Attlee's Labour Government, will, in time, tend to undermine the position of this wealthy and privileged caste by creating a class of able and educated young men who will perceive the barrenness of the Orange position, and will not easily be fobbed off with the cry of 'No Popery'. Already, after 37 years of Unionist rule, there must be many people who are weary of the Unionist Party, and would welcome a change of government. But these are problems for the people of the Six Counties themselves and they must be left to solve them in their own way. Our task is simply, by withdrawing the threat of external coercion, to permit Northern politics to evolve in a normal and peaceful way.

Once we have taken the steps outlined earlier in this paper to reduce tension between North and South and to create the conditions in which a unity of wills can grow, then we should say no more in public on the subject of Partition than is necessary, but should let commonsense and goodwill do their work. It would be a good thing if every man who contemplates speaking on Partition in public should ask himself the question – 'Will my speech really help to unite Ireland?' We should, however, keep ourselves well informed on the problems of the North for knowledge will help to protect us against mistakes of policy such as we made in the past.

There will be plenty of work for us to do in the South, which will assist in bringing both parts of Ireland together. We must develop our economy to the highest degree of efficiency of which it is capable. We must raise the educational and cultural level of our people as high as we possibly can. Finally, we must strengthen those principles of tolerance on which our free society rests, in order to ensure that our problems are faced fully and openly, and that the natural talents of our people find full expression. Tolerance is the key to a United Ireland.

The problem of uniting our people is a new and difficult one for Irishmen and the old ways of thinking are very little help to us in tackling it. Indeed, they have obscured the problem from us for more than 35 years. In tackling this problem we will need the gifts of perseverance, restraint, moderation and, above all, charity. It is possible that once we set our people on the road of peace and mutual understanding their journey to national unity may be a short one, but we must not expect it. The odds are that the road will be long and difficult and we cannot even be sure that it will lead to unity. But of one thing we can be quite certain: there is no other road.

Notes

1   Originally published as Donal Barrington, 'Uniting Ireland', *Studies* vol. 46, no. 184 (winter, 1957), pp. 379–402.

2   Frank Gallagher's *Indivisible Island* (Dublin, 1957) set out the Nationalist case for a United Ireland that Barrington challenges here. Gallagher asserted Irish Nationalist rights and values as timeless; his book made little effort to understand Unionists; he refers to these throughout as 'Tories'. See Graham Walker, 'The Irish Dr Goebbels: Frank Gallagher and Irish Republican Propaganda', *Journal of Contemporary History* vol. 27, no. 1 (January, 1992), pp. 149–65.

CHAPTER 18

Fifty Years of Irish Writing (1962)

Sean O'Faolain

Sean O'Faolain argued that twentieth-century Irish writing fell into two parts: a period of growth from 1900 and one of decline that began to operate immediately after the Free State was founded in 1921. At that stage the general mood was romantic, nationalist, fervid, critical of others, especially one's opponents, whether native or foreign, but not very self-critical. Independence, he argued, had been accompanied by 'a nervy sensitive, touchy, defensive-aggressive, on-guard mentality'. The resultant censorship was a 'blending of the moral and the patriotic: the desire to protect from corruption this infant nation born out of so much hardship'. One of the striking effects of this was the comparative failure of the modern Irish novel: 'If one were to exclude Joyce – which is like saying if one were to exclude Everest – and Liam O'Flaherty, how little was left!'[1]

When the editor of *Studies* kindly invited me to write an article on the fortunes of Irish literature over the past 50 years I presumed that the main interest of anything I might have to say would lie in the fact that I am an Irish writer who was born in 1900, which implies, I suppose, that, within the limitations of my personal oddities and idiosyncrasies, what I here say cannot fail to be, at any rate to some degree representative of the views of the generation after Yeats. In other words, I am very happily presenting myself and my views as a type specimen. I feel obliged to say this at the outset, to give myself full freedom of expression by making it quite clear to my readers, especially to readers outside Ireland, that some of the things I have to say must be displeasing to my host. I might otherwise seem to be taking an unfair advantage of his hospitality.

I do not propose to say much about the earlier part of the last 50 years. What was written in that period, say 1910–21, is well known and has been much discussed. It was the heyday of the Abbey Theatre. The riots over *The*

Playboy were over and the battle won – the play was now being produced without opposition, largely through the tough courage of Yeats and the gallant support of his players. Prose was flourishing – Moore, Stephens, Canon Sheehan, Somerville and Ross, lesser entertainers like George Bermingham, and, to move on a bit in years but still within the general 'period', Eimar O'Duffy, Shan Bullock, Conal O'Riordan and others. I am aware that to move on outside date brackets is always tricky in dealing with a literary period but, in the first place dates and periods rarely coincide in literary history (For example, the eighteenth-century period in English literature did not end with the year 1800.) And, the second, and for our purposes, more important point here is that the whole story of latter-day developments in Anglo-Irish letters is very much a story of pioneering and overlapping (Joyce's *Dubliners*, for example, appeared in 1914 but he is alien to most of our literary traditions before him, though he was fully contemporaneous with Yeats as a young Dubliner). Poetry, too, in the opening ten years of our chosen 50 was flourishing – Yeats, Clarke, Higgins, Campbell, Seamus O'Sullivan, though here again I am overlapping dates, to keep the sense of period Clarke and Higgins both were born in 1896. Clarke did not publish his first book *The Vengeance of Fionn* until 1917.

The general mood of that period, before the establishment of the Irish Free State, was romantic, nationalist, fervid, critical of others, especially of one's political opponents, whether native or foreign, but not very critical of ourselves – apart from the sort of rather superficial satire one got from plays like William Boyle's *The Eloquent Dempsey* – and it was quite uncritical in matters literary, historical and what would nowadays be called sociological. This absence of a deep-cutting critical objectivity was, I think, the great weakness of the so-called Irish Literary Movement. It made it, as some of us at the time kept on saying worriedly, without being able to do anything about it, a movement of feeling rather than of thought. As one looks back over the prose of the period one sometimes wonders whether our writers ever took off their green glasses. Exceptions will, no doubt, be offered, such as O'Duffy and O'Riordan, yet, on re-opening such novels as *The Wasted Island* or *Adam of Dublin* I, for one, still feel that nothing in them is at all as tough and clear-sighted as, say, *The Real Charlotte* (Somerville and Ross) or *A Drama in Muslin*. This last, and to most readers I feel sure, unexpected title, may make my point clear.

George Moore was a flippant Bohemian; the novel is not a good novel; it is melodramatic, often absurd, even penny-noveletteish; yet to what other novel of that time can one go for such a clear observation of the formative social factors behind, and responsible for, the grimness of Dublin life as depicted, but never explained – it was not his interest – by Joyce in the *Portrait* and *Ulysses*? Moore, trained by Zola and Flaubert saw, displayed and eviscerated – an amazing feat for a man normally without an iota of responsibility in his composition – the real forces, social and economic, which had infected Ireland with the state of spiritual paralysis that so disgusted Joyce and produced in contemporary Irish writing so much verse that if not actually a form of compensatory escapism is dangerously close to it. To the Irish Literary Movement, taken by and large, the evil enemy was England, holding down and frustrating all that was lovely and worthwhile in the Holy Land of Ireland whose beauty the poets endlessly chanted. Moore, whose relations with Ireland were consistently those of *odi et amo* with at times an almost psychopathic stress on the *odi* – saw that the real source of infection was the native middle classes, and – religion apart – all their tawdry, snobbish, and provincial, social values. Events were to support Moore's contention to the full.

This leads me to explain why, as I see things, the story of Irish writing since 1900 falls into two parts: growth and decline.

Though nobody could have observed it at the time, the causes for this decline began to operate immediately the Irish Free State was founded, in 1921. Their effects were, however, held at bay for a time by the continuing momentum of nationalist excitement persisting after the revolution was over. Seán O'Casey's plays illustrate this. His *Juno and the Paycock* was staged in 1924, and his *The Plough and the Stars* in 1926, both of them dealing with the revolutionary period which was finished and done with. It is true that there was a theatre riot over the latter play, but nobody attached any special significance to it. If anything one took it for a good omen. It was like the old days of the *Playboy* riots. It promised a continuity of tradition. '*Plus ca change*,' we said. But we were wrong. It was not *la même chose*. There was a fundamental difference between the circumstances surrounding O'Casey and those surrounding Synge. One might build on the two riots a parable of the reasons for the later decline in Irish writing.

In the old days – to keep, for the moment, to the example of the theatre – an elite had been in the saddle. The whole of Yeats' outlook had been aristocratic though nationalist, just as he had always been both European and Irish, as excited by the *Axel* of Villiers de l'Isle Adam as by the peasant folktales of Biddy Early. He had said several times that his sort of theatre should be as hard to get into as a secret society. He liked small audiences. The poetic drama he admired could never have become popular, and insofar as the Abbey Theatre did become a popular or people's theatre, he felt that he had failed to create what he set out to create. So, he had always struggled against the popular taste for so-called 'realistic' drama. In spite of every inevitable concession to that taste he dominated his ambiguous creation as a poet with a poet's ideals. This all began to change immediately a native government was established. The type of people who had, long ago, protested against Synge's *Playboy* had had no political power. The people who objected to O'Casey had political power. (It is to be remembered that the new Irish Government decided to subsidise the Abbey Theatre; which, at the time, seemed to us all a splendid gesture. Disillusion was to come slowly with the gradual realisation that when governments give money they receive influence in exchange.)

Moreover, in those 'old days' the Catholic Church had had only a limited amount of political power because the government had been an alien and non-Catholic government, and the foreign Gallio, like all pro-consuls, had kept the ring with the tolerance of total indifference. Now the Church could wield almost unlimited power because the native government was composed of men who respected, loved, and feared it. It is evident that the new intellectual atmosphere depended on the sophistication, cultivation, and tolerance of both the native government and the Church, the new elite. Unfortunately, centuries of depression had bred in both not only a passionate desire for liberty – each with its own interpretation and its own aims – but the antithesis of that natural desire. It had induced a nervy, sensitive, touchy, defensive-aggressive, on-guard mentality as a result of which patriotism became infected by chauvinism and true religious feeling by what most Irish writers after 1921 tended to call 'puritanism'. I imagine that I am describing something which happens commonly in all countries which have emerged from a revolutionary phase, and that it does not involve any special criticism of Ireland or the Irish nature. (An intellectual Jew in contemporary Palestine, an intellectual Cypriot in Cyprus, would probably nod his head in understanding and sympathy if he were to read my summary.)

The simplest illustration of what happened was the establishment of a severe literary censorship in 1929. Its aim was, and its aim no doubt still is, a blending of the moral and the patriotic: the desire to protect from corruption this infant nation born out of so much hardship. Within 20 years thousands of books were banned as indecent or obscene. It will be noted that the reason or banning was not political and it was social (and religious) only in so far as books and periodicals were and still are banned if they advocate, or advertise, contraception, abortion, or the artificial insemination of humans. Within recent years this early fervour for banning has been much abated, thanks to the nomination of intelligent censors, following prolonged protests by writers and the general public. Most of the books now banned are ephemeral and their absence from the public libraries and bookshops is no loss. This may be acknowledged and welcomed as a sign of a growing sophistication in contemporary Ireland.

But there have been two particularly bad results for Irish literature; within a few years there was scarcely an Irish writer of distinction who had not, at least once, been declared the author of obscenity, and he was – and still is – denied recourse to the courts of the land in self defence. But the worst feature of the censorship has been that with it there arose a private censorship all over the country in the form of a witch-hunt which no librarian or bookseller could dare to resist by stocking books objected to by these unofficial censors. Demos was in the saddle.

To form a just picture of this new intellectual atmosphere it is essential to grasp one other point. The revolution of 1916–21 had been a social revolution. This fact lifts the history of Irish writing over the past 25 years out of its apparently local setting and puts it in its proper place as part of a general world tendency. The idealists who inspired the people to rise against British rule were – as I have said – unaware of the social forces they were working with and releasing. In the nineteenth century these forces had been personified by the impoverished farming community in the Land League's fight for decent conditions of land tenure. In our day the social forces behind the last stage of the Irish Revolution were personified by the sons and daughters of those farmers – surplus children squeezed into the towns and cities, and finding there that all the power and most of the wealth was in the hands of people of a different religion, racial origin, or political loyalty. Seán O'Casey's plays are thus an exactly true statement of the Irish Revolution whose flag, he clearly felt, should be, not the tricolour, but the plough-and-the-stars flag of the urban labouring classes.

We must, finally, understand that the class that came to power and influence was not a labouring class; the more able among them were *petit bourgeois*, middle-men, importers, small manufacturers – the modern counterpart of Moore's nineteenth-century middle classes – forming a new twentieth-century middle class to fill the vacuum created by the departure or depression of the earlier alien middle class. These men, naturally, had had very little education and could have only a slight interest in the intellectuals' fight for liberty of expression. They were ordinary, decent, kindly, self-seeking men who had no intention of jeopardising their new-found prosperity by gratuitous displays of moral courage. In any case, since they were rising to sudden wealth behind protective tariff-walls they had a vested interest in nationalism and even in isolationism. The upshot of it was an alliance between the Church, the new businessmen, and the politicians, all three nationalist isolationist for, respectively, moral reasons, commercial reasons, and politico-patriotic reasons, in themselves all perfectly sound reasons. The effect on letters was not good. The intellectuals became a depressed group. Possibly they were also infected by the atmosphere around them.

For completeness let us try to look sympathetically on the other side of the picture. Ireland is not a publishing country. All but a number of books, so few that it would be an exaggeration to call them a handful, are published abroad, apart from all primary school texts and most secondary school texts.

Practically all our mental food is therefore imported: good food but not native. If there is such a thing as a racial Irish quality of life it is very difficult for it to resist almost overwhelming external influences, since this local way-of-life is not equipped intellectually to support it. The intellectuals cried out for a bold, adventurous, and thoroughly modern system of popular education, but both the Church and the State feared the results. It is to be said that the Irish way-of-life, though poor, indeed impoverished as to institutions fit to represent it – e.g. publishing houses, periodicals, rich universities – is atavistically powerful, spiritually obstinate, strongly resistant, in a great many ways appealing; it represents precious and lovable qualities, and is eminently worth preservation, provided it expresses itself in achievement and not merely in emotional declaration. The intellectuals' position is that it cannot and will not preserve itself by negative methods, and that it is, in practice, now as in the past, being undermined and corrupted by a lack of moral and intellectual courage.

We can now look at Irish writing against this social, political, and religious background. First, the theatre:

As we look back over the plays produced in the Abbey Theatre since the First World War we find that the theatre was still lively almost up to 1932. (This suggests that the momentum of the revolutionary stimulus went on for some ten years.) The lists include first productions of plays by Lady Gregory, Brinsley McNamara, Padraic Colum, Daniel Corkery, Shaw, Lord Dunsany, Lennox Robinson, George Shiels, Seán O'Casey, T. C. Murray, Yeats, Wilde, Rutherford Mayne, Teresa Deevy, Denis Johnston, and Paul Vincent Carroll. Lady Gregory died in 1932. From then onward two or three plays of distinction were produced but no outstanding name is added to the list. In 1935 Yeats, who was ageing and ailing, felt that the theatre needed younger men. His friend, the poet Frederick Robert Higgins, was appointed director; so was Frank O'Connor; and a significant name also appeared among the directors, an ex-Cabinet Minister, Mr Ernest Blythe. Mr Hugh Hunt, now producer at the Old Vic Theatre, London, was brought in as producer, and from 1935 to 1938, the combination of Higgins, O'Connor and Hunt gave the theatre a new and exciting spurt. It is of interest that in those three years the Abbey produced several non-Irish plays – including plays by Shakespeare, Flecker, Toller, Shaw, André Obey. Yeats died in 1939. O'Connor, feeling unable to cope with influences of which he disapproved, resigned in 1939. Higgins died in 1941. Mr Blythe became Managing Director. Thus, there remained on the Board, to represent old tradition, only Mr Lennox Robinson. Otherwise the bridge with the past was down.

Unless we imagine that literature exists in a vacuum we must see what sort of official influences played on the theatre at this period. I will give two examples. In 1932 when the Abbey Theatre visited the United States the usual hyper-patriotic societies there protested against some of the plays, including O'Casey's, and at home deputies were prompted to ask awkward questions in the Dáil. In reply to one questioner on this issue, Mr de Valera said (26 April 1933) that the Government had made indirect representations to the Abbey Theatre, and that it was hoped that if the Company visited America again plays of the kind objected to by the American-Irish would not be produced. In that year the official subsidy was reduced. In 1934 a similar angry question received a similar reply, de Valera then saying that such plays damage the good name of Ireland. Yeats stood his ground, and was attacked bitterly by the popular press.

The second significant incident occurred in 1938 when the Board of the Theatre decided that plays in the Irish language should henceforth become a regular feature of the work of the Theatre. This, I hold, was a retrograde step artistically, however laudable from the patriotic point of view, since there happened to be no Gaelic-writing playwrights worth mentioning and most of the trained actors could not speak Gaelic. The result showed itself in 1942 when the Government again intervened to ask the Theatre to take over the work of an existing company of Gaelic players called 'An Comhar Drámuíochta' (The Drama Cooperative). After this, so far as I know, no junior players were employed unless they could speak Gaelic, an accomplishment which had as much to do with acting as if they could dance the *can-can*. I record this incident solely to give the reader my impression of the lowering of intellectual standards after Yeats.

Let us now try to define the precise effect on the arts. Fundamentally what had happened was that a social concept of the function of literature was beginning to replace the 'individualist' concept. Compare Yeats, taking him as representative of the first 25 years of the Anglo-Irish revival. Yeats had loved all art that was remote and uncommon, 'distinguished and lonely'. He had seen the element of nobility in the simplest people but he had never permitted his affection for familiar life to be confused with a preoccupation with the common or the popular. Thus, writing of the Theatre he had said:

> The modern author, if he be a man of genius, is a solitary, he does not know the everchanging public well enough to be its servant. He cannot learn their convention; they must learn his. All that is greatest in modern literature is soliloquy, or, at most, words addressed to a few friends.

This dislike of 'realism' had always been with him. He sought always to sublimate reality, and it was in that search for a dissolvent of the flesh that he had formed the distinction between character, that is, the social, public, moral thing, formed by and for the purposes of organised society, and personality, which is what appears in all the great moments of drama when this social, functional thing drops away and a man's spirit burns with the 'pure gem-like flame'. So, he had found inspiration in the ancient mind of his people, but it was not a political mind, or a social mind, but a mystical memory, linking man to those ages when life was still a unity, before he became fissured by rationalism and splintered by what we nowadays call psychological analysis.

One could easily demur at much of this. The theatre, after all, is the most sociable of all the arts. And, as I have indicated in my opening remarks, there was already too much of this withdrawal-from-life in the first period of the Irish Literary Movement. At any rate our new, ambitious, hardfaced democracy understood none of this aristocratic concept. It understood only 'realistic plays', political plays, representationalism, characterisation, explanations, social comedies and tragedies. It is to the credit of some Irish playwrights resident in Ireland that they took the risks of some sort of criticism and satire, and it is to the credit of the Abbey Theatre, even in its decline, that it staged some of these plays. But what we have had even of this 'some sort of criticism and satire' has been so feeble as to extinguish the value of the terms I have used ('realistic', 'political', 'representational', 'social') to describe the sort of plays the new public wanted. Because the new audiences did not really want any of those things; they wanted those things in an ersatz form: plays that merely gave the illusion of being political, realistic, social, critical, and so on. They were ready to laugh at plays dealing with the surface of things. They were not ready for plays that opposed what might be called, for short, the new synthetic orthodoxy, or at any rate diverged radically from it, let alone that denied it or rejected it. No social-realistic drama – whether comic or tragic – can thrive in this atmosphere. Mr Brendan Behan, for instance, whether good, bad or indifferent, could not have broken through in Dublin. He first had to break through in London or New York.

But there are even greater and deeper dangers in the writers' battle for honesty. The danger of becoming embittered, or twisted, threatens creativity itself, and here we come to the real battleground of contemporary Irish writing. For the first time Irish writers have had to *think* themselves into personal release. Disillusion is also a form of revelation. There is no longer any question of dishing up local colour. (The Noble Peasant is as dead as the Noble Savage. Poems about fairies and leprechauns, about misted lakes, old symbols of national longing, are over and done with.) We need to explore Irish life with an objectivity never hitherto applied to it – and in this Joyce rather than Yeats is our inspiration. But to see clearly is not to write passionately. An artist must, in some fashion, love his material, and his material must, in some fashion, cooperate with him. It is not enough for an artist to be clinically interested in life: he must take fire from it. This has been the great rub in Ireland for some 30 years. It is not confined to Ireland. Everywhere today, as I see it, literature is facing the same problem: How to transmute into permanent forms a life that one sees critically rather than lovingly.

If this really is an universal problem, why is it so? I think it is so because writers everywhere feel that life no longer has any sense of Pattern and Destination. The argosies set out. They forget why. To give the most naive example possible of Pattern and Destination: time was when novelists moved their men and women, with a sense of completion, towards a home and a family, in love and marriage. Countless is the number of novels and plays shaped about the thwarting of this journey. All the hypocrisy of the Victorian novel, its sentimental, evangelical piety, its evasiveness exposed itself in this 'Destination' which everybody knows today is only a starting point, another challenge, another problem. No writer dares to play this old tune today. The result is that men of genius have been writing as the matador kills bulls, by virtuosity or by savagery – Joyce, Hemingway, Anouilh, Aymé, Bazin, Julien Green, Mailer, all the writers of the *roman nouveau*; or they impose Pattern and Destination by sheer force. Lagerkvist by his symbolism. Mairaux by his mysticism, Sartre by his Existentialism, Bernanos, Greene, or Mauriac by their Catholicism, the later O'Casey by his Communism. One may be lost in admiration of this forcible handling of intractable material, though one does sometimes wonder whether humanity has not emerged from their work literally man-handled, moulded to shape, intellectualised, not men but puppets. The regionalists are in the happier position. Faulkner may still find Pattern and Destination about him, or imagine he can find it.

An Irish writer might expect to find old patterns persisting in his region also. But the dilemma has here taken a particularly sardonic form. My countrymen are so satisfied with their sentimental Pattern that they have no interest in Destination. Everything having been solved they have no further to go – except to Heaven. They are frustrated by the illusory completeness of their own conventions. The novel elsewhere may be frustrated by the certainties of men lost; here it is frustrated by the certainties of men saved. We read with an excited absorption the work of Catholic novelists elsewhere – that is, novelists who work within the frame of the struggle between God and the Devil, rather than the struggle of man with material evil or impersonal misfortune – and we observe that they deal with characters who are wilful, rebellious, passionate, arrogant, conscious, persistent, reckless men who put theology to the test of experience, either to uphold it or not as their experiences prompt. We turn, hopefully, to the potential material of Irish novels on the lines of Bernanos or Mauriac. We discover to our dismay that no error has been so great as the popular conception of the Irishman as rebellious, passionate, reckless, wilful, and so on. We are, in effect, very much in the same position as Hawthorne who just managed to squeeze one novel – and it is not really as fine a novel as the professors say; he lacked courage to push his concept of life to its end – out of equally unmalleable material, in a society where, also, sin was furtive, convention rigid, courage slight and honesty scant.

One of the most striking effects of all this on Irish letters in the period before us is the comparative failure of the modern Irish novel. If one were to exclude Joyce – which is like saying if one were to exclude Everest – and Liam O'Flaherty how little is left. We have, of course, plenty of honourable efforts (perhaps, I might suggest, like my own efforts) but of anything like top-notchers (Joyce's *Portrait* aside) how many others would the really serious critic want to put beside, say, Elizabeth Bowen's Irish novel *The Last September* or whichever one, two or three of O'Flaherty's he would choose for this test? My explanation for this I have already given – that Irish life in our period does not supply the *dramatis personae*, ready for the hard conflicts, the readiness to take anything *jusqu'au bout* in either full or at least some awareness of what is at stake, without which dramatic themes for the novel are missing. We produce spurts of spirit. They end in laughter (the great national vice and virtue) or exile.

This may be why, on the other hand, the short story has thriven in the meantime, and this is probably the best product of our period. The successes here have been so numerous that I need not even mention names. They have been wise to choose the smaller, yet revealing themes in the absence of the larger, more dramatic ones.

The Irish novelist who has been most persistent in mining for revolt and passion has been Liam O'Flaherty. He has found his passionate creatures in the west of Ireland and in the Revolution. His best-known novels *The Informer* (1925), *The Assassin* (1928), *The Martyr* (1932) are in the middle of our period. Each deals with the revolutionary upheaval, which was a godsend to all Irish writers until, as in the theatre, the vein became exhausted around 1932, ten years after the Revolution ended. In that year O'Flaherty wrote *The Puritan*, a study of the new Irish rigorism, and thereafter he chose, with one exception, which was a failure, historical subjects. It is most revealing that all of O'Flaherty's work is shot through by a wild romanticism – to put it crudely, the romanticism of the noble savage. He had to write in this way to gear himself and his characters to action. Since he is so much a Romantic one should not expect intellectual as well as emotional rewards from his work. I regret their absence – as I do in Hemingway: it is an equally pointless regret.

I think my reader will begin to realise the difficulties of writing in a country where the policeman and the priest are in a perpetual glow of satisfaction. He must, however, also see that, to a real extent, Irish novelists have failed to solve a problem. I will illustrate this problem by quoting the comment of an intelligent American critic on his first visit to Ireland. He said: 'This seems to be a very prosperous, comfortable, well-to-do country. We do not get that picture from your writers. Why not?' His comment was not wholly fair. He ignored Emigration, to make but one point, and other things that do not immediately strike the eye. Still, I have failed to present an intelligible picture of contemporary Irish society – acquisitive, bourgeois, unsophisticated, intellectually conservative and unadventurous, rigidly controlled on every side – if the answer to that 'Why not?' is not apparent. I will underline it only by pointing out that the change-over from a stratified society – ranging from aristocrat to outcast – to a one-class society, where there are not native aristocrats and no outcasts (except the writers?), and where the hard, traditional core is in a farming population, rarely induces a fertile awareness either among people or writers. And awareness in literature is an essential. Even before the Revolution Irish writers – Joyce, Shaw, Wilde, dozens besides – felt this, insofar as our awareness was then (as they saw it all going down the drain of politics and nationalism). They left Ireland for the more interesting life of the island next door. Unawareness itself is, it may be added, not a theme for any writer: it is a negative; it eliminates the element of self-conflict, which alone gives meaning to any theme.

One other obstacle, and of all perhaps the most difficult to surmount, has come between the Irish writer, whether poet, dramatist, or novelist, and his normal material in Irish life. It may be expressed in the words of the poet, Robert Greacen, in a poem significantly entitled *Written on the Sense of Isolation in Contemporary Ireland*. Having called up the 'unfettered great in heart and mind who gave no inch to fate' – Swift, Burke, Sheridan, Congreve, Goldsmith, Moore and Yeats – he says:

> Yet all of these the world for subject took
> And wed the fearless thesis to their book.

We are, it would seem, only just beginning to learn how to be, as Yeats was, European though nationalist. Hitherto, Irish writers, still tuning-in, as writers always do, to the intellectual stations of the world did so almost like men in an occupied country listening to forbidden voices. The writer who had the feel of the world rose, hitherto, from his grapevine, excited by the sense of the world, then turned to his page to write as he felt. . . . But with what? With whom? What characters would think and speak for him, in his poem, play, or novel? As I have said, the *dramatis personae* were otherwise engaged. Perhaps this is now changing?

I feel profoundly that Greacen's point has much to say about the last thirty years of Irish poetry. There is no loss of technical skill, if anything a far greater verbal sophistication has arrived in Irish poetry over the last 30 years than existed previously. There is no decline in receptiveness. The later work of Austin Clarke, Patrick Kavanagh, Padraic Fallon, Valentin Iremonger, Thomas Kinsella, Robert Farren, to name only a few, show poetry just as much on tiptoe, ready for flight, as it ever was. All that is lacking is not significant subject, but width of personal vision –and one rarely hears a modern idiom, a modern speech. The voltage of poetry (of any art) must do more than illuminate the local, or bring the barque of the mind happily home. Poetry is a lighthouse calling us to far seas. Clarke, for all his intense nationalism and smoored piety, often speaks with a far-echoing voice, as understandable to any part of the world as to us. I have always felt that Denis Devlin was a great loss to us: he wrote with a full response to the fullness of life everywhere. So, frequently, does Iremonger.

This need for a larger vision shows itself most poignantly in modern Irish poetry in the Irish language. Within my knowledge I am aware of only three Gaelic poets who are not utterly lost in the Gaelic mist, trying to extract ore from long-exhausted mines, symbols worn threadbare by the first phase of the Irish Literary Movement. Those three are Máire Mhac an tSaoi (now Mrs Conor Cruise O'Brien), Tomás Tóibín, but above all the Seán O'Riordáin of *Eireball Spideóige*, a delightfully fresh-minded poet irrespective of place or language. Here, again, it is not the subject or theme (as with the novelist) which is important; it is the freedom and scope of the imagination, dealing with any subject. For where the novelist is contained by character the poet is not – he is his own character, his own subject. This O'Riordáin has instinctively grasped and is thereby, liberated at once from the old trap of writing *about* Ireland.

The lesson of our time is that Irish writers cannot any longer go on writing about Ireland, or for Ireland, within the narrow confines of the traditional Irish life-concept; it is too slack, too cosy, too evasive, too intense. They must, or perish as regionalists, take, as writers everywhere do, the local (since they know its detail most intimately) and universalise it, as Joyce did – as Kavanagh can do it even when he is writing about a potato-field or O'Riordáin about a hospital-nurse. It is a matter of bravely and clearsightedly accepting the tensions of one's own being, or relentlessly challenging the life about one with their sharpest questions, of looking, then, far and wide, in time and place, for others who have been in some like conflict – a Stendhal, Balzac, Hawthorne, Forster, Joyce, Trollope, Yeats, Frost, Hardy, Lampedusa, Lorca, Cavafy, Zhivago, whoever it may be anywhere at any time who, one feels, might ironically sympathise – saying to them, 'That was how it seemed to you! Here is how it strikes me', and seize one's pen, *for them* and one's self.

Men of genius accelerate the processes of time for their country, *if* (which is a challenging, and often the most dismaying conjecture) they can cope with their country. The problem is up to the writers themselves. Nobody outside can help them; nobody inside will help them. They will not evade it by exile – Ibsen did not, and did not wish to. (He had other reasons for his exile.) Nobody need pity them either, since by the grace of God and the savagery of Oliver Cromwell their language is now the English language and if they have anything worth saying that they can say well, the periodicals and publishers of Britain and America are waiting for them with open arms and purses. If they feel that exile is absolutely necessary, they may, alone among the writers of the small countries of the world, emigrate freely. What they have to cope with either way is complex enough. But was there ever a writer whose life and work was plain sailing? Their main worry must be that their worst enemies are impalpable and insinuating self pity, bitterness, sentimentality, cynicism, their own unsophistication, barren rage, even their love of country, their love of friends (It was Ibsen who said that he had to leave Norway because friendship was too expensive: meaning that, for friendship's sake one refrained from saying things that should be said.) It is improper for any critic to probe into these struggles. They are delicate, intimate, and fearful.

Notes

1   Originally published as Sean O'Faolain, 'Fifty Years of Irish Writing', *Studies* vol. 51, no. 201 (spring, 1962), pp. 93–105.

CHAPTER 19

Inherited Dissent

The Dilemma of the Irish Writer

(1965, abridged)

Augustine Martin

This article appeared early in Augustine Martin's academic career; he subsequently became Professor of Anglo-Irish Literature at University College
Dublin, Artistic Director of the Abbey Theatre and a member of the Seanad.
He was an early champion of John McGahern and, as also illustrated below,
a trenchant critic of the overweening influence of Joyce and Yeats upon
emerging Irish writers. As editor of the leaving certificate anthology *Soundings*,
first published in 1969, he defined how poetry was taught for more than a
quarter of a century in Irish schools. *Soundings* was a bestseller when it was
republished in 2010. Martin contributed several articles on the intellectual
politics of Irish literature to *Studies*.[1]

The relations between the Irish artist and his society have been strained and
uneasy since our literature emerged from the nineteenth century. One could
make a nasty collection of comments from the writings of Irishmen, since, say,
the publication of George Moore's *The Untilled Field* in 1903, down to Mr
Austin Clarke's *Flight to Africa*, 60 years later. These comments would refer to
the apparent difficulty which the literary artist finds in living among and writing about his countrymen. For Joyce, Ireland was among other things the old
sow that ate her farrow; a country dedicated to the banishment of her artists.

This situation is sometimes puzzling to innocent students who can find no
case of an artist who was actually banished, and who are puzzled to find that
some of our most trenchant satirists occupy positions of public trust in Irish
society. Another collection might also be made, a great deal more massive

and amorphous than the first, illustrating the image of Ireland which such writers have projected down through the decades. This image of Irish society, promoted in fiction, drama and poetry would be found to be consistently unflattering; it would also be found that it had undergone very little essential change since the turn of the century. Raymond Mortimer, surely an alert observer, in reviewing the late Michael Farrell's *Thy Tears Might Cease* stated it thus:

> The best Irish writers of Farrell's generation (unless they were Protestants) believed that independence would remould their country nearer to their hearts' desire. Now they complain that it has become provincial, complacent and philistine – a waterlogged boat slowly sinking, in which the priest and the publican grow sleek, while the dwindling population seek to escape. Presumably they exaggerate, but what room is there for intellectuals in a society that bans their books?

This passage puts one side of the picture very neatly: the artist as a pariah, at odds with his smug, philistine society. In essentials it hardly differs from the image of Ireland put out by Joyce and Moore in the early years of the century. It is the picture of Ireland that continues to dominate our literature; unquestionably this is the sort of situation which the majority of literary foreigners expect to find in Ireland. As an image it is certainly as well established as the nineteenth-century image of the imbecilic peasant and hard-riding gentry which Croker, Lover and Lever had impressed on an overseas reading public, and which George Moore was so rightly anxious to discredit.

Now the universality, stamina and persistence of this twentieth-century 'waterlogged boat' image poses two allied questions. Firstly, is it a true image? Has the spirit of the nation stood still in a state of complacent and sluggish decay for all this time? Or alternatively, has the image itself become moribund? The writer has consistently chastised his society for being lifeless, inert and complacent. Is it possible that the writer may have himself fallen victim to these very vices in being satisfied with outmoded stereotypes of a society which has, in the meantime, shaken off its lethargy and moved forward unnoticed by its literary chroniclers. To pursue this second alternative a little further: there have been considerable and noticeable changes in both the temper and the pattern of Irish life, particularly since the war. In such areas as industry, housing, agriculture and education these changes have rapidly accelerated over the past ten years. Have any, or all of these social changes been reflected in contemporary Irish writing? And if they have not – as I believe they have not – Why?

This essay is an attempt to answer these questions, to examine the relationship that exists and has existed between the Irish writer and his society, to glance at some of the more urgent problems and difficulties that confront the young creative writer in Ireland today. And lest my position may be misunderstood in this land where secret novelists and poets are said to abound, I write not as a practitioner but as an onlooker, a reader, and a critic in a small way. From this point of vantage it appears to me that Irish writing has reached some sort of crossroads, a time demanding reappraisal and renewal and perhaps a greater degree of intellectual awareness than has been necessary for some years past. It is being said, for instance, by responsible commentators – e.g. Robin Skelton in *The Critical Quarterly* – that there is a revival of literature going on in Ireland today. If this is so, then the need for the sort of definition mentioned above is all the more urgent.

TRADITION AND ENVIRONMENT

The creative consciousness of a writer is normally under pressure from two forces: on the one hand there is the literary tradition which he has received from the past, remote or proximate, and on the other there is his environment, the society in which he lives and which must inevitably become his subject matter. Ideally both forces should cooperate: under the control of his own inspiration the tradition ought to furnish him with models, suggest technical possibilities, indicate areas of life and experience which he might explore; at the same time it ought not to come between him and the living scene which is in one way or another to be his material. This is ideally the case, but in practice the two forces do not always fuse profitably. Literary history is strewn with the corpses of talented writers who allowed an inherited mode or sensibility to blind them to the realities of their own age and place. At the end of great literary movements there is always this period of decline, when otherwise competent writers continue to work through a derived rather than an experienced sensibility.

It is easy to see the progressive decay in romantic sensibility from Tennyson through the pre-Raphaelites and the Decadents down to the Georgian lyricists. It is not merely a matter of semantic decadence – though it is in the gradual dislocation of word and meaning that it is most clearly manifest – it is a general process which involves the uncritical acceptance of second-hand imagery, symbols, postures, thought patterns, ideas – even opinions. When this condition sets in, the time has come to renew the creative apparatus, break with the immediate past or – at least take a more ruthlessly selective attitude towards it – seek more remote, less dominating models, and open up new areas of the mind and the landscape for exploration. Eliot did this for English poetry in the teens of the century and now he, in turn, has become part of the tradition. Young English poets are, at the moment, struggling to get free from his very powerful influence. We, in

Ireland, could perhaps afford to watch the process with amused detachment were it not for our own parallel and even more urgent predicament. In fact our own modest tradition has fallen under the immense and crippling shadows of Joyce and Yeats; and when two such giants throw their shade over a social landscape as small as Ireland's things are likely to get very difficult for the fledgling writer who is trying to bring that raw material into artistic focus.

THE INFLUENCE OF JOYCE AND YEATS

It would be difficult to exaggerate the influence of Joyce and Yeats on the young Irish aesthete of today. Having travelled the world their reputations have come back to Ireland to receive, in full, belated homage. Great effort has been put forth by the younger generations to see that justice be done to their vast achievements. The activities which now surround the Martello Tower, and the Sligo Summer School, while admirable in terms of piety, have served to intensify the influence exerted by both writers on the creative consciousness of an emerging generation. This influence manifests itself in various, subtle ways; in the works of younger writers their names keep recurring like pious invocations in the latest publications of Ewart Milne, Richard Weber, Basil Payne, James Liddy, Desmond O'Grady and Roy McFadden there are formal allusions to the works of Yeats and Joyce. One could also instance the proliferation of their more celebrated phrases – both on the literary pages and in the literary pubs – 'silence, exile and cunning', 'signatures of all things', 'the old sow that ate her farrow', 'forge in the smithy of my soul' and then Yeats's 'dog that praised its fleas', 'rocking the cradle of genius', 'words alone are certain good', 'the foul rag-and-bone-shop of the heart', 'call the muses home', 'a terrible beauty', 'no petty people'. When Brendan Behan died Roy McFadden, as if in an attempt to clinch my conviction in the matter, commemorated him with such lines as

> A broth of an Irish boy no doubt
> But, Joyce be with us, don't neglect
> The learning of the intellect. . .

This man, in fact, is now become a god. Surely Eliot has not got such a cultish grip on the younger English writers. A great deal of water has flowed under London Bridge since Anthony Blanche recited 'The Waste Land' from Sebastian's balcony!' But we are a small country, rather given to extremes of rejection or adulation, and we have received a good deal of flattery from abroad of late. The result is that these two great writers have become a pair of benevolent *incubi* for the young writer who is trying to find his feet.

If Joyce and Yeats were orthodox, typical writers, their influence might be a great deal more salutary: if like Wordsworth, Shakespeare or Thomas Mann they had absorbed and transfigured the pieties of their country's ethos into art, then their successors might have selected with greater ease from the many lessons bodied forth in their work. But, in different ways, both writers repudiated the social and religious pieties of Ireland, both were philosophical eccentrics, Joyce in particular, seeing Dublin as a 'centre of paralysis', deals destructively with his material and the vision of Ireland which he embodies is so grievously compelling that one is inclined to forget that it is so intensely personal and subjective. Two generations later this fierce personal vision is capable of coming between our eyes and the Irish scene – which has changed out of recognition since then – and even colouring our view of it. This is an example of a literary tradition becoming so strong as to impair the second factor – the dialogue between author and environment. The resulting tension in the mind of the Irish writer has been stressed by Benedict Kiely in his admirable survey, *Modern Irish Fiction*, where he writes:

> Irish literature and particularly the modern Irish novel is tugged this way and that now by the rejection that meant so much to Joyce, now by the acceptance that contains as a skin contains an apple in the stories of Daniel Corkery.

Here tradition and environment come together in one ineluctable, complex pressure on the novelist. Mr Kiely, no doubt, has not only seen the tension at work in the writings of others, but perhaps has had to control it within the rigorous equilibrium of his own excellent novels. It would be false and over dramatic to say that the Irish artist had to choose between two sharply divided, ready-made attitudes to his society, between rejection and acceptance; but the 'tug', however subconsciously, is still there. In his struggle for expression he must cope with this antecedent tension, and this tension will be one of the factors in determining his final attitude towards his material. Consequently the question is not whether he will be sympathetic or hostile to his society. The real question is whether his hostility or acceptance will be derived or experienced. Will it be the result of a highly fashionable traditional bias, or will it be the result of a hard personal confrontation with the realities of that society. Will it be literature nourishing itself on its own entrails, or literature drawing its sustenance from the springs of life?

It is only natural that a tug between Corkery and Joyce should result in a clear victory for Joyce. When Ernest Boyd set out to compare *The Portrait of the Artist as a Young Man* with *The Threshold of Quiet* he was really laying aside his critical judgement temporarily. It is not just that rejection is more attractive and dramatic than acceptance; it is simply that Irish fiction has had its James Joyce and still awaits its Thomas Mann. It is human to look around for someone to fill the role, and in 1922 it was natural to elect Corkery for the honour. Early last year (1964) a critic in *The Irish Times* cast Joseph Brady, author of *In Monavalla*, for the part. But the plain fact is that he does not measure up; and so far the forces of rejection are winning hands down – on sheet merit at that! They have been at work much longer than many of us care to admit, and the movement cannot be laid solely at the door of Joyce.

THE SOURCES OF DISAFFECTION

Thirteen years before Stephen Dedelaus pronounced his *non serviam* George Moore's alter ego, John Rodney in *The Untilled Field* had made his choice:

> He was leaving Ireland. On this point his mind was made up, . . . He had enough
> of a country where there had never been any sculpture nor any painting, nor any
> architecture to signify. They were talking about reviving the Gothic, but Rodney
> did not believe in their resurrection or in their renaissance, or in their anything . . .
> he was going . . . to where there was the joy of life, out of the damp, religious
> atmosphere in which nothing flourished but the religious vocation.

This stance of national and religious apostasy on the part of the Irish artist in the person of Moore/Rodney was rapidly reinforced by Moore's immediate successors. Yeats, Stephens, AE and, of course, Joyce expressed in different ways their distrust of Catholic Ireland as a centre of artistic energy. Yeats, Stephens and AE abandoned different forms of Protestantism for a more mystical religious concept, while Moore and Joyce left Catholicism for a religion of art. It would be impossible, and presumptuous to try to unravel or pronounce upon the individual subtleties of faith and dialectic which dictated these several defections. One point, however, might be noted – that each of them replaced his original faith with blends of the mystical and aesthetic. They seem to have been needled into apostasy by a Christianity which at that time, in both systems, appeared to be extremely philistine, anti-intellectual, disciplinarian and above all anti-mystical. It was Christianity smug in the dry complacency of nineteenth-century apologetics, suspicious of everything outside devotionalism and observance. It would take too long to establish the point by argument, but a quotation from Father Martin D'Arcy SJ (in his preface to the poems of *St John of The Cross*, translated by Roy Campbell) provides in dependent witness to the official frame of mind:

As is well known, many leading Protestant divines refused to give mysticism a place within the Christian faith, and for a period Catholic spiritual writers advocated a vigorous practice of the virtues in preference to what savoured of illuminism and quietism. In the last 50 years – he writes in 1951 – this open or veiled hostility has changed into a marked degree of appreciation.

This 'veiled hostility', prevalent in the Christian world at large, was if anything more intense in Ireland. And as the artistic impulse is essentially mystical it might explain the recoil of so many Irish artists. To some extent it might explain why so many obviously intelligent men turned enthusiastically to Madame Blavatsky's incredible cult of theosophy; it helps to explain the movement of Stephens, Yeats, Russell and others towards Celtic paganism. As Austin Clarke points out, three orthodox Christian authors of 'acceptance', Pearse, MacDonagh and Plunkett attempted to set up a counter-trend of Christian mysticism. But the minor nature of their talents and the finality of a British firing squad severely limited their influence. Younger writers were affected by a spirit which seems to have been almost inherent in the age: in his *Drums Under the Window* we find the young O'Casey reading Fraser and Darwin as if they were sacred books; later it was Marx – always it was the doctrinal catalyst of an antecedent dissent.

By now nearly all the greater builders of our tradition have been mentioned, and the balance has been heavily weighed in the direction of revolt and rejection. The image has been that of the artist as maverick, if not exactly pariah. It might fairly be said too that the cleavage between artist and average society has been a genuine, a spontaneous thing rather than a perverse cult of withdrawal. The standard of literature produced is guarantee enough that a solid impact between artist and material had been consistently made. Further evidence of this spontaneity is shown in the reaction of artistic Ireland to the Insurrection in 1916. Yeats, with that honesty which characterised his social attitudes, made a public confession of his previous blindness in a poem which became the finest existing tribute to his country's dead; Russell concurred; Stephens celebrated it in two passionate books; O'Casey saluted it in one splendid play – the rest were excused by death or exile.

In fact the teens of the century promised greatly, producing a steady upsurge of positive writing. Corkery, Padraic Colum and that now neglected fiction writer Seamus O'Kelly were taking up the torch from a tradition which had been predominantly Anglo-Irish and Protestant, and the dialogue between sow and farrow began to lose much of its acrimony. But abruptly the kissing had again to stop. The ugly horror of the Civil War broke in and the quarrel was renewed. When the smoke settled the air was heavy with disillusion. The dominating figures of O'Flaherty, O'Connor, O'Faolain who had shared the dream of a free and beautiful Ireland made no secret of their disappointment that – in Mr Kiely's phrase – 'the birth of a terrible beauty in 1916 ended only in the establishment of a grocer's republic.' Ironically O'Connor and O'Faolain began as pupils of Corkery; but being sincere and original writers they absorbed from him all that was consistent with their own visions and then went their own ways. Austin Clarke, once a dutiful son of the same cultural matrix, returned from England in the 1930s and lamented over a land:

> . . . where every woman's son
> Must carry his own coffin and believe
> In dread, all that the clergy teach the young.

It may be significant also that while his two brilliant pupils dominated the 1930s with fiction and controversy, the old master, Corkery, lapsed into silence – his only contribution to the decade being in 1939, *Earth out of Earth*, his final book.

This 'echo of learned controversy' obscured somewhat the merits of two considerable novelists who emerged in the early years of the decade, Kate O'Brien and Francis MacManus. It was a pity, because both of them reflected a calm contemplative relationship with their material. If we except Miss O'Brien's one impatient swipe at the newly formed censorship board, we can see them both as novelists of 'acceptance' in the healthiest possible sense. Both showed a deep penetrating understanding of the society they depicted, its social standards, its religious leaven, and both succeeded in exposing it to the roots with a relentless, yet placid, objectivity. In most other respects they were and are utterly different writers, though they share the unjust neglect of their countrymen. Yet the attitude of disinterested contemplation, free from either enthusiasm or bitterness – surely the ideal state for the realistic artist – bore fruit in the 1940s when a post-revolutionary, post-civil-war generation had come of age. They were jointed by Mary Lavin – for whose pen a 'grocer's republic' might have been specifically invented – Michael MacLaverty and later Benedict Kiely; all of whom found a calm exploratory attitude to Ireland quite natural. In their work there was no dramatic hostility, no sharp sense of disillusion nor, on the other hand, no wild doctrinaire enthusiasm. Bryan McMahon's celebration emerges organically from a folk tradition in which he had steeped himself, and on the other side of the coin Patrick Kavanagh's harsh, affectionate, implacable investigations in *Tarry Flynn* and *The Great Hunger* came direct from life as it was lived, owed nothing to bookish pre-suppositions. Even the satirists, Mervyn Wall and Flann O'Brien, exhibited a spirit of delightful liberty. Wall's brilliant and self-mocking anticlericalism had nothing of

Joyce's or Clarke's fierce, bitter involvement; O'Brien made it a point to mock at Joyce, and at all that was pompous and pretentious in his cult.

The only two considerable figures of the 1950s, James Plunkett and Thomas Kinsella spoke with clear, individual voices; and they might be seen as forerunners of the present 'movement' which we alluded to at the outset. But it is only fair to stipulate that while the movement may break down, or be found not to exist, both these writers have staked indisputable claims to distinction, and that much of our hope for the future of Irish writing is centred on them both.

This has been a rapid and rather crude survey of the modern Irish tradition, carried out as a search for a single theme – the writer's relationship to his country, and implicitly his attitude towards his tradition. It has roughly demonstrated that *in fact* there is no question of a consistent, monolithic attitude; that different men and different generations have reacted individually, differently: that the movement has been broadly from rejection to enthusiastic acceptance, back to disillusioned rejection, back to calm detached acceptance, down to the present time.

THE HARDENING 'CLICHÉ'

But while the scene has varied in detail, the more spectacular figures form a near-continuous line of dissent down through the half century: Moore, Joyce, O'Connor, O'Casey and, most significantly, Austin Clarke whose influence on the present is incalculably powerful. Furthermore, these dissentient writers have been so influential that they have conveyed the *impression* of a monolithic attitude. Because the most vocal of our writers have been dissentient and distrustful of Irish values it has been assumed, both at home and abroad, that all sensitive Irish artists feel the same. The image of which we have spoken has formed and the tendency has been to read Irish literature in the light of the image, often importing ideas and ascribing prejudices where they have no relevance or meaning.

A recent example will serve to show how intelligent readers can fall victim to this error. When John McGahern's brilliant first novel *The Barracks* was reviewed in an English Sunday paper, the critic immediately assumed that the author implied a hostile comment on rural Irish life. It is an erroneous assumption, for there is no writer – with the possible exception of MacManus – more free from didacticism than McGahern. This would be insignificant, however, if it were not for the manner in which the reviewer seized on one detail in the book to clinch his point. In describing the scene around the village church the author mentions an authentic detail – rosary beads twined round the church railings. As every Irishman can tell the beads are lost property which have been picked up off the ground and displayed where their owners may find them. But the reviewer, apparently mistaking the custom for a superstitious rite, wonders sadly what one can do for people who piously twine rosaries round railings. The reader in this case has fallen victim to a *cliché*, because the vision of Ireland which the misreading implies is the result of a powerful and relentless *cliché*. He has seen something in an Irish novel which was not there; he has mistaken Mr McGahern who was born in 1935 for Mr O'Connor who was born in 1902.

It has become firmly established in the majority of literate minds that Ireland is a backward, insanitary, inert, despairing country; a people priest ridden and superstitious, which despises its artists and intellectuals, treats its autocratic, avaricious and crafty clergy with a sanctimonious servility; a people soaked in dreams and booze, fixated backwards on the events of Easter Week 1916, blind to the meaning of the present and the future, without economic hope, helpless in the face of emigration, ignorant of the facts of life, overcome with a Jansenistic fear of sex and the body, bemused with the opium of past splendours – yet in spite of it all, a people friendly, poetic, with a certain gentle unreliable charm. This set of traits cannot be ascribed to the pages of any one writer: they are the cumulative end-product of half a century of writing which was by turns hostile, embittered and penetrating [. . .].

Notes

1   Originally published as Augustine Martin, 'Inherited Dissent: The Dilemma of the Irish Writer', *Studies* vol. 54, no. 213 (spring, 1965), pp. 1–20.

CHAPTER 20

Pluralism and Northern Ireland (1978)

John Brady SJ

John Brady argued that there was a need to modify those aspects of law and public administration that seemed to give the State a markedly Catholic character. A carefully framed divorce law would, he argued, be for the common good. The Irish prohibition on the sale of contraceptives in the wake of the 1973 McGee ruling was described as 'bizarre'. Brady argued that to abstain completely from all efforts to influence the decisions of mixed marriages – the abandonment of Ne Temere – would be 'an appropriate gesture'. He also made the case for inter-denominational schooling in the North. Various companion articles in the same issue of *Studies* also made similar arguments. The author at the time of publication was Director of the College of Industrial Relations.[1]

There are two principal reasons why a discussion of pluralism in Ireland is important at the present time. It is relevant to the sense of contentment and well being of the citizens of the Republic, and to the wise administration of the State. Secondly, it could be helpful towards a resolution of the Northern Ireland problem. Regarding the evolution of the Republic, it would appear that for the foreseeable future there will be a greater diversity of beliefs, moral judgements, attitudes and behaviour patterns than was the case in the past, and a more open expression of this diversity. There is more diversity within the Catholic Church in the aftermath of the Second Vatican Council. The other Christian Churches have some distinctive viewpoints and values, again more openly expressed than was formerly the case. There are adherents of other religions to be considered. Agnostics and atheists may object that the State is too overtly Christian in its Constitution and laws. The evolution of Irish society would appear to require that a more conscious pluralism be developed both in attitudes and habits of thought, and also in legal and administrative structures. There is a danger of some loss of values which have been a traditional feature of Irish society. There is also the possibility of gain in a more mature acceptance of responsibility in the conduct of one's personal life, and in social unity based on reconciliation and mutual acceptance of diverse but sincerely held positions. The general direction in which Irish society hopefully might evolve would be towards a greater sensitivity on the viewpoints and needs of minorities, while retaining the distinctive quality of life which is ultimately based on a high level of Christian belief and practice.

The relationship of pluralism to the Northern Ireland problem is a debatable and hypothetical one. The relationship is debatable because it is held by some that Northern Unionists are not really interested in what happens in the Republic, but only in maintaining their own position. On the other hand, the extent to which the Republic is a mirror image of Northern Ireland must be of concern to anyone who thinks some form of unity is the long-term solution. Genuine dialogue with Northern Unionists would help clarify the issues. Northern Unionists assert that there is much about the Republic which they dislike and find alienating. It is necessary to look at the expression of these dislikes and fears and examine to what extent they represent a genuine divergence of viewpoint from our own which ought to be met. In many ways, some manifest and some less obvious, the evolution of the social fabric of the Republic has reflected the views and attitudes of the 95 per cent Catholic majority.[2] If we seriously believe that some form of link between the two parts of Ireland could be the long-term answer to the problem then we should start running our society as if there was a 25 per cent Protestant minority to be taken into account. This would be a very worthwhile exercise for its own sake and would help to focus thought on areas where the standpoint of the civil legislator ought to be different from that of the Catholic Church leader. Secondly, it might over time bring a constructive response from Unionist leaders in Northern Ireland, and create a situation where some form of link could be openly discussed.

Although this may seem at present a remote possibility, the reasons why it is of importance are worth stating. Ten years after the beginning of the disturbances there is no sign of any genuine and lasting peace coming to Northern Ireland. Violence is on the decrease, but the social and political causes out of which it came still remain. It is very doubtful if Northern Ireland can attain a permanent peace within the United Kingdom. The people of Britain no longer have the rather tenuous sense of common identity with the people of Northern Ireland which they may have once had. A psychological barrier has come down between Northern Ireland and Britain; the people of Britain are tired of that troublesome and alien place beyond the Irish sea, where people have attitudes quite incomprehensible to their own way of thinking. They do not want to know any more and wish the problem would go away. That this is so can be inferred from private conversations, discussion or the lack of it in the media, and even from the level of interest in parliamentary debates on Northern Ireland affairs. While there may be no actual demand in Britain that Northern Ireland cease to be part of the United Kingdom, the level of apathy and indifference is a very poor basis for a long-term political settlement.

Secondly, Northern Ireland has still not escaped from a political impasse in which a majority try to manipulate the instruments of democracy so as to maintain permanent control within their own hands. The point that the minority has enough power to refuse to be manipulated has not been grasped. Hence political life remains abnormal and sterile. Northern Ireland continues to be a politically neurotic society, one in which the principal and perennial object of discussion is how political life is to be organised and constitutionally channelled. This is an enormous waste of energy and a diversion from the normal tasks of politics in achieving economic and social progress. There would be a great liberation for the people of Northern Ireland if they could achieve a political order which would be acceptable to all sectors of the population and would free energies for creative purposes. It is very doubtful if this can be attained within Northern Ireland alone without reference to the rest of the island.

THE PROBLEM OF IDENTITY

The underlying problem is that the Northern Ireland Unionist or Loyalist is defining his identity in a way that is deeply divisive. In thinking of himself as British and Protestant, he excludes any possibility of identification with members of the other tradition in Northern Ireland who think of themselves as Irish and Catholic. In as much as he insists that the political structure must reflect closely his own concept of self-identity, he guarantees the continuation of a deeply divided society, fraught with tension. If you define your vital interests in a way that another party with whom you have to deal finds oppressive and objectionable, then you have the classic conflict situation, the human predicament, in which each side struggles for what it regards as its rights. The only way out is to pause and re-define your vital interests. In the present case this would involve the Northern Irish Unionist or Loyalist coming to think of himself as primarily Irish, although belonging to a distinctive tradition in the island which differs markedly from the majority Nationalist and Catholic tradition. This distinctive tradition requires a separate political structure with a high degree of autonomy. It does not have to exclude a link with the rest of the island based on a mutual acceptance of common interests, and it does not have to exclude a full participation on terms of equality of the Northern Nationalist and Catholic in both the affairs of an autonomous Northern region and of the whole island.

There are in fact many thoughtful Northern Unionists and Loyalists who have come to an awareness of this need, and are in the process of redefining their self-identity in terms of a distinctive Irishness. They will admit in private discussion that some form of unity in the island is the long-term answer. Perhaps the time will soon come when the question of what political links might be acceptable can be discussed openly. What citizens of the Republic can do in the meantime is to make it clear that we do not wish to govern Northern Ireland against the wishes of a majority of its people, but that we would welcome a federal link of a loose kind which would be an expression of common Irish identity while preserving the distinctive traditions of both parts of the island.[3] As an earnest of our seriousness about this we should modify those aspects of law and public administration which may seem to give the State a markedly Catholic character. We should try to show in practice that we do not regard 'Irish' and 'Catholic' as somehow almost synonymous, but that we have a broader concept of Irishness which includes and welcomes the Irish Protestant tradition in both its Northern and Southern forms. Such an effort is bound to be a gradual and time-consuming process, requiring extended reflection and debate within the Republic, and some willingness on the part of politicians to lead and guide public opinion in sensitive areas. The idea that such changes as might need to be made can be considered in the context of some future conference at which the Republic, Northern Ireland and Britain would be represented is not realistic. There are several important areas of discussion which touch on human rights, and which should in no way be seen as part of a negotiation process. The correct stance is that either we demonstrate willingness to change unilaterally, or, if we do not want to change in some area which is important to Northern Unionists, we make a clear statement that a diversity of practice between North and South would be acceptable, and that no effort would be made to impose uniformity in the event of a federal link between the two parts of the country.

It is remarkable that ten years after the conflict in Northern Ireland began there are no guarantees to the people of Northern Ireland given by the Republic on the record, apart from the guarantee about the status of Northern Ireland being changed only by majority consent given at Sunningdale. If a Unionist were to consider voting for a federal link with the Republic for the sake of peace in the island, there are many issues of importance about which he is completely in the dark. Would the marriage law of the Republic apply to Northern Ireland. He does not know. Would his children need Irish in order to apply for a public position, or would article 8 (3) of the Irish

Constitution be applied to make English the exclusive official language in Northern Ireland. No one has bothered to tell him. Would compulsory redistribution of land take place in Northern Ireland, or would security of tenure in land ownership be guaranteed. Again, no reassurance has been given, despite the well-identified conscious or subconscious fears of the planter stock in Northern Ireland. When one considers the lack of any guarantees from the Republic, combined with the obviously careful and deliberate refraining on the part of British governments from giving any guarantees of continued economic support over a lengthy transition period should the people of Northern Ireland decide to change their status, one sees that the people of Northern Ireland may choose between things as they are or the void. The notion of the people of Northern Ireland having a choice about their status turns out to be a mindless application of the idea of democracy to a case in which the substance of a democratic choice does not exist. The substance of a democratic choice does not exist because neither Government has elaborated the elements of a genuine proposal. The ambiguity of Britain's position is very obvious. To create a high degree of economic dependence and offer no alternative to it once the political link is altered, is in effect to take away freedom of choice. The ambiguity of the Irish Government's position is also striking. To advocate political unity as a solution while having no firm proposals on a wide range of matters of concern to Northern Unionists is to be less than serious about the nature of possible political and administrative links between the two parts of the island. There is also the question of the general ethos to be sought for in a federal Ireland and how both parts of Ireland might evolve towards it. The need for a conscious search for pluralism is of course much more urgent in Northern Ireland than the Republic. One wonders, for example, does it ever occur to Unionist politicians that when they go out of their way to speak of the Republic as a 'foreign' country, they not only sound ridiculous, but also deliver a scarcely concealed insult to their fellow Ulstermen of Nationalist tradition, by implicitly telling them that they are foreigners in their own country? The need for thoughtful Northern Unionists to seek for a pluralist understanding of their own position and that of the Nationalist minority and to make an adequate political response to the present situation is very urgent. The 60 million people in these islands who want a solution to the Northern Ireland problem have some rights to have their view considered, and cannot be kept waiting much longer. A response is needed from the Republic also, one of evolving its own internal ethos in such a way that a federal link with Northern Ireland would become possible, and present less difficulties and fears in the mind of the Northern Unionist. Let us look at some of the areas in which a response might be made.

CHURCH AND STATE

The general issue of Church-State relations underlies most specific questions in which evolution is needed. It is not particularly helpful to talk vaguely about the separation of Church and State, and anyone who uses this expression ought to specify what he means. In the Soviet Union the separation of Church and State means the total exclusion of the Churches from all involvement in education, provision of social services and health care, and cultural life. In the United States it has led to serious and unwarranted difficulties for Catholic schools through the denial of state financial support. The characteristically Irish development of Church-State relations has combined a juridical separation with a wide exercise of the principle of subsidiarity, the support of the State for Church-run schools, hospitals, and social services. This has applied both in the Republic and in Northern Ireland, and much good has come from it, in fact it is arguable that the level of social provision achieved in this way has been much higher than it could otherwise have been with the resources available. This tradition can be maintained and developed while seeking a more pluralist society by having a greater diversity in the types of institutions through which social provision is achieved. Regarding matters of law, the arguments put forward by Fr Gabriel Daly, Louis McRedmond and Mary Redmond underline the point that the post-Vatican II position of the Roman Catholic Church is that a full correspondence between Catholic moral teaching and the law of the land is neither necessary nor very desirable. The Church is a free society and should not seek, directly or indirectly, to enforce its own moral view by coercive law. The Catholic hierarchy are on record as stating this position very clearly.[4] There seems to be a reluctance on the part of politicians and political commentators to accept that they mean what they say, but it should be presumed that they do. There are areas where legal reform is badly needed, but where it has been put off on account of the sensitivity of the issues, and the matters of conscience involved. Politicians ought to take their courage in their hands, and seek for a consensus among the three major parties as to what ought to be done. Then they should propose the agreed changes to the people, stating the reasons in detail. The Irish people are very mature politically, and if the major parties unite in putting a well reasoned case to them they are likely to accept. If a referendum was required, an agreed proposal would be likely to be passed. The experience with the amendment of Article 44 certainly suggests this strongly. One feels that the difficulties of making changes are often overstated perhaps as an excuse for putting off action in difficult matters. It is always so easy to blame the bishops.

Obviously the whole area of marriage law is the major area which needs attention. The combination of outdated law and evolving social trends has left a situation which can fairly be described as an unholy mess. If it is accepted that this state of affairs is the kind of situation one starts out from, and not some model situation which really would be best left as it is, it might be easier to get agreement on changes. The bizarre position which persists concerning the law controlling contraceptives in the aftermath of the *McGee* case is well known and has been adequately treated in a previous issue of *Studies*.[5] Marital breakdown is an increasing feature of Irish life, and neither Church nor State can cope with it properly. There is a fundamental ambivalence about the attitude of both Church and State to marriage. In a country which has no divorce procedure of either Church or State there should be strict requirements for entry into marriage; it might well appear that in fact no one should be allowed to marry before the age of 23, as this is the average age at which full emotional maturity is attained. Marriage before this age is distinctly hazardous, and the likelihood of breakdown is considerable. Yet young people are allowed to enter into marriages which are ill advised, and left stranded in a marital no man's land when the inevitable breakdowns come. There is not likely to be much support for a strict stand against premature and ill-advised marriages, and in any event it would not be a complete answer to the problem. Marriage counsellors regularly meet cases where both parties have tried in good faith to make a marriage work, yet total and irreversible breakdown occurs. There are other cases of marital infidelity and desertion which amount also to a definite breakdown.

The civil legislator, contemplating the Roman Catholic Church's position on divorce, the views of the Protestant Churches which allow for private conscience in the matter, and an agnostic position, has reasonable grounds for the view that a carefully framed divorce law would be for the common good. It should not make divorce easy but it should make it possible as a last resort, where definitive marital breakdown is proven. The argument that this would have bad social consequences is of dubious value. Consequential morality is almost always bad morality. It is almost always wrong to sacrifice the good of human persons in need to some vague notion of the general good. It is not clear, to say the least, how insisting that someone who has experienced definitive marital breakdown by the age of 26 must remain alone for the rest of life advances or safeguards the common good.

If a divorce law were to be introduced it should be done in the context of a comprehensive reform of marriage law which would establish the status and rights of each partner in a manner compatible with the best of modern thinking. This would be a vast task, yet one of the greatest importance for the future welfare of society. A great deal of human misery is caused by the morass of outdated, inadequate and confused marriage law which bedevils anyone who has the misfortune to get into marital difficulties. This thoroughgoing reform of marriage law is one of the urgent needs in the search for a pluralist society, and the viewpoint of the civil legislator should be quite distinct from that of the Church leader.

The question of mixed marriages requires an initiative from the Roman Catholic Church as part of its commitment to a pluralist society. The discouragement of marriages between Protestants and Catholic by all the Churches was one of the reasons why the planter stock in Ulster never assimilated with the native Irish, in contradistinction to previous settlement patterns. This constitutes a specifically Church responsibility for the recurring tension and strife in Northern Ireland. Roman Catholic insistence on the children of mixed marriages being brought up as Catholics has accelerated the decline of Protestant numbers in the Republic, which in turn has added to Northern suspicion of the Republic. A magnanimous gesture is called for. It is necessary to balance the social and political welfare of the whole people of Ireland and the achievement of a Christian social order against the religious merits of a fairly small number of people being brought up as Catholics rather than Protestants. The appropriate gesture is to abstain completely from all efforts to influence the decision of parents of mixed marriages as to which tradition they will rear their children in, and to leave the matter entirely to their own conscience. The view which is sometimes put forward that the Catholic Church is obliged by a command of Christ to insist that children of mixed marriages be brought up as Catholics is not well founded theologically, especially in the light of the Decree on Ecumenism of Vatican II. The other Christian Churches are there recognised as having in themselves the means of salvation, even if not the fullness of these means, and their members as Christians and brothers in the Lord. In these Churches the command of Christ that men be baptised and have the Gospel preached to them is fulfilled. It is theologically sound and reasonable to take the view that where grave reasons exist it could be the right course to refrain from asking for any undertakings in mixed marriages and to leave the outcome in God's hands. These grave reasons exist in Ireland. The conflict situation in Northern Ireland is a scandal to the whole world, in the fullest biblical sense of that term, some thing that keeps men from making the commitment of faith. Protestant spokesmen have said repeatedly that in this matter a generous stance by the Catholic Church would be an important contribution to reducing tension and mistrust. This gesture is of symbolic importance and should be made.

EDUCATION AND PLURALISM

Another area in which an initiative is called for is inter-denominational education. The theme of education and pluralism is discussed in detail by Fr

Paul Andrews in his article.[6] Suffice to note here that there is a recommendation about inter-denominational education in the Report on Violence in Ireland prepared by a Working Party set up by the Irish Council of Churches/Roman Catholic Church Joint Group on Social Questions.[7] The recommendation is that the Churches should promote pilot schemes and research projects to find effective ways of bringing together Protestant and Catholic young people at school level. This recommendation should be put into effect, chiefly where it matters most, in Northern Ireland, but also in the Republic. There are no insuperable difficulties about educating Catholic and Protestant children in the same school and examples of this can be found both in the history of Irish education and in current practice. In the circumstances of Northern Ireland the putting into practice of the idea would require a deliberate and comprehensive effort not to make education a medium for imposing the culture, values, sense of history and tradition of the majority on the minority or *vice versa*, but to seek an impartial and ecumenical stance in all these areas. The teaching of religion could be carried out in separate class groups, but the situation justifies some pilot work in the ecumenical teaching of religion, that is to say, teaching Catholics and Protestants together from the same text books which are written from an ecumenical standpoint of respect for each tradition, and which explain the divergences in understanding and the common Christian heritage.

There are three reasons why some boldness in this area is called for and required. Catholics and Protestants do not mix enough socially in Northern Ireland, and this is part of the total problem. Socialising at school age would help to break down the barriers between the communities. The O'Donnell research showed that there are marked differences between the real and assumed stereotypes that the Catholics and Protestants of Northern Ireland have of each other, and that these stereotypes are acquired mainly from parental and traditional sources.[8] Inter-denominational education could be a means to reduce these stereotypes, and hence the patterns of behaviour which flow from them.

Secondly, the MacGréil research produced some significant results bearing on the issue. To the question 'Do you agree or disagree that the position and influence of the Catholic Church in the Republic of Ireland is a real obstacle to Irish unity?', 41 per cent of Dubliners answered affirmatively, and this included a majority of those under 30 years of age, of males, of those with university education and of those with the highest socio-economic occupational status. To the question 'In your opinion have separate Catholic and Protestant Schools (Primary and Secondary schools) been a major cause of division in the Northern Irish Community?', 61 per cent of respondents replied affirmatively. There was little variation between the opinions of Roman Catholics and of the major Protestant denominations on the issue. Fr

MacGréil comments that this is a case where it appears that the Church is associated with a disintegrative role in society, and that such an image has a high potential for alienation from the Church, if not from religion.[9]

These results should suggest to the reflective Catholic Church leader that a response is called for from the Catholic Church in Ireland *vis-a-vis* the Northern Ireland situation. The needed response is a demonstration that the Catholic Church is prepared to pursue its legitimate interests in education through participative structures, at least in some instances and on an experimental basis. Over time experience will be gained on what forms of participative structures are satisfactory in ensuring that the religious and moral upbringing of children is safeguarded. The very strong parental and traditional influences that prevail in Ireland, and especially in Northern Ireland, give grounds for thinking that no undue risks would be taken with the faith formation of the children of the present and the future. There is a witness value in the Catholic and Protestant Churches collaborating in the education of children which could be helpful in the Northern Ireland context. There is no need to think in terms of dismantling the existing school systems. There are new situations arising frequently from urban growth requiring new schools, and some at least of these could be inter-denominational, with Catholic and Protestant representation on the management board, and with a mixed staff. By collaborating in this way the Churches would be saying in deeds rather than words that they do not wish to perpetuate the divisive social structures of Northern Ireland.

The third reason why boldness is called for relates to the nature of the ultimate solution to the Northern Ireland problem. That solution must include the Protestant and Unionist population abandoning the concept of safeguarding its vital interests by exercising a monopoly of political, economic and social control in Northern Ireland. It is that quest for monopoly control which is the root evil of Northern Ireland, as it is a concept which is totally unacceptable in the late twentieth century. The Protestant people of Northern Ireland have paid a high price in terms of human suffering for their unacceptable modes of political thought. So has the Catholic population and all the people of these islands have had to bear a heavy burden of lost opportunity. In place of that unacceptable and divisive concept, there has to be created a political society in which vital interests are safeguarded by constitutional rights and a participative political structure. The ultimate test of a new political order would be that it would not make any difference whether there was a majority or a minority of Protestants in Northern Ireland, precisely because the guaranteeing of vital interests and rights would be completely divorced from the counting of heads. To get such a radical switch of political thinking will be very difficult, but it is absolutely necessary for ultimate peace. A political order which is a calculated and sustained insult to one third of those who live under it is no basis for peace. In biblical terms, a society divided against it self cannot stand; the Protestant people of Northern Ireland, like the people of Jerusalem over whom Christ wept, do not know the things that are for their peace. To get peace, it is necessary to lose one's life in order to find it, to let go of an outdated and disastrous political means to safeguard vital interests, and to seek them in a new way which is non-divisive and based on equality of rights under a constitution designed to enable people with fundamentally different aspirations to live peacefully together.

Granted the difficulty of such a change of political outlook, any witness that the Catholic Church can give that it does not regard control as the only way to safeguard its own vital interests is important. Northern Protestants tend to look at the Catholic Church as exercising a kind of control in the Republic which is the counterpart of the control they themselves exercise over many aspects of life in Northern Ireland. The comparison is far from exact, but there is a need for counter-witness to it. Participation in shared and ecumenically based activities is the best counter-witness, and education is the major area offering opportunities for it.

It is necessary to have a vision of the long-term answer no matter how difficult it may seem to be to attain it. The Swiss experience is an interesting case in point. Switzerland has cultural differences far more pronounced than anything found in Ireland, and the distribution of Catholics and Protestants has a marked territorial basis; people still talk openly of Protestant and Catholic cantons. There is a history of religious tension in Switzerland lasting down into the early twentieth century. Yet because of a good federal constitution it is possible today for this most diverse and pluralist nation to live peacefully and to be among the best run countries in the world, and the most successful economically and socially. It has been possible over the past 20 years to make the transition from having an overall Protestant majority to having an overall Catholic majority without a ripple of tension, because no one needed to feel threatened in any way by the transition. The most useful thing that could be done at the present juncture in Northern Ireland would be to send all the leading politicians to Switzerland for three months to study in depth the working of Swiss political institutions, and to observe Swiss society. It might just generate a vision of what Ireland could be like, and enable a break to be made with the truly dreadful sterility of political life in Northern Ireland.

CONCLUSION

Finally, it is important that those of us in the Republic who like the people of Northern Ireland, and who genuinely would welcome an all Ireland dimension to economic, social and political life, should say so frequently. It has been asserted fairly regularly by British journalists in recent years that they have detected that there is no real desire for Irish unity, a fear of involvement with Northern Ireland, and a dislike of Northerners among citizens of the Republic. That such attitudes exist cannot be denied. Ireland has never lacked men and women who put their short-sighted self interest and the desire for a quiet life before the long-term welfare of all the people of the island. However, they are not representative and Irish history has not in its decisive moments been made by them. There are also those who would welcome a link between North and South, and who would have an open attitude of mind towards the necessary adjustment.[10] There are those who like Northerners of both traditions, who admire their intelligence, their dry humour, their candour and capacity for hard work. When one has accepted the notion of cultural pluralism, which Professor Liam de Paor treats in his article, as an enriching thing, it becomes possible to enjoy differences and not to fear them.[11] One can accept the people of Northern Ireland as they are, while longing to see them liberated from an endemic conflict situation, so that they can find their true selves. From this liberation could spring a great upsurge of creative energies, not only in Northern Ireland but in the whole island, as the transition is made to a lasting peace based on a just and generally accepted political order. If these essays on pluralism help even a little towards the emergence of that new stage in Irish history the contributors will feel that the work of writing them was most worthwhile.

Notes

1   Originally published as John Brady SJ, 'Pluralism and Northern Ireland', *Studies* vol. 67, no. 265–6 (spring, 1978), pp. 88–99.

2   A fair-minded treatment of the experience of the Protestant community in the Republic may be found in Jack White, *Minority Report* (Dublin, 1975).

3   Cf. Address by Dr Garret FitzGerald TD, then Minister for Foreign Affairs, to the International Consultation Mixed Marriage held by the Irish School of Ecumenics in Dublin, September 1974; published in Michael Hurley (ed.), *Beyond Tolerance* (London, 1975), pp. 188–193.

4   The call for serious public debate about the impact on society of proposed changes of law, which was made in this statement, deserves a better response than it has got. The clear distinction between a clerical contribution to such a debate, and the propounding of Catholic moral doctrine, needs to be kept in view. cf. Statement on Public Morality issued following the meeting of the Irish Catholic Bishops' Conference at Maynooth, 14–16 June 1976; reproduced in *The Furrow* (July, 1976), pp. 444–5.

5   James O'Reilly, 'Marital Privacy and Family Law', *Studies* vol. 66, no. 261 (spring, 1977), pp. 8–24. Cf. also William Binchy, 'A Reply to Mr O'Reilly', *Studies* vol. 66, no. 264 (winter, 1977), pp. 330–5.

6   *Violence in Ireland, A Report to the Churches*, (Dublin and Belfast, 1976), pp. 86–7.

7   A useful pilot project in the teaching of religion has been initiated by the Department of Education, New University of Ulster, Coleraine, under the direction of Dr John Greer. Protestant and Roman Catholic teachers cooperated in producing curriculum material with an ecumenical dimension, suitable for use in both Catholic and Protestant schools. The trial use of the material produced encouraging results. The project could be developed further, but is currently at a standstill due to lack of funds.

8   E. E. O'Donnell, *Northern Irish Stereotypes* (Dublin, 1977), pp. 147–66.

9   Michael MacGréil, *Prejudice and Tolerance in Ireland* (Dublin, 1977), pp. 385–7.

10 Ibid., p. 378. A 64 per cent majority of respondents regarded the political unity of Ireland as desirable, and 54 per cent would find a federal solution acceptable or desirable.

11 One of several articles on pluralism and Northern Ireland contained in the same themed issue, Liam de Paor, 'Cultural Pluralism', *Studies* vol. 67, no. 265–6 (spring, 1978), pp. 77–87.

CHAPTER 21

Upstairs, Downstairs

The Challenge of Social Inequality (1983)

John Sweeney

Writing in the midst of the 1980s economic crisis and under the shadow of
the Northern political crisis, Sweeney argued that the economic success that
followed economic development in 1958 had created an Irish society that was
more relatively unequal than before. His themes were social inequality, social
segregation and the justifiable anger of dispossessed youth. When this article
was first published John Sweeney was the Founder-Director of the Jesuit
Centre for Faith and Justice, and living in the Ballymun flats. He is no longer
a member of the Jesuit order and is currently works as Senior Social Policy
Analyst for the National Economic and Social Council.[1]

'Things fall apart, the centre cannot hold.'

I begin with a stylised story. The characters are fictional but a resemblance
with reality is strictly intentional!

Jerry is bored. Propped against the entrance to the block of flats he has an
easy view of the Garda station. The way the squad car leaves the yard warns
him that something interesting may be afoot. Jerry left school last year, in
time to take part in the excitement of the H-block campaign. He had always
felt out of place in school. There was the odd nice teacher but the whole
place seemed to put him down. As there is still another year to go before he
can draw the dole, he is helping out in stores at the local supermarket. That
kept him from going into town this afternoon with his mates. Mick is hoping
to show off his skills with a motorbike. Jerry is afraid for him but half hopes
he will put it off. A ride on one of those new Kawasakis would allow him to
sleep tonight with some sense of achievement.

Above Jerry, in the gathering dusk, Aer Lingus's last flight to Brussels climbs to gain its cruising altitude, it carries a full load of civil servants, businessmen and interest-group representatives. There is more than one brief case open as a meeting the following day gets its preparation. The sense of purpose in the plane means no one is looking out of the window. If they were, the neat patchwork of Priorswood and Bonnybrook, the space-age complex of Ballymun and the sprawling swathes of Finglas would only remind them that Dublin's physical expansion has been swallowing one thousand acres of land a year. For, from high up, it seems that Jerry lives in a fairyland. The street and house lights are coming on and trace an intriguing network of lines and curves. You would have to travel through the estates in a car to see and feel the effects of heavy unemployment and inadequate amenities. The airport road forces no such experience on travellers to Brussels! If somewhere in their files are digests of a recent OECD Report and of a NESC-commissioned study telling them that, nationally, unemployment among the under-20s is double the national rate and that, in Dublin, unemployment on local authority housing estates is twice the city-wide average, nothing they have seen in the day just ending reminded them of that. The traffic from their homes in south Dublin to Ballsbridge was slightly worse than that from their offices to the airport. Social segregation by housing areas is an abstract problem which, as planners, they may have to think and talk about. Traffic flows are everyday experiences that they must *do* something about.

Ironically, it was the same event in the previous year which served both to inject a brief sense of purpose and belonging into Jerry's life and to give middle-class, professional Dublin actual experience of the social division in their city. The H-block campaign gained enthusiastic adherents in Jerry and many other unemployed, working-class young people. They readily protested the British Government's cynical acceptance of the trickle of deaths in Northern Ireland because their experience, too, is of a society indifferent to the gradual wastage of their lives. Their sense of history is no stronger than that of more prosperous Dubliners, but their need to belong to some movement, where the glorious exploits of the few compensate the many for their drudgery, is. Middle-class Dublin, on the other hand, was aghast at the extent to which a cynical Republican element was able to mobilise Jerry and his friends to find excitement on Dublin's streets. For a while, it seemed as if the local authority estates which the Irish Bishops described, in 1975, as 'social time-bombs with slow-burning fuses' were about to explode. However, Toxteth remained a Liverpool experience, for the time being. The same images of cars burning and shop windows crumbling that enter the nightmares of the passengers to Brussels, are part of the daydreams of Jerry and his friends.

Jerry and the passengers to Brussels are, of course, fictional characters. However, the shape of the story is an attempt – however clumsy – to communicate the tenor of some recent research on society in the Irish Republic. For example, a major study of Dublin's development in recent decades was carried out by UCD's Department of Urban and Regional Planning, at the request of the National and Economic Social Council (NESC). It reflected: '. . .Dublin has been for long and remains still a socially divided city. . . . The social dichotomy between the affluent ascendancy and the tenement population, both resident in the historic city, has yielded to a more dispersed but still polarised society . . . The evidence of increasing affluence amongst the expanding middle classes contrasts sharply with the relative poverty of some of the public housing areas. . . . The fact is that too little is known about the impact of planning policies on social groups within the urban context . . . It is hoped this study will lead to . . . a more humanising urbanism and help offset existing and new social antagonisms. The study is strongly influenced by the belief that "if cities do not begin to deal constructively with poverty, poverty will deal more destructively with cities".' (NESC Report, no. 55, published in September 1981. It quotes Robert McNamara in the 1975 World Bank Report).

A second research document, published by the Economic and Social Research Institute in April 1982 (Paper no. 109), had studied the even broader phenomenon of income distribution at the national level. Once again, and gratefully, the authors' dependence on funded research – and, therefore, care to present their findings with as much analytical rigour and as little contentious passion as possible – has *not* prevented them from allowing readers glimpse how they *feel* about what their research has unearthed: 'Our own appraisal . . . is that social class differences are so deeply implanted in Irish society as to be self perpetuating. . . . Prospects for basic change in the 1980s are rendered almost nil by social group differentials in educational participation. Taxation on capital and inherited wealth (has drifted towards the inconsequential . . . Ireland may enter the twenty-first century with an upper middle class so privileged and so securely entrenched as to hearken back to its nineteenth-century predecessors.'

We have probably always thought of social class as more a British phenomenon than an Irish one. The greater density of population, and the longer, deeper ravages left by industrialisation, on the neighbouring island afford moments in her history when class identity appears to have been the moving force rather than a sense of Britishness. The Catholic, Nationalist, community of Ireland, while it always contained within it people from different social worlds (the Protestant, Unionist community too, but that is of less relevance to this article on society today in the Irish Republic), seems – by contrast to the

British experience – to have been more homogeneous, more steadily united by the need to make common cause against the arrogance of a colonial power.

The First Programme for Economic Expansion, introduced in 1958, gave an acceleration to the industrialisation process, however, which has given a potentially new divisiveness to the significance of where citizens of the Irish Republic live and go to school. This is something on which the two reports just quoted are in complete accord. Let us return to Jerry and the plane. Jerry feels little sense of solidarity with the Irish people on their way to Brussels. Bigger price increases for Irish farmers. Projects to be approved by the Social and Regional Funds. Jerry is waiting to be allowed to graduate *to the dole*. If he remains in his neighbourhood or in that neighbourhood where he is given a house when, after two children (or three?), his turn on the housing list comes he may be on the dole for the rest of his life. 'One of the consequences of the spatial grouping of social characteristics is that areas become identified with problems and the mere presentation of a person's address may be sufficient to categorise that person within a particular stratum of the urban milieu.' (NESC) The older people in the plane above Jerry are aware of the competition for employment. With the national unemployment rate approaching 15 per cent (end of 1982) and beginning to affect Leaving Certificate holders and even third-level graduates, not just early school leavers like Jerry, the personal anxiety most often affecting concentration in the plane on the morrow's business focuses on childrens' schooling. Should Gráinne be put into a fee-paying primary school Could Dermot do with some extra tuition in this, his Leaving Certificate, year:

> Education in the 1920s (made) only a slight impact on a person's adult situation . . . By the 1970s . . . educationally determined skills and qualifications differentiated between skilled and unskilled manual workers, between professionals and routine service workers . . . new employment possibilities [are] largely limited to those with family resources sufficient to secure the credentials that [govern] access into the newly consolidated advantageous positions of white-collar employment. (ESRI)

A society where a rising number of scarce employment positions are filled, not by virtue of inheritance and property ownership, but by those who possess the necessary credentials testifying to education and training, punishes the Jerrys of this world with idleness, and discomforts those within the system because their childrens' futures are insecure.

I THE FACT OF SOCIAL INEQUALITY

It is in the area of housing that the existence of two Dublins, two Corks, two Limericks – in short, of two Irelands – can be most plainly seen. When your schooling is local, and no job awaits to introduce you to a wider world, as is the case with many working-class young people today, the immediate neighbourhood assumes crucial significance. When a bishop asked a candidate for confirmation from an inner city parish 'Who made the world?' and was told 'the Corporation', the child was not being impertinent. In the child's experience, houses were built and maintained, streets repaired and cleaned, playgrounds provided and removed, men given employment or not – all, by the Corporation!

The challenge that our growth in population (nearly half a million additional people between 1961 and 1979) and its preference for urban environments (46 per cent lived in urban areas in 1961, 60 per cent by 1979) have presented to local authorities has been enormous. It is the Dublin metropolitan area's three local authorities which have borne the brunt of the consequent demand for new housing. The County Council's draft development plan (1980) forecast an increase of 348,000 in the population of the Dublin sub-region between 1979 and 1991. More than half of this (181,000) is expected to come from migration into the area, as the process by which the Eastern seaboard's share of the national population grew from 23 per cent in 1926 to 37 per cent in 1979 continues. The remainder is accounted for by the natural increase of the existing population. Yet the total housing demand is even greater than this population *increase* suggests, because population *movement* within Dublin is also reckoned to continue. In 1926, 85 per cent of all Dubliners lived 'between the canals'. In 1971, that geographical heartland accounted for only 18 per cent of the population of the city and its suburbs. The number of people actually living in the city centre has halved over that period as some of Europe's worst housing was demolished and replaced by office blocks. Alternative accommodation has been provided chiefly on the city's perimeter for the displaced population. This pressure is relentless, especially as the inflated value of land in the city centre makes it possible to provide two public housing units ten miles from the city centre for the price of one in the inner city.

Housing

The enormous demand for housing, reflected, for example, in the 35,000 names on council waiting lists around the country (1981), has not been matched by any proportionate growth in the priority accorded the provision of housing within public expenditure. Of the major headings under which the social expenditure of public authorities is classified, housing has increased the least since 1960. There has been a greater willingness to rely on the private sector here than in the fields of health, social insurance or education. Hence, tax relief on mortgage payments and loans and grants to first-time purchasers of new homes have been important instruments of policy. Yet they have done little to ease the demand for public housing. In the absence of controls on the price of building land, some of the benefit of these measures to boost private construction has been passed on to land speculators, and the mortgage millstone weighing on home buyers has not been lightened by as much as it could have been. In the absence of annual readjustments of the loan that can be made in line with rising house prices, and of the income limits qualifying for a grant in line with inflation, the ability of people on low incomes to entice funding agencies to grant them a mortgage has been weakened.

With an increase in their responsibilities out of all proportion to the increase in their resources, local authorities have cut corners and attempted to squeeze the most houses out of given financial funds. Thankfully there has been only one Ballymun, where the Department of the Environment (then of Local Government) stepped in to provide 2,866 flats in one fell swoop using factory-built units that kept the construction cost at around £10 million. There *has* been a succession of developments like Finglas, Tallaght and Darndale where young families are not placed in high flats but the emphasis still seems to be on providing shelter rather than laying the foundations of a community. These visually depressing estates fall victim to the lack of planning whereby the public sector virtually creates a new settlement of many thousand people but the facilities and amenities they need remain the responsibility of the private sector. If there is a high level of employment and good money in the community, the shops, supermarkets and clubs follow quickly. Where unemployment and social welfare dependency is high, the amenities appear in dribs and drabs and a long time after the estate has been built. Sometimes, 14 years later a large urban community does not have the equivalent services and facilities of a rural town one fifth its size.

It is the lack of success with which our society and its institutions have met the demand for new homes arising out of our contemporary population movements that the UCD study commissioned by *NESC* highlights. Its authors painstakingly examined the 193 District Electoral Divisions of the Dublin metropolitan area for 42 characteristics on which the 1973 Census supplied data. They concluded (as quoted above) that Stumpet City is still a divided community. Fully one third of the population, the 11 per cent resident in the inner city and the 22 per cent in local authority housing estates, lived in areas characterised by 'multiple social deprivation'. Jerry is not alone! They conducted surveys in 1979 in both types of area which suggested that their deprivation relative to the expanding middle-class areas was not significantly easing.

Deprivation

What sort of deprivation do they describe? While in their own words it is 'multiple', 'a spatial grouping of (unfortunate) social characteristics', etc., housing, education and employment get special attention. For example, let us take housing. In the inner city there are still many old buildings and it is not unusual for their dwellers, frequently elderly, to be in single rooms and without a bath or shower. Thirty-eight per cent of the population there were classed as 'overcrowded' as against fifteen per cent in the Dublin sub-region as a whole. On the local authority estates overcrowding continues to be the problem but for the different reason that large families are being raised in houses with few bedrooms. In one electoral ward in Ballyfermot, for example, 52 per cent of the population was in families of six or more persons but only 0.3 per cent of the dwellings had six or more rooms. On the education front, it emerged that the educational achievements of the adults living in both types of area were far behind those people in the rest of the city. For example, in 1974, 73.6 per cent of those in the inner city had completed national school only as against 24.4 per cent in the Killiney/Kill o'the Grange area. The more alarming finding, however, was that such concentrations of low educational achievers were tending to be self-perpetuating. For the school attendance, school performance and entry to third-level education of young people were also far behind the national norm. Of young people in the appropriate age group, one per cent entered higher education in 1978–9 from Dublin 1 (North Inner City) and Dublin 10 (Ballyfermot) though the national norm was approaching 20 per cent. In Dublin 18 (Foxrock, Carrickmines, Cabinteely) the percentage was 34:

> A child is educationally disadvantaged from the beginning when there is a low level of parental education. This is compounded where parents are hostile or apathetic to education and where cultural norms reinforce the lack of interest in education or where peer groups impose sanctions inhibiting access to, and acceptance of, further educational opportunity. (NESC)

Jerry got no encouragement from family or mates that would have made him overcome an already deep-seated distaste for schooling and remain on after his 15th birthday. There was no one to reflect with him that school leavers without a school certificate are three times as likely to remain without a job as holders of a Leaving Certificate (National Manpower Service Report on 1981 school leavers); or that a survey conducted among the unemployed in Britain – where, in times past, Jerry would have gone to find a job – found that 85 per cent of them had left school at or before the age of 16, with the proportion rising to 95 per cent when only the *long-term* unemployed, were considered.

II THE GENERATION OF SOCIAL INEQUALITY

These educational differences between communities within Dublin are much more disturbing than mere differences in quality and type of housing stock. For there is still great public faith in a good education as both the individual's passport to a better future and as something which brings benefit to the community at large. The precise mechanisms through which this individual and collective benefit is realised are not as clear in the popular mind but, somewhere, the notion that education results in a job rather than unemployment, or in a more satisfying job rather than a dead-end one, is probably strong. Similarly, it is probably also believed that a higher level of education in the national community as a whole increases the total supply of jobs, partly because there will be more initiative in the population leading to the greater probability of self-employment, partly because there will be more productive workers for employers and a greater incentive to them (especially foreign) to rely on an Irish workforce. The context that the NESC and ESRI reports reveal to the education-for-employment debate is, therefore, very important.

When a person is tempted to think that the present social problems afflicting certain housing areas will die away as those areas 'settle down' – as have Cabra, Crumlin and Ballyfermot today whose situations were once as bad as those of Finglas, Coolock and Darndale – they may not be aware of how crucially they are assuming that unemployment levels will return to those of the 1960ses, 1950s and 1940s. It has been little studied but a new housing area probably 'settles down' when a sufficient number of its residents are content, have at least some discretionary spending power and see some results from attempting and demanding what community life in their area needs. If a large number are on social welfare, the resources and will to improve the neighbourhood are difficult to generate. Heavy emigration before 1960, and sustained economic growth from 1960 to 1973, contributed to keeping the numbers on welfare smaller and more geographically diffused than seems to be the case now at the beginning of the 1980s. Unemployment, like so much else, is distributed unevenly. And it is difficult to present education as the solution. Raising the educational level of the national workforce may be necessary to *maintain* existing employment levels (it is also, or course, commendable for non-economic reasons) but it is unlikely to bring more employment when international competitiveness for jobs based on exporting is so sharp. Prescribing more education for this person or that social group as the way to enable them 'get on' presumes – in the context of a widening gap between the number of people looking for work and the number of jobs available – that the rest of the competition is not also upgrading its educational standing.

Neither the passage of time nor more education can be relied on, at the present time, to ease the degree of social inequality that has our society sick. It is the way in which trends in the level and nature of employment have affected different social groups that constitutes – in the eyes of this writer – the common finding of most import in the two Reports. The NESC-commissioned study paints a picture of defined geographical areas and occupational groupings suffering disproportionately from nationally-induced changes in Dublin's occupational structure. The labour force in the inner city and on local authority housing estates is disproportionately dependent on the supply of blue collar, unskilled manual jobs. It is precisely these types of job that have been disappearing from the national economy in general, and the inner city in particular. The IDA estimated that 10,000 manufacturing jobs disappeared from Dublin 'between the canals' over the six-year period, 1973–8. One quarter of those new jobs reappeared in new factories on the city's perimeter. The rest were sacrificed on the altar of 'industrial restructuring' built by free trade. Even the large employers that stayed, e.g. Guinness' and the Dublin Port and Docks Board (which could hardly move!), contributed to the decline in demand for unskilled labour as the introduction of labour-saving machinery typically resulted in fewer jobs with a larger proportion of them being for white collar workers. In fact, over all, the new jobs arising out of information processing in all its forms more than surpassed the number of jobs lost in goods production. One reflection of that is that the land space devoted to offices increased by 100 per cent over the same period (1966–74) that the square footage devoted to industrial purposes fell by 30 per cent. It was little benefit, however, to the inner city residents that they lived cheek-by-jowl with the booming information industry. Its offices (civil service, banking, insurance, etc) employed people with the necessary educational and training qualifications but they, the local people, did not have them. So the curious situation arises in which 'inner city residents either fail to find work, or commute outwards, while thousands of incoming commuters, usually in private cars, clog the city streets in day time'. (NESC)

Viewed in isolation, the disadvantage at which the workforce in parts of Dublin finds itself is inviting preferential treatment for those areas in educational and industrial training policies. The Department of Education and AnCO certainly *have* their part to play. The breadth and perspective which the ESRI Report adopts on the matter, however, cautions modesty on their part for the root of the problem lies much deeper. It is the wave of change that the 1958 First Programme for Economic Expansion unleashed, and the way in which the more powerful groups in Irish society have ridden that wave, that have produced the relative disadvantage of such communities as Dublin's inner city. As fundamental a reordering of national priorities might be needed to end this involuntary poverty.

The mechanisation of agriculture with the consolidation of policies aimed at encouraging large, commercial farms, and the pursuit of export-led industrial growth, has been occasioning a profound change in Irish social structure since 1960. While the volume of wealth our economy produces each year grew remarkably, there was relative stagnation in the total number of people at work. In broad terms, workbenches in agriculture and in industries made defunct by free trade were swapped for more productive ones in exporting industry and offices. The total number of workbenches grew by only 128,000 over the 22-year period, 1961–82 (April), a number that the estimated new entrants to the workforce would fill in less than six years at present rates. Of this barely rising number of work positions, the proportion providing people with the experience of working for some one else rather than in self-employment has been rising. Of the male workforce, for example, 56 per cent were classified as employees in 1961, but 69 per cent in 1979. Finally, of these employee positions, the prospects facing candidates for white collar and skilled manual niches have been much, much rosier than those facing candidates for semi-skilled and unskilled manual jobs. Between 1961 and 1979, 172,000 *more* of the former were needed, but 35,000 *less* of the latter.

Without having to open the ESRI Report someone reflecting on these trends in the level and nature of employment might begin to guess the role the educational system has been increasingly adopting. They could summarise the trends as follows: (a) there is sharpening competition for the available workplaces; (b) more of those workplaces now involve approaching an employer rather than being 'fixed-up' by one's family; (c) more employers are now looking for brain rather than brawn.

The outcome they might guess at, therefore, in advance of reading any study of the Irish educational system, is that the competition for employment has produced an associated *competition for education*. The race has begun in earnest and many hope to reach the finishing line with superior educational or training credentials so that some employer will surely take them on. Jerry may not know it but, by leaving school at 15, he may have saved himself from the considerable (to him) exertion of more schooling in order to arrive at the same place, namely, the dole queue.

In drawing attention to the extent to which the middle class have been the quickest to respond to the new competition for employment posts the ESRI Report is helping us understand the 'why' of the considerable inequalities in the upper reaches of the educational system which researchers like Dale Tussing and Pat Clancy have done so much to document. Why, for example, with less than 10 per cent of the eligible age group, the upper middle class accounted for 38 per cent of new entrants to the universities in 1979, while the working class, with 52 per cent of the eligible population, provided only 14 per cent of the universities' intake. The introduction of free secondary schooling in the mid-1960s *did* enable many working-class children remain on longer in school. However, the middle class was not caught napping and responded with such alacrity to the new premium that the transformation of the economy put on credentials that working-class children emerge, after longer schooling, at the same relative disadvantage as before in the job market. The advantage children from higher-income groups enjoy is cumulative. Even at primary level and up to the end of junior-cycle secondary schooling, when participation rates for *all* social groups are high, the children of the lower-income groups can be slipping behind. A poorer diet, more difficult home conditions, an unhealthy neighbourhood (e.g. lead-poisoning from dense traffic), the middle-class assumptions and sympathies of the curriculum, etc., etc., can lead to frequent absence from school and poor concentration while present. When the minimum school-leaving age is attained, it is the children of semi-skilled and unskilled manual workers who begin to leave in the largest numbers. Schooling has proved a joyless experience and more money is needed in the home so that even the chance of part-time earnings cannot be missed. By the time the Leaving Certificate is attempted, the social group differentials in participation are so pronounced that policies directed at equalising access to third-level institutions can, at best, have a marginal impact. The bulk of those from working-class and lower middle-class backgrounds have already been removed from the pool of potential students in higher education.

The ESRI authors express their understanding of how social inequality is being maintained and deepened by reflecting:

> Irish society, once dominated by the structuring principle of family-owned property, was by the 1970s differentiated sharply according to class-linked packages of skills and qualifications attained mainly through education. The newer and more advantaged opportunities in white-collar or skilled manual employment were disproportionately assumed by the already privileged middle-class and (large) farm families.

Plus ça change plus c'est la même chose! They voice a main conclusion:

> The current middle-class domination of the upper levels of secondary and of all of third level education needs to be challenged by effective policies to ensure an

equitable share in educational opportunities to those from working-class and lower middle-class backgrounds.

III THE RESPONSE TO SOCIAL INEQUALITY

There is, certainly, much that can be done to give children brought up on small farms or in deprived urban areas a fairer chance in the educational race. While schools cannot be expected to single-handedly redress the damage that home and the wider community can cause young people, public funds and the attentions of the teaching Religious Orders should be asked, and expected, to discriminate in favour of the schooling of poorer children. The quality of a society is gauged by the treatment accorded its weakest members. If the better off have to shoulder a greater part of the expense of their own children's schooling, because the priorities governing the allocation of public monies and the talents of teaching Religious Orders shift to favour the least well off, that should not be interpreted as a 'zero sum' game, namely, that they have lost what others have gained. It is their right, and the right of their children, to live in a society where social classes are not in an uneasy war. If they short-sightedly insist that their taxes should underwrite their children's schooling, rising demands on the public purse for compensation for vandalism, extra policing, additional health and welfare services, etc. – not to mention their own investment in burglar protection – may see the priority of security taking every bit as much money from their pockets as a shift in educational policy threatened to take.

However, if priority attention to schools in deprived areas is not to be just a further attempt to regulate the poor, i.e. to contain them and prevent (what some would argue are needed) jolts to the social system, a second, and even more important, area for change is in the nature of the schooling that working-class and lower middle-class children receive. The influx of these children to the educational system after the introduction of free secondary schooling has not been matched by any significant revamping of the content or methods of teaching the secondary curriculum. Of every five children who enrolled for some form of post-primary education in 1975–6, three sat for the Leaving Certificate in 1980 and one enrolled in a third level institute that autumn. Yet, how much of the education that the four who did not enter a third-level college, especially of the two who did not even reach the Leaving Certificate year, was moulded by the needs of the one student who did continue in full-time education? The statistics recording the stream-lining that the educational system is affecting nationally conceal, of course, very different experiences on the part of the various types of schools. In Secondary schools, only one in four had left before the Leaving Certificate year; in Comprehensive schools it was two in four, and in vocational schools three in four. Even taking those who actually got to the Leaving Certificate in 1980 as a group together, the significance of the type of school attended emerges again in the quality of the results obtained and the uses to which they were put. Fee-paying secondary schools got one third more of the students into higher education than non-fee-paying schools, and twice the proportion that community and vocational schools managed. All this poses questions for educationalists, among those questions the ESRI authors surely have in mind when they stress the responsibility for greater equity that rests on the educational system. Have schools sufficient freedom to foster the interests and development of their students in the light of the actual life chances facing them? How should a school respond to the probability that 20 per cent of its students will be gone before their third year, and 75 per cent before their sixth year, with a fair proportion of those leaving early facing a life of intermittent unemployment?

These questions challenge those working in schools whose intake is primarily from the lower-income groups. Educationalists in secondary schools, and fee-paying ones especially, have probably been the most vigorous and successful in responding to the needs of *their* students. The disproportionately large slice of third-level and employment posts that their graduates obtain witnesses to the drive and creativity with which they motivate their students to work for those credentials so necessary to forward advancement today. The passengers on the Brussels flight are no fools, nor is their motivation in any way to be decried. Parents who did not want the best for their children would be strange indeed, and to be prepared to meet the costs of fee-paying primary and extra-curricular schooling, in addition to fees at secondary level, can, in fact, in the present imbalance between the demand for, and supply of, good employment posts, be the best thing for their sons and daughters. If a working-class or small farm family were suddenly to have the financial resources of, for example, a professional family, it is hard to see them making decisions about their childrens' schooling markedly different to those which the upper middle class have been making to date. Policies that discriminate in favour of society's weakest members are based, plausibly, on an understanding of human solidarity where fuller recognition of the dignity of the poor enhances life for everyone. Policies, however, that set out to fetter society's strongest members – even if public institutions were not dependent on such people in order to implement their policies – are not so easily defensible. They can penalise healthy instincts (such as the desire to do the best for one's children and try to enlist envy as a sentinel for ensuring greater equality.

Questions posed to educationalists by the extent of social inequality in our country today are of one type. Those posed to that large and diverse group, from government ministers to trade union leaders, who are more directly responsible for social policy, are of quite another. The extent to which the upper middle class are, in the word of the ESRI Report, 'entrenched' in the upper reaches of the educational system is clear. What response society should make to that is not. One familiar demand is that the Jerrys of this world be equipped with the weapons they need to scale the embankments where the privileged are entrenched. Their schools should be provided with whatever extra facilities (by way of lower pupil-teacher ratios, remedial facilities, extra-curricular activities, dining rooms, etc.) are needed to compensate for their rougher environments, so that more of them might be motivated, and able, to get a good Leaving Certificate. Much improved grants, then, at third level would compensate for the costs and foregone income that presently deter many a working-class young person from continuing in full-time education.

Fundamental doubts have already been raised, however, about the effectiveness of such policies and whether they really go to the root of the problem. They are likely to prove ineffective because, while assisting the weak, they do nothing to ensure that the upper middle class do not maintain their lead. Differentials can be maintained with as much tenacity in education as in matters of income or housing! If the primary reason why students from lower-income groups remain in full-time education is to better their employment prospects, *and* if nothing happens to increase the over all supply of desirable employment posts, their expectations can be cut to pieces as children from more privileged backgrounds prove to have the additional command of foreign languages, social skills or just plain higher grades that employers are demanding by the time they leave the educational system.

The root of the problem surely lies in the scarcity of desired employment positions. It has occasioned the growing use to which the educational system is being put in determining who fills them. Policies aimed at lessening social inequality will get the best results if they focus on measures that widen the number of respected occupational niches. There is a danger that the hat will be thrown at full employment in the 1980s. The depressed state of the international economy, technical change in manufacturing industry (suggesting that the employment engine of the 1960s and early 1970s is no more), evidence that other industrial countries are not coping much better with unemployment, the deep-seated imbalance in the public finances – all are invoked to gain public acceptance of the present high level of unemployment. Yet continuing high unemployment, and the rising proportion of those on the dole who are out of work for a year or more, is driving a wedge in Irish society between a large group who suddenly realise they have a lot which they could lose, and a significant minority who realise that they have very little to lose. Increasing social conflict will not be checked by social welfare.

The present administration of unemployment assistance, and of welfare payments in general, is probably doing more to cement a second-class citizenship than to 'bring in' to society those whom the economy is excluding.

It is true that traditional avenues of employment creation seem blocked. The State has little money, foreign companies are fewer and being courted by more suitors, the trades unions are trying to maintain their members' real living standards. Yet, a time when old answers no longer carry conviction is a time to begin fresh thinking. In an encyclical *On Human Work* the present pope, John Paul II, is saying that our economy is built on mistaken premises in the first place. What would an Irish economy where labour had priority over capital, and the workers' needs priority over the organisation of work, look like? That document's invitation to press on with the democratisation of work places and participative planning at the national level can be allied with contemporary interest (especially on the part of women and young people) in work sharing and flexi-time to produce fresh approaches to the now endangered national goal of full employment. Nothing will produce a turn around in Jerry's life so much as his being able to substitute waiting for the dole with the experience of purposeful work where he is treated as a person and able to contribute to his family, community and country.

The theme of work, its availability, and the satisfaction and remuneration it brings with it, may seem an unusual theme on which to end an essay on social inequality. Those with an interest in selling machines and the consumer delights that machines produce have familiarised us with notions that work is on the way out and the leisure society about to enfold us all. The passengers to Brussels and Jerry would smile. The former because, more often than not, they bring a brief case full of work that must be done at home with them in the evening. The latter because leisure is long hours propped against different walls. This writer is prepared to back the hunch that 'human work . . . is probably the essential key to the whole social question'. (*On Human Work*) Surrendering to the market, therefore, such fundamental decisions as how many work, in what and how, is a recipe for social disaster. Jerry can vouch for that.

Notes

1 Originally published as John Sweeney, 'Upstairs, Downstairs: The Challenge of Social Inequality', *Studies* vol. 72, no. 285 (spring, 1983), pp. 6–19.

CHAPTER 22

T. K. Whitaker (1984)

Raymond Crotty

Raymond Crotty challenged the official history of post-1950s economic development as represented by T. K. Whitaker in a review essay published during the 1980s economic crisis. It appeared three years before his seminal *Ireland in Crisis: A Study in Capitalist Colonial Development* (1986) which argued that much of the wealth that had been generated in Ireland, from the Elizabethan enclosures onwards came about through political manipulation of land values as distinct from actual economic production. Crotty was a farmer who became an agricultural economist. He wrote extensively on Irish economic development and Ireland's involvement in the European Union to which he was opposed.[1]

T. K. Whitaker was born in Co. Down in 1916. He entered the Civil Service in Dublin in 1934. He reached the apex of the service in 1956, when he became Secretary of the Department of Finance. He served in that capacity until 1969, when he became Governor of the Central Bank, a position he held until 1976. In that year he was elected Chancellor of the National University of Ireland. T. K. Whitaker's *Interests* is a collection of his papers, essays and speeches. Most of the papers have already been published, but there are important new ones.

That the author is a person of very exceptional talent is clear from the present publication no less than from his successful career. But there have been other Secretaries of the Department of Finance and other Governors of the Central Bank, to some of whom the author pays tribute in an 'In Commemoration' section of this book. Yet none of these has played nearly so prominent a role in the public life of the State as has T. K. Whitaker during the 28 years since his appointment as Secretary of the Department of Finance. Neither in Ireland nor elsewhere (apart perhaps from Confucian China is there a parallel for the dominant role that the civil servant, T. K.

Whitaker, has played in Irish public life. The major political role played by Whitaker has usually been reserved in western states for politicians, or occasionally for commercial or press magnates. Army generals have frequently seized by *coups d'etat* in the former colonies the power that was thrust on T. K. Whitaker. *Interests* helps to explain the author's remarkable prominence in Irish politico-economic affairs.

The time and place were right for Whitaker in 1956. Keynesianism was the new economic orthodoxy – an intellectually respectable set of arguments for cutting the state free from the old, Pickwickian strictures of balanced budgets. It was argued, under the Irish version of the Keynesian rubric, that if it had been in order for the Allied powers to borrow in order to wage and win a war, it was incumbent on Irish governments to borrow for nation building. This was a policy that, in Ireland, had more than usual attractiveness, and more than usual scope. The emigration of half of six generations – and almost by definition, the more critical half – had dulled Irish perceptions about possible defects in such a policy. Emigration also, by making possible over a protracted period both extreme financial rectitude and extreme political stability, ensured for the Irish State a quite exceptional borrowing capacity.

The first coalition government, which came into office in 1948, had embarked on sustained public sector deficit financing. The policy came unstuck in the mid-1950s, with a balance of payments deficit that, relative to national income, remained unequalled until the late 1970s. The politicians, in the ensuing crisis, were ready to abdicate responsibility to the technocrats, led then by T. K. Whitaker. The essence of Whitaker's innovation was to redirect a portion of the deficit-financed public expenditure towards encouraging exports in order to safeguard the vulnerable balance of payments situation. Less emphasis was given in government programmes to houses, schools and hospitals, and more was given to factories, hotels and offices, so as to ensure a supply of foreign funds that was adequate to sustain a rate of economic growth that was more rapid than previously and that was sufficient to maintain the workforce at a level no lower than that to which it had fallen in the crisis of the mid-1950s. Any reservations that might have been entertained about the soundness of sustained government borrowing – and they were few in a society stripped by emigration of its dissidents – were stifled by the then current Rostovian notion of an 'economic take-off' – a blissful levitation that was the due reward of competently managed countries. If that did not stifle the doubts of an exceptionally uncritical society about the long-run consequences of the policy, there was the much quoted Keynesian aphorism: 'in the long run we are all dead.'

Now, 28 years after T. K. Whitaker became Secretary of the Department of Finance and 26 years after he wrote and published *Economic Development*, we are not all dead, but alive; and the economy has 'taken off' like the proverbial lead balloon. A public debt that hardly existed in 1956 has grown and, relative to the size of the economy, has become larger than the public debt of any other country. Moreover, it continues to grow more rapidly than any other country's public debt. About one quarter of all demand in the economy now comes from that part of government and other public authority spending that exceeds current revenue and that is financed by borrowing. Irish public debt has increasingly sloshed over into external borrowing, as a result of which Ireland, from having in 1956 a considerable net income from assets held overseas, has now to pay abroad, in interest and dividends, more per head of the population and more relative to Gross National Product than any other country. Borrowing by Irish governments is now, as it was not in 1956, critically dependent on further foreign borrowing, but, as the author points out, Ireland now has 'almost exhausted our foreign borrowing potential' (*Interests*, p. 101).

The number getting a livelihood in Ireland, after a 20-year period of stabilisation, has recommenced the downward course which that number, uniquely among the countries of the world, has followed since the 1840s. There is one vital difference between the position now and what it was in the 1950s. Then the half of the Irish who, since the 1840s, have failed to get a livelihood in Ireland, could emigrate. Now they cannot. Now with the country's population growing more rapidly than in the pre-Great Famine decades, the point made by Whitaker in 1956, when population was declining, seems particularly ironic: 'It has also to be realised that economic development here is made all the more difficult by the population situation and calls for greater sacrifices than in a country with an increasing population.' (*Interests*, p. 52).

Interests, as an exegesis of the policies and of the thinking that informed policies in Ireland during the past 30 years, is useful in understanding what has gone so disastrously wrong. Those policies and that thinking are not to be faulted in detail, for on points of detail Whitaker's position is impregnable. The weakness lies with the premisses, where the defects are enormous and glaring. Whitaker, as well as current western orthodoxy, is preoccupied with capital and with saving to provide capital (*Interests*, especially chapters one and two). Yet the whole Irish experience for the past 160 years throws doubt on the assumed relationship between capital formation and social well being. Capital formation was more rapid in nineteenth-century Ireland than in most countries, but its social consequences were disastrous. Irish capital formation, in flocks and herds, like automation now, made people 'redundant' and caused the starvation of millions. There has never been anything like as much capital formation as is occurring now in Ireland's fellow former capitalist colonies of the Third World, yet never have so many people endured so much poverty as is being endured in these countries now.

The sustained reversal of the 140-year-old decline in the number of people able to get a livelihood in Ireland, or reduction in the quantity and degree of poverty in the other former colonies, are pro-found problems of economic development. Capital formation, if it has any relevance to these problems, has much less than Whitaker accords it. The economic underdevelopment that is characteristic of Ireland and of all the other former capitalist colonies, which comprise the Third World, is a hitherto intractable problem. It is one that will yield, if at all, to a more creative, imaginative empathy than is to be expected from a person who, at the age of 18, joined the Irish Civil Service, and spent the rest of his working life there. Nor is that creative, imaginative empathy likely to be engendered in such a person within Merrion Street's corridors of power, insulated as these are from the emigration the inflation that is not offset by index-linked salaries and pensions, and from the redundancies and unemployment that are the common lot of the plain people of Ireland.

The new material in *Interests*, especially chapter four, is mainly concerned to distance the author from the unfavourable course of Irish economic events during his recent, retired years. It is understandable that he should wish to do so; but it is important, if there is to be a chance of avoiding chaos in the looming crisis, that it be realised clearly that the country is reaping in 1984 what was planted in 1956. There have been shifts and tacks in the conduct of Irish public affairs meanwhile. But it is misleading to describe these, as the author does, as 'turning points', marking major policy shifts. To quote just one important fact to illustrate the basic continuity of policy before, during and after the Whitaker era: During the first five years for which the necessary data are available, 1953–7, which also mark the immediate pre-Whitaker era, annual public sector borrowing averaged 7.6 per cent of national income. That was precisely the same proportion in the last five years of Whitaker's term in the Department of Finance, 1965–9. However, netting out the service of existing public debt, with relatively the same gross borrowing in both quinquennia, the additional resources available for providing public services were the equivalent of 3.4 per cent of national income in the earlier, and 1.9 per cent in the later period. The cost of servicing a public debt, which was negligible when Whitaker became Secretary of the Department of Finance, had become of much greater significance when he left to become Governor of the Central Bank. The continued need for public sector deficit financing together with compound interest have thereafter ensured the accelerating growth of the cost of servicing debt. Irish producers respond to the higher taxes that go to servicing debt rather than to providing current services by raising their prices, a procedure that was facilitated by Dr Whitaker in his role of Governor of the Central Bank. These higher prices, triggered off by the taxes to service public debt and made possible by monetary expansion, reduce Irish competitiveness and result in larger balance of payments deficits. These require for their financing more borrowing, especially of foreign currency. There has been a very close correlation between debt service costs and balance of payments deficits throughout the past 30 years. The rising cost of servicing public debt and the resulting balance of payments deficits, which are the cause of the disarray now in the Irish public finances, were implicit in the policies of *Economic Development*, of 'Capital Formation, Savings and Economic Progress', and of the other papers of an economic character in *Interests*.

The author's term, 'turning points', can justifiably be used for only two fundamental changes in the course of those events that now profoundly dominate Irish life. The first of these was when, as a result of price changes in Britain 160 years ago, cattle and sheep became more profitable than people on Irish land. Since then, little more than half those born in Ireland succeeded in getting a livelihood in Ireland; the others starved if they did not emigrate. The second turning point occurred ten years ago when, just as suddenly as the earlier, profoundly important price change, emigration from Ireland virtually ended, so that the half of the population who, for 160 years, have failed to get a livelihood here can no longer leave. The social forces contained in the new departure are as powerful as those contained in the old one of the 1820s. Whether these forces are harnessed constructively, or are allowed to wreak social havoc, as the old forces did in the nineteenth century, will depend on the conduct of public affairs in Ireland during the remaining years of the twentieth century. Judging from *Interests*, the prospects are not bright.

It is fitting, as a Down man, that Dr Whitaker should have included two chapters on the North of Ireland situation. There, Protestant and Catholic struggle with each other for jobs and houses, the Protestants determined to retain what privileges they have, and the Catholics to end their disabilities. That frequently fatal struggle, reminiscent of similar struggles between blacks and whites, and between Hindus and Muslims elsewhere, makes sense only in an island where less than half as many get a livelihood as 140 years ago. Most of the decline in jobs occurred in the 26 of the island's counties that opted for political freedom but that, like all the other ex-colonies, failed to use that freedom to provide better for their people. With its public finances in disarray after 36 years of sustained public sector borrowing and with the half of its population that, for 140 years, has failed to get a livelihood here no longer able to emigrate, the Republic is likely to witness in the immediate future the same alienation of the landless and jobless half that now affects many of the Catholic third in Northern Ireland. It would be remarkable if these casualties of a failed social order in both parts of the island did not coalesce. If and when that occurs, Ireland is likely to conform to the pattern set in virtually all of the other ex-colonies, by placing a general rather than a civil servant in control.

Notes

1   Originally published as Raymond Crotty, 'Turning Point or On Course?', *Studies* vol. 73, no. 291 (autumn, 1984), pp. 233–7. Also see R. Crotty, *Ireland in Crisis: A Study in Capitalist Colonial Development* (Brandon, 1986).

CHAPTER 23

Moving Statues and Irishwomen (1987)

Margaret Mac Curtain

Margaret Mac Curtain's article was, in effect, a response to a response to the 1985 moving states phenomena by other Irish writers located within a historical and cultural analysis of Marian devotion in Ireland. In so doing she captured a sense of the emotional landscape of mid-1980s Ireland. 1985 – the year of the Kerry Babies Tribunal – was 'a year that had not been kind to Irish women'. This followed the divisive politics of the 1983 Referendum on the Right to Life of the Unborn. Dr Mac Curtain lectured in Early Modern Irish and European History in University College Dublin from 1964 to 1994, and was prioress of Sion Hill Dominican Convent.[1]

INTRODUCTION

It rained all through the summer and early autumn of 1985, and the statues moved at Ballinspittle, Mount Melleray, Asdee, Ballydesmond, Courtmacsherry, and over 30 small Marian shrines in different parts of the country. There were reports of moving or speaking statues, ones that showed visions of heavenly light during that untowardly long spell of unceasing rain in July, August and September. By October the statues had become stationary again and the coach firms, the burger vans, the temporary benches and car parks around the grottoes gradually disappeared.

What was the Spirit saying to the Irish Church? Can it even be assumed that the Spirit of God was speaking through a series of events? A number of journalists, some theologians and Churchmen, and a group of psychologists gave the subject serious attention. The media, both Irish and British, including a remarkable photo-book taken during the last week in August, *Ireland, A Week in the Life of a Nation* (London, 1986) covered the crowds at the different shrines intent on encapsulating the out-of the-ordinary. Canon Denis O'Callaghan, Parish Priest of Mallow and former professor of moral theology at Maynooth College, addressed audiences on the subject, neither dismissing the crowds' eyewitness accounts superciliously nor yielding to any pressures to sanction their alleged authenticity.

The observers from the Applied Psychology Department of University College Cork offered a substantial explanation at the phenomenological level. They claimed in relation to the Ballinspittle statue of the Blessed Virgin (which attracted unusually large crowds during the night hours) that it was a problem of eye focus where the onlookers were unable to fix a bright object against a dark background. Staring at the statue fixedly gave the onlooker the experience of seeing it shimmering or moving backwards and forwards. This mass experience they termed the 'Ballinspittle syndrome' but they did not address the question: why the power of the imagination to form such images occurred just then?

WHAT THE JOURNALISTS THOUGHT

Journalists probed the reality of the phenomenon with acuity. Some had attended the gatherings as spectators in Ballinspittle or elsewhere, writing for newspapers and periodicals throughout Ireland and Britain. Colm Tóibín, a freelance journalist, assembled in book form the impressions of a group of journalists and invited other writers to contribute by analysing what was occurring on a cultural level, and draw some inferences. Of the four women who contributed to the book, *Seeing Is Believing* (Laois, 1985), two, June Levine and Isabel Healy, had gone to Ballinspittle and they narrate the effect on the bystanders and on themselves of the moving, five-foot-eight, statue of Mary, placed high up above the road. The other two women, Mary Holland and Nell McCafferty did not visit the shrine. In their contributions they endeavour to situate the reported sightings of the statues within the context of female experience in Ireland in recent years. For Nell McCafferty the moving statues of the Virgin Mary were symptomatic of 'the desolate situation of Irish women'. In Mary Holland's estimation 'the crowds at Ballinspittle are a salutary reminder of how divided our society has become'. With the trained ear of sensitive journalists they sensed that the occurrences were in a subliminal way connected with issues that affected women's lives in the area of what Nell McCafferty termed 'the war of the womb'. Both referred to the aftermath of the 1983 8th Amendment to the Constitution, the incorrectly-styled Abortion Referendum. Both listed a series of tragic incidents connected with unwanted pregnancies, singling out the Kerry Babies Tribunal, which had occupied the media for months of 1985, as an example of the public humiliation that women in this country had to undergo. Both situated the moving statues of Mary in the context of female oppression in Ireland. For Nell McCafferty the occurrences were a predictable superstitious reaction; for Mary Holland, 'the crowds at Ballinspittle dramatise the problem facing the Church . . . for the yearning after old certainties goes beyond religious practice to reflect an unease with the quality of life in Ireland and with a society which, it now seems to many people, has failed them materially as well as spiritually.'[2]

The stranger to Irish politics could well suppose that in the mid-1980s our society was traumatised around women's issues and that large sections of that society were caught between the competing claims of Catholic morality and secular modernisation of our civil legislation in areas of birth-control, illegitimacy, marriage and divorce.

NOT THE FULL EXPLANATION

For other contributors to *Seeing is Believing*, explanation of the phenomena went wider. Notably in the essay by the folklorist, Daíthí Ó hÓgáin. 'A Manifestation of Popular Religion', there is an effort to place the sightings in the context of iconophily. He reminds the readers of the role statues have played in pre-Christian culture and traditions as heroic images, as represen-tations of deity, as oracles that spoke or moved. After the death of Christ, the place of Mary in iconography of the mother-symbol, and the almost sacred character of the Icon and the 'Luke' portraits were firmly established in western religious consciousness. Parallel to the statues, in pagan and Christian memory, was the notion of prodigies, signs, portents, foretelling disaster, signs associated with the Apocalypse of John, indicating a popular perception of some approaching catastrophe. Because of historical circumstances statues in Ireland were a fairly recent introduction in Christian Catholic worship associated with the building of churches from the mid-nineteenth century onwards, thus the phenomenon of moving statues, well-documented in western European religious history is not familiar to the Irish psyche. Ó hÓgáin concludes his observations by noting: 'It would seem to be of far greater value if we searched for the underlying causes which lead people to notice such things at some times and places rather than others.'[3]

Something certainly happened at the level of religious and psychological experience in Ballinspittle and found a response in men as well as women. Even if it can be decided that it was the imagination playing tricks on the crowds that gathered nightly, such an acknowledgement – that the imagina-tion of hundreds of people was exploding into tantric or semi-magical images, – allows us to comment on the event in a less dismissive way than if we approached it with an uncompromisingly scientific explanation. After all, the episodes were communal events, and many people who came there experienced simultaneously a sensation of a Marian statue swaying or dissolving into other images, such as St Joseph, Padre Pio, – for June Levine, a young Rabbi. Not everyone was bewitched; but those who went realised that the *social* happening they witnessed had a significance that so far has defied a totally satisfactory analysis. To explain the phenomenon away in terms of a diagnosis consonant with 'normal' secular views of mental health is to miss the nuances. Some kind of fuse ignited the imagination around an object of popular devotion during those weeks, and there occurred a disjunction of spiritual vision, or a suspension of conventional faith. It took place in the context of lay devotion. No Catholic rituals, no masses, no official presence of Church authorities occurred at the grottoes. The statues that moved were of Mary, a woman, in a year that had not been kind to Irishwomen.

My purpose in the following pages is to follow the line of investigation opened by the women journalists and examine what has been happening to the spirituality of Irishwomen as they encountered the challenge of secularisation and feminism.

IRISHWOMEN IN THE 1980S

In 1969 the Women's Movement was entering consciousness all over the world. In Dublin's Fownes Street, a group of women met regularly in a support group whose goal was to launch the movement upon a society more open, more liberal than at any previous period in the twentieth century.[4] The 1960s had been a buoyant, optimistic decade in Ireland, North and South. The closing session of Vatican II in 1966 with its call for *aggiornamento*, had released spiritual energies among priests, laity, and religious women and men. The Catholic Church was seen to be embarking on a new enterprise, one of dialogue and engagement with the contemporary world. The weekly radio discussions of Seán Mac Réamoinn from Rome and the television exposure of large sections of Irish society to the minds of the world's finest theologians contributed to a new awareness among Irish people. Irish society was about to take its place among the member-states of the European Community and it was to face, among other challenges, the hitherto unknown one of secularisation.

For many Irish Catholics there was perplexity. To a society as highly sacramentalised as the Catholic Irish the new demands of vernacular liturgy resulting from a changed model of Church caused bewilderment. There was a sense of loss which affected devotional practice and religious observance alike. It is in this period that Professor J. A. Murphy, a specialist in twentieth-century Irish history, perceives 'a collapse of the kind of solid Catholic church-going practices that were there up to 1960 or so'.[5]

The Women's Movement inserted an added tension into the Irishwoman's faith-life. The splendid mutterings of the Latin Mass became the vernacular whose language was, to ears sensitised by consciousness-raising exercises, disconcertingly sexist. Confession was, throughout the 1970s, supplanted by the therapies, Gestalt, Co-counselling, Psycho-synthesis, and never regained its old ascendancy. As the decade moved on, the Catholic Church in Ireland began to be considered by groups of women, religious as well as lay, as unattractively male-dominated. Two alternatives presented themselves to women: they closed ranks around the Church they loved and clung to their familiar devotional practices; or they embraced the ideology of the Women's Movement wholeheartedly, and identified with feminism.

THE SEARCH FOR FEMINIST SPIRITUALITY

In an article 'Secularisation: A Healing Process?' (published in *Studies* in 1985) Ursula Coleman examines the effects of dualistic thinking upon our experience of the sacred and the secular, sealing them off from each other.[6] She applies her methodology to the Women's Movement in contemporary Ireland and arrives at the conclusion that feminism is, at this point of time, perceived to be opposed to religion because it is identified with a secular philosophy. She traces the growing polarisation which has occurred since our membership into the European Community. There is a better deal for women in paid employment, social welfare, equal work opportunity but, she adds, 'in the really contentious issues . . . the discussions relating to contraception, sex education, unwanted pregnancies, pre-marital sex, the abortion trail to England, the need for civil divorce, Irish people have divided.' As she views it the Women's Movement has become part of that divide, finding itself at odds with the Catholic Church. 'It was seen to be waging war against what was sacred. The response, therefore, was a defensive one. The Catholic Church and the Women's Movement became enemies.' Thus the 1983 Referendum was a watershed in attitudes which polarised women among themselves.

Feminism is more than the Women's Movement however: it is a way of interpreting life and it has a protean quality in its diversities. There is a radical agnostic, even atheistic feminism which rebels against male authoritarian structures and, unable to contain the critique from within the institution, forces the feminist to leave; or, as Hanna Sheehy Skeffington once declared, 'to read or think oneself out of the Church is a hazard of being a feminist.'

Feminism is also a 'therapy of the soul', to borrow a phrase from James Hillman, the psychoanalyst, and as such he insists 'it tends to ignore that gender question'. He sees feminism as a structure of consciousness, and like the ecology movement it has much to offer in perceptive insights. The soul, he argues, does not know whether it is rich or poor, learned or ignorant, male or female.[7] Feminism thus understood pertains to men as well as to women and it offers profound insights to the contemporary Church in its self understanding of liberation.

Many Irishwomen who have left the devotional practices of their youth are now genuinely seeking a spirituality that meets both their search for a God who is not patriarchal, and for a continuing revelation of God's presence in the world – not in opposition to past traditions but evolving out of them. In Ireland it is to Celtic models that the feminist search is turning more and more. One such model has been studied as a Leaving Certificate textbook by thousands of Irishwomen, unaware that in the person and autobiography of Peig Sayers there are to be found clues that lead into the heart of Celtic spirituality, and supply an agenda for becoming a free spirit.

THE FAITH-WORLD OF AN IRISHWOMAN

Broadly speaking the religious experience of Irishwomen is uncharted territory. It may be discovered in diaries, letters, recorded conversations if researched awarely and it appears in the occasional autobiography that spans the century between 1870 to 1970, frontier decades for Irishwomen in their long stride towards self-awareness. 1878 bestowed on them the Intermediate Certificate; 1973 gave entry into the equality of the European common market community.

Following a tentative methodology, I shall endeavour to discover the faith-world of the Irish rural woman using whatever personal sources are at hand. Peig Sayers (1873–1958) in her *Autobiography* and in her subsequent *Reflections of an Old Woman* gives us glimpses of the spiritual resources on which she drew, when as a young bride she came from the mainland to live on the large Blasket Island off the Dingle peninsula. It was an Irish-speaking world and she lived on that rocky island for over forty years of the present century as wife, mother and neighbour in a community which her own testimony has rendered famous. For Peig Sayers her encounter with the supernatural was one in which she sharply differentiated her superstitious world of ghosts and spirits of which she was a supreme story-teller from the central mysterious path of her life. For Peig the significant guideline of her actions was always 'whatever God has destined for me, I will receive it': this as a young 13-year-old parting from her loved mother for nearly three years. The note is clearer in the incident of her son's fatal fall from the cliff. Unable to leave the house because of her sick husband she cannot accompany the boats in their search for the body. 'It was they who were surprised when they found where he was – not hundreds of yards out at sea – but high up on a smooth ledge, his exact size, and he was laid out as quiet and composed as if 12 women had taken charge. No living person knew how he had happened on that ledge with the blue sea all around. No one but God alone.[8]

Peig's deepest conviction that she was 'a bauble in the hands of the Maiden and her Son' is reminiscent of Teresa of Avila, and another of her sayings is biblical: 'God always opens a gap of support.' When her son, Micheál, is going to the States she enjoins on him: 'Let nothing cross you that would diminish the love of God in your heart.' Her faith in Mary's powers of intercession with her Son were unshakeable; her identification with the Sorrowful Mother complete. She lost four children and her husband before middle age. 'I remember bending to my work with my heart breaking. I used to think of Mary and the Lord – the hard life they had. I knew I had a duty to imitate them and bear my sorrow patiently.'

CELTIC SPIRITUALITY

Peig Sayers' God was pre-eminently the Spirit who infuses nature: she had an intense sense of the presence of God. Her favourite form of refreshing her own spirit was to be by herself looking over the harbour out to sea on a clear day, enjoying the wheeling gulls and the brief smoothness of the waters that so often claimed the lives of the fishermen. This facility in contemplating God in nature is the essence of Celtic spirituality which John Macquarrie describes thus:

> The sense of God's immanence in his creation was so strong in Celtic spirituality as to amount almost to a pantheism . . . But perusal of typical Celtic poems and prayers makes it clear that God's presence was even more keenly felt in the daily round of human tasks and at the important junctures of life. Getting up, kindling the fire, going to work, going to bed, as well as birth, marriage, settling in a new house, death, were occasions for recognising the presence of God.[9]

On reading her *Autobiography* the reader is left with a sense of a human being who has succeeded in integrating the different strands of her life in a deep meaningful way. Her ability to observe her own grief and to describe herself and the way of life on the Great Blasket was truly remarkable. She was esteemed by the other islanders for her neighbourliness and for her capacity to enjoy good company and laughter. Her sense of Heaven was that of the conviviality of friends gathered, talking together and telling stories; her concept of God as final judge daringly familiar: he was *An Rógaire*, The Rogue. There is a tenth-century poem called 'St Brigid's Heaven' translated by Sean O'Faolain in *The Silver Branch* which finds echoes in many of Peig's reflections and epigrams:

I would like to have the men of Heaven
In my own house;
With vats of good cheer
Laid out for them . . .
I would like a great lake of beer
For the King of Kings.
I would like to be watching Heaven's family
Drinking it through all eternity.[10]

Peig Sayers' life, like that of many country women, was of necessity one removed from Church-going, frequency of mass and sacrament, and from the hearing of sermons. Like her neighbours she lived, when times were bad, in poverty and frugality of food. What then has she to offer the town-dweller in the way of getting 'to know God'?

The answer is in her own life, written and lived. There is a sense in which the quest for feminist spirituality must veer towards the side of the oppressed and the poor if we want to find God. The world of the late-twentieth century, including Ireland, is one of structural conflict in which keeping large masses of people poor is a key element. Women and children suffer grievously in such circumstances. For women there is a growing recognition that the issue of oppression will not go away, has not disappeared, and needs to be confronted daily.

If Peig Sayers on her rocky island has any spiritual meaning for the contemporary Irishwoman, it is about finding a knowledge of oneself that comes from within the soul and within the culture, one which steels the will and detaches the spirit from all sentimentality. To be a kindly neighbour sharing house and bread, to be steadfast in the face of loss as great as hers, to remain true to her roots which she discerned had to do with her essential identity, and to add to that, serene old age, and the reputation of being the best storyteller in Ireland: what more salutary antidote to a moving statue could there be than the spirituality of Peig Sayers?

Notes

1   Margaret Mac Curtain, *Studies* vol. 76, no. 302 (summer, 1987), pp. 139–47.

2   Daithí O'hÓgain, 'A Manifestation of Popular Religion' in *loc. cit.*, pp. 66–74.

3   Mary Holland, 'Ballinspittle and the Bishops' Dilemma' in *loc. cit.*, pp. 45–8; Nell McCafferty, 'Virgin on the Rocks', pp. 53–8, in Colm Tóibín, *Seeing is Believing* (Dublin, 1985).

4   The best account of the early years of the Women's Movement in Ireland is in June Levine, *Sisters* (Dublin, 1982).

5   John A. Murphy, 'What it means to be Irish', in *Boston College Magazine* vol. XLIV, no. 3 (1985), p. 23.

6   Ursula Coleman, 'Secularisation: A Healing Process?', *Studies* vol.74, no. 293 (spring, 1985), pp. 26–37.

7   Laura Pozzo, *Interviews with James Hillman* (London, 1984), pp. 70–4.

8   Marie Ní Chinnéide (ed.), *Peig*, (Áth Cliath, 1963), translated by the author; cf. Bryan MacMahon, Peig, *The Autobiography of Peig Sayers of the Great Blasket* (Dublin, 1981).

9   John Macquarrie, 'Paths in Spirituality', quoted in M. Maher (ed.), *Celtic Spirituality* (Dublin, 1981), p. 7.

10   W. R. Rogers, 'Introduction', p. XII, in his edition of Peig Sayers, *An Old Woman's Reflections* (Oxford, 1978).

CHAPTER 24

Reflections on Current Discontents

(1989, abridged)

Tom Garvin

Here Tom Garvin challenges the negative assessment of Irish social and economic development promoted by Raymond Crotty. He outlined empirical evidence that life in Ireland had improved; Irish people lived longer, were in better health and were clearly better off according to a range of economic indicators. In a reply article Frank Sammon SJ criticised Garvin for not addressing questions about social inequality that were at the heart of various critiques of Irish developmental modernity in *Studies*. Garvin's article in turn challenged the fatalism of some such accounts. It rehearsed some of the arguments of his 2004 book: *Preventing the Future: Why was Ireland so Poor for so Long?* Tom Garvin is Emeritus Professor of Politics at University College Dublin.[1]

Since the arrival of the current time of economic troubles in the Republic of Ireland in 1980, it has become fashionable to see the Republic as an economic, or (at best) a moral failure. Some British and Ulster Unionist commentators see it as the former, while some southern Catholic ecclesiastical commentators seem to see it as the latter. Many well-known journalists in the Republic appear to view it as both. The exaggerated optimism which accompanied the economic progress of the 1958–80 period has been followed by an equally exaggerated pessimism, a pessimism which may even have helped to aggravate the situation.

As early as 1982, Joseph Lee described the Republic rather depressingly as the country in Europe which had made the least economic progress since the First World War. Essentially he was comparing the Ireland of 1918, bloated with the farmers' war profits, with the wrecked economies of 1918

Germany and France. His complaint was that the Ireland of two generations
later did not show the dynamism of continental countries which had suffered
and enjoyed the stimuli of war-driven booms. According to Lee, the Ireland
of 1982 was an impoverished little country, staggering along and unable to
break out of a vicious circle of dependency, debt and poverty. It could be
argued, rather unkindly, that choosing 1918 as a base year makes Ireland's
performance look weaker than, say, taking the year 1845. Things in the
Ireland of 1988 are far better than they were in 1845, and Germany's progress
since that date appears positively sluggish by comparison.[2]

More recently, Raymond Crotty, in a book which is an extraordinary
mixture of insight and whimsy, has consigned the country to the ranks of the
exploited, pre-capitalist, communal and helpless Third World. Crotty
seems at times to believe that the Ireland of the late 1980s is in some sense as
poor materially as the Ireland of the 1840s.[3]

Social comment in Ireland is commonly marred by an exaggerated moral-
ism, that is, a propensity to prefer a moral lesson to any real understanding
of our collective circumstances. It is also frequently cretinised by what may
be a national cultural proclivity towards exaggeration in the interests of
telling a good story. This is not to suggest that recent times in the Republic
have not been bad: they have. I happen to believe that the real problem
involves getting people to admit that much of the fault lies in their own
culture, their habits, their attitudes and their assumptions about the causes
of wealth and poverty: some Irish people have a self-defeating 'mindset' that
is encouraged by some lay and ecclesiastical opinion formers. This 'mindset'
assumes that the way to cure poverty is to spread what little wealth exists
around more evenly. I further believe that this formula is one which will
ensure a general, if egalitarian, poverty for all. I also suspect that some
people wish subconsciously if not consciously to see such a state of affairs
come about.

Be that as it may, in this essay, I would like to offer a few tentative answers
to a few more concrete questions: in particular, how well off are Irish people
generally, and are their material conditions improving or deteriorating
relative to those of other nations?

A NATION OF MODERATE WEALTH

The first decision to be made is about the universe of comparison, or the
appropriate group of countries to compare the Republic of Ireland with.
Ireland has been, historically, a relatively rich country by world standards,
at least since the later years of the nineteenth century. In recent years, she
has always been in the top 30 or so independent states in income per head

outside the Communist world, the universe being the 160 or so independent or quasi-independent political entities in the world.

Twenty-four of these countries are over one million in population and are not oil provinces with no significant non-oil economies. In 1985 they ranged from, at the opulent end of the scale, Switzerland and the United States, to, at the poorer end, Malaysia and Portugal. Even these latter were very wealthy by general world standards. Ireland can also be usefully compared with the 12 rich nation states that, in 1988, comprised the European Community.

A second decision involves choosing indicators of well being or riches. The usual, even somewhat overworked, summary statistic offered by comparativists is, of course, Gross National Product (GNP), usually divided by the population and offered as a *per capita* number (GNPPC). A statistic of this kind hides many kinds of discrepancies and anomalies. A country which elects collectively to have large numbers of children *à l'irlandaise* will naturally generate a lower GNPPC figure than one which chooses to have small numbers of children *à l'allemande*. A healthy, well-fed and richer population will live longer and generate an 'artificially' low GNPPC figure because of the larger number of older people in the population. For local peculiar reasons, Ireland's GNPPC has historically been deflated significantly by both of these effects.

GNP itself is a pretty tricky concept to operationalise, for several reasons. International GNP comparisons in US dollars, or any other common currency denominator, will always be misleading to the extent that exchange rates do not reflect the internal purchasing power of currencies; the main effect seems to be that absolute income disparities are overstated. In Ireland's case, the country's GNP is made appear somewhat smaller than it actually is in internal purchasing power. 'Black economies' exist everywhere, and may amount to a significant proportion of GNP. Finally, in the case of very poor countries with large subsistence sectors, there can be serious measurement problems, but this is not a point of much importance in the present argument. Bearing these caveats in mind, I have used GNP as a preliminary yardstick. Later I suggest some other indicators of collective well being.

Ireland's GNPPC of US$4850 in 1985 made it the twentieth richest country in the non-Communist world, and that her income per head was about 54 per cent of the mean GNPPC of the 24 richest. She was slightly richer than Spain and less than one third as rich as the proverbially opulent United States. She was twice as rich as Portugal, nearly one-and-a-half times as rich as Greece, but noticeably poorer than Trinidad, New Zealand and Italy. She was as rich as Israel. Comparative GNP data (1957–85) also indicates that this picture has not changed dramatically in the last 30 years.[4] Since 1976, Ireland's relative standing has improved slightly during a period of sluggish growth generally in the western countries compared with the period 1945–73, an era which is already being seen retrospectively as an economic *belle époque*. In 1957, Ireland's relative standing was rather better, ranking 17th in GNPPC, her GNPPC as a percentage of the mean GNPPC of the 24 countries being 59 per cent. Her shift down the scale since then has been mainly due to the extraordinary recoveries of the defeated Axis countries of the Second World War. Japan, in particular, has shifted from a position of abject poverty and physical ruin to one of great economic strength and extraordinary productive capacity. In real terms, Japan's wealth per head has probably more than quadrupled, admittedly from a very low starting point; in 1957, she was much poorer than Ireland. Spain has done well, as have the lesser-known cases of Finland, Austria and Trinidad. Interestingly, Finland and Austria have done relatively better than the better-known cases of West Germany and Italy. Ireland's figure of 882 per cent probably represents rather more than a doubling of wealth per head, not a despicable performance, and one that gives her a ranking of 14th out of 24 in progress made since 1957, just above Portugal and well ahead of the mature economies of the United States, Belgium, the United Kingdom, New Zealand and Israel.

To sum up, the figures indicate that Ireland held her own in the economic stakes during the last 30 years, and even marginally improved her relative standing. She has maintained a place somewhere in the global lower-middle class: no money for fripperies such as Olympic stadiums or ICBMs, but scarcely 'Third World' either.

A PETIT-BOURGEOIS EUROPEAN COUNTRY

It is somewhat startling to note that, in 1957, the United Kingdom was the richest of the countries of today's European Union (omitting Luxembourg) and that Spain and Portugal were far poorer than Greece.[5] Ireland ranked eighth, her GNPPC being 75 per cent of the mean for the 11 countries. In 1976, her GNPPC had sunk to 55 per cent of the mean of the 11, but it rose again to 68 per cent by 1985. Her rate of growth since 1957 has been the eighth highest of the eleven, ahead of Portugal, the United Kingdom and Belgium, but far behind Spain and Italy, the coming leaders of the Mediterranean tier.

Ireland's GNPPC as a proportion of the United Kingdom's rose between 1957 and 1976 from 46 to 68 per cent, but has dropped down since then to about 57 per cent, reflecting Ireland's recent stagnation and the economic acceleration of the United Kingdom under Thatcher. I suspect that one source for the tone of desolation in the voices of some Irish and British

commentators on Irish economic travails is a common British-Isles paro-
chialism which prevents either from looking any farther than Thatcher's
London. The Irish economy has not collapsed, but has stagnated in the 1980s
in common with those of many other European countries. Looking at the
country in a wider perspective, it has rather improved its relative position in
the last generation, and the rate of relative improvement is growing.

A HEALTHIER COUNTRY

GNPPC is a tricky measure, and often a deceptive one. The United States
is a fabulously rich country, but it has pockets of poverty within its territory
which many poorer European countries would not tolerate. Its health
services are not always as effective as are those of many poorer countries,
and its housing problems, despite the efforts of many local and federal
administrations over the years, are far more serious than, say, Ireland's. As
the *cliché* has it, man does not live by bread alone, and measures of, for
example, public health are in some ways better indicators of a nation's
physical and material well being than GNPPC. Ireland happens to be
among the two or three best-fed countries in the world in calorie intake.
Despite Northern Ireland, murder rates are low, although not as low as they
used to be. Life expectancy is a good example of a non-economic indicator
of welfare, and the life expectancy of women is even a better one. In
underdeveloped countries, women tend to die as early as, or even earlier
than, men. This is due to uncontrolled and unplanned childbearing in a
context of inadequate obstetrical services, bad diets and poor education. By
way of contrast, in developed countries women far outlive men, partly
because of women's natural longevity, partly because of men's greater
willingness to take physical risks, indulge in alcohol and tobacco, and partly
because of the stress of work.[6]

Malaya, as it then was, gives us the horrific statistic for the 1950s of 57
years as an average life expectancy of women, a classic 'third world' statistic.
At that time, the European Catholic countries in particular tended to have
lower life expectancies for women, reflecting the relative underdevelopment
of these regions of the continent. By 1985, this contrast had virtually disappeared. Spain's figure showed a spectacular improvement, and Ireland's is
also impressive. A very great improvement in public health occurred in all
these countries, and Ireland's progress was better than most. In this statistic
at least, Ireland, along with Trinidad, Spain, Portugal, Belgium, Austria and
Greece has clearly travelled from nearly 'Third World' conditions to those
of the 'First World'. However, it should be recalled that the Americans and
Scandinavians enjoy still longer life expectancies. Life expectancies are also,

of course, linked in part to cultural factors such as preferences in diet, use of tobacco and even, perhaps, attitudes toward life and death. It appears that some advances in this area are due to the willingness of some cultures to change their habits of living, in particular to change diets and cut down on alcohol and tobacco. It is not clear that the Irish have yet reached that point.

Another statistic commonly used in assessing levels of public health is the infant mortality rate (IMR) or the number of children out of every thousand born who do not survive the first year of life. Ireland has historically been unusual in that mothers tended, on average, to be older than elsewhere, thus aggravating obstetrical problems. Also, Ireland's ethical opposition to abortion in any circumstances has perhaps resulted in a rather higher IMR. Despite these circumstances, Ireland's IMR has been at or near the average of the developed countries over the last 35 years, and it has shrunk along with those of the other countries because of advances in medical science, improved public awareness of health care and improved public hygiene. In Ireland, the average age of motherhood has come down, which has helped bring down the IMR.

A century ago, commonly one infant in four died within a year of birth even in 'advanced' western countries; an IMR of 250 was commonplace.[7] It is only since the Second World War that infant mortality has become uncommon in the west. Most of Ireland achieved statehood in 1922. In that year the Irish Free State had an IMR of 69, while Northern Ireland had one of 77, as did England and Wales. Switzerland's figure was 70, Sweden's was 63, and Denmark's was 82. These figures were actually rather good by the standards of the period. France had an IMR of 90, Italy one of 128, while the German Reich had a figure of 130. Austria had an appalling rate of 156. These figures make our current discontents look indeed trivial and give us some vague idea of the misery which millions endured two generations ago quite apart from the horrors of war.

GNP figures, and even public health statistics, fail to capture these historical realities. The Ireland of 1922 was possibly one third as rich as she is now in gross GNP terms. Many of the jobs people were willing to do to earn a living at that time would scarcely be regarded as jobs at all by the more advanced society of the 1980s; much of the population eked out a miserable living as 'relatives assisting' almost equally impoverished peasant farmers, as maidservants and menials often in virtual peonage, as sweatshop workers in conditions of great squalor, or as grossly underpaid workers in transportation, public administration and other services. More subtly, the society was far more unequal than it is today, the gap between rich and poor being far wider and social hatreds far more intense.

I realise that this will surprise some readers, and it is a picture that is somewhat difficult to substantiate, given the difficulties presented by historical data on incomes. However, the circumstantial evidence to support it is very considerable. Welfare services were fewer, redistribution of wealth was minimal and the skilled working and middle classes were small. The classic pattern of opulence in the midst of general poverty, so evident in present-day underdeveloped countries, was very much present in the Ireland of two generations ago. In agriculture, there was a small number of (much envied) great cattle ranchers, but most farmers were poor and pre-commercial, their farms far smaller and less developed than those of today. Housing was primitive by modern standards. It was common for local authority houses to be built (in so far as they were built at all) without bathrooms, because bathrooms were unheard-of luxuries.

The Ireland of 1922 was riddled with diseases that are now almost forgotten. Tuberculosis was commonplace, and it was medical science that rid most of the country of that disease in the 1950s. Preventive medicine has done wonders in Ireland, but no one seems to know it, in part because Irish journalists apparently could not be bothered to write it up. Many congenital disabilities which commonly condemned many people to a lifetime of incapacity and social isolation are now spotted in infancy and routinely cured or alleviated. Levels of nourishment are far higher.

Social advance is associated with education. An intellectually incompetent population will have few chances to progress economically, and will also remain unhealthy because of ignorance. Education is also a useful measure of general well being. In 1925, the Irish Free State had 518,000 children receiving elementary education in the under-equipped and overcrowded primary schools of that era. A very large proportion received no further schooling whatsoever, and perhaps half did not even receive the minimum free schooling required by law. As elsewhere in the world, farmers in particular were often hostile to schooling beyond an age where children could be of help as 'relatives assisting' on the farm. A paltry 25,488 pupils proceeded to secondary school, and only a few thousand received any third-level education.

In 1969, the figure for primary education was about the same, but school attendance was far more rigorously enforced, and it is possible that real levels of primary education had expanded by more than a third. The number in secondary schools had increased from 25,488 to 144,425, or nearly six fold in a generation and a half. The classic pattern of transition to a post-agrarian society was evident; people were having fewer children but were educating them more. Interestingly, the figure for secondary education had remained almost static until 1955, but had accelerated rapidly after that.[8] Various reasons for this exist, but one salient reason was the passing from power of the revolutionary generation of Irish political leaders, who apparently displayed little enthusiasm for the education of the population beyond levels common in their own youth; there is nobody as conservative as a successful revolutionary. Third-level education followed a similar pattern. In 1922, the Free State had under 4,000 privileged young people receiving third-level education; by 1968, that figure had expanded to 22,484. The number of third-level students in 1985–86 topped 55,000. The number of students in third-level education in the Republic is now double the number receiving second-level education in 1922.[9]

CONCLUSION

Social progress in Ireland since 1922 has been considerable. It has sometimes been hampered by lack of economic means, and it has been badly slowed by political instability and ideological hostility at times. The entire 20-year process by which independence was achieved and consolidated between 1917 and 1937 was expensive and probably delayed many desirable reforms by decades, much as the instability in Northern Ireland has slowed economic progress in both parts of Ireland in innumerable ways in the past 20 years. The relationship between revolutionary violence and social and economic progress in Ireland in this century has probably been negative. Progress in the Republic occurred when the revolutionary *élan* grew weak, that is, in the 1950s. Since then, it has been impressive in many ways, occasionally even outstripping the United Kingdom; for example, more of each age cohort now go forward to third-level education than do so in the United Kingdom.

However, during most of the 1980s, the economy has stagnated, in part because parallel obsessions with redistribution ('social justice') and with winning elections by subsidising key groups of voters dominated Irish politics from 1977 until recently and undermined business confidence at first and eventually the collective morale of the country. There are welcome signs of repentance in the last few years, but few have yet admitted that the episode may have been quite unnecessary and may have cheated us of the best part of a decade's economic growth and social progress.

The real danger, however, is a psychological one: the tendency to downgrade past achievement is deeply rooted in the sub-culture of Irish journalism, and a kind of dime-store moralistic radicalism is too commonly permitted to take the place of fairmindedness and solid research. It is a moot question to what extent Irish newspapers have, over the years, contributed to the demoralisation of the community, not so much by concentrating on 'low standards in high places', but rather by ignoring the extraordinary progress that has been made by the country in many fields. Perhaps they have not looked closely enough at the lowish standards Irish journalists, like other highly unionised callings in this country, sometimes tolerate from their own colleagues.

Notes

1   Originally published as Tom Garvin, 'Wealth, Poverty and Development: Reflections on Current Discontents', *Studies* vol. 78, no. 311 (autumn, 1989, abridged), pp. 212–325.

2   Joseph Lee, 'Society and Culture', in Frank Litton (ed.), *Unequal Achievement* (Dublin, 1982). pp. 1–18.

3   Raymond Crotty, *Ireland in Crisis* (Dingle, 1986).

4   Bruce Russett et al. (eds), *World Handbook of Political and Social Indicators* (New Haven., 1961), pp. 149–57; World Bank, *World Development Report* (Washington, 1977), pp. 184–5; *World Development Report* (New York, 1987), pp. 194–5.

5   Bruce Russett et al. (eds), *World Handbook of Political and Social Indicators* (New Haven., 1961), pp. 149–57.

6   Ibid., pp. 196–8, *World Development Report* (New York, 1987), pp. 258–9; Ibid, p. 200–1, *World Development Report* (New York, 1987), pp. 258–9.

7   Infant mortality figures from B. Mitchell, *European Historical Statistics: 1750–1975* (New York, 1975), pp. 127–34.

8   Schooling figures from ibid., p. 764.

9   Third-level figures: ibid., p. 775; Higher Education Authority, *Report, Accounts and Student Statistics 1985–6* (Dublin, 1987), p. 48.

CHAPTER 25

Growth and Decline of Churchly Religion (1994)

Tony Fahey

This article exemplifies a recurring theme in Irish sociology and *Studies*, the apparent decline of religiosity and the secularisation of Ireland. This article stands out for its analysis of the options facing the Church in Ireland, whether to continue to dilute itself across a secularising society or whether to focus mainly on observant Catholics. At the time of writing Tony Fahey was a researcher at the Economic and Social Research Institute. He is now Professor of Social Policy at University College Dublin.[1]

INTRODUCTION

The Catholic Church's mission is both prophetic and evangelising: it must bear witness to the truth *and* spread it. This dual mission can be paraphrased in terms of quality and quantity. Witness is a matter of the content and quality of the Church's message, evangelisation is a matter of quantity: the numbers of people who accept the Church's teaching. These two issues are often in tension with each other, and even in Ireland today, I am sure there are many Catholics who would be happy to see the Church decline in quantity if that were to mean an improvement in the quality of Catholic faith and practice. Here, however, I want to focus on the question of quantity. Not because I think quantity is the more important, but because it may help to clarify thinking by treating it separately. I will try to do three things: first, look to historical patterns in the quantitative rise and decline of religions in modern times in western countries; second, position Catholicism in Ireland within those patterns; and third, look at the lessons and challenges for Irish Catholicism today which emerge from the lessons of recent history.

RELIGION AND MODERNITY

The modern world, it is often felt, is unfriendly to religion. There is too much individualism, too much change and confusion in social values, too much interest in material things and too little respect for authority for religion to thrive. Sociology has long supported this view by arguing that secularisation is a more or less inevitable companion of industrialisation and modernisation. The 'secularisation thesis' has pointed to factors as diverse as urbanisation, the loss of community, industrialisation, institutional differentiation, the growth of technical rationality, consumerism, materialism and cultural pluralism as causes for the long-term decline of religion in modern western societies.

There is truth in the secularisation thesis but also over-simplification. It is true that as institutions in western societies have become larger and more complex, they have become more secular. Institutional complexity means that no single, simple vision of how things are is capable of coping with all elements of the system at once. Religions thereby lose their presidency of the system and become but one institution among many. Government, the courts, business, the arts, science and education develop distinct structures within which religions have less and less say. It is also true that many people in western countries are largely irreligious: they know little or nothing about organised religion, rarely if ever participate in religious services, and generally consider as eccentric and slightly puzzling those who display strong religious commitment. It does seem that the great majority of people in western countries have at least a vague, uninformed belief in the existence of God, but barely perceptible nods of this kind in the direction of the divine hardly amount to what one would require before one would call people 'religious'.

Growth of Religion

It is, however, wrong to say that religion has been steadily and irreversibly withering since the advent of the industrial age. This is so partly because formal religion was often more absent or superficial in the daily lives of ordinary people in the past than we tend to assume – the pre-industrial era was by no means a golden age of Christian religious adherence. But the image of constant decline is also inaccurate because Christianity has had some remarkable successes in modern times, even if it also has had its defeats and reverses. One of the great sites of success was the United States, which is not only the leading industrial nation but also the most liberal, individualist, consumerist and pluralist society of the modern age. At the declaration of independence in 1776, according to a recent study, as few as 17 per cent of Americans were members of any Church.[2] By 1870, the rate of religious adherence had jumped to 35 per cent and by 1980 it had increased further to 62 per cent. The Catholic Church appears to have been the single biggest beneficiary of this growth. Between 1880 and the early 1960s the number of Catholics in the United States showed a massive absolute increase (from around 6 million to 44 million) and an equally impressive relative growth (from about 8 per cent to about 23 per cent of the population). The prosperous 1950s and early 1960s were an especially strong period of expansion for the Catholic Church in America. Vocations to the priesthood and religious orders grew rapidly and popular belief and practice remained high (about 70 per cent of American Catholics attended Mass weekly in the 1950s).[3]

Europe, on the whole, has been less loyal to Christianity in recent decades than has America, but even here the trend in religious adherence is much more complex than the cruder secularisation accounts suggest. There have been many sustained episodes of Christian, and especially Catholic, expansion since the French Revolution. Some of them, as in Ireland and parts of Eastern Europe, have left a vibrant, if sometimes unpleasant, legacy, while others have fizzled out and gone into freefall at various times. The picture becomes especially complex when we look within national boundaries at variations in religious adherence by gender, social class, region, ethnic affiliation and so on. These suggest that, over the modern industrial age, the encounter between religion and secularism has by no means always left religion with the wooden spoon. Rather it has created a shifting, many-shaded mosaic in which the Christian Churches have sometimes shown themselves able to meet the challenge of modernity, even if at other times they have hardly put up a fight.[4]

Society and Individual

In the course of modernisation, therefore, we have to distinguish between the fate of religion at the societal and individual levels: *societies* secularise even as *people* often (but not always) do not. As religions become less 'official' or less 'established', in some cases they can become more popular, while in others they become less so. Christianity has had its successes over this period, but these have not come in the form of state *concordats* nor assertions of Church control over major social institutions. They have come through winning the hearts and minds of large numbers of believers as far as the conduct of their personal lives is concerned. Indeed in America, it is precisely the secular structure of society (as reflected, for example, in strict Church-State separation) which has allowed high levels and diverse forms of personal religious affiliation: religiosity is a private matter and its presence or absence has little formal effect on the citizen's standing in the society at large. The first lesson which emerges from the recent history of religion, therefore, is that there really is no such thing as a modern Christian society but there can be, and are, large numbers of modern Christian people. This, then, brings us to what is the really intriguing question about present-day quantitative aspects of religious rise and decline: the variable success of religion among individuals in modern societies. As it loses influence at an institutional level, how and why does it retain such a strong hold among some people and fail so totally among others? The facile, and common answer, is that religious adherence is a function of backwardness: religious faith is little more than ignorant superstition or an other-worldly compensation for worldly failure, all of which falls away when people are prosperous and educated. This explanation is simply wrong: religion in recent times has shown itself not to be strongly associated with disadvantage. While it may sometimes appeal to the poor and oppressed, it can also sometimes appeal strongly to the well off.

Strictness and Strength

A more interesting approach to the variable individual-level success of religion refers not to the social characteristics of individuals but to the types of religion and Church which are on offer to them. In 1972, in an influential contribution in this vein, the American sociologist Dean M. Kelley published a book entitled *Why Conservative Churches are Growing*.[5] This book focused on what he saw as the seismic shift in American Protestantism in the 1960s – the decline of the large 'mainline' Protestant Churches and the growth of smaller, more conservative denominations. His explanation for the success of the conservative Protestant denominations was quite simple – they were growing because they were strict, and the stricter they were the more they grew. In his view, there was strong demand in the United States for what we might call good old-fashioned religion, that is, religion of conviction and commitment, where questioning and doubt were ruled out and where liberal, ecumenical openness to other faiths, or to those of no faith at all, was shunned. The mainline denominations, in his view, had abandoned real religion in this sense: they had become soft and liberal and had increasingly merged into their secular environment. As a result, their place was being taken by the hard, aggressive 'upstart sects' who met the challenge of secular liberalism head-on by preaching an uncompromising fundamentalism.

Kelley's lead has given rise to a new school of thinking about religion in social research, a kind of 'economics of religion'.[6] This school argues that the appeal of religion is rather like that of an upmarket consumer commodity. If it is to 'sell', it must have a well-defined brand image or identity (i.e. it must be different in clearly visible ways from other belief systems, especially the non-religious ones), it must be costly (i.e. it must make real demands on the believer), and it must have definite benefits. As with the possession of upmarket consumer goods, the principal benefit which 'real religion' gives to believers is the feeling of belonging to a privileged élite of some kind. In addition, most commodities have certain inherent use values (religious affiliation can have internal aesthetic or psychological value alongside the external group membership it confers, just as a Mercedes is an effective mode of transport as well as a status symbol). The key argument of religious economics is that religions thrive when they get the right balance between 'brand image', costs and benefits, and they fail when they do not (and, of course, success and failure here are measured purely in quantitative terms, without any reference to quality or theological authenticity).

In the case of the Catholic Church in America, according to this approach, the balance was just right up to the Second Vatican Council but then was knocked out of kilter.[7] The traditional identity of Catholicism was ruined as Latin and ornate ritual were abandoned, traditional dogmatism softened and the distinctiveness from other belief systems blurred by ecumenism and the flirtation with liberal thought. Costs were restructured in a damaging way as the Church relaxed some rules (e.g. the easing of rules of fasting in Lent, on Fridays and before receiving Holy Communion) while it gave new dogmatic status to others that had already been abandoned by many American Catholics (especially regarding contraception). And the benefits were correspondingly reduced as the sense of distinctiveness in being a Catholic was eroded, and as the psychological rewards of such diverse things as ritual, faith in the miraculous and the security offered by the Church's own certainty in its teaching were taken away by a wide range of reforms and internal quarrels over doctrine. The same pattern occurred in the priesthood and religious life: the identity and benefits of the priestly and religious life were reduced as a new emphasis was placed on the Church of the laity, while the costs were maintained (even raised) with the continued insistence on celibacy in the face of a new cultural belief in the centrality of sexual expression to normal healthy life.

The economic approach to religion may be particularly suited to America, its country of origin. There the 'market' in religion is more open and pluralist than in most other countries, so that people actually choose their religion to a greater extent than elsewhere. It also raises many questions: why 'brand images', costs and benefits change, why certain costs are deemed acceptable and others are not, and how various religious 'products' gain or lose value as benefits. Despite these and other limitations, however, the economic approach is useful in focusing attention on the individual-level dynamics of religious rise and decline, as opposed to movements at the institutional level. Indeed, the more religion declines at the institutional level – the more the old religious monopolies are broken – the more relevant the language of choice, of competition and of the 'market' in religious ideas and allegiances becomes.

CATHOLICISM IN IRELAND

We can now attempt to position Catholicism in Ireland within the patterns just outlined. The revival and consolidation of Catholicism in Ireland since the early 19th century was, of course, a striking instance of Catholic quantitative success in modern times – and it was of added importance because of the role of the emigrant Irish in promoting Catholicism throughout the English-speaking world. Catholic success in Ireland, while by no means unique, was in some ways exceptional. Irish Catholics became more Catholic than most, especially in their devotionalism and acceptance of Catholic doctrine. More unusually, Irish society became increasingly Catholic. From the 1920s to the 1950s, the Church's role in national self-definition, in law and the constitution, in social policy, education, health care, and in many other areas grew – to the extent that, in some areas (such as schooling), the Church *was* the institutional system to an exceptional degree. This partial sacralisation of Irish society reflected the homogenisation and decreasing complexity of Irish society.

Since the 1960s, both levels of Catholic success in Ireland – the institutional and the individual – have been beset by difficulties. Firstly, it seems inescapable that the Church's institutional influence is steadily in decline, notwithstanding the defeats of the 'liberal agenda' in the abortion referendum in 1983 and the divorce referendum of 1986. The institutional system is now too big, diversified and complex for the Church to have the same control as it had in the past. Indeed even in the 1940s and 1950s, the Church's rather unhappy experience in trying to shape developments in health insurance and the mother-and-child health scheme showed how even modest institutional development could outstretch the Church's ability to keep up. In any event, the Church has now lost much of its former role as president or overseer of institutional life, and is becoming but one more lobby struggling to have its voice heard in conflicts over social development. It has occasionally responded creatively to that challenge – as, for example, in the work of the Conference of Religious on Social Justice, or of Trócaire on Third World development, both of which are distinguished by their reliance on lay professionals to give a hard technocratic edge to their work.

As with other Churches in other countries, however, it is at the second level – individual adherence to Catholic teaching and ritual – that the real question for the future of the Catholic Church in Ireland lies. Popular adherence has remained high, but there are indications of a significant shift away from Catholic doctrine and practice. This is especially so among those born since the 1950s, both at the top and bottom of the social scale (i.e. those with university education at one end and the working-class unemployed at the other).[8] Undoubtedly, some of this quantitative decline may be occurring among those whose faith was superficial and of poor quality. But some of it may be occurring among conscientious objectors who have developed genuine doubts about the moral or spiritual value of Catholicism, a form of decline with much more serious implications.

There is no inevitable or inherent force in modernisation which suggests that the Church is bound to shrink. It is possible for religions to pluck adherents from the midst of the modernisation process, as Catholicism often did in the past and as the 'upstart sects' are doing today. The question for the Catholic Church in Ireland is whether it has the vigour and inspiration to become one of the upstarts again, or whether it is an ageing, sclerotic institution entering its twilight years.

CHALLENGES

How, then, is widespread personal religious faith and commitment to be won and maintained in the future? I cannot answer this question; I can only reflect on what it means. To return to the language of religious economics, the basic challenge is to strike an effective balance between identity, costs and benefits. That challenge is by no means simply a matter of reducing costs – of making Catholicism 'easier' – nor of blurring identity by accommodating wholeheartedly to larger social trends. If the success of 'upstart sects' elsewhere is a guide, dogged conservativism might be a better strategy, though opinions will differ on the implications that would have for the quality of the Church's message. However, even in quantitative terms, conservativism too can lead into a dead end, especially if conservatism is taken to mean blind, immobile adherence to old ways. Effective conservativism is creative and responsive: it modernises and moulds itself to new circumstances, even if at the same time it clings to core symbols of tradition and rejects much of the language and imagery of modernity.

Having looked very briefly at the lessons of history, I will venture to summarise what we can learn from the past about how Irish Catholicism might underpin its future. Firstly, Catholicism must be a 'high tension' belief system, with some element of spikiness in its relationship with the world around it, and with a distinctive Catholic aspect to that spikiness. It must, in other words, remain a religion, and a recognisably Catholic religion at that, rather than a social doctrine peppered with vague 'god talk'. Secondly, to preserve its identity, Catholicism must look to its traditions. Catholicism is branded by its traditions, and if it jettisons that branding, it will lose its place in the marketplace of beliefs and ideas. Finally, it must respond creatively to its changing environment, so that it rides the waves of social change rather than be swamped by them. Tension and spikiness can lead to isolation and decline if it is too pervasive, or if it leads to an attitude of all-embracing damnation of everything new. Tradition needs to be renewed rather than simply preserved. The nineteenth-century Catholic Church showed what creative adaptivity could mean: it was exceptionally effective in harnessing the motors of modernity to its cause, even as it condemned many aspects of the modern world.[9] That extraordinary creativity needs to be repeated today if the Church is to thrive.

I will mention only one issue to illustrate the difficulty of what is involved – the Church's relationship with women. One striking aspect of the Church's current difficulties is the almost total collapse of vocations to the female religious life. From about the mid-nineteenth century to the 1960s, in Ireland as in many other parts of the Catholic world, female vocations easily outnumbered male vocations, and were one of the main strengths of the Church's evangelising effort. In Ireland today, however, not only is the total number of vocations low, but also only about a quarter of them are female, a sharp reversal of the gender balance of earlier decades.[10] Women still show slightly higher levels of adherence to Catholic belief and practice than men. However, the difference is waning, especially among younger women and married women with jobs outside the home, and there is a growing sense of lukewarmness in women's relationship with the Church.[11]

Women in the past have been the key transmitters of the faith to children, so if they go, the Church goes. The Church will have as much difficulty coping with the gender revolution of the last three decades as it had with the industrial revolution of the last 200 years. To hold on to women is somehow to come to terms with feminism. But to come to terms with feminism is to challenge many central aspects of patriarchal Catholic tradition, and thereby to risk that loss of identity which could undermine the Church. We thus come back to the tension between quality and quantity, and between competing views as to the essential qualities which Church teaching should possess. It will take great wisdom and grace to resolve this tension in a way that will further all aspects of the Church's mission at once.

Notes

1   Originally published as Tony Fahey, 'The Church and Culture: Growth and Decline of Churchly Religion', *Studies* vol. 83, no. 332 (winter, 1994), pp. 367–75.

2   Roger Finke and Rodney Stark, *The Churching of America 1776–1990: Winners and Losers in Our Religious Economy* (New Jersey, 1990), p. 16, p. 92.

3   James J. Hennessey, *American Catholics: A History of the Roman Catholic Community in the United States* (Oxford, 1981), p. 175; James P. Dolan, *The American Catholic Experience: A History from Colonial Times to the Present* (New York, 1985), p. 139.

4 Hugh MacLeod, *Religion and the People of Western Europe 1789–1970*, (Oxford, 1981).

5 Dean M. Kelly, *Why Conservative Churches are Growing* (New York, 1972).

6 See, e.g. Finke and Stark, *op. cit.*; Laurence R. Iannacone 'Religious Markets and the Economics of Religion', *Social Compass* vol. 39 no. 1 (1992).

7 Laurence R. Iannacone, 'Why Strict Churches are Strong', *American Journal of Sociology* vol. 99, no. 5 (1994); Finke and Stark, *op. cit.*

8 Michael P. Hornsby-Smith and Christopher T. Whelan, 'Religious and Moral Values', in C. T. Whelan (ed.), *Values and Social Change in Ireland* (Dublin, 1994).

9 Tony Fahey, 'Catholicism and Industrial Society in Ireland', in J. H. Goldthorpe and C. T. Whelan, *The Development of Industrial Society in Ireland* (Oxford, 1992).

10 See e.g. Council for Research and Development, Vocations Returns 1992, St Patrick's College, Maynooth.

11 Hornsby-Smith and Whelan, *op. cit.*

CHAPTER 26

Catholicism and National Identity in the Works of John McGahern (2001)

Eamon Maher

John McGahern was first championed in *Studies* in 1965 by Augustine Martin. That same year McGahern was sacked from his teaching job following the publication of his second novel *The Dark*. This owed much to the personal intervention of the Archbishop of Dublin, Dr John Charles McQuaid. If McGahern's relationship with the institutional Church was fraught his engagement through his writings with Irish Catholicism remained nuanced. The focus of this interview was upon Catholicism and national identity in his work. Eamon Maher is the author of several works on McGahern including *The Church and Its Spire: John McGahern and the Catholic Question.*[1]

Eamon Maher [hereafter EM]: John McGahern, it is a great privilege to welcome you here today. I won't embarrass you by enumerating your many achievements as a writer, the prizes awarded you, the reputation you enjoy at home and abroad. Rather, I'd like to focus our discussion on the theme of Catholicism and national identity in your works, a theme which is, in my view, central to everything you write. We might start by discussing the environment in which you were brought up. Was yours a typically Irish Catholic upbringing?

John McGahern [hereafter JMG]: Yes. I mean it was the only upbringing I knew and in that sense you can't consider it typical. The Church dominated everything.

EM: Your parents would have been religious?

JMG: I think my mother was very spiritual. My father was very outwardly religious.

EM: Rituals like you describe in many of your novels were commonplace?

JMG: The Rosary was said every evening. I always liked that sentence about the medieval churches, that they were the Bibles of the poor. *The Church* was my first book and I would think it is still my most important book. At that time, there were very few books in the house. The only pictures we could see were religious pictures, the Stations of the Cross. The only music we would hear was religious hymns; and it's (*the Church*) all I came to know of ceremony, even of luxury – the tulips that used to come in the flat boxes when I was an altar boy, the candles, the incense.

EM: These memories stay with you.

JMG: Yes, but also one of the problems for a novelist in Ireland is the fact that there are no formal manners. I mean some people have beautiful manners but there's no kind of agreed form of manners. For a novelist there has almost to be an agreed notion of society. In that sense, I often think that you could never find Jane Austen writing poems or short stories. And it's through the Church that I first came to know all I'd know of manners, of ceremony, of sacrament, of grace.

EM: Some people might be surprised that you paint such a positive picture of your relations with the Church.

JMG: I would think it is neither positive nor negative – it's just a fact. I remember when *The Dark* was banned I went on *The Late Late Show* from, of all places, The King's Hall in Belfast. I was expected to attack the Catholic Church and I said that I could no more attack the Catholic Church than I could my own life. I remember there was a Unionist in the audience and he got up and said: 'There's a man, whose book has been banned by the southern Government, who has been sacked out of his school by the Archbishop of Dublin and he comes down here to Belfast and gets up on his hind legs and praises the Catholic Church.' He says: 'Could Moscow do a better job of brainwashing than that?!'

EM: Speaking about Archbishop John Charles McQuaid, you were in Scoil Eoin Bhaiste in Clontarf at the time. He actually intervened with the parish priest, the Manager of the School, didn't he?

JMG: Actually, the Manager was a charming man. He was a Fr Carton and I don't think he had any interest in Catholicism or spirituality. He came from the rich family that supplied all the potatoes to the Dublin market and he loved whiskey and food. He complained to me constantly about 'them bowsies of doctors'. I was, I suppose, spiritual at the time and I equated spirituality with a priest. I was a bit shocked when he said to me one day in the school yard: 'If you listened to those bowsies of doctors, life wouldn't be worth living!' I thought that a priest was supposed to have a more elevated view of life.

EM: I just wonder, John, if the religious instruction you received as a child had a detrimental impact on your spirituality?

JMG: No, I mean I have nothing but gratitude to the Church. I would think that if there was one thing injurious about the Church, it would be its attitude to sexuality. I see sexuality as just a part of life. Either all of life is sacred or none of it is sacred. I'm inclined to think that all of life is sacred and that sexuality is a very important part of that sacredness. And I think that it made a difficult enough relationship – which is between people, between men and women – even more difficult by imparting an unhealthy attitude to sexuality. By making sexuality abnormal and by giving it more importance in a way than it has – by exaggerating it.

EM: It was always the way in this country that religion and sexuality were entwined and that practising Catholics were expected to obey the rules handed down from on high.

JMG: Yes. When I was in my 20s it did occur to me that there was something perverted about an attitude that thought that killing somebody was a minor offence compared to kissing somebody.

EM: And then of course the Papal encyclical, *Humanae Vitae*, came along and it caused a lot of pain for many sincere Catholic couples who were trying to avoid having children.

JMG: In a way, I had left Catholicism at that time, but the debt remained. And of course it was a very simple form of Catholicism and to a certain extent I always thought that as well as being my most important book the Church was also my first fiction. I think fiction is a very serious thing, that while it is fiction, it is also a revelation of truth, or facts. We absolutely believed in Heaven and Hell, Purgatory, and even Limbo. I mean, they were actually closer to us than Australia or Canada, that they were real places.

EM: A physical state?

JMG: I remember writing once that there was an orchard beside the bar-racks, Lenehans' orchard, and somehow in my imaginings of Heaven, Lenehans' orchard was some place around the entrance.

EM: It may have had something to do with the Garden of Eden.

JMG: I don't know, maybe it had.

EM: Elizabeth Reegan, the main character in your first novel, *The Barracks*, suffers much and yet is receptive to the beauty of nature and the cycle of life. Her exclamation before her death of 'Jesus Christ!' as she looks out one morning at the spectacular countryside seems to me to be something of an epiphany. What is the role and meaning of revelation in your novels?

JMG: I don't think that the writer can say that. That belongs to the reader. I mean all the writer tries to do is get his words right and in order to do that you have to think clearly and feel deeply. I like a thing that Chekhov said: 'When a writer takes a pen into his hand he accuses himself of unanswerable egotism and all he can do with decency after that is to bow!' I also think that the only difference between the writer and the reader is that each of us has a private world which others cannot see and that it's with that private world that we all read. It's a spiritual, private world. And the only difference between the writer and the reader is that he (the writer) has the knack or talent to be able to dramatise that private world and turn it into words. But it's the same private world that each of us possesses. Joyce once described the piano as a coffin of music and I see the book as a coffin of words. A book, in fact, doesn't live again until it finds a reader and you get as many versions of the book as the number of readers it finds.

EM: Speaking as a reader, I find that passage particularly moving where Elizabeth looks out on that splendid Roscommon vista which up until then she had never fully taken in. Now, when she is close to death, the beauty strikes her with poignant force.

JMG: That's a dramatic problem. When you're in danger of losing a thing it becomes precious and when it's around us, it's in tedious abundance and we take it for granted as if we're going to live forever, which we're not. I think there's a great difference in consciousness in that same way in that when we're young we read books for the story, for the excitement of the story – and there comes a time when you realise that all stories are more or less the same story. I think it's linked to the realisation that we're not going to live forever and that the way of saying and the language become more important than the story.

EM: In an interview you did once with Julia Carlson, you remarked how amazing it was that a Catholic country like Ireland should have produced so many writers who were lapsed Catholics. But is this fact all that surprising? Maybe the writers would have been more Catholic if the country had been less so.

JMG: That was a very hurried interview and it was never revised or corrected. I mean I think that's a fact and I think that we had a very peculiar type of Catholic Church here in that it was a fortress church. Very much like an army, it demanded unquestioned allegiance. I remember reading in Proust's letters where they were trying to throw the *curé* off the school committee and Proust says that he should remain if for nothing but the spire of his church which lifts men's eyes from the avaricious earth. Elsewhere in that same letter he describes the eighteenth-century Church in France as 'the refuge of ignoramuses'. I would think that the Church, the personnel of the Church I grew up in – which I separate from the sacraments, the prayer, the liturgy – I would suspect might even have been a refuge of ignoramuses also. Proust said also that he agreed with Tolstoy that one would never have thought when looking back at the eighteenth-century Church that one would see the revival of spirituality that was seen in the 19th century. Proust stated as well that Baudelaire was intimately connected with the Church, if only through sacrilege.

EM: Yes, that's an interesting comment with regard to Baudelaire, who was the quintessential *poète maudit* and yet was also very spiritual.

JMG: But you can't commit sacrilege if you believe in spirituality.

EM: In the same interview with Julia Carlson you pointed out that Irish identity was very confining. To be Irish was to be against sexuality, against the English. How do you think our national identity has evolved since the 1960s?

JMG: I think I was remarking on something that I would see as childish. Trying to define yourself as being against something is poor, I think. The way I see it is that all the ol' guff about being Irish is a kind of nonsense. I mean, I couldn't be anything else no matter how hard I tried to be. I couldn't be Chinese or Japanese.

EM: Strangely enough, it's almost becoming 'sexy' to be Irish, which certainly wasn't the case a few decades ago.

JMG: Well, that's just another version of the same thing. What's interesting is to be human, to be decent or moral or whatever. Everything that we inherit, the rain, the skies, the speech – and anybody who works in the English language in Ireland knows that there's the dead ghost of Gaelic in the language we use and listen to and that those things will reflect our Irish identity. And I actually see it as being very childish for anyone to have to beat their breast and say 'I'm Irish!' I mean, isn't it obvious?

EM: You present a very different picture of Ireland from some of your contemporaries like Brian Moore, John Broderick (who was a cousin of yours, I believe), Edna O'Brien and Frank McCourt. What is your opinion of their depiction of Irish mores?

JMG: Well, I can't speak for them.[2] I would think that I write out of my own private or spiritual world. I would see my business as to get my words right, and I think that if you get your words right you will reflect everything that the particular form you're writing in is capable of reflecting. And, in fact, I think that if you actually set out to give a picture of Ireland, that it would be unlikely to be interesting, that it would be closer to propaganda or journalism. Because when an author starts a book, he has no idea where it's going. It's a voyage or a work of discovery. And I have a suspicion that if the tension wasn't there for the writer that it wouldn't be there either for the reader. Art is a mysterious thing, the fingerprints of the writer are all over it and you can't fake anything from the reader. If the tension's not there, the reader will sense that it's actually not dramatised, not thought out, not felt. There's a very interesting analogy that Auden made where he said that while the scientist knows his work, the work doesn't know him. Whereas the work always knows the writer.

EM: But even as a reader – you would read fiction – there must be Irish writers whom you admire.

JMG: Oh yes, many. When I was young both Beckett and Kavanagh were writing and publishing and they were for me the most exciting writers at the time. They weren't the most fashionable – O'Faolain and O'Connor were the most fashionable. And I would think that Kate O'Brien is a most important writer and she was considered nobody then. I like strange people: I like Ernie O'Malley, I like Tomás O'Crohan's *The Islandman*. I like Michael McLaverty, some of Corkery's short stories. I mean the obvious ones are Joyce and Yeats.

EM: Joyce and Yeats cast a shadow over Irish writers who came after them. You inherit a certain literary tradition – before you become a writer, you're a reader – which has to influence you.

JMG: Yeah, sure. But I don't consider them shadows. In fact, I would think that they're an enormous source of sustenance and pride. In a sense Yeats was a terribly important figure because he made it difficult for the mediocre to get a footing. Not only was he a brilliant poet but he almost single-handedly established a tradition that wasn't there before. In fact, he paved the way for Joyce and Synge, and you could say even Beckett. I see some of Beckett's works as full of Yeats. I think the play *Purgatory* is very close to *Waiting for Godot*. I edited for a French publisher John Butler Yeats' letters and there's a charming letter where John is very upset that Willie has rejected his play for the Abbey because he said it had no system. John Butler Yeats was drawing a portrait of Synge at the time and he was complaining to the latter about Willie's rejection of his play. Synge said: 'You should go back and ask him if his plays have a system!'

EM: You often portray characters who are veterans of the War of Independence. Men like Reegan (*The Barracks*) and Moran (*Amongst Women*) are disenchanted with the Irish Free State, which is ultimately the fruit of their struggles. In Moran's words, it has resulted merely in 'some of our johnnies in the top jobs instead of a few Englishmen'. Is he echoing your own view of the situation here?

JMG: No, not really my view, but my father fought in the war of Independence and one of my uncles. He (the uncle) was expelled out of the IRA. He won a King's scholarship, he was a very intelligent man, a pedant. He got expelled out of the IRA for insisting that they all learn Irish after the war was over. He joined the Blueshirts then. To a certain extent, Moran is an imaginary figure but he is also based on a number of people. That was, in a way, a prevalent reaction – in that the dream didn't become the reality. A lot of it was confused with their youth which would end anyhow. It was also the most exciting and dramatic time of their lives. I think they had a kind of dream – you see it in O'Malley's *On Another Man's Wound* too – that they were bound together by something bigger than themselves. And then normal life restored itself and the Church and the medical profession got power. And, if anything, the country got poorer.

EM: Yes, as often happens after a conflict like that, it was a minority that benefited.

JMG: And it was a very unattractive minority, I think, that did well out of the State, in that they were the shopkeepers, the medical profession, the Church. People were looked down on that had to go to England to earn a living as if they had committed sin in some way, as if it was any virtue to have the luck to remain on in Ireland.

EM: In the modern context, we have a 'new' type of country now with the Celtic Tiger, which is also benefiting a minority.

JMG: Ah, I think a lot more people are better off now. I think it's a wonderful thing and that they don't have to go unless they want to go abroad.

EM: Because emigration, as far as you'd be concerned, was a major problem. And then you had to emigrate yourself.

JMG: I thought that romantic notion of the writer having to go abroad was foolishness, even when I was young. It looked like a nonsense to me that someone like Larkin or Evelyn Waugh – I think Larkin is a great poet – or Thomas Hardy would have to go abroad to be an English writer. I remember saying once that I thought a person could write badly in Ireland as well as anywhere else – you didn't have to go abroad to write badly!

EM: I suppose once more, because Joyce did it, it became fashionable.

JMG: It's a sign of an inferiority complex. It is our country now and we don't have to apologise to anybody. In fact, I remember when *The Dark* was banned I was friendly with the very distinguished editor of *The Listener*, Joe Ackerley, and he said that it was marvellous about the scandal surrounding the book, that it would boost sales. I actually didn't think that at all: I was quite ashamed. You know, it was our own country and we were making bloody fools out of ourselves. When I was young in Dublin we thought the Censorship Board was a joke and that most of the books banned were like most of the books published: they weren't worth reading anyway, and those that were could be easily found and quickly passed around. There's no fruit that tastes so good as the forbidden fruit. And then I was actually a bit ashamed to be mixed up in it and I would refuse to make any protest about it. In fact, it's well known that the people in Paris wanted to make a protest and that Beckett was approached. He said that first of all he would have to read the book and then to ask McGahern if he wanted a protest. And only for Beckett I would never have been asked that. When they asked me, I said that I didn't want a protest, that I was enormously grateful to them and to thank them and Mr Beckett, but that I thought that by protesting one gave it too much importance.

EM: You were amazingly low key. I mean you were a *cause célèbre* at the time and you did nothing to highlight the wrong that was done to you.

JMG: Ah, I don't think it was a virtue: it was pride more than anything. I wouldn't like to claim too much credit for it.

EM: Does the writer of fiction have a role to play in forging a national consciousness in your opinion?

JMG: Not deliberately. The only role a writer has is to get his words right and to do that, as Flaubert said, you have to feel deeply and think clearly . . .

EM: And write coldly.

JMG: In order to find the right words. But think clearly means coldly. I think that if you do that, you will reflect everything that is worth reflecting. Whereas when you set out to reflect something you end up reflecting nothing. There's a very interesting thing that Scott Fitzgerald said: 'If you start with a person, you end up with a type, but if you start with a type, you wind up with nothing.' You set out to discover something in your writing and it is through the attempt to discover that you reflect. If you have your mind made up about something, you'll reflect nothing.

EM: So really you are a wordsmith and what emerges is there for the reader to interpret, accept or reject.

JMG: I think that if it is good work – and that's for the reader to decide – it actually does become the history of our consciousness.

EM: Anthony Cronin has suggested that you, in common with Edna O'Brien, persist in misrepresenting Ireland – which Cronin sees as urban, open and secular – by portraying characters who are dominated by rural values, taboos and religious repressions. What is your reaction to this critique?

JMG: Well he's (Cronin) a reader and he's attacked my work from the beginning, as he has every right to – in fact, I'd defend his right to do that – but I would see in that the vulgarity of making subject matter more important than the writing. In fact, a writer doesn't really have much choice over his subject matter in that the subject matter claims him/her, and that all that matters is what he does with the subject matter. The quality of the language, the quality of seeing and thinking are the important things, not whether it's rural Ireland, or whether it's in Foxrock or in bohemian Dublin. I think that all good writing is local, and by local I don't differentiate between Ballyfermot and north Roscommon. If the writer gets his words right, he'll make that local scene universal. The great Portuguese writer, Miguel Torga, said the local is the universal, but without walls.

EM: In his *Irish Journal*, Heinrich Böll wrote that for someone who is Irish and a writer, there is probably much to provoke him in this country. Has this been your experience?

JMG: I would think that to be a writer anywhere is always a difficult thing because you have the same problem of finding the right words. I read Böll's book and liked it, but I thought it was a love affair with Ireland, and it was a fantasy world. It was very charming because of that, but it was a dream world – and every world is to a certain extent a dream world.

EM: The strange thing about Böll, as I see it, is that when he's actually writing about Germany he's extremely cutting and his observation is very acute. Whereas he seems to have glossed over completely the more unsavoury aspects of Ireland, the poverty, emigration – he has this notion of emigration as being almost a romantic thing for the Irish.

JMG: Well, of course, he knows more about Germany, almost certainly. That's why family rows are the worst, because everyone knows too much about one another and can inflict wounds that an outsider wouldn't be able to inflict.

EM: Do you think that the Peace Process will succeed?

JMG: I've been asked that many times and I think that Northern Ireland is fashionable because of the violence. When I was growing up, there were two sectarian states, one here and one in the North. Despite public claims and utterances, they were very happy with one another: one could point the other out in self-justification. I know people from both sides of the divide in the North and I don't actually understand the Northern situation because I think that it's an emotional situation. It's sectarian and you need to be brought up in it to understand it. It just seems strange and foreign to me. It doesn't engage me personally. I don't think it's right that people should be killing one another. From my point of view, life is more sacred than any idea.

EM: You speak about two sectarian states. Do you feel that the Irish Republic was in its own way sectarian?

JMG: When I was growing up it was completely Catholic, sectarian. It was almost like a theocracy.

EM: You were accused on a number of occasions of portraying Protestants in a sympathetic manner.

JMG: Yes, that's right. I grew up very close to the Rockingham Estate and there were many Protestants there. They dwindled: I think that the marriage laws had a big impact on them. They were a very attractive people to me. Everybody had good manners, they were better off and, of course, some of them did convert to Catholicism in order to get married. I write about that in 'The Conversion of William Kirkwood'.[3] I remember saying on French television once about the North of Ireland that it was a very mysterious place to me, that it seemed to me that the Catholics hated the British and they looked down on the people in the South as degenerate and the Protestants hated the people in the South and they looked on the British as being degenerate. They conducted their warfare in Washington, London and Dublin and the one place where they wouldn't talk to one another was in the North of Ireland. I didn't think that anything would happen in the North of Ireland until they were actually kept up there and talked to one another, which seems to be what is happening now, whether it will endure or not. I live beside the border and I have a cousin who was a diocesan examiner and he tells me that to examine religious doctrine in the schools when you go six to seven miles across the border, Catholicism is 40–50 years behind the times in the North of Ireland. He was talking about 15 years ago.

EM: I'd say the situation isn't dramatically different today.

JMG: When you grow up in the South, you have a different experience altogether. There's a very nice statement of David Hume's: 'I never discuss religion,' he says, 'Because its basis is faith, not reason.' I would apply the same thing to the North of Ireland.

EM: A final question to you, John. We've just come to the end of the first year of the new millennium. What sort of Irish identity do you see emerging in the coming decades?

JMG: I don't know. It'd be a wise man that would try to predict that. It doesn't really interest me because I believe that the real adventure is a spiritual adventure and that that's a human adventure. One's Irish experience is given and it's what one does with it that counts. That's just the accidental place (Ireland) that life happens and it's the only place and it's the place we love and it's passing. We will have an identity, but I think we wouldn't have it long if we started worrying about it.

EM: John McGahern, thank you very much for your time and patience.

Notes

1   Original published as Eamon Maher, 'Catholicism and National Identity in the Works of John McGahern', *Studies* vol. 90, no. 357 (spring, 2001), pp. 72–83.

2   In some written notes that the author submitted to me he supplied the following answer to a similar question that is worth reproducing here: 'I read a few of Moore's novels. The craft and care are obvious, and have to be respected. But I never found in Moore what I look for in writing. *Angela's Ashes* interested me much more. I found it a very strange book, a mixture of farce and clearly honed American evocative writing and literary pretension. A work it reminded me of was Synge's *Playboy of the Western World*, also a farce. It was farce as a great kick at misery and passive suffering. If it's not a farce then the concluding chapter is in serious bad taste and the whole book a sort of porridge.'

3   This short story appeared in *The Collected Stories* (London, 1992), pp. 331–50.

CHAPTER 27

Forty Years On (2003)

Mary Kenny

Only a small proportion of writers in *Studies* were women. In this article Mary Kenny reflects on the achievements of four decades of Irish feminism from the vantage point of her own shifting views over time. She is a journalist and playwright and the author of several books including *Goodbye to Catholic Ireland*, a social history of twentieth-century Ireland.[1]

A useful way of examining the last 40 years in the lives of Irishwomen, I thought, was to examine the changes I have seen in my own life in that time. Not that my own life is typical: but then no individual life is typical. But since I was involved in founding a feminist movement in Ireland (the Irish Women's Liberation Movement) and since my trade involved reporting and writing commentaries on the lives of other women, there may be some illuminations in an autobiographical approach.

In 1962 I was 18 years old, and had been out of school for two years. I was a difficult and rebellious schoolgirl, disruptive and prone to sowing disorder among my fellows. Disruptive behaviour in schoolchildren is now also associated with the wrong food additives – too many items in their diet carrying the letter 'E', I believe – or with a syndrome known as Attention Deficit Disorder, which in turn is treated with a pharmaceutical drug marketed as Ritalin. Whether it be better to treat difficult and naughty children with psychology and pharmaceuticals than to fetch them a metaphorical clip around the ear and tell them to be on their way is yet to be tested, since all the care lavished on naughtiness has not yet reduced or corrected disorderly conduct; but this is merely one measure of the ways things have changed. And it is a symptomatic measure. For child-centred education had not yet been developed in 1962, and the 'therapeutic' approach to human conduct had not yet been implemented.

In any case, I had worked for my living since the age of 16, and this was not considered at the time a particular hardship. There were individuals I knew, but a few years older than I, who had left school at 12; although this was not exactly legal, it was at times allowed in practice, sometimes on the understanding that the young person was entering an apprenticeship.

The question of university education really did not arise for the majority in 1962. It was simply assumed that this would be for the exceptionally clever, those 'scholarship girls' who always came top of the class, and shone at brainy subjects like maths. I felt mildly critical of Maeve Binchy's otherwise adorable novel *Circle of Friends* for this reason: Maeve is an accurate social observer, but it seems to me that the assumption, in the story, that normal young folk in Dublin all went off to university together was élitist. There were only two conditions, broadly speaking, under which young women, in particular, went on to college for the generation born in the early 1940s: one was where the girl was exceptionally clever, and had parents who valued and encouraged that cleverness. The other was when her parents were in easy enough circumstances to pay for her to be at university, rather than in work. Of course there were exceptions: there always are, but among the group of my contemporaries, born around 1944, this was the pattern. My sister, born in 1933, found at a reunion of her classmates from a Dominican boarding school in the 1970s, that only two women in 25 had gone on to further education. The majority had become secretaries, which was the usual choice of profession for middle-class young women at the time; although the more glamorous aspiration was to become an air hostess, which carried an almost impossible stamp of prestige.

When our feminist movement was founded in 1970–1, we claimed that women had been short-changed in education and opportunities. I am now of the view, quixotically, that our analysis was insufficiently Marxist: for educational expectations in Ireland were more class-prejudiced than gender-prejudiced. Working-class boys were even more excluded from further education than middle-class girls, as Finola Kennedy shows in her indispensable study, *Cottage to Creche*.

And I have to say, in tribute to the Loreto nuns, that although they did not, at the time, offer the expectation that most girls would have the chance to go to university, they nonetheless did take the education of women seriously. They did seem to think it was very important to work hard and pass exams; and they highly esteemed pupils who were conscientious in their studies. At no time did I ever pick up the utilitarian assumption that a particular aunt of mine held, that 'sure, girls will only get married – what's the use of spending money on educating them?' This notion was simply not on the agenda. Indeed, marriage was hardly ever mentioned as an aspiration, which is perhaps logical from consecrated virgins. Occasionally, we might be told that we were 'the mothers of tomorrow', but that was as far as it went. The idea, which was very much to the fore in American culture at this time – and so brilliantly attacked, and exposed, in Betty Friedan's *The Feminine Mystique* (1963) – that women were defined by their sex role, inside and outside of marriage, was not in play.

In this, the Irish nuns of that generation were the inheritors of Miss Beale and Miss Buss, the formidable Victorian spinsters who pioneered serious-minded education for women. Sometimes I have reflected that some aspects of feminism were the continuous and direct result of convent education, in which we saw women manage great estates and in effect international corporations: for the Mother Superior and the Mother Provincial were also the inheritors of the tradition of the great Abbesses of the Middle Ages.

In 1962, having worked as a waitress, a filing clerk, a typist and a secretary, I resolved to go off to France as an *au pair* girl, which was the beginning of a different kind of education, which is jestingly referred to as the 'University of Life'. My peers from school were starting their first training courses, or, indeed entering colleges or universities, as some did, after all. Of my four closest school friends, one entered her parents' business, one went on to do an English degree, one entered office life, and one attained that dizzy glamour of becoming an Aer Lingus stewardess. All of them married, though 50 per cent of the marriages in this group were later dissolved.

Much has been said about 'the sexual revolution' of the 1960s, but the real sexual revolution which occurred in Ireland was in the sudden and indeed welcome increase in marriage. As has been widely documented, the Irish had been most reluctant marriers, ever since the famine period of 1845–50. The extreme reserve about marriage reached its nadir in the 1950s when the Catholic bishops were constantly wringing their hands about the dearth of marriages, and lashing into the 'selfish bachelors and over-cautious "old maids"' who would not embark on wedlock. Not that it was an exclusively Catholic problem: Irish Protestants were just as resistant. An interesting indicator of this was the 'Lonelyhearts' advertisements in the Dublin *Evening Mail*, a newspaper which reached both Catholic and Protestant readers, and in which notices from the Guild of the Holy Rosary sat cheek by jowl with those of the Freemasons' Lodges. The age of those seeking spouses often seemed mature, and the most common self-description was the use of the word 'respectable'. 'Business gent, 35, respectable, wishes to meet respectable girl.' 'Respectable working-class girl, RC, wishes to meet respectable working-class man, strict TT.' 'Working man, 36 years, steady job, good appearance, would like to meet respectable working girl, 30 years, with view to matrimony.'

Then, in the 1960s, this altered. As we all know, social trends began to 'loosen up' by about 1958, perhaps particularly with the election of Pope John XXIII. Television broadcasts commenced in Ireland in 1961, the same year, coincidentally or not, that the contraceptive Pill appeared. Sex, for many Irish young people, still meant marriage, and from the early 1960s, the national newspapers featured a riot of wedding, and a plethora of engagement photographs. Between 1951 and 1971 the percentage of married men in Ireland between the ages of 25 and 34 climbed from 33 per cent to 58 per cent (and to its peak of 66 per cent in 1981, from which it has since fallen, with the acceptance of cohabitation). Among young women, the increase from the 1950s to the 1970s was 54 per cent to 74 per cent. Finola Kennedy is no doubt correct in presuming that much of this change was economic: the 1960s saw a mini-Celtic Tiger effect, as emigration slowed down, and more opportunities for work were available. People could afford to marry. And they did.

In France, I experienced a culture shock which was at once liberal and reactive. I was exposed to a politically disputatious society which was only beginning to come to terms with the Algerian troubles; and among the young, was challenging the 'authoritarianism' of General de Gaulle. The Catholic Church in France, by 1963, had already relaxed the more informal rules which were still in situ in Ireland: young women went into the Church bareheaded and people took the Eucharist standing, and in the hand. The political and ecclesiastical aspect of French life struck me as progressive and radical, but domestic life was rigidly archaic.

Indeed, in terms of the everyday, Irishwomen were in many respects more liberated, for life in Ireland was easy going and meals were not exacting. At that time, we were content to have a boiled egg for our evening meal, or sausages on toast. In France, the exquisitely high standards of cuisine and the domestic arts meant that women slaved all day long shopping, cooking, presenting and cleaning. I thought it was appalling. I still think that household drudgery is a horrible source of female oppression, although how civilised life and a pleasant dwelling can be maintained without someone skivvying away to maintain it, I do not know. Moreover, some of the most radical feminists of my youth have, paradoxically, turned into some of the most accomplished homemakers: I would mention here my friend June Levine, who once said that marriage was an institution invented by the patriarchy to keep women down, and who today is not only married, but maintains one of the most beautiful homes, and the most delightful tables, I know.

When I returned to Ireland in 1969 – having in the meantime worked as journalist in London, after two years in France – it was a society in the throes of a modernising process. The 1960s had been a successful decade for marriage, and for an increase in fertility too; but also a challenging one for the old rules. Many of the laws and regulations in Ireland had failed to evolve largely, I now think, because neutrality during the Second World War had held back social change. The changes for which we in the feminist movement campaigned had largely been brought about in other European countries because of the modernising impact of wartime: the 'marriage bar', in which women were obliged to resign from their jobs in the State sector and often in civil society too, had operated in the United Kingdom until it was swept aside by the sheer need of getting women into the workforce in 1939–45. True, there had been a return to enforced domesticity in the 1950s, but certain advances had been retained. Even the custom of women wearing trousers was less usual in Ireland than in Britain, if one looks through the women's magazines of the 1940–80 period.

The 'sex revolution' as such, was also beginning to have its impact, and this was, I would say, almost wholly due to the introduction of the contraceptive Pill. The Pill introduced the idea that sexual intercourse did not necessarily have any consequences; and this, in a way, was a new idea in the history of humankind. Contraceptive devices had been known previous to 1961, of course; but all of these devices were interruptive of the sex act in some way. The contraceptive Pill completely separated sexuality from fertility, and in that sense, it not only ushered in a sexual revolution; it was the enabler of the revolution in biology, and the whole spectrum we now have in assisted reproduction, from IVF to cloning. The Vatican was right to treat the introduction of the Pill as a crisis: it was. This is still not an easy question to resolve. Women are entitled to some control over their fertility. But the mechanistic view that prevails among the population lobbies and the birth-control gurus occludes not only moral considerations, but at the deepest level, female sensibilities. It was June Levine who said to me in 2002: 'They [the mechanistic birth controllers] don't seem to understand that the baby is part of the sexuality.' The fruit of the womb is not, after all, so easily separated from the transmission of life.

And so the 1970s and 1980s were a time in which the modernising changes of the 1960s were being carried further. Attitudes changed, as we hoped they would, to unmarried mothers, and some of my generation became single mothers, either through choice or circumstance. Sometimes this choice also included some pain which could not be resolved by a mere change in the law. A friend of mine who gave birth to her daughter in 1974, could never bring herself to tell her own father about the child, and he died without ever knowing. Changes were brought about to assist the deserted wife, whom we thought a particularly pitiful victim. But, as all social welfare reformers have learned, eventually, that it is a fine balance to relieve distress without creating 'a poverty trap'. How do you help the abandoned wife, or the single mother, for that matter, without providing a financial incentive for more men to desert their wives, or more mothers to choose not to marry? Difficult.

Looking back on those years, almost all our own lives were tempestuous in some way. Liberation was not as easy as it looked. Raising children was not as easy at it looked. Deciding not to have children was not as easy as it looked. 'Lifestyle choices', whether these be cohabitation, marriage, divorce, or homosexuality all brought their own sorrows.

The Irish economy zigged and zagged upwards and downwards. Social changes went on apace, and there were many bitter disputes over the abortion and divorce referenda. Both of these have been surveyed so comprehensively that it would be otiose to revisit these in any detail; but I had come to disagree with many of the canons of feminism – although not all – and I recall many fierce debates among friends and contemporaries. The first abortion referendum, in 1983, was particularly sharp: it was the first time that such a contentious, personal, morally and emotionally laden subject had been so publicly aired in Ireland. In its own way, it was another end of innocence: a woman wrote to the *Irish Times* saying that until now she had never heard the word 'abortion' except in connection with the failure of a cow to calve. At the same time, I would not disparage these referenda, for it is important for a society to discuss, and clarify, its own values, even where such discourse is divisive.

As the 21st century dawned, it has often struck me how successful young Irish women now seem. This is very evident in the public media, particularly through radio and television, where confident and articulate young women abound. Some commentators lament that there are not yet enough women in political life, but since the majority of women have no great interest in politics, it will never be otherwise – unless we were to usher in some 'Equality Agenda' based on an artificial construct of quotas and coercive social engineering. There is always a tension between freedom and equality: too much emphasis on equality must mean a restriction on freedom, and those of us who were women's *liberationists* must usually put liberty before equality. Women must be free not to have to vote, to stand for parliament, or to engage in political life, just as they must be free to do so. Those women among my own peers, such as Gemma Hussey and Nuala Fennell, who went into politics in the 1970s and 1980s, prospered reasonably well: but they chose to quit politics with the conclusion that for the most part the game isn't worth the candle. Nuala described the life of a backbench TD as 'cannonfodder'.

But I am pleased to see young women now expecting to go to university, and to have free accession to the trades and professions, and to have a self-confident attitude to earning their living. I think in many respects the lives of young women in Ireland in 2003 hold much promise; it is also my impression that young women continue to be, as they always have been, very open to the spiritual.

Yet they too will have their own problems, sorrows and pains. Some of the problems arising in their lives are the direct consequent of the advances we thought we were making: for example, we affirmed the right for women

to take on mortgages, and women duly won that right. However, in consequence, the price of housing has been unwittingly increased, and now it is
almost impossible to purchase a home without two incomes: and sometimes
extremely difficult to do so even with two incomes. It is good for young married women to have the choice to have a job, but that in no way minimises
the difficulty of holding down a job, while raising children and trying to keep
a marriage together. When that class of 1962 gets together, we also perceive
that much of the extreme coarseness, the indigestible media vulgarity, the
in-yer-face advertising and even, perhaps, an element of sexual harassment
and date rape, are also fallout from the candour and freedom which we once
affirmed.

And wherever something is gained, something is also lost. An old 'Sixties'
feminist said to me as the century came to end: 'Life is materially better than
in our youth. But it is also less poignant.' I think this is so: it was the struggle,
and not the goal, that turned out to be the exciting part.

Notes

1   Originally published as Mary Kenny, 'Forty Years On', *Studies* vol. 92, no. 365 (spring,
2003), pp. 7–12,

CHAPTER 28

Paisleyism

A Theological Inquiry (2004)

Neil Southern

Studies since its inception has published many articles on religion; 1912 saw the publication of two articles on Islam. In recent years it has included ones on immigrant African Pentecostals, and this account of the relationship between Paisley's theology and Unionist politics. Many articles on the Northern crisis had advocated pluralism and ecumenism; these pointed to weak understandings of Unionist perspectives south of the border. This article draws on interviews with leading members of the Democratic Unionist Party including Iris Robinson and Nigel Dobbs. At the time of writing Neil Southern was a research associate at the University of Ulster. More recently he has been a Facilitator in a community peace-building programme in Northern Ireland.[1]

Revd Dr Ian Paisley is responsible for creating an ideology which has made a huge impact on the thinking of many Protestants in Northern Ireland. Whilst the Free Presbyterian Church, of which Paisley is moderator, is a relatively small denomination, having around 15,000 members, his Democratic Unionist Party (DUP) is an extremely important factor in the ideological development of political Protestantism. Indeed, the DUP's success in recent elections has made it the leading Unionist party – an electoral result for which Paisley has waited 32 years. Clearly, Paisley offers a brand of Unionism and Protestantism that appeals to many Ulster Protestants. Therefore, given the grip that Paisleyism has on Northern Irish affairs, it is a system of ideas and values which cannot be ignored – nor escaped.

Yet, what is often underemphasised is that Paisleyism arises from a blend of deep-seated and intensely held theological views which, by their very nature, have done nothing to discourage ethnic division. Indeed, it has been through the vehicle of politics that Paisley's religious ideas have poured into the Protestant community. As a result, when Paisley articulates a response to the Belfast Agreement (or any move toward harmonisation of community relations) which is condemnatory and denunciatory, his reaction is principally conditioned by theological concerns before the secular aspects of ethnicity enter the equation. To put it another way: Paisley's anti-Catholicism as a theological factor is of greater relevance to Paisleyite ideology than the political factors which are grounded in his antipathy towards Irish nationalism. And this ought not to be surprising given the fact that Paisley and the leadership of the DUP describe themselves as being fundamentalist in their religious convictions, claiming to be 'saved' and 'born again' evangelical Christians.[2] Thus, given the strong religious credentials of these politically high-profile individuals, it is not surprising that a theological interpretation of the ideology can be made.

One of the most distinguishing features of the theology that motivates Paisley and his religious supporters is the way in which they interpret the Bible literally. In common with other fundamentalist religious groups whose sacred text is central to their personal and collective lives, Ulster's fundamentalists view the Bible as a divinely inspired document which contains a list of God's unchanging laws.[3] Placing an emphasis on the Old Testament's covenantal theology which conditioned the social, political and religious relationship that the ancient Israelites had with God, evangelical Democratic Unionists and Free Presbyterians believe that Northern Ireland should follow suit. They treat the covenant that God established with the Israelites to be archetypal and to serve as an example of the covenantal expectations God places upon all those with whom He is prepared to enter into covenant. The immutability surrounding God's rules in the Old Testament mean that the Ten Commandments must be honoured, and covenantal fidelity maintained, if a people are continually to receive divine blessing. It was for this reason that for many years the DUP followed a policy of sabbatarianism in the local councils it controlled in Northern Ireland. A theology that had sabbatarian implications meant that, from the 1970s to the early 1990s, civic amenities could be closed on a Sunday. Hence, non-theologically minded Protestants in DUP-controlled councils found themselves following council rules whose origins lay in the millennia-old theology of the Old Testament. This social policy, which can be seen as an attempt by the DUP to use the forum of local politics as a vehicle for furthering their religious beliefs, was eventually put on the DUP's back burner when it was realised that secular Protestants who vote for the Party do not want an unpalatable theocratic element to be part of the political deal.

Looking at the example of Old Testament Israel in terms of the conduct that secured God's favour and that which brought His condemnation,

Paisleyites are inclined to point out how important it is that Protestant Ulster forsake its apostate path and return to the God-fearing faith of its fore-fathers. Accordingly, ecumenism is the worst of Protestant sins because it involves communication and interaction with Catholicism. Arguing by anal-ogy to the captivities of Israel and Judah by the Assyrians and Babylonians, Paisleyites believe that an apostate Protestantism that has abandoned the 'true' faith and which is basking in its secularity could be chastened by God. Interestingly, fundamentalists adopt a political understanding of God's chastening: such chastening, it was suggested, could take the form of a Gaelic Irish captivity – or in the political vernacular – an all-Ireland. The purpose of chastisement within the divine plan is to humble a people and bring them back to a true and dedicated worship of God. This religious and political perspective on covenantal faithfulness is well demonstrated in the following comment by DUP MLA and former MP Revd William McCrea:

> I was reading a portion of scripture recently where Israel forgot its maker and I believe that Ulster, it is sad to say, has forgot its maker . . . I believe that God can use many an instance to the means of chastening God's people and to bring them back to a place of blessing.[4]

Similarly, the following remarks by the prominent Free Presbyterian minister and former DUP activist, Revd Ivan Foster, refer to the partition of Ireland as being an example of God delivering His Ulster Protestant people from pending oppression just as He did those who followed Moses out of Egypt:

> I have always believed that the intervention, the divine intervention, the providential intervention of God at the turn of the century when Ulster was preserved from going into a society that was predominantly Roman Catholic was a favour, an answer to prayer. And I have also said the day we lose it, is a day when you can see in that loss the frown of God, because whatever favour He showed our fathers, He is obviously taking away from us . . . I do believe that an all-Ireland political entity can but mean chastening for the people of God.[5]

What can be discerned in the comments of McCrea and Foster is the centrality of the Old Testament to their religion and politics. The Old Testament provides the fundamentalist with a context within which his exper-iences can make perfect sense. Israel's history, in terms of its internal crises and its external problems associated with the national struggle for existence, are appropriated by the fundamentalist as a means of understanding his own situation. If Israel's apostasy and covenantal failings provoked God's displea-sure and subsequent chastening, then Ulster's apostasy and increasing

Godlessness could qualify it for the same treatment. Like Israel of old, whose enemies threatened them with the political humiliation of subjugation, so too are God's people in Ulster conceived of as being threatened by similar forces whose intent is the same but who differ only in name and racial type. Whilst Catholics in both religious and political spheres constitute an obvious enemy to the Paisleyite, the Protestants who are involved in the ecumenical movement are just as dangerous.

Protestant participation in ecumenical endeavor is, of course, a particular hate of Paisleyites, because it represents decay from within. The institutional fraternising of elements of Protestantism with what is believed to be its age-old adversary, along with a general de-sacralising of the Protestant consciousness, are seen as ways of inviting God's condemnation which the fundamentalist is at pains to avoid. As a result, many of Paisley's sermons and the religious literature produced by the Free Presbyterian Church carry warnings about that which is likely to befall a people who, in the main, have turned their back on God. Similar to the Israelite prophet whose job it was to bring to the people's attention the disastrous consequences that would follow the nation's backsliding, Paisley's jeremiads are often political in nature and are patterned on a shock and restore strategy. Illustrating the Paisleyite's theological view of the covenantal relationship that is believed to exist between God and His people in Ulster is a passage from *The Revivalist* wherein Paisley warns:

> Our beloved Province is entering a very serious situation. The onslaught of the devil . . . is manifested on every side . . . Ulster is going to be made an example of the results of ecumenism in the pulpit and treachery in the State. The same situation that occurred in Israel in the days of Ahab and Jezebel is occurring at the present time in our Province, and God's judgements will continue to be upon us if we turn not our whole heart . . . unto Him.[6]

The remedy for this appalling state of affairs is genuine repentance and a rejection of the sin of worldliness. Paisley's portentous comment, therefore, is intended to alarm and produce anxiety for it sets about explaining the religious and political awfulness in the Province in terms of human transgression and, of course, makes mention of the inevitable visitation of God's judgement upon Protestantism as a lawful consequence of its waywardness. It is an ominous warning of pending adversity that provides us with a glimpse of the fundamentalist's conception of God as retributive judge of unrepentant sinfulness.

It should be noted how the fundamentalist commandeers portions of the Old Testament – which, because of the literalist approach to biblical interpretation, forbids any notion of these portions being theologically out-of-date, and gives them a Northern Irish spin. The thematic strains of the contemporary narrative are just the same as these Old Testament passages i.e. transgression of covenant, cost of sin and the need for repentance, but the Paisleyite simply de-contextualises them and re-applies them to his own historical circumstances. Similar to the cries of the Jewish prophets for God's deliverance of His people either from the national shame of captivity, or the national decline associated with spiritual lukewarmness, Ian Paisley follows suit.

Evidently, when Paisleyism takes its theological cue from the Old Testament a host of problems make their presence felt. While in ancient Israel the divine prescription was, at times, aggressive annihilation of the 'other', for the Paisleyite in Ulster it is bitter denunciation. If Israel was hostile toward its bordering heathens, then Ulster Protestantism can afford to be antipathetic towards Catholicism, Irish nationalism and basically anything Paisleyite fundamentalists conceive of as being contrary to biblical truth. If God's decree demanded that the Israelites adhere to a policy of separatism, then the fundamentalist in Northern Ireland can but do the same. Such factors make it easy for Paisley to preach a message that justifies various levels of division whether from his pulpit or soapbox – irrespective of its hard-hitting consequences at the level of community relations in Northern Ireland.

The fondness that the Paisleyite has for the Old Testament is accompanied with a commitment to the teachings of the Protestant Reformer, John Calvin (1509–64). Religious fundamentalists who occupy the senior positions in the Democratic Unionist Party, and who also belong to conservative evangelical denominations in Northern Ireland, adhere to the theology of Calvinism.[7] The roots of their Calvinism lie in Calvin's *The Institutes of the Christian Religion* (1536) and the methodical articulation of Calvinism by the Synod of Dort 1618–19. The point of researching the theology of a political and religious group who are, in this case, Calvinistic, is because aspects of this theology are thought to play a part in creating the matrix within which the inflexibility and acerbity of Paisleyite ideology is formed. Again, due to the fact that seriously minded religious people are involved in Northern Irish politics, theology is not confined to the private domain but instead makes its mark on society at large.

What is of particular significance is how the principles of a theology like Calvinism fashion the mentality of Calvinists and give structure to the interaction they have with other groups. It ought to be borne in mind that the Calvinism of John Calvin or the Synod is not, metaphorically, a 'soft' or cuddly theology; rather it is perhaps the most powerful theological assertion concerning the mind of God and His eternal purposes. It could be described as a systematic theology which sees God in a position of total sovereignty, and humanity in a position of total depravity – without, it should be stressed, any middle ground.[8] Within the context of those whom I have researched, Calvinism seems to lend itself quite easily to the believer viewing life in rigidly black and white terms. It is a theology that conceives of humanity as being split into two categories, namely, the elect and the unelect. And as a consequence of God's plan of predestination, the spiritual status of each group is fixed and unalterable. As Calvin declares in *The Institutes*:

> We call predestination God's eternal decree, by which he determined with himself what he willed to become of each man. For all are not created in equal condition; rather, eternal life is foreordained to some, eternal damnation to others. Therefore, as any man has been created to one or the other of these ends, we speak of him as predestined to life or death.[9]

Calvin goes on to state that it is a matter of God's inscrutable and incomprehensible will that He decided to devote to destruction and give over to damnation human beings who are to be denied salvation.[10] A person might be excused for thinking that these passages which outline Calvin's idea of double predestination reflect a mind that borders on a 'cold-blooded' conception of God, wherein the image – that all important element which affects our disposition and helps fashion our attitude – that Calvin conjures up, is of a deity who selects, or chooses, *certain* undeserving sinners while ignoring the rest. It is an interpretation which emphasises the judgmental and clinical properties of God at the expense of the sort of virtues, namely, generosity, compassion and mercifulness that we might associate with a God who has ensured that salvation – whilst not accepted universally – is at least potentially available to all. For Free Presbyterian Revd David McIlveen who has gained a reputation in Northern Ireland as an individual who considers himself duty-bound to make social protests in defence of what he believes to be the Bible's position on social issues, God's election is a simple matter:

> the biblical position is very clear that we have been chosen in Christ before the foundation of the world . . . we know that certainly before man was born and before the world was created that God had chosen His people in Himself, that's an undeniable fact.[11]

In addition to the self-understanding that one belongs to the elect, the idea that God has predestined individuals to perform a role in this world can have an empowering effect.[12] It immediately places upon the shoulders of the Calvinist the burden of responsibility. Thus politically active Calvinists like Ian Paisley and those within the ranks of the DUP can argue that in

God's eternal plan they have been predestined to be politicians and party activists. DUP MLA and MP, Iris Robinson, put her involvement in politics down to God's will: 'I was called into politics. I prayed about whether I should get involved or not, and I got a very strong word that I [God] will give thee a victory over thine enemies.'[13]

As a consequence, an individual's political endeavors must be underpinned by saintly obedience as a way of ensuring that he or she dispenses one's religious duties in a God-approved manner. Free Presbyterian and DUP MLA and MP, Nigel Dodds, makes this clear in the following comment:

> I believe I have been called [by God] to do this particular type of work and I will be called to give an account of how I have managed my time and my stewardship, and my opportunities for elevating and promoting the cause of Christ on earth . . . in my family, in my neighbourhood, in my political life as well.[14]

Dodds believes the politics of Democratic Unionism in Northern Ireland to be a localised part of promoting the cause of Christ on earth. According to this theology, the individual has a divinely appointed duty to uphold certain values and defend certain beliefs. Thus Robinson and Dodds' comments tell us something about the interplay between religious zealotry and dedicated political endeavour within the DUP. Paisleyites are inclined to argue that, just as it would be ludicrous to place a Godless man in the Christian ministry, so too would it be foolish to put an unbeliever in a position of political authority. This is because a politician's lack of spiritual regeneration is thought to have negative political consequences. The following comment by Free Presbyterian Minister Revd David Priestly gives us an insight into the fundamentalist's view of the dangers that surround unChristian leadership:

> If you take David Trimble and this peace deal, he's been sucked in. He's been carried along by the Government's plan because he's no spiritual light. He's no understanding of the situation of the spiritual struggle that's gone on here for hundreds of years . . . But if you get a man who knows his God, knows his history, knows what the struggle has been about down through the centuries in this land, he will take a bolder stand in the political realm.[15]

Priestly's comment informs us that in the absence of Christian leadership (we should not ignore the Calvinistic framework within which Priestly, as a Calvinist, makes his comment) politics can become a very dangerous endeavor. Trimble is someone in whom Paisleyites like Priestly can place no confidence. And, we should stress, the reason for his criticism is to be understood primarily in theological terms and not merely because Trimble has moved the Ulster Unionist Party in a direction that Priestly finds distasteful – bad politics, as it were, is a consequence of bad spirituality.

We need, then, to treat seriously religious beliefs and theological ideas and therefore be prepared to view Calvinism in the context of its capacity to transform psychologically the minds of those individuals who subscribe to this brand of Protestant theology. In terms of predestination and election, Calvin's (and Paisley's) God is discriminatory and selective, and has a people on earth that have a higher spiritual rank and status from those who have less than little. It could be argued that an uncritical absorption of Calvin's teaching on predestination, along with its inter-connected image of the Divine personality, might inspire adherents of the creed to become pitiless, uncharitable and inflexible, and it could be said, the chronic sufferers of a hardness of heart. In essence, individuals cannot afford to ignore the possible role that their own conception of God has to play in conditioning their conception of the 'other'. Set within the context of a rigid Calvinism, then, the presence of harshness and aggressiveness within Paisleyism is perhaps a little better understood.

Clearly, the proclivity Paisleyites have for the Old Testament and the predilection they possess for Calvinism, are two dimensions of their theological profile that are well suited to a context of ethnic conflict. And from an historical perspective this is hardly surprising given the fact that the theology which justified the Israelite conquest of Canaan had, at times, a brutally militant and xenophobic aspect to it, and Calvinists (particularly of the John Knox variety) in the sixteenth century were familiar with militancy and the realities of religious xenophobia as an unavoidable factor in the survival of their creed. Additionally, the portrayal of God is one which confirms that He has made a qualitative distinction within humanity – ethnically in terms of the Israelites being a chosen people, and spiritually in terms of Calvinistic election. It should not be too difficult to gain a comprehension of how both theological strains can act as an impediment to reaching, for example, political agreements. Similar to the situation in contemporary Israel (where religious Zionist parties adopt a theological opposition to the sort of political settlement which would be favourable to Palestinians), when laid bare, politically active fundamentalists in the Paisleyite tradition are the most vociferous opponents of political negotiation and accommodation because of concerns that emanate from their theology.[16] Let us now conduct the final part of our inquiry into the theological roots of Paisleyism in Northern Ireland.

There is an apocalyptic mood that prevails in the minds of Paisley and his religious followers, which causes them to have a fixed eye on the future. This is due to their belief that we are living in the 'Last Days' when biblical prophecy will be fulfilled in historical developments. The 'Last Days', of course, is a time fraught with varying degrees of anxiety. This is because the eschatological reading of these fundamentalists is, in the main, one that can be described as being post-tribulationist. Simply put, this means that they anticipate having physically to go through the trials of the tribulation period mentioned in the Bible. Indeed Paisley gives us an insight into how he conceives of the future as being a period of spiritual and physical hardship:

> We are moving into a time when the ecumenical movement is going to force the pace as far as organised Christianity is concerned. And when the Protestant churches are eventually absorbed into the Roman system then there will come about again a whole series of persecutions across the world . . . If the ecumenical movement achieves its goal every person who refuses to conform in so-called Christian countries will come under the persecuting power and influence of that system . . . There's going to be more suffering, there's going to be more torments, there's going to be more trials for the true Church of Jesus Christ.[17]

Accordingly, and decipherable from the above quotation, a post-tribulationist futurology which confirms that the Church will experience the adversity of the tribulation must at the same time have some indication as to the historical movements through which the perceived forces of evil will operate. Decoding eschatological portions of the Bible, these fundamentalists are in no doubt as to which movements will be found in the camp of the enemy. In reference to Revelation chapter 17, verse 5, Paisley has this to say:

> Here we have a woman – not the true Church of Christ, but the Antichrist – this harlot woman . . . Here we have the greatest indictment ever made of the Roman Catholic system. It was this chapter that opened the eyes of the Reformers to the real significance of Romanism – it's a chapter that's dodged by the evangelicals of our day.[18]

Given that the above comment lacks syntactical ambiguity, we are provided with an uncut insight both into Paisley's theological beliefs and his indefatigable ideological drive to convey his feelings without any form of prudential censorship. Paisley wants to leave his readers in no doubt that, as far as he is concerned, Catholicism is a religious enemy, and is unperturbed by the fact that many may feel his comment to be a sign of overt bigotry. A charge of bigotry is not in any way difficult for a man like Paisley to swallow. He believes that the Bible is supportive of his stance against Catholicism and that if other Protestants had his religious insight, they would adopt a similar approach. Notably, Paisley considers his interpretation of this aspect of biblical prophecy to be so important that he aims his criticism at the 'evangelicals of our day' who are at odds with Paisley's interpretative notions.

These quotations help us to understand how Paisleyite perceptions of Catholicism are moulded by a particular reading of prophecy. This prophetic dimension to Paisleyism should not be underscrutinised, because it is another set of religious ideas which, when analysed, enables us to piece together the theologically underpinned world view of these fundamentalists.

It could be argued, then, that the real driving force behind Paisley's constantly produced anti-Catholic dynamic, is not so much derived from a looking back to the sixteenth century, when doctrinal disputes between Protestant and Catholic led to bitter division, but rather from a looking forward through the lens of Bible prophecy into the future, where, it is believed, there will be a Catholicism intent on destroying the 'true' Church. If the Bible – which to the fundamentalist, we must remember, is the literal word of God in matters past, present and future – is considered to portray the Catholic Church as seeking the destruction of 'true' Protestantism, then absolute separation and virulent denunciation become theological imperatives.

That biblical prophecy plays an influential role in Paisleyite ideology is plain to see and informs us as to the spiritual depth to the ideology's anti-ecumenism and its abhorrence for this attempt at Church unity. To such fundamentalists, their literalist understanding of the Bible means that biblical principles – prophetic or otherwise – cannot be compromised and therefore can in no way be sacrificed in the interests, say, of entering into dialogue with the Catholic Church as a way of encouraging better relations across the religious divide. Improving community relations, moreover, by means of ecumenical association is, for Ian Paisley, much too dangerous a religious project. Paisley cannot accept the basic premise from which the other ecumenically inclined Protestant Churches operate, namely, that the Catholic Church is a Christian church.[19] Obviously, Paisley's prophetic conceptions render this premise totally impossible. We are then left confronting the reality of the impact Paisleyite theology has on the sectarian edifice in Northern Ireland because his message is one that does not countenance reconciliation with the Catholic Church as being theologically permissible. His eschatological convictions function to justify his separatist instinct which, because of his participation in politics, stretches its tentacles well beyond the realm of religion. Therefore, the theological components that are to be found at the core of Paisleyite ideology play a part in the production of political paralysis in Northern Ireland.

If fundamentalists like Paisley are to be understood properly, then the religious ideas that they embrace must receive serious inspection. As the charismatic force behind Paisleyism, Ian Paisley's political charisma is indebted to the zeal which derives from his unwavering belief that he interprets the Bible correctly and, accordingly, represents authentic Christianity in all areas to which his life is devoted. But such devotion has left a legacy of both political division within Unionism and religious division within Protestantism and, of course, has done nothing to encourage reconciliation between Protestant and Catholic in Northern Ireland.

Notes

1   Originally published as Neil Southern, 'Paisleyism: A Theological Enquiry', *Studies* vol. 93 no. 371 (autumn, 2004), pp. 349–62.

2   Lionel Caplan, *Religious Fundamentalism* (London, 1987), p. 15.

3   Ian Paisley, 'Why No Free Protestant Would Swallow The Ecumenical Pill', *Sermon, Martyrs Memorial Production* (Belfast, n.d.).

4   Interview with Revd William McCrea, 19 November 1998.

5   Interview with Revd Ivan Foster, 1 December 1998.

6   *The Revivalist* (October 1985), p. 2.

7   This fact was established as a result of interviewing senior members of the DUP.

8   Boettner provides a definitive and comprehensive account of Calvinism from the position of a Calvinist. Loraine Boettner, *The Reformed Doctrine of Predestination* (New Jersey, 1932).

9   John Calvin, *The Institutes of the Christian Religion* (London, 1968), p. 926.

10   Ibid., p. 931.

11   Interview with Revd David McIlveen, 24 November 1998.

12   Walzer stresses the way in which Calvinism radically transformed the thinking of its adherents with its provision of a theologically based ideology which affected all aspects of society and not only the religious. Michael Walzer, *The Revolution of the Saints* (New York, 1974).

13   Interview with Iris Robinson, 14 April 2000.

14   Interview with Nigel Dodds, 17 August 1999.

15   Interview with Revd David Priestly, 5 September 2000.

16   Raphael Mergui and Philippe Simonnot, *Israel's Ayatollahs* (London, 1987).

17   Ian Paisley, 'The Conspiracy to Indoctrinate the Children Attending State School', *Sermon*, Martyrs Memorial Production (Belfast, n.d.).

18   Ed Moloney and Andy Pollak, *Paisley* (Swords, 1986), p. 405.

19   Dennis Cooke, *Persecuting Zeal: A Portrait of Ian Paisley* (Dingle, 1996), chapter 4.

CHAPTER 29

The Doghouse No Longer Feels Lonely

(2008–9)

Fergus O'Donoghue SJ

The preoccupations of journals can sometimes be best gleaned from editorials, particularly so in the case of *Studies* where decisions on what to publish ultimately rest with the editor. Throughout a century of existence various editors have published statements of intent, calls to arms on various social issues; editorial commentary has more recently included postings on the *Studies* website. This 'article' compiles four successive editorials that appeared during 2008 and 2009 as Ireland's economic crisis and its various crises of accountability became increasingly evident. Fergus O'Donoghue was the Editor of *Studies* from 2001 to 2011.[1]

EDITORIAL

Autumn 2008

The wet spring and summer of 2008 was a time when several Irish fantasies ended: the dream of being an infinitely prosperous nation, of being able to rely on the absolute security of property values, of being exemplary Europeans and of being well governed.

The iconography of the period was simple: we were accustomed to seeing countless photographs of politicians socialising with property developers, but this could not convey the strangeness of a time when a Taoiseach was forced from office, when most politicians expected us to vote for the Lisbon Treaty on their word alone, and when a well-known writer equated Ireland in the 1950s with Russia under Stalin.

There was also a sense of history having repeated itself: in 1977, the Republic's largest political party bought a general election with policies we could not afford, thus leading to ten years of economic misery. In 2007, the same party, this time in coalition, had guaranteed its re-election by spending the State's entire surplus and promising that prosperity would be permanent. Arrogance peaked when people's fears were not addressed and we were told, more or less, to shut up and vote 'Yes to Europe'.

National self-definition as the 'Island of Saints and Scholars' and 'My Four Green Fields' had been replaced by belief in permanent prosperity. We, in the Anglophone West, felt so happy that we needed to read accounts of other people's unhappy childhoods, thus creating a new literary genre: 'misery lit' (sales have declined recently by over 30 per cent). Self-definition is dangerous (Britain once boasted of ruling 'the largest empire the world has ever seen' and Spain called itself the 'spiritual reserve of Europe'), but we are drawn to it, somewhat compulsively.

Who actually takes part in the discussions about national identity? Panellists on RTE radio and television talk shows are usually middle aged and middle class, with a south Dublin bias. Radio phone-ins are usually filled with complaints. Newstalk 106FM and local radio offer a wider perspective, but this is an area where writers could offer very original viewpoints.

Writers, however, have to make a living. Very few Irish writers can live by writing alone. Some become internationally famous; some write very popular fiction, which is ideal for film adaptation; others find security in academic life, particularly in the United States. Exile is now a lifestyle choice rather than a statement of ideological independence, whilst emigration has faded as a theme in Irish life and literature. Adaptations of classics and writing detective stories may be lucrative, but are not innovative and are unlikely to be lasting.

We need help in making sense of our present. Demonising the past is a waste of time, as we face rising levels of violence, drug abuse and alcohol consumption. Unlike some far more important countries, we have never fallen victim to the corrosive effects of national pride. We have managed, however inadequately, to sustain two very dissimilar languages. We are still involved in the drama of belief and unbelief, even though our intelligentsia is largely secularised and harbours some pockets of frenzied anti-Catholicism.

Where do we get a sense of belonging and what are our sources of self-respect? In a very sudden shift, we discover that property can be a burden and that very large cars invite contempt rather than envy. As, once again, we revise our self-image, some of the best tools for reflection are found not in novels, but in contemporary short stories, such as Ann Enright's new collection *Taking Pictures* (which evokes modern urban Ireland from a feminist perspective and shows far more insight than the dreary novel which won her the Booker Prize) or Claire Keegan's depiction of modern rural Ireland in *Walk the Blue Fields* (2007), in which the title story brilliantly revives the stock fictional figure of the Irish priest.

Reading good short stories is not the worst way of passing gloomy times.

Winter 2008

The Christmas shopping season began very early this year, not only in Ireland, but in most of Europe. We were not really enthused by having the Christmas lights switched on during the early days of November, but recognised it as part of a desperate effort to encourage commerce, and maybe even some comfort shopping.

We are, however, bewildered by the swift change in our economic situation, angry with our government and unable to understand exactly what has gone wrong. Self-congratulation has been replaced, almost overnight, by national self-denigration. Last year's prophets of gloom were lonely and were treated with scorn; they have been proven right.

If we are absolutely honest, we will admit that our government suffered from a very strong commitment to our own new Credo: complete trust in the construction industry and utter faith in the inherent benevolence of market forces. In the midst of all the current negativity, it helps when we remind ourselves that the mistakes we made are international, rather than uniquely ours, that Spain is even more depressed than ourselves and that Iceland's uninhibited love affair with international banking has led to disaster.

When the Celtic Tiger was roaring, we became distracted. The homeless and drug addicts do not vote, so we forgot about them. The response to crime was to lock criminals up, rather than try to rehabilitate them. We needed immigrants to keep the economy moving, but we ignored the presence of people who were 'trafficked' here. Trafficking involves the smuggling *and* exploitation of people from poorer countries. It is an international scandal and is the downside of globalisation. It is grimy and not very newsworthy, so it receives little attention.

The celebration of selfishness, expressed in the building of gated communities and in advertising campaigns that appealed to our egoism, briefly became a national characteristic. The ideal Irish man or woman was portrayed as young, expensively dressed and groomed, self-centered, fast moving, forgetful of and/or contemptuous toward the past, devoted to consumerism and contentedly godless.

Godlessness is basic to this worldview. It is fashionable and fits into the mainstream of contemporary European thought, which emphasises that religion is private as well as personal. Green policies become a substitute religion, even to the extent of regarding humanity as a polluting rather than a sinful entity.

As the recession began to bite, during the summer of 2008, our government went on holiday and then returned to work, uttering prophecies of doom. A rushed Budget then hurt the oldest and the most vulnerable amongst us. The ensuing uproar took everybody in government by surprise. How can our politicians have become so remote from the rest of us?

Our Green Party is usually regarded, and seems to regard itself, as being above criticism. Its leaders are given some of the attributes of living saints, but all its Dáil deputies stood to applaud a very unjust Budget, thereby showing that they may have sold their souls for power.

As jobs vanish and many mortgage holders find themselves with negative equity, appeals to patriotism are hollow, not least when they come from people who live in great comfort. There is, of course, no longer any appeal to religious motivation. Our continued commitment to Third World issues, even when we have been at our most materialist, is proof of the fundamental decency which it the stance of the vast majority of Irish people. It is this trait, rather than any other, on which our leaders should rely.

Spring 2009

The doghouse no longer feels lonely; in fact, it is becoming rather crowded. Catholic clergy have been in it for ages, but now we have been joined by bankers, builders, property developers and government leaders who, like us, used to be the toast of the nation, but are now some our most execrated citizens. Irish Catholicism has long been described, by its critics, as 'toxic', but even that word seems insufficient to describe our banking culture in the sour aftermath of our love affair with property and banking, which, only recently, had replaced our belief in faith and motherland. We had fooled ourselves into thinking that the free market form of capitalism was near-perfect and we overlooked our decline in social capital, not least in civility, because we no longer had 'time': time for family, for friends, for church. Many of us worshipped American models of living and working, but forgot that the United States is marked by its strong respect for religion.

We are experiencing something akin to being hit by a truck. A few of us heard it coming and gave warnings, but they were ignored, or, in an infamous remark by one very senior politician, advised to consider suicide. Being people of extremes, we now make the mistake of tarring all bankers, developers and politicians, because of the actions of a minority of their colleagues, just as we did with the Catholic clergy.

Do we expect too much from our government leaders in Ireland? Are we being unfair to expect creative and inspired leadership from dynastic politicians? Many of them have, after all, inherited their parliamentary seats; some of them are the third generation in occupancy. Most of them have a strong sense of entitlement (not least to large salaries), so they are both angry and upset when their judgement and experience are questioned. Our government is trying to cope with the local effects of an unprecedented international financial crisis, which demands harshness with the leading bankers, builders and property developers who have been its close friends for more than a decade.

We may, unfairly, expect too much from our leaders, in the way some fans expected musical innovation in U2's latest album. U2 has done nothing musically new for about 20 years, but continues to make vast amounts of money: each new release sells in huge quantities and also boosts sales of the back catalogue. Our government thought that it, too, had hit on a winning formula and promised us endless prosperity; its only problem would be directing the flow of revenue. Important visitors were told all about our wonderful economy and were cued to praise it, exactly as an adult gives the expected warm response to a child's accomplishments.

The past, in this way of thinking, has nothing to teach us, as was illustrated, last year, by a newspaper columnist, who contrasted the 'headscarf-wearing, Mass-going' Irish grandmothers of yesterday with the 'tanned, gym-going' grandmothers of today. The disparaging contrast is not that far removed from truth, but overlooks the extreme reluctance of the headscarved grandmothers to live beyond their means and their realisation that hard times were part of the life cycle. Hard times, according to our leaders, were gone for good: the present was wonderful and the future could only be better. The small country that had been bottom of the pile had come to the top of the heap, and was going to stay there.

National discourse today has degenerated into recrimination, so we overlook the many positive legacies of the Celtic Tiger years: an educated and experienced workforce, a more cosmopolitan country, towns that look smart rather than shabby. Our return to the default setting of 'most distressful country' prevents us from seeing what has been accomplished and what is attainable.

It is taken for granted that our political system is corrupt. Such cynicism is dangerously corrosive. We need a healthy democracy, abandoning clientist models of central and local governance. In our over-centralised Republic, we need to recover the autonomy of local government. We should realign our political groupings and realise that the 'nudge, wink and slap on the back' tradition has expired.

We have many talented public servants, entrepreneurs and politicians. They will be allowed to use their talents to the full only if we resolve to involve ordinary citizens in governance, to end clientism and to regard membership of public bodies as a way of serving the nation rather than benefiting from patronage.

Being stuck in anger, as we are now, can only be a transitional stage. For the health of our democracy, we must move beyond it. It would be helpful if our Government, which did a lot to create the present crisis, ceased its hectoring and, in its own *mea culpa*, apologised for its mistakes.

Summer 2009

One hundred years ago, John Redmond was by far the most famous living Irishman. Today, he is almost forgotten: streets, buildings and institutions are not named after him. Redmond is regarded as representing a dead end in Irish history. One hundred years ago, Nano Nagle was overlooked, though the Presentation Sisters were working in nearly every large town in Ireland. Nine years ago, she was voted the Irish Woman of the Second Millennium.

John Redmond and Nano Nagle were committed Christians. Most of us, like them, were brought up believing in God, but nearly all of us were brought up to believe in progress. Believing in the constant betterment of humanity has been part of the western intellectual tradition since the Enlightenment, making sin and redemption less attractive concepts. This attitude has survived the dreadful 20th century, the most violent in human history. Uncounted millions died in warfare and in revolutionary or post-revolutionary violence. The collective memory of such misery and loss was blotted out in the consumer boom that began in the 1960s and stopped only recently. The one exception to the desire to forget was the Holocaust, which was studied seriously from the 1960s onward, after the initial horror had been absorbed. Nano Nagle would not have been surprised at human depravity. John Redmond, who lived in a calmer age, might have been more optimistic.

Very few lives have happy endings, but we continue to fool ourselves about this very grim reality and go to films where all ends well, or watch television series where desperate situations can be resolved within an hour. The daily struggle and the blessed monotony of life do not sit well with the 'happily ever after' mindset, so we are open to becoming consumers: of things, of time, of each other.

The collapse of communism in 1989 left no challenges to the belief that our destiny is to possess and that our aim in life should be self-fulfilment. Western democratic capitalism was seen as the perfection of human history, rather than the latest (and therefore temporary) manifestation of human endeavour. Atheism seems both logical and sensible in such a situation: we are in charge of our destiny and, if we pull together, everything will work out for the best. We respect religion, but we should not be bothered by it, other than when it provides rites of passage. Its claims to truth may be discounted, because all truth is relative and my desires are the only things of which I can be sure.

Needless to say, the hubris that comes from the latest western *Zeitgeist* is challenged by those who refuse to regard our culture as the pinnacle of human history, who do not admire our lifestyles and who look at our empty churches with dismay.

In Ireland, we usually come late to the feast, so we became wholehearted consumers just as western capitalism began to falter. Knowledge of history has weakened, being replaced by a fascination with genealogical research (which may tell us a lot about our ancestors, but less about their culture and religious beliefs). We have no general sense of how we arrived where we are, nor of the people and groups whose endeavours led us here.

Reflection does not come easily to us Irish people; we are much better at literature and drama than we are at theology and philosophy. Given our slowness to reflect, we are liable to accept the very latest thinking, but would be stronger and much wiser if we remained proud of our roots.

There are two traditions in Irish nationalism, but one is often emphasised to the almost total exclusion of the other. Constitutional and revolutionary nationalism both arose as an enraged response to systematic injustice; one can only be understood in relation to the other. The Churches played a fundamental role in creating the country we have, but today there is a widespread opinion that a secular Ireland would be a much happier place. Religious orders built much of the medical and educational infrastructure of Ireland, but they are characterised, without exception, as being oppressive and exploitative.

There is often an uneasy feeling that we are accepting a one-sided interpretation of the past, but we are unable to articulate our discomfort and, instead, murmur something about the good priests, nuns or brothers we have known. We need occasions, such as the many local commemorations of the 1798 Bicentenary or the celebration of the Easter Rising anniversary in 2006, if we are to express our real feelings. Patriotism is wonderful, except when evoked by cash-strapped governments.

A healthy democracy is assured only when we accept our many-sided past and have a critical attitude towards our present. Our current crisis reminds us that the best politicians are those who respect us and who show it by offering us no slogans and no easy answers.

Notes

1   Originally published as four separate editorials: Fergus O'Donoghue, *Studies* vol. 97, no. 387 (autumn, 2008), pp. 249–50; vol. 97, no. 388 (winter, 2008), pp. 369–70; vol. 98, no. 389 (spring, 2009), pp. 5–6; vol. 98, no. 390 (summer, 2009), pp. 121–2.

CHAPTER 30

Immigration and Social Cohesion (2009)

Bryan Fanning

The 2006 Irish census identified a population of 4,239,848 persons. Of the 'usually resident' population, 610,000 or 14.7 per cent of the total were born outside the State. Of these, approximately 10 per cent were 'non-Irish nationals'. Just over 10 per cent of children in Ireland in 2006 were born in other countries. This article is one of a number published in *Studies* since 2002 on immigration. Many of these examined immigrant experiences of racism and social marginalisation. This article summed up a decade of responses to asylum seekers and other migrants by the Irish State. It criticised a lack of emphasis on integration, explaining this as partly the result of a wider dominance of economic development goals over concerns about social cohesion.[1]

Irish media discussions about social cohesion and immigrants have been mostly limited to sporadic alarmist accounts of white flight from some residential areas although this has been in the main a lazy recycling of the experiences of other countries; concrete instances of difficulties faced by some immigrant children in securing access to school places have also been documented. All such accounts correctly infer that integration occurs, or not, within specific communities and localities. Precise information on how immigration has impacted on most such communities in the Irish case remains slight. The focus of this article is upon institutional barriers that seem to impede a focus on future social cohesion. The Irish debate on integration has been mostly fairly abstract; the first government report *Integration: A Two Way Process* (2001) emphasised mutual rights and responsibilities, but not concrete issues which might affect how immigrants were received by any given community.[2] The second, and still most recent, integration document, *Migration Nation* (2008), again emphasised principles of integration but committed to only a handful of concrete actions, some of which were dropped at the first whiff of budgetary restrictions.[3] Irish debates on immigration developed in the shadow of events in other countries; 9/11 recast immigration as a security debate; the 2001 Bradford riots and those in 2005 in Paris suggested the urgency of investing in social cohesion but these lessons were drowned out by new anti-multicultural orthodoxies. 'Fortress Europe' responses to asylum seekers cast immigration as a security problem rather than social policy challenge.

Irish responses to immigration have to a considerable extent been dominated by security perspectives, specifically influenced by the expanding remit of the Department of Justice, Equality and Law Reform for asylum policy, 'reception and integration' and 'immigration and naturalisation'. But the business case for large-scale immigration was articulated on behalf of the social partners. The 2006 National Economic and Social Council (NESC) report *Managing Migration* in effect defined integration in terms of labour market participation.[4] Securocrats justified restrictions upon migrant rights and entitlements with scant consideration about how the human misery these caused might subsequently impede integration. Economists prioritised economic growth above social cohesion and presumed that a *laissez faire* approach to integration was sustainable, never thinking that migrants were real people with real families, the crooked timber of humanity rather than disposable factors of production. Both mindsets worked against a focus on social cohesion.

THE SECURITISATION OF IMMIGRATION

In retrospect it seems that responses to asylum seekers in the late 1990s were remarkably heated compared to subsequent attitudes towards immigrants, even if the former were so far fewer in number. The 2006 Census recorded over 400,000 recent immigrants but the arrival of 3,883 asylum seekers in 1997, following 1,179 in 1996, was portrayed as a crisis by some politicians and officials; in media accounts Ireland was being 'swamped', something no newspaper headlines proclaimed subsequently about immigration. By the end of the decade the total number of asylum seekers in Ireland was less than 10,000. Over time they constituted a smaller and smaller proportion of overall immigration. Ireland had ratified the UN Convention on the Rights of Refugees in 1956 and had periodically admitted groups of refugees, Hungarians in 1956, Chileans in 1973, Vietnamese in 1979 and Bosnians in 1991 – an official total of some 2,333 persons.[5] Some of these did not stay in Ireland very long; the Hungarians went on hunger strike demanding relocation to the United States or Canada, at the heart of this were administrative difficulties in meeting their needs, but the small Vietnamese and Bosnian communities grew over time through family reunification. Ireland only got around to putting its obligations to refugees on a legal footing in 1996 when the Refugee Act was passed with all-party support.

However, the rapid rise in the number of asylum seekers was used to justify non-implementation of much of the Act. Amendments to the Aliens Act (1935) introduced on 29 June 1997 (the last day in office of the outgoing Government) increased the powers of immigration officers to determine whether 'aliens' should be allowed to enter the country. The revised Act was implemented in a heavy-handed manner; although the amendments expressly did not apply to persons entering the state from Northern Ireland or Great Britain, some 600 of these were refused entry into the country during the first two months. About 20 had applied for asylum but were not permitted to enter the country by officials.[6] The asylum issue was portrayed by politicians and by officials as an administrative crisis. In 1999 the vista of asylum seekers queuing overnight outside the Mount Street 'one stop shop' established to process their claims was scathingly criticised both by Michael McDowell, later Minister of Justice, Equality and Law Reform, and by Liz McManus, then a Junior Minister. Her statement that the Government's asylum policy was a 'shambles', prompted new restrictions on asylum seekers rather than reforms aimed at meeting their needs. A new dispersal policy was introduced aimed at sharing the burden of asylum seekers. The political rhetoric that emerged in response to administrative difficulties depicted asylum seekers as 'bogus' refugees and as welfare scroungers.

Subsequent policy changes made the Department of Justice almost entirely responsible for the welfare of asylum seekers. Existing welfare entitlements were replaced by a system of 'direct provision' that limited support for asylum seekers to basic accommodation, meals and cash allowances of £15 weekly for adults and £7.50 for children. In effect social policy became an instrument of border policy. Direct provision was designed as a punitive system, and was found in a number of studies to cause extreme poverty. From 2000 to 2009 these low rates of payment remained frozen whilst most other benefits rose with inflation year on year. In this context asylum seekers depended considerably upon NGOs, religious organisations and community groups for help to integrate.

For the first few years of the 21st century Irish immigration debates continued to be preoccupied with national security, with controlling, deterring and being able to expel unwanted guests of the nation. A raft of legislation did much to criminalise and make dangerous the act of seeking asylum. McDowell, as Minister for Justice, Equality and Law Reform, sought to undermine and then remove the constitutional right of the Irish-born children of immigrants to citizenship, interpreted by the High Court in 1987 as a right to remain in the State with their families. The 1987 ruling had allowed for the regularisation of a significant number of asylum seekers and other immigrants with Irish-born children. A 'policy decision' was made to begin to refuse leave to remain to asylum seeker families in the knowledge that this would trigger a further test case in the Supreme Court.[7] In April 2002 the 1987 ruling was overturned in the High Court (*Lobe v. Minister of Justice*). On 23 January 2003 the Supreme Court upheld this ruling, in essence holding that the Irish citizen child of non-citizens could be deported with its parents unless the non-citizen parent agreed to be deported without their child. This ruling was effectively superseded by the June 2004 Referendum on Citizenship that removed the existing birthright to citizenship from the Irish-born children of non-citizens.

The *Irish Nationality and Citizenship Act* (2001) superseded the *Aliens Act* (1935). Significantly it systematically replaced the term 'alien' in Irish legislation with that of 'non-national'. The term began to be used by the Department of Justice Equality and Law Reform in security debates; in reports about crime, human trafficking and illegal immigration, and by the Department of Enterprise and Employment to describe immigrant workers. By 2004 the 'national/non-national' dualism had become the prevalent common-sense conceptual framework for debates about immigration.

The 2004 Referendum undermined a definition of social membership set out in Article 45.1 of the 1937 Constitution which states:

> The State shall strive to promote the welfare of the whole people by securing or protecting as effectively as it may a social order in which justice and charity inform all the institutions of the national life.

Here, a concept of domicile entitlement, distinct from citizenship, was emphasised. It had been articulated in social welfare legislation that referred to 'every person in the state' rather than citizens of the State. On top of this the 2004 Social Welfare (Miscellaneous Provisions) Act restricted considerably the entitlements of 'non-nationals' to benefits such as children's allowances. These political and policy responses to immigrations deepened constitutional and legal distinctions between citizens and non-citizens. In essence, the Referendum outcome marked the end of a phase of Irish immigration policy, but not of a mindset preoccupied with deepening distinctions between Irish citizens and immigrants and with little or no focus on integration or social cohesion.

IMMIGRATION AND THE ECONOMY

In 2004, in what turned out to be a radical act of social engineering, Ireland became (alongside the UK and Sweden) one of the three EU member states that did not impose any restrictions to the free movement of workers from the eight new Central and East European EU member states. The UK counted 290,000 arrivals between May 2004 and September 2005. Ireland, with less than one tenth of its population, issued about 160,000 new social security numbers between May 2004 and November 2005: some 86,900 to Polish migrants, 29,500 to Lithuanians, 14,600 to Latvians and 29,900 to those from other new EU member states. By 2005 Ireland's proportion of 10.4 per cent foreign born (as estimated by the OECD) exceeded that the United Kingdom (8.3 per cent). The 2006 Census identified some 610,000 or 14.7 per cent of the total population (4,239,848) as born outside the State, and approximately 10 of the total population as 'non-Irish nationals'.[8] In less than two years some of Ireland's largest immigrant communities had established themselves from scratch.

In the post-2004 period political and policy debates focused upon the benefits of immigration to the economy; the 2006 NESC Report, *Managing Migration*, advocated large-scale and ongoing immigration, whilst noting that there were 'virtually no empirical data concerning the social, or even economic, integration of minorities, and scant academic analyses of the social impacts of immigration'; the Report implied that Irish policy amounted to little more than a leap of faith in immigration-fuelled economic growth.[9] In 2008 the newly established Office of the Minister of State for Integration Policy published its first (and only to date) major report. *Migration Nation* located the case for large-scale immigration explicitly within a developmental nation-building narrative:

> The important point for all Irish citizens to understand is that immigration is happening in Ireland because of enormous recent societal and economic improvement, beginning in the 1990s, but built on an opening to the world created by the late Seán Lemass as Taoiseach (Prime Minister) in the 1960s.[10]

For decades after independence the national conversation was dominated by questions of cultural and religious reproduction, how to ensure that the Irish language and Catholicism (key components of the majority Irish identity) were successfully passed from one generation to the next. Irishness so constituted had emerged radically before independence and conservatively dominated post-independence ideals of social cohesion. What became the Republic of Ireland defined itself as a mono-cultural society notwithstanding the existence of small indigenous cultural minorities. There was little in Irish history to suggest that the dominant homogeneously imagined community would prove as radically open to immigration as it had been to emigration.

Cultural nationalism, however, had offered scant protection against emigration and social decline. Developmental modernisers held out the hope of social cohesion based upon economic security.[11] The prioritisation of economics above culture emerged as the defining nation-building project of the last half century. It coincided with secularisation and the removal of essentialist nationalism from the political mainstream in response to the Northern conflict; these arguably culminated in a generic modernity incapable of conceiving the integration of immigrants or indeed Irish citizens in terms of anything other than labour market participation. Whilst Irish responses to immigration were legally and cognitively structured in terms of distinctions between 'nationals' and 'non-nationals' what it meant to be Irish was by no means clear after some 50 years of developmentalism. As put by Bertie Ahern at the launch of *Managing Migration*:

> While it is no easy task to state clearly what it means to be Irish today, there are certain aspects of our community and Republic which, I believe, deserve respect and understandings from those who have come amongst us. That extends clearly, to the rule of law and the institutions and practices of constitutional democracy. It includes the characteristic features of community life in Ireland, including the unique place of the Irish language, Irish literature, music and folklore, and our religious and spiritual sense.[12]

A lightly held sense of tradition aside – *Riverdance* rather than blood and soil nationalism – Irish society was apparently much the same as any western country, generically modern in its rules of belonging. *Migration Nation* and *Managing Migration* de-emphasised cultural rules of belonging in favour of economic participation. *Managing Migration* argued that from the 1960s government policies concerning trade liberalisation and foreign direct investment began to improve the domestic economic situation and hence, eventually, reversed the net loss of population due to migration. Weak economic performance during the 1980s was accompanied by a net outflow of migrants, a trend that was reversed in the mid-to-late 1990s. Economic growth during the 1990s saw the rapid expansion of the labour force from about 1.4 million in 1994 to just over 2 million in 2005. This increased labour demand was met initially by Irish nationals who had been previously unemployed or outside the labour market by returning Irish migrants, and as these reduced as a proportion of in-migration by non-Irish migrants; by 2004 Irish returnees constituted less than 25 per cent of total immigrants. *Managing Migration* claimed that ongoing immigration was likely to make Irish society more resilient and adaptive:

With Irish growth rates and employment projected in the near future to follow the impressive trend set during the last decade, migration will certainly remain a key feature allowing the labour market to react to changes in demand and further boosting Irish competitiveness. As such, Irish unemployment is expected to remain low, especially compared to other EU countries. This will be a significant advantage to Ireland in the expanded European Union.[13]

In effect the Report endorsed large-scale immigration whilst inferring that 'in the unlikely event of economic downturn' immigration levels could be controlled. However, the kind of measures suggested and since introduced (limiting work visas to areas of labour market shortage) could only apply to non-EU migrants.[14] NESC advocated following the example of Canada and Australia in setting language and educational criteria for admission. Immigrants would be expected to 'invest' in these factors prior to applying to entry. This would 'shift the burdens of settlement' (i.e. the cost of integration programmes) from the host country back to the would-be-immigrants, and 'shifts the locus of adjustment from the country of destination back to the country of origin'.[15] In essence it was proposed to accept where possible only those migrants with the required human capital capabilities to meet developmental rules of belonging; the market would handle integration.

INTEGRATION AND SOCIAL COHESION

The initial security phase of immigration policy worked against integration in a number of respects. To take one example, Africans now comprise Ireland's second largest immigrant community but many are former asylum seekers who were not allowed to work for years. The State proactively impeded their efforts to integrate by excluding them from the remit of employment and social inclusion programmes. A 2008 ESRI study found that black people participating in the Irish labour market have an unemployment rate that is nine times that of Irish nationals, and are seven times more likely to report experiencing discrimination.[16] Arguably, African immigrants seem 'hungry to participate' in civil society because of rather than in spite of their experiences of insecurity.[17] As a relatively established (pre-2004) immigrant cohort Africans have been at the forefront of bottom-up immigrant political participation. Rotimi Adebari, a former asylum seeker was elected as town councillor in 2004 and mayor of Portlaoise in 2007. He credited his success, as do many public representatives, to community involvement. Some 40 immigrant candidates stood for election in 2009; about half of these were African; research currently underway finds that most of these like

Adebari, are active in a wide range of local community organisations.[18] African candidates in 2009 were typically involved in capacity-building roles in immigrant community groups, active church members and involved in a number of (Irish) organisations in their local communities.

Two reports published by the Joseph Rowntree Foundation suggest lessons for the Irish case. *Immigration and Social Cohesion in th UK* (2008) finds that new immigration has contributed to the pressures on social cohesion arising from the economic and social transformations of the 21st century; it emphasised a role of central government of supporting local communities in meeting the needs of new migrants.[19] A key finding was that the challenges of integrating new immigrants depended mostly on local factors: 'the story in each locality about who belongs there.'[20] The lesson for Ireland is that concrete actions in specific communities matter more than national-level integration or anti-racism rhetoric. *Immigration, Social Cohesion and Social Capital* (2006) defined social cohesion as 'a process of developing social relationships, community bonds and common status in British society'.[21] It criticised how predominant security perspectives had undermined a focus on concrete measures to achieve such cohesion at a community level. Within government the security focus had cognitively undermined social policy, community-based and civic leadership approaches to integration.[22] An influential 2006 US study by Robert D. Putnam argues that large-scale immigration undermines trust and reciprocity in host communities; people tend to hunker down in response to such change.[23] Each of these studies suggests that large-scale immigration imposes social costs upon host communities and potential damage to social cohesion. Each counsel against complacency and emphasise the need to continually invest in the social fabric at a community level.

In the Irish case this translates into a crucial role for local government, community partnerships, voluntary organisations, NGOs and churches. The voluntary and religious sectors grasped this from the outset. These have, as best they could and without State support, supported vulnerable migrants and have campaigned against the damage to social cohesion wrought by security approaches to migration. Influenced by the latter, the State endeavoured to exclude migrants from the remit of social inclusion policies and programmes. Encouragingly, *Migration Nation* acknowledged a 'strong link between integration policy and wider State social inclusion measures, strategies and initiatives'.[24] A strategic approach to social cohesion requires that measures for citizens and immigrants must be melded into a common vision of integration-as-social-inclusion. This may not be welcome news in the midst of an economic crisis. A society that shirks investing in integration when times were good faces particular challenges in doing so during lean times, but also risks potential long-term costs if it neglects to do so. However, the main institutional barriers to integration and social cohesion are more likely to be cognitive rather than financial.

Notes

1 Originally published as Bryan Fanning, 'Immigration and Social Cohesion', *Studies* vol. 98, no. 391 (autumn, 2009), pp. 273–83.

2 Department of Justice, Equality and Law Reform (Dublin, 2001).

3 Office of the Minister of Integration, *Migration Nation: Statement on Integration Strategy and Diversity Management* (Dublin, 2008).

4 National Economic and Social Council, *Managing Migration in Ireland: A Social and Economic Analysis* (Dublin, 2006).

5 Bryan Fanning, *Racism and Social Change in the Republic of Ireland* (Manchester, 2002), p. 97.

6 Paul Cullen. 'Refugees, Asylum and Race on the Borders', in Ethel L. Crowley and Jim Mac Laughlin (eds), *Under the Belly of the Celtic Tiger: Class, Race, Identity and Culture in the Global Ireland* (Dublin, 1997), p. 105.

7 Donnocha O'Connell and Ciara Smith, 'Citizenship and the Irish Constitution', in Ursula Fraser and Colin Harvey (eds), *Sanctuary in Ireland: Perspectives on Asylum Law and Policy* (Dublin, 2003), p. 265.

8 For census figures see www.cso.ie

9 National Economic and Social Forum, *Managing Migration in Ireland* (Dublin, 2006), p. 148.

10 Office of the Minister of Integration, *Migration Nation: Statement in Integration Strategy and Diversity Management* (Dublin, 2008), p. 8.

11 Tom Garvin, *Preventing the Future: Why Was Ireland so Poor For So Long?* (Dublin, 2004).

12 Address at launch of *Managing Migration*, see www.taoiseach.gov.ie

13 NESC, *Managing Migration*, p. 93.

14 Ibid., p. xx.

15 Ibid., p. 14.

16 Philip J. O'Connell, and Frances McGinnity, *Immigrants at Work: Ethnicity and Nationality in the Irish Labour Market* (Dublin, 2008).

17 Theophilus Ejorh cited in 'Political Activism and the Irish-African Community', *Indymedia Ireland*, 22 July 2006.

18 Research by Bryan Fanning and Neil O'Boyle since published as Bryan Fanning and Neil O'Boyle, 'Immigrants in Irish Politics: African and East European Candidates in the 2009 Local Government Elections', *Irish Political Studies* vol. 25 no. 3 (2010), pp. 417–35.

19 Mary Hickman, Helen Crowley and Nick Mai, *Immigration and Social Cohesion in the UK* (York, 2008).

20 Ibid., see www.jrf.org.uk.

21 David Robinson and Kesia Reeve, *Immigration, Social Cohesion and Social Capital* (York, 2006).

22 Ibid.

23 Robert D. Putnam, '*E Pluribus Unum*: Diversity and Community in the Twenty-First Century', *Scandinavian Political Studies* vol. 30 no. 2 (2006), pp. 137–74.

24 *Migration Nation*, p. 9.

CHAPTER 31

No Cheap Grace

Reforming the Irish Church (2010)

Séamus Murphy SJ

The autumn 2010 issue of *Studies* contained a number of landmark articles on the institutional failures that permitted and covered up clerical sexual abuse. Several were unambiguously critical of what the accompanying editorial referred to as 'a toxic culture of fear'. Fear of authority encouraged priests to keep their heads down and not challenge authority. Fear of scandal encouraged secrecy. The resulting hypocrisy and the almost complete disregard for the safety of children had led to widespread disgust and disillusionment. This necessitated, the editorial continued, a profound change in attitude at the highest level of the Church. Séamus Murphy SJ is a former member of the editorial board of *Studies*. He currently teaches philosophy at Loyola University Chicago.[1]

The Ryan and Murphy Reports have sent shock waves through the Irish Catholic Church, and reverberated as far as the Vatican. The horror and outrage they generated are so strong that many people may, after expressing their horror and outrage loudly and vehemently, want to pass on to less stressful matters.

Where does the Irish Catholic Church go from here? First, it has to learn from the reports. Second, it has to consider the implications for the Church as community and as institution. In what follows, I offer some reflections, mainly in response to the Murphy Report.

LEARNING

Reform will not be easy. Some has been carried out, and those who did it deserve credit. But it will take some time and much work for the reform to put down deep roots. Setting up appropriate structures is necessary; it is also relatively easy. Changing people's mentality may be a lot harder. When hard and humbling lessons have to be learned, some will resist all the time, and all will resist some of the time. Resistance to learning, not necessarily malicious so much as a wanting to go into denial about unpleasant realities, must be factored into calculating what reform will cost.[2]

The issues are morally too important for such resistance to be tolerated or for the rest of the Church to throw up its hands, helplessly, in the face of inertia, which is the predominant way of resistance. As well as change of structures, there must also be a revolution of mind and a conversion of heart: this is what Pope Benedict seeks in appealing for spiritual renewal of the Irish Church.[3] He calls for penance, fasting, prayer, reading of Scripture, confession and other means to be practiced by Irish Catholics for 12 months 'in order to obtain the grace of healing and renewal for the Church in Ireland'.[4] What he says indicates that he sees prayer as no easy option: Irish Catholics, lay and clerical, have to undergo the tough spiritual discipline of putting themselves humbly before God in order to learn what to do. In a memorable phrase of Pastor Dietrich Bonhoeffer, who gave his life in opposition to the Nazis, there is no 'cheap grace'.

FACTS

It starts with facing three simple facts: (1) a large number of priests sexually assaulted children during the last 40 years, (2) their superiors made no serious effort to punish or prevent them, and (3), if it were not for media *exposé*, it would still be going on. We can quibble with, add nuance, or contextualise each fact, but we cannot let nuance and context make us lose sight of them.

On (1), it might be thought misleading to say 'a large number of priests sexually assaulted children'. It is true that only around 4% of priests have been accused of child molestation, true that priests do not make up a disproportionate number of sexual abusers, and obviously true (given these two facts) that clerical celibacy has nothing to do with it. Even so, the fact remains that the number of priests involved is large: not large relative to other categories of men who abuse, but far too large.

Sexual assault on a child by any adult is seriously wrong. Such assault by a priest is arguably more evil than the same act by almost any other person, since it may inflict, in addition to the other harms, a particular spiritual damage on the child. The damage it inflicts on the Church is dreadful: and here I refer not to the Church's public image, but to the spiritual and moral lives of Catholics and other Christians. The priest is a sign or symbol; and just as a good priest's faith, celibacy and fidelity are powerful signs of the presence of God, so too a priest raping a child is a powerful sign of a diabolic power.

On (2), no doubt it is simplistic to say that bishops and superiors 'made no serious effort to punish or prevent abuse'. Anecdotal evidence suggests that tough action was taken in some cases; but the Murphy Report reveals those cases to be the exception rather than the rule. Why bishops and religious superiors acted as they did is still mysterious; none have offered a serious public explanation for why they failed in the 1970s and 1980s. There was great emphasis, at the time, on bishops listening to advice; perhaps the advice from psychologists and Canon lawyers turned out to be bad. There was much emphasis in the post-Vatican II era on not being harsh, heavy-handed, or 'legalistic'; perhaps the bishops were trying to be compassionate with human weakness. Was this all wrong? Presumably, no; but the fact remains that they failed to stop priests from assaulting children, and failed to remove offenders from the priesthood. It was not wrong for bishops to be compassionate and hopeful of forgiveness, healing and redemption – and it was wrong not to realise that those were not the only virtues required.

On (3), giving the media credit for bringing the matter to light may stick in the throat of some. Secular media culture is cool towards religion. In the case of the Catholic Church, the media is wary at best and is often aggressively hostile. It shows no parallel interest in any similar problems among the Irish Protestant churches or the Jewish or Muslim communities. It pays no comparable attention to child sexual abuse in families. Until very recently, no parallel vehement denunciation was hurled at State institutions caring for children when those children are maltreated, and no similar standard of accountability has yet been applied to police or social workers or journalists. The secular media loves issues that can be presented as Church-State clashes, and is enthusiastically on the other side to the Church. It shows little understanding of historical context, and justifies its own past silence on paedophile crimes with the risible claim that it too lived in terror of the Catholic Church. In fact, from the 1960s on, the Irish secular media was vociferously hostile to the very idea of sexual self-discipline and to the claim that bishops should exercise authority. Given the findings of the Reports, the media must share in culpability for what was done to children because of its discrediting of those values, as well as its general neglect, prior to 1990, of the issue of sexual abuse of children. All this is true. Yet the fact remains that if it were not for the media, the appalling abuse would still be continuing, and still be effectively cloaked.

AGENDA FOR CHANGE

Bishops, priests and laity all have to change if the Irish Church is to be reformed. Saying that may arouse defensiveness. There appears to be defensiveness (mixed with fear) among some clergy, although it is hard to know how widespread it is.

The same statement may also arouse an angry defensiveness among some laity, who may deem talk about change in the laity an attempt to shift responsibility from priests and bishops. But such a mentality, however much encouraged by certain kinds of media reporting, would reflect a scapegoating attitude to clergy, and possibly even a kind of hypocrisy, given that more than 95 per cent of sexual assaults on children are carried out by laymen. Sexual abuse of children by 'practising' Catholics also hurts the Christian community: when the Pope wrote to the Irish Church, he did not think it was made up only of clergy.

Bishops may also get defensive. Yet perhaps they might bear in mind the story a certain Irish bishop once told of how, when he was consecrated bishop, a well-wisher said to him: 'You'll never eat a poor meal again, and you'll never hear the truth again.' Irish bishops may rarely have heard more truth spoken to them than in the last few years, and while it has been stressful, it has not all been harsh.

BISHOPS

Perhaps the most important thing for a bishop to start saying aloud to himself is: 'The buck stops here.' Although accountable to the wider Church, the bishop is not a mere branch manager of a corporation, and his power is not something delegated to him from the Pope. He too is a successor of the apostles and shares in the governance of the Church.[5] He must govern his own diocese; he cannot shift the responsibility to the Vatican or blame Canon Law. Norms and structures can be put in place and many already have been established.[6] But they cannot substitute for the proactive leadership of the bishop.

Given that the governing role of the bishop is so crucial, it is necessary that a certain mindless conservatism be banished. I give two examples. There are bishops for whom being called 'Your Grace' or 'My Lord' matters a lot, and whose diocesan website is more focused on him and his homilies than on where the layperson can go with allegations of sexual abuse or how she can learn more about the Catholic faith. In these times, such a man is unfit to be a bishop. My second example is that if a diocese lacks the resources needed for 21st-century ministry, including appropriate expertise, lay participation, and evangelising outreach, it should be amalgamated with another diocese. About 10 of the 26 Irish dioceses should go.[7] Bishops' governing styles and diocesan structures are meant to serve the people and their needs, not be ornamental medieval relics.

The Murphy Report on the Dublin Archdiocese expressed its bewilderment and incomprehension at the fact that diocesan authorities had neither observed nor applied Canon Law in the cases of priests credibly accused of serious delicts or crimes. It is good that this has been said forcefully.[8] About six years ago, there was an ill-informed media debate over the relative priority of Canon Law and Civil Law, with loud calls for Canon Law to yield precedence to Civil Law.[9] The Murphy Report has revealed the true state of affairs: Canon Law, far from obstructing Civil Law, has hardly figured at all in response to clerical wrongdoing. What is shocking is not that bishops did not report abusers to the civil authorities, but that they generally failed to apply to those abusers the very law they were themselves responsible for enforcing. This was a serious failure in governance.

One of the curious things about cases prior to the 1990s is that laypeople often complained to bishops or religious superiors, but not to the police. It is somewhat unfair that at present only bishops and clergy who knew about abuse cases are being criticised for not reporting it to the police; parents are generally not being criticised. However, even if unfair, criticism of those bishops and clergy is deserved. For surely, where laypeople complained to the bishop, but not to the police, they were expressing a belief that the Church had the ability as well as the duty to punish the wrong and redress the injustice perpetrated by one of its priests. They were giving the bishop the opportunity to deal decisively with the matter, and trusting him to do so. That trust has been sadly betrayed by weak bishops. The laity has rights as well as duties, as is outlined in Canons 208–31 of the Code of Canon Law, including a right to be protected from dangerous or unbalanced priests. The bishop is the person with the primary duty of protecting his people from predatory priests.

It has been claimed, by one Irish Canon lawyer, that a bishop is a kind of father to his priests, so he should never report their criminal actions to the civil authorities. That claim presumably entails that the bishop, if questioned by the police, should refuse to answer questions that might incriminate the priest. One has to assume too that the canonist thinks a 'fatherly' bishop should never kick his 'sons' out of the priesthood. Morally, that amounts to a proposal to conceal crime. One hopes that his is an isolated view. However, given the shrill tone in media circles, one senses that many people have simply put their heads down and are waiting for the storm to pass. Although probably a minority, I suspect there may be more who think as he does.

First, if the bishop is a kind of 'father', he is meant to be father to all his people, laity and clergy alike. If he is particularly solicitous for some, it must surely be for the most vulnerable, and the scandals have shown us how very vulnerable children were. The proposal that the bishop shield or protect the priest is based on the idea that bishops should always side with the priest against complaints from the laity, regardless of their nature or provenance. As well as proposing a morally outrageous bias, following such advice would amount to an abdication of episcopal governance.

Second, the Catholic Church explicitly endorses the rule of law.[10] On other matters, bishops have often called on people to assist the police by reporting criminal wrongdoing. It is incomprehensible that a Canon lawyer would suggest that the law be subverted. Even if there is no clear obligation in Civil Law to report such crimes, the claim that a bishop should neither report it nor cooperate with police investigations amounts to a proposal to subvert the spirit of the law, Civil and Canon.[11]

Third, the Church is not to be identified with the clergy. The Church's abiding interest lies in being living witness to the gospel of Jesus Christ, and that interest embraces the layperson equally with the priest. The proposal that the bishop should conceal the priest's putative crime involves a shameless partisanship, a clericalism gone mad, and a gross violation of the equal rights of the laity. The priest has a right to some support from his bishop; and the layperson has a right to it too. If the priest can look to the bishop for mercy and compassion, so too can the injured layperson, particularly a child. There is no way the priest's claim could outrank the layperson's claim.

No evidence has been offered that any bishop was intentionally complicit in crime. It seems rather that bishops were weak and scared, confusing charity with 'niceness', thinking of compassion and mercy and redemption as soft and gentle things, quite disconnected with the toughness of justice. Yet tough justice is as much part of the Christian message as mercy and compassion. Since he must govern, and since he cannot govern except in justice and fairness, the bishop cannot function as the accused priest's counsellor, confessor, or advocate. He cannot identify the Church's interests with the priest's interest: the Church's interests are in justice and, to the degree appropriate, in mercy.[12] It is not the bishop's business to interfere with the justice to be meted out to the civil authorities; and it is his business to see to it that justice is done in the canonical forum.

Media insistence that Civil Law takes priority over Canon Law would have discouraged bishops and their advisers from utilising law in this matter, and, in the light of the Murphy Report, that is the last thing the bishops need. The fact that the media has paid little attention to that Report's criticism of failure to apply Canon Law, must not be allowed to encourage a mentality that sees the responsibility for dealing with criminal priests as belonging to the State alone. The Church must govern itself, not merely because it has a duty to vindicate the rights of priests' victims, but also because its own historical experience warns against allowing itself to be reduced to full accountability to the State.[13]

The following is a kind of litmus test for Church governance. Consider the case of a priest against whom there is significant evidence of sexual abuse of a minor, but where the Director of Public Prosecutions, doubtful of securing a conviction, has decided not to prosecute. Where the bishop (in line with current custom) has held off on canonical proceedings while a civil prosecution was pending, the State's decision should make him more inclined, not less, to initiate canonical proceedings. Even if such proceedings fail to lead to a conviction in a canonical court, the recent widespread failure to use Canon Law has created a situation where the Church must, not merely display, but also rebuild its own determination to deal vigorously with paedophile priests, and particularly in cases where the State is unable to do so. This is part of an appropriate response to the Pope's call to bishops to 'grow in solidarity with your people and deepen your personal concern for all the members of your flock'.[14]

For bishops, that means (among other things) that they may not take it that determination of a priest's guilt or innocence is solely a matter for the civil authorities, as if the Church were merely a department of the State. Besides, a bishop who has reasonable grounds to believe that one of his priests is a danger to children is morally obligated, regardless of whether the priest has been convicted in any court, to ensure that the priest does not come in contact with children.

OF LAW AND LAWYERS

Two erroneous views about law have played a role in the sad saga. One is the legal positivist view that law is autonomous, not significantly connected to morality. The other is the anti-law or antinomian view that the Church is about love and charity, so there is no place in it for something as cold and impersonal as law.[15]

On amoral law, the Murphy Report refers to one Dublin Canon lawyer, chancellor of the archdiocese in the 1970s, who – like the other Irish canonist mentioned above – held that the diocese had no obligation to report criminal priests to the civil authorities, and opposed initiation of canonical proceedings against such priests. One wonders what he thought the function of law was. Did he think it had nothing to do with morality? Why did it not occur to canonists such as they that law was not just a set of administrative tools to keep the organisation going, but also a means of protecting people's rights?

While there were also sane Canon lawyers, their reaction to such morally intolerable stances among their colleagues was weakly ineffectual at best. At the time of the ill-informed debate about relative priority between Canon and Civil Law, other Canon lawyers did not make their voices heard. Yet canonists must have known more about what was going on than other priests. Perhaps some rethinking of role is needed here too, for in the wretched history in question, the Canon lawyers were like Sherlock Holmes's 'dog that did not bark in the night'.

The other aberration was far more common. Since Vatican II, many a theologian, particularly moral theologians, regularly taught and preached that God and the Church were 'about love, not about law'. It has been a theme much preached on by priests. There is an acceptable interpretation of that slogan. But the question must be asked: did the huge emphasis placed on it generate an anti-law culture in clerical circles (even among canonists), bringing the very idea of law into such disrepute that, when evidence of serious delicts was presented to bishops, they hardly thought about using the law? Given the evidence, the authors of the Murphy Report would have been justified in concluding that the Irish Catholic Church had become a lawless church. That did not happen overnight; yet once again, the dog did not bark.

No doubt there are bad laws, where law needs to be tempered by love, and the letter of the law by equity. But it is also true that love needs to be informed by law. It is precisely because it is a rather cold and impersonal thing that law can provide a guide to objectivity in cases where love and conflicting emotions can bias us. We need law.

PRIESTS

Since the time of the Fr Brendan Smyth episode in the early 1990s, it has not been easy to be a priest in Ireland. When the nauseating details of his abuse of children were publicised, some priests were insulted in the street. However, as the laity's initial shock wore off, a calmer mood prevailed, as it was realised that not every priest is an abuser. Many priests have commented on how supportive regular church-goers have been towards them personally in recent years. At the same time, the revelations have distressed and demoralised priests. A few priests have had false allegations made against them, and have had to endure the humiliation and anxiety of lengthy suspension. Even if exonerated, they may live with the fear that another accusation, no matter how unfounded, may – on the principle of no smoke without fire – cause people to start viewing them as tainted.

Some priests are tempted to react defensively, seeking to circle the wagons and stonewall. While just as appalled at the behaviour of criminal priests, they may become focused on their own rights as a priority. Though understandable, such a reaction would be short-sighted, since it would obstruct bringing about the very thing that would be most likely to assure them justice, namely, a calmer and more reasonable public atmosphere on the issue and a more balanced and predictable approach on the part of diocesan authorities.

As the Pope's *Letter* highlighted, there is a need for renewal in the Irish Church. It is more than just a matter of weeding out bad apples and having bishops take effective charge. Priests themselves must play a supportive role in this. Better structures are in place today. All that is required is that people use them. But that may turn out to be a big requirement. Individual priests and religious who want to make the scandals and the abuse a thing of the past must ask themselves: Am I prepared to be a whistle-blower? Like other bosses, bishops and religious superiors are prone to be jealous of their prerogatives and likely to resent 'do-gooders' as interfering. One can only hope they learn better, but, in the nature of things, whistle-blowers are not popular. As regards clerical whistle-blowers, they appear to have been few. Far from being rebellious, most priests and religious were too submissive, passive, and deferential to authority. Those who knew of no abuses are in the clear; those who did know, and who said nothing, bear some moral responsibility. Some of Brendan Smyth's Norbertine confreres must have had an idea that he was molesting children; they do not seem to have made any effort to push the weak Norbertine abbot into taking decisive action, let alone agitate to get him removed from office because he would not act. A tough bishop may not be popular with his priests; but the Murphy Report should bring home forcefully to every Irish priest that much of the current misery arose from their superiors being ineffectual. The scandals warn priests: Worry more about weak bishops than about tough bishops.

As things currently stand in Ireland, it may soon be the case that a child will be safer with a priest than with most other male adults. That is a good change, but it may at present have too much the quality of a frightened reaction to vivid scandals. The change needs to put down deeper roots. In particular, clergy have to undergo a conversion.

First, priests need to renew their own faith: this has been one of the topics raised by the current and previous popes in relation to these issues. Priests are called to be men of God.[16] Yet some priests hardly ever make retreats or have spiritual direction. How then can they know whether it is God or something else that they bring to others?

Second, priests must deepen their commitment to celibacy, so that its spiritual and moral meaning shines out for themselves and others. The paedophile scandal is one of those cultural signs that points to the necessity of re-valorising the virtue of chastity or sexual self-discipline. Our society needs it. The sacrifice that a priest makes in accepting celibacy has, in addition to its many meanings, acquired a new meaning: that of expiation for the sexual sins of others, particularly those of other priests. The Church, the people of God, needs that sacrifice and expiation.

Third, priests have to take ownership with respect to dealing with scandalous behaviour by fellow priests. In a certain sense, priests have to give bishops permission to lead, and support them when they do lead.[17] Too often, priests and religious can be selfish in their attitude to authority: their main concern is that the bishop or superior not interfere with their comfortable routine or solipsistic lifestyle, so they do not want strong leadership. The same selfish desire not to be disturbed can come into play when the priest or religious hears rumours of scandalous or even criminal behaviour by a fellow priest or religious. Not wanting to get involved, or feeling it's 'somebody else's job', he or she may well not report it to the bishop or superior, much less follow up later to find out what action the bishop or superior took.

That culture has to change. It is not clericalism; it is laziness, combined with cowardice, and it is often powerfully rationalised by claiming to want to be 'charitable' and not be harsh in one's judgements of others. There is a certain kind of spirituality still around, that emphasises a charity quite disconnected from the demands of justice. It is also fortified by the 'love, not law' culture discussed earlier. But given bishops' failure to take Canon Law seriously, reflecting an attitude that must have been shared by many priests, one can only conclude that the love contrasted with law was weak and spineless. 'Love in action can be a harsh and dreadful thing compared with love in dreams,' the spiritual director Father Zossima says in Dostoevsky's *The Brothers Karamazov.*

In his *Letter* to the Irish Church, Benedict XVI calls upon us all to do penance and pray for a full year 'in order to obtain the grace of healing and renewal for the Church in Ireland'.[18] He then goes on to invite us to resort to the sacrament of reconciliation. The Pope's advice is good. But it would be easy to 'spiritualise' what he is asking for into something soft and unchallenging. That will not reform the Church. The priest or religious who has honestly admitted that he or she would be unable to be a whistleblower now knows what to fast and pray for in the coming months. So to does the priest addicted to affection or sexual gratification, who has been 'two busy' (or proud) to go to a colleague or Sexaholics Anonymous. They also know what to bring to confession. The sacrament of reconciliation is concerned, not just with one's sinful acts, but also with the ways we betray Christ and his people by not working to become the disciples he has called us to be.

Notes

1 Originally published as Seamus Murphy, 'No Cheap Grace: Reforming the Irish Church', *Studies* vol. 99 no. 395 (autumn, 2010) pp. 303–16.

2 One of the best books on the issue of clerical paedophilia is still Philip Jenkins, *Pedophiles and Priests* (Oxford, 1996).

3 See *Pastoral Letter of the Holy Father Pope Benedict XVI to the Catholics of Ireland* (hereafter *Letter*): In confronting the present crisis, measures to deal justly with individual crimes are essential, yet on their own they are not enough: a new vision is needed, to inspire present and future generations to treasure the gift of our common faith.

4 *Letter*, n. 14.

5 See Vatican II, *Lumen Gentium (Dogmatic Constitution on the Church)*, nn. 21, 27.

6 Automatic reporting of credible complaints against clerics or other Church personnel to the civil authorities, whether police or child protection agencies, appears to be largely accepted. A bishop who fails to do so should be required to resign.

7 See Vincent Twomey, *The End of Irish Catholicism?* (Dublin, 2003).

8 The Pope's letter sharply criticises the bishops for failure to apply Canon Law. See *Letter*, nn.4 and 11, where there are five references to this failure, one linking it to the importance of impartiality and another linking it to respect for people's dignity.

9 There is no clash between Civil Law and Canon Law, any more than between French Law and Spanish Law. They have their distinct zones of competence, and neither has 'priority' over the other in any general sense. See *Code of Canon Law*, c. 22, with commentary on it in John P. Beal, James A. Coriden and Thomas J. Green (eds), *New Commentary on the Code of Canon Law* (New York, 2000).

10 See for instance, Vatican II, *Gaudium et Spes (The Church in the Modern World)*, nn. 74–5; John Paul II, *Centesimus Annus (The Hundredth Year)*, n. 44 (1991); *Catechism of the Catholic Church*, nn. 2238–342; and *Code of Canon Law*, c. 22.

11 In his letter, the Pope directs the Bishops to 'continue to cooperate with the civil authorities', thereby tacitly endorsing the current policy of reporting allegations of sexual assault on minors by Church personnel to the police (*Letter*, n. 11).

12 'Any institution that wants to proclaim justice must first itself be just', Synod of Bishops, *Justice in the World* (Rome, 1971).

13 In the contemporary western world, there are groups, some influential in the secular media, who aim at eliminating the Church's influence and scope for action: the scandals have been a Godsend to that agenda. In view of these considerations, one can only deplore an Irish Catholic bishop's remark a few years ago that Civil Law was superior to Canon Law. Where would he think his duty lay if it became legally obligatory for priests to report the confessions of paedophiles to the police?

14 *Letter*, n. 11.

15 See Ladislas M. Örsy, 'Theology and Canon Law', in the introduction to Beal, Coriden and Green, *New Commentary on the Code of Canon Law*, pp. 3–4.

16   The address of Archbishop Dolan of New York at Maynooth, 27 May 2010, is particularly good on the base-line frame of mind for a priest. See www.catholicbishops.ie

17   See *Letter*, n. 10.

18   *Letter*, n. 13.

Index

Abbey Theatre, 187–8, 189, 192–4
abortion, 16, 190, 248, 258
  referendum, 245, 267, 288
Act of Union, 163–5
Adebari, Rotimi, 314–15
AE, *see* Russell, George
age of consent, 85–8
agriculture, 97, 102, 129, 156, 201, 231, 259
Ahern, Bertie, 3, 22, 313
Aiken, Frank, 11
Aliens Act 1935, 310–11
Anglicisation, 79, 137–8
Anglo-Irish culture, 14, 183, *see also* literature
Anglo-Irish Treaty (1921), 25, 138, 162, 167–9
  negotiations, 169
Asquith, Herbert, 24–5, 27–8
asylum seekers, 17, 309–11
  former, 314–15
  and security, 309–11
  welfare of, 310
Auden, W. H., 276

banking, 156–7, 231, 303, 304
Barber, Noel, 17
Barrington, Donal, 10, 14, 161–86
Barry, Kevin, 173
Bartley, P., 122–5
Beales, H. A., 157–8
Beckett, Samuel, 277, 279
Behan, Brendan, 194, 203
Benedict XVI, Pope, 319, 321, 327
Bentham, Jeremy, 7, 91, 137, 138, 143, 150

Beveridge Report, 9–10, 158–9
bigotry, 167, 173, 177, 298
Binchy, Daniel A., 6, 7, 105–17, 146–9
Birrell, Augustine, 22, 24
bishops, role of, 321–4
Blythe, Ernest, 192
Boland, John Pius, 24
Böll, Heinrich, 280
Bonhoeffer, Dietrich, 319
Boundary Commission, 169
Bowen, Elizabeth, 196
Boyd, Ernest, 204
Boyle, William, 188
boy scouts, 43
Brady, John, 13, 210–21
Brady, Joseph, 205
Bruton, John, 3, 22
Bukharin, Nikolai, 79
Burke-Savage, Ronald, 11–12, 14
Busteed, John, 7–8

Cahill, Edward, 119–31
Calvinism, 294–7
Canavan, J., 122–3
canon law, 127, 320–7
  and civil law, 321–5
capitalism, 9, 60, 95, 98, 113, 121, 157, 240–1, 304, 306
Carrigan, William, 83–4, 86–70
Carrigan Report (1931), 17, 83–91
Carson, Edward, 27, 50–1
Casement, Roger, 66
Catholic
  emancipation, 165, 166
  social thought, 5–6, 9, 119

Catholic Church, 190, 210, 217–20,
    247–8, 262, 267–9, 299, *see also*
    Church–State relations
  in Europe, 264
  in France, 286
  in the USA, 264, 266
  reform, proposed, 318–29
  social provision by, 215
  and women, 248, 269
Catholicism, 1–3, 5–6, 16, 143–4,
    271–82
  in Europe, 121, 125
  in Germany, 114
  in Ireland, 120, 121, 126, 139, 211,
    267–9
  and nationalism, 164–5, 174
Celtic Tiger, 30, 278, 286, 303, 305
censorship, 187, 190–1, 207, 278–9
Chadwick, Edwin, 159
Chekhov, Anton, 274
child
  abuse: 83–5; clerical, 16–17, 319–27,
    see also Murphy Report; Ryan
    Report
  labour, 40–2, 143
Churchill, Lord Randolph, 166
Church–State relations, 9, 122–3,
    126, 129, 211, 215–16, 320
citizenship referendum (2004), 311
civil war, 21, 25, 78, 120, 138, 163,
    168, 206
Clarke, Austin, 188, 198, 200, 206–8
Clarke, Thomas, 57, 67
Clery, Arthur, 3–4, 17, 40–4
Collins, Stephen, 3, 21–30
Coleman, Ursula, 248
Colum, Padraic, 52–3
Commonwealth, 184
communism, 4, 6–7, 110, 112, 115, 137
  collapse of, 306
Connolly, James, 12, 29, 55, 60
Connolly, Violet, 6
Constitution (1922), 121, 130
Constitution (1937), 6, 13

Article 8, 13, 213–14
Article 44, 129
Articles 2–3, 13
Articles 41–4, 13
Articles 41–5, 129
Article 44, 215
Article 45, 311
Jesuit influence on: 119–32; draft
    document, 126–30
contraceptives, 13, 85, 88–91, 216
  the Pill, 286–7
Convent of Les Dames Irlandaises,
    Ypres, 70–6
Corcoran, Timothy, 2, 41
Corkery, Daniel, 5, 7, 204–7, 277
Cosgrave, W. T., 3, 8, 83, 86
Costello, John A., 10, 169
Coyne, E., 122–3
Crawford, Virginia, 5
Criminal Law Amendment Act 1935, 88
Cronin, Anthony, 280
Crotty, Raymond, 16, 238–43, 254
Cúchulainn, 32–3, 65
Curragh mutiny, 25, 163–4, 170

D'Arcy, Martin, 205
Davis, Thomas, 62–3, 66–7, 141, 163,
    183
Davitt, Michael, 3, 41, 43, 46
Democratic Unionist Party, *see* DUP
de Paor, Liam, 13, 221
de Valera, Eamon, 2, 8, 10, 28, 86, 91,
    119–31, 167, 169, 193
Devlin, Denis, 198
Devlin, Joseph 50
Diarmuid and Gráinne, 33
Dillon, John, 24
divorce, 2, 13, 216, 246, 248
  referendum, 288
Dodds, Nigel, 296
DUP, 290–2, 295–6

Easter Rising, 3, 11–12, 27–30, 52,
    54–6, 57–69, 79

economic
    development, 8, 96, 240–2, 253–60
    growth, 155, 230, 239, 260, 309,
        312–3
    liberalism, 150–2
    internationalism, 96–7
    policy, 7–8, 151–2
    theory, 151–2
    underdevelopment, 241, 257, 259
Economic Expansion, First Programme
    for, 226, 232
Economic and Social Research
    Institute, *see* ESRI
education, 259–60
    and the Constitution, 126–7
    for girls, 284–5
    inequalities in, 230–6
    inter-denominational, 217–20
    university, 232, 284
elections, general 260
    1906, 24, 49
    1910, 24
    1932, 86
    1933, 87
    1949, 10
    1977, 301
    2007, 301–2
    in Germany, 106, 116–17
    in Northern Ireland, 170, 177, 179
Eliot, T. S., 202–3
emigrants, returning, 313
emigration, 155–6, 197, 209, 230, 239,
    241–2, 267, 278, 280, 286, 302
employment structure, 231–2, 236
Enright, Ann, 302
Enterprise and Employment,
    Department of, 311
ESRI, 225–6, 230–3, 235–6, 314
European Community, 247, 248, 255

Fahey, Tony, 16, 262–70
family, 9
    and the Constitution, 6, 127–9
Famine, Great, 81, 285
Fanning, Bryan, 17, 308–16

Farrell, Michael, 201
fascism, 4–6, 105–17
feminism, 16, 247–9, 269, 283–9, *see
    also* Women's Movement
Ferguson, E. C., 176
Ferguson, Harry, 17
Fianna Fáil, 22, 130
Fine Gael, 5, 22
Finlay, Thomas, 8
First World War, 26–7, 46, 52, 70–7
FitzGerald, Garret, 3, 12–14
Fitzgerald, F. Scott, 279
foreign policy, 183–4
Foster, Ivan, 292
Free Presbyterian Church, 290–3
Free State, 21, 22, 78–80, 83, 101,
    188–9, 277
free trade, 7, 9, 93–4, 98, 231–2

GAA, 180
Gaelic culture, 7, 60–3, 66, 133–44,
    147–8
Gaelic League, 7, 51, 61, 67–9, 147
Gallagher, Frank, 161, 172, 176–8
Gallagher, Michael Paul, 15
Garvin, Tom, 16, 253–61
Geoghegan, James, 86–90
Geoghegan Committee, 87–90
Gill, Henry, 4, 70–7
government borrowing, 239–42
Government of Ireland Act 1920, 167
Greacen, Robert, 197
Green Party, 304
gross national product, 240, 255–8
Gwynn, Denis, 4, 45–53

Hawthorne, Nathaniel, 195–6
Hayek, F. A., 9, 15, 159
Healy, Isabel, 245
Hewitt, John, 182
Higgins, Frederick Robert, 192
Hillman, James, 248
Hitler, Adolf, 6, 105–17
    anti-Semitism, 110–13
    and Catholicism, 114

early life, 107–8
and the First World War, 109–10
Mein Kampf, 6, 106–7
oratory, 105–6
Holland, Mary, 245–6
Home Rule, 24–6, 28, 40–1, 49–52, 62,
    67, 139, 163–7, 171, 172, 184
Home Rule Bills
    1886, 23
    1893, 23–4
    1912, 25, 51, 164, 184
housing, 4, 15, 41, 50, 157, 224, 227,
    230, 257, 259
    local authority, 224, 227–9, 231,
        259
Hume, David, 282
Hunt, Hugh, 192
Hyde, Douglas, 61, 69

immigrants
    integration of, 314–16
    Irish-born children of, 310–11
immigration, 17, 308–16
    from EU member states, 311–12
industrialisation, 97, 181, 225–6, 263
infant mortality, 258
Inglis, Tom, 15
IRA, 10, 22
Ireland, as a Catholic state, 13, 29, 120,
    128, 205, 213, *see also* Catholic
    Church, Catholicism
Ireland Act 1949, 170–1, 179
Iremonger, Valentin, 198
Irish Brigade, 70, 74, 76
Irish Citizen Army, 55, 60
Irish identity, 149, 213–14, 275–6, 282,
    312
Irish language, 138–9, 141, 144, 148–9,
    276
    plays, 193
Irish literary movement, 188–9, 194,
    198
Irish Nationality and Citizenship Act
    2001, 311
Irish Party, 3, 22–4, 28–9, 51

Irish Republican Brotherhood, 25, 27,
    50–1, 60, 62, 67
Irish Volunteers, 27, 46, 51–2, 60

John XXIII, Pope, 285
John Paul II, Pope, 237
Joseph Rowntree Foundation, 315
Joyce, James, 18, 47, 48, 188–9, 194,
    198, 200–1, 274
    influence of, 203–5, 277
Justice, Department of, 85, 87–91
Justice, Equality and Law Reform,
    Department of, 309–11

Kavanagh, Patrick, 198, 207, 277
Keegan, Claire, 302
Kelley, Dean M., 265
Kennedy, Finola, 16–17, 83–91, 284,
    286
Kennedy, Kieran, 15
Kennedy, Sr Stanislaus, 14
Kenny, Enda, 22
Kenny, Mary, 16, 283–9
Keogh, Dermot, 6, 119–32
Kerry Babies Tribunal, 245
Kettle, Andrew, 46
Kettle, Larry, 51
Kettle, Tom, 3–4, 40, 45–53
Keynes, John Maynard, 8–10, 93–104,
    150, 154
Keynesianism, 8–9, 239
Kiely, Benedict, 204, 206–7
Kilmainham Jail, 46, 58
Kinsella, Thomas, 198, 208
Kipling, Rudyard, 49

Lalor, Fintan, 62, 64
Land League, 41, 46, 49, 191
Larkin, Emmet, 15
Larkin, James, 50, 51
Lavin, Mary, 207
Lee, Joseph, 253
Lemass, Séan, 3, 8, 54–6
Lennon, Brian, 13, 15
Levine, June, 245, 287

Lisbon Treaty, 301
literature, *see also* poetry, short stories,
    theatre
    Anglo-Irish, 188, 193, 206
    Irish: 31–9, 186–99, 200–9; and
        1916, 206–7; and mysticism,
        32, 38–9, 205–6
Lueger, Karl, 109
Lynch, Patrick, 8–9, 14, 150–60

MacBride, Seán, 10–11, 169
Mac Curtain, Margaret, 16, 244–52
MacDonagh, Thomas, 35, 52, 206
MacEoin, Seán, 22
MacEntee, Seán (John F.), 3
MacGréal, Michael, 218–19
MacLaverty, Michael, 207
MacManus, Francis, 207
MacNeill, Eoin, 3, 12, 25, 51–2, 54,
    59–60, 67
Maher, Eamon, 271–82
Mannheim, Karl, 158
Mansion House Committee, 169–70
marriage, 285
    and the Constitution, 122–3, 126–7
    law, 127, 213, 215–17
    mixed, 217
Martin, Augustine, 12, 200–9
McCafferty, Nell, 245–6
McCrea, William, 292
McDermott, Seán, 56
McDonagh, Thomas, 3
McDowell, Michael, 310
McErlean, J., 122
McFadden, Roy, 203
McGahern, John, 208–9, 271–82
    Amongst Women, 277–8
    The Barracks, 208, 274–5
    The Dark, 271–2
McIlveen, David, 295
McMahon, Brian, 207
McManus, Liz, 310
McQuaid, John Charles, 2, 119, 271, 272
McVerry, Peter, 16
Meleady, Dermot, 21

Mill, John Stuart, 137, 139, 150
Mitchel, John, 62, 64–5, 67, 68, 141
monopolies, 152, 156–7
Moore, George, 188, 200–1, 205
    A Drama in Muslin, 188–9
Mortimer, Raymond, 201
moving statues, 16, 244–51
Murphy, J. A., 247
Murphy, Séamus, 17, 318–29
Murphy Report, 17, 318, 320, 322–6
Mussolini, Benito, 5, 101, 108, 115

Nagle, Nano, 306
National Economic and Social Council,
    see NESC
nationalism, 4 , 10–12, 63–7, 138–9,
    147, 162, 164, 168, *see also under*
    Northern Ireland
    constitutional, 1, 10, 23, 168, 307
    cultural, 7, 147, 313
National University of Ireland, 24,
    46–7, 49, 238
National Volunteers, 25–7
Nationist, 48
Nazism, 6, 106, 110, 113–15, *see also*
    Hitler, Adolf
NESC, 224–6, 228–31, 309, 312, 314
New Deal, 152–3
Nolan, Dom P., 75
Northern Ireland, 161–86, 210–21, 242
    conflict, 13, 211–12
    culture, 181–3
    discrimination in, 174–8
    education in, 175, 181
    government of, 167–8
    housing in, 175–6
    identity in, 212–14
    nationalists in, 176–81, 213–14
    politics, 169, 212
    social services in, 184–5
North–South
    cooperation, 173
    relations, 213–14
    trade, 180–1
novels, Irish, 196–7

Oakeshott, Michael, 151
O'Brien, Conor Cruise, 10–11, 49
O'Brien, Edna, 276, 280
O'Brien, George, 2, 8–10, 49
O'Brien, Kate, 206
O'Callaghan, Denis, 244–5
O'Casey, Seán, 181, 190–1, 195, 206
   Juno and the Paycock, 189
   The Plough and the Stars, 189
O'Connell, Daniel, 7, 133, 139–43,
   146–9
O'Connor, Frank, 142, 144, 148–9,
   192, 206–9, 277
O'Donoghue, Fergus, 17–18, 301–7
O'Donovan Rossa, Jeremiah, 66
OECD, 224, 312
O'Faolain, Sean, 7, 133, 139–42, 144,
   146–9, 187–99, 250–1
O'Flaherty, Liam, 196, 206
O'Hanlon, Fergal, 173
O'Hanlon, Gerry, 14–15
Ó hÓgáin, Daíthí, 246
Oldham, C. H., 7–8
O'Malley, Ernie, 277, 278
O'Neachtain, Seán, 37
O'Rahilly, Alfred 5
Orange Order, 50, 163–6, 172, 175, 177,
   185
   views on the Catholic Church, 167
Organisation for Economic Co-operation
   and Development, *see* OECD
O'Riordáin, Seán, 198

Paisley, Ian, 290–300
   theology of, 291–9
Parnell, Charles Stewart, 23, 46
partition, 10, 25–6, 28, 62, 161–85, 292
   origins of, 162–4
patriotism, 3, 5, 12, 23, 43, 63–5, 68,
   190–1, 193, 304, 307
peace process, 281
Pearse, Patrick, 3, 11–12, 29, 31–9, 51,
   57–9, 61–9, 206
Plunkett, James, 208
Plunkett, Joseph Mary, 3, 52, 206

pluralism, 2, 13, 210–21, 263
poetry, *see also* literature
   Anglo-Irish, 35–7
   Irish, 197–8
Polyani, Michael, 152
population growth, 227, 240
Presbyterians, 166
Priestly, David, 296
property
   developers, 301, 304
   ownership, and the Constitution,
   127–9
prostitution, 88
   juvenile, 83–5
protectionism, 8, 93–4, 98, 102
Protestantism, 14, 16, 25, 42, 138
   American, 265
   English, 121, 136, 163, 170
   in Northern Ireland, 164–6, 172,
   174, 177–85
   political, 139, 290
Proust, Marcel, 275
Puritanism, 136–8, 142, 144, 190
Putnam, Robert D., 315

Redmond, John, 21–30, 163, 171, 306
Redmond, Mary, 13
Refugee Act 1996, 310
refugees, 309–10
religion
   appeal of, 265–6
   growth of, 263–4
religious
   education, 5, 13
   experience: 246; women's, 249–52
   observance, 15–16
   worship, freedom of, 122, 126, 128
Robinson, Iris, 296
Robinson, Lennox, 192
Roche, Stephen, 88–91
Roosevelt, Theodore, 42, 152–3
Rosenberg, Alfred, 113–15
Royal Irish Regiment, 75–6
Russell, George (AE), 5, 36, 78–82,
   205–6

Russia, Soviet, 6–7, 98, 101–4
Russian Revolution, 78–9
Ruttledge, Patrick, 87, 90
Ryan, John A., 154
Ryan Report, 17, 318

Sammon, Frank, 14, 253
Sayers, Peig, 249–52
Second World War, 60, 256, 286–7
secularisation, 263–5
self-sufficiency, national, 93–104
Shaw, Francis, 11–12, 30, 57–69
Sheehy, Eugene, 49
Sheehy, Mary, 49
Sheehy Skeffington, Francis, 48, 49, 52
Sheehy Skeffington, Hanna, 248
short stories, Irish, 196, *see also*
    literature
Sibbett, R. M., 164, 167
Sinn Féin, 1, 2, 15, 22, 27–9
Skidelsky, Peter, 8
Smyth, Brendan, 17, 325–6
social
    deprivation, 229
    division, 245
    inclusion, 16, 309
    inequality, 223–37
    policy, 128, 157–9
    progress, 256–60
    welfare, 14, 228, 230, 236–7, 287, 311
Social Welfare (Miscellaneous
    Provisions) Act 2004, 311
Southern, Neil, 290–300
Somerville, Peter 7
Somerville and Ross, 188
Soundings, 200
Stephens, James, 188, 205–6
Studies
    editorial policy, 14
    objectives, 1
    and 1916, 3
    subject matter, 1–2, 8–9
suffrage, women's, 4, 40–1, 43
Sweeney, John, 15–16, 223–37
Switzerland, cultural differences in, 220

Synge, J. M., 181, 277
    Playboy of the Western World, 188–90

Táin Bo Cúailnge, 31–2, 34, 38, 64–5
television, 285
theatre, 192–4, *see also* literature
Thornley, David, 12, 14
Tierney, Michael, 2, 5–7, 133–45, 146–9
Tóibín, Colm, 17–18, 245
Tone, Wolfe, 12, 42, 59, 62, 64, 66
Trimble, David, 296–7
Tuairim, 10, 13–14

Ulster Unionist Party, 10, 27, 170, 297
Ulster Volunteers, 50–1, 62
unemployment, 10, 100, 155, 224, 226,
    229–30, 236–7
    assistance, 237
unification of Ireland, 11
United Irishmen, 163, 166
Unionists, 10–11, 16, 28, 48, 50, 162–4,
    168, 171–86, 211–14, 253, 290, 296
utilitarianism, 136–7, 148, 152

Valéry, Paul, 103
Vatican II, 14, 210, 215, 217, 247, 266,
    320, 325
votes for children, 40–4

war, *see* civil war, First World War,
    Second World War
welfare state, 9–10, 153
    British, 150, 158–9
    in Northern Ireland, 185
Whitaker, T. K., 8, 16, 238–42
Wilson, Sir Henry, 163
women
    oppression of, 245–6
    in politics, 288
Women's Movement, 246–8

Yeats, W. B., 34, 36, 69, 181, 188,
    189–90, 192–4, 197, 206
    influence of, 203–5, 277
Young Irelanders, 163